ALE, EDI, & IDOC
Technologies for
SAP™
2nd Edition

Check the Web for Updates

To check for updates or corrections relevant to this book, visit our updates page on the Web at http://www.prima-tech.com/support.

Send Us Your Comments

To comment on this book or any other PRIMA TECH title, visit our reader response page on the Web at http://www.prima-tech.com/comments.

How to Order

For information on quantity discounts, contact the publisher: Prima Publishing, P.O. Box 1260BK, Rocklin, CA 95677-1260; (916) 787-7000. On your letterhead, include information concerning the intended use of the books and the number of books you want to purchase.

Arvind Nagpal

with

John Pitlak

SERIES EDITORS &
CERTIFIED SAP R/3
APPLICATION CONSULTANTS:

Gareth M. de Bruyn
Robert Lyfareff

ALE, EDI, & IDOC
Technologies for

SAP™

2ⁿᵈ Edition

A Division of Prima Publishing

A Division of Prima Publishing

Prima Publishing and colophon are registered trademarks of Prima Communications, Inc. PRIMA TECH is a registered trademark of Prima Communications, Inc., Roseville, California 95661.

ISBN: 0-7615-3431-8
Library of Congress Catalog Card Number: 2001086785
Printed in the United States of America

00 01 02 03 04 H H 10 9 8 7 6 5 4 3 2 1

Publisher
Stacy L. Hiquet

Associate Marketing Manager
Heather Buzzingham

Managing Editor
Sandy Doell

Project Editor
Cathleen D. Snyder

Technical Reviewers
Johan Marneweck
Harshad Sonar

Copy Editor
Kate Talbot

Interior Layout
Marian Hartsough Associates

Cover Design
Prima Design Team

Indexer
Sharon Shock

Proofreader
Kim V. Benbow

Dedication

*This book is dedicated
to my mother, Veronica S. Pitlak,
and to my father, the late John A. Pitlak.*

—John Pitlak

*I gratefully dedicate this book to my dear wife, Ritu,
my little darling, Anika, and both our parents.
Ritu, I could not have done this without your full
cooperation, support, and persistence.
Dear Anika, winter is almost over
but I hope we can still catch some snow
and make that snowman you wanted.
To our respected parents,
your continuous encouragement, belief in me,
and blessings have made this book a reality.
I could not have asked for a better family.
I love you all; thanks for making my dream a reality!*

—Arvind Nagpal

Acknowledgments

Preparing the second edition of Arvind Nagpal's excellent book proved to be a lot more work than I expected, even though most of my effort was simply updating it to SAP version 4.6. I had a lot of help, though. As editor, Cathleen Snyder kept me as much on track as she could, and Kate Talbot's copyediting did a lot to improve the style and clarity of the presentation. The technical editors, Johan Marneweck and Harshad Sonar, helped prevent a number of errors from creeping in, and made suggestions that added detail and clarification to many points. I greatly appreciated the comments and suggestions of the series editors, Gareth M. de Bruyn and Robert W. Lyfareff.

My career working with SAP R/3 has been a challenging and rewarding experience, and I would like to thank the following individuals for helping make it so. Dave Schnell of Computer Sciences Corp. brought me into my first SAP implementation and started me down this road. John Reed at Ecommquest has been of valuable assistance at a couple of points in my SAP career. Lately, it has been my pleasure to work with John Amos, Stephanie McDoulett, and the other fine folks at McKesson Corp. Their cooperation made it possible for me to undertake the work on this book.

Lastly, and perhaps most importantly, I want to thank my better half, Jan McConnell, for her support and tolerance of my hectic schedule and general harriedness of late. She is, quite simply, the best.

—John Pitlak

First and foremost I would like to take this opportunity to thank all of my readers for making the first edition of this book a remarkable success. I am indebted to every single one of you for making this book appear on the bestseller list at several online bookstores. I have enjoyed receiving e-mails from several of you who have shared your experiences in implementing the SAP Cross Application technologies, and I expect the same to continue with the second edition of the book. Your input and appreciation have helped us launch the second edition of the book, which covers up to version 4.6 of SAP. As the ALE, EDI, and IDoc technologies continue to be the standard for interfacing SAP to the external world, I hope you will find this edition a big help in your implementation.

Doing a book of this magnitude requires a team effort. First of all, I want to thank Matthew Carleson and Debbie Abshier of Prima Tech for giving me an opportunity to do this book and share my knowledge with the SAP community. Thank you Cathleen Snyder and Heather Buzzingham for helping with the second edition of this book. Your excellent comments and suggestions were invaluable. Thank you to Kate Talbot for keeping me straight on my corky English. Johan Marneweck and Harshad Sonar, your technical review was a big help in ensuring the correctness of this material.

I want to take this opportunity to thank several other individuals who have guided me in building my SAP career thus far. Thanks to Dr. Mike Spano of IBM, for introducing me to the world of SAP; to Dr. Thom Hodgson of North Carolina State University, for your expert advice on my masters thesis on SAP EDI; to Mike Perroni of BFI Houston and Jeff Cassel of AMP Inc., for keeping me challenged with real-world problems; to Hari Adusumilli and Paul Leing, for giving me an opportunity to teach at SAP America; and to all my students whose questions, input, and appreciation guided me along the path of writing this book.

Finally, I would like to thank SAP America.

—Arvind Nagpal

About the Authors

John Pitlak is an independent consultant who has helped a number of large corporate clients implement EDI and ALE in their SAP R/3 environments. His career path has been diverse, to say the least. After narrowly avoiding a Ph.D. in history, he found employment in Washington, D.C. as an economist, and later as a certified public accountant, before landing in information systems. As a consultant to the EPA, he participated in some of the early federal government EDI initiatives. Relocating to New Mexico in 1993, he continued to consult for the Department of Energy before beginning an eastward commute to Virginia to work on an SAP implementation in 1995. Since then, he has lived the rootless existence of the SAP consultant, becoming knowledgeable about the dining possibilities and airport vagaries of numerous major metropolitan areas, and loving it.

Arvind Nagpal is an active leader in the e-business and B2B integration community today. He has over twelve years of experience in the IT industry and six years of SAP experience. As an advisor and instructor, he consults with several Fortune 500 companies and teaches at SAP America. His in-depth knowledge has helped companies implement successful and scalable ALE and EDI systems. Mr. Nagpal enjoys the continued support and admiration of his clients and students, most of whom still call on him for advice in such SAP cross-application technologies as ALE, EDI, business framework, Internet commerce, and workflow. After completing the first edition of this book, Arvind joined Rapidigm as the Director of e-Business Services, focusing on delivering end-to-end integrated e-business solutions to help companies leverage their investments in the ERP systems.

About the Series Editors

Gareth de Bruyn's background includes over seven years of SAP experience, from ABAP development to configuration and business process definition, as well as project management. His experience ranges from the intricacies of the SD module all the way through MM, PP, and variant configuration, as well as aspects of CRM. He has taught SAP courses to employees and mentored many individuals in ABAP. Last year he led one of the first US implementations of SAP on the

Linux operating system, from the ERP software to BW and CRM middleware. A native of South Africa who was raised and educated in the United States, de Bruyn believes that mySAP technology is revolutionizing international business. De Bruyn has a Bachelor of Science degree in Chemical Engineering, Biomedical Engineering emphasis, from the University of California. He currently works for his own firm as an independent SAP consultant. He plans to earn a law degree to unite his technical and international business skills to capitalize on this global opportunity. When he is not working on MIS challenges, you can find Gareth working on his home theater or playing with his two dogs, Max and Isabel.

Robert Lyfareff is a veteran of several successful SAP installation teams over the past four years. Coupled with his formal training in computer science and electrical engineering, this unique SAP experience enables him to write about real-world business situations and issues. What excites and challenges him about his work is the integration and modification of business practices and the new technology. Currently, he works as an independent SAP consultant and author.

About Prima Tech's SAP Series

The demand for SAP programming and support expertise is exploding. Prima Tech's SAP series is designed to prepare IT professionals for a successful career using the world's leading ERP application. From ABAP/4 programming to preparing an effective organizational structure for the support of an SAP installation, to providing guidance on becoming an SAP consultant, Prima Tech's SAP series is the most comprehensive resource available for IT professionals. For more information on this and other SAP books and resources, see Prima Tech's Web site at http://www.prima-tech.com.

Contacting the Authors

You will learn something new about SAP practically every day, and working through this book probably won't be enough to make you perfectly comfortable with every SAP function you might need to use. If you find you can't locate the information you seek in SAP's help utilities, feel free to contact one of us via e-mail at arvindnagpal@yahoo.com or pitlak@acm.org. We hope to help you become more proficient with SAP, and will strive to apply our experience in ways that will help you achieve SAP proficiency at a faster rate. Good luck!

Contents at a Glance

Contents

Chapter 19 Introduction to ALE Technology 379

PART VII   THE SAP ALE INTERFACE. 391

Chapter 20 The Outbound ALE Process 393

Chapter 27 ALE Process Troubleshooting and Recovery. 533

Chapter 28 Managing ALE Process
Performance and Throughput 547

SECTION THREE IDOCS 557

PART X IDOC BASICS 559

Chapter 29 IDocs from the Outside 561

Chapter 32 Programming in the IDoc Interface 617

Chapter 33 Customizing the Interface
for New or Extended IDocs 669

PART XII   ARCHIVING IN THE IDOC INTERFACE 697

Chapter 34 Archiving IDocs and Deleting Work Items. . . 699

Introduction

In any SAP implementation, integration between business processes within a company and across companies is very important for a successful implementation. Within a company, integration must include interfacing with legacy systems, communicating with third party products, and integrating business processes across distributed SAP systems. The two most commonly deployed technologies for this type of integration are ALE (*Application Link and Enabling*) and EDI (*Electronic Data Interchange*) technologies, which make use of the popular IDoc (*Intermediate Document*) interface for exchanging data.

EDI provides business process integration across companies by exchanging business documents such as purchase orders, invoices, and shipment notices in electronic form, using industry standard formats such as ANSI X12 (*American National Standards Institute*) and EDIFACT (*Electronic Data Interchange For Administration, Commerce, and Transport*).

ALE, which is SAP's proprietary technology for integrating distributed business processes within a company, has been available in SAP since release 3.0. ALE was designed to link one SAP system to another SAP system, but the ALE architecture lent itself to being used to link SAP systems to non-SAP systems without any modification. The flexibility of ALE technology has proliferated into several application areas, and today many third-party products use it to exchange data with SAP. The underlying architectures of the ALE and EDI technologies are quite similar. Both make use of SAP's proprietary IDoc interface, which defines the format and structure of the data that is exchanged between two systems. Although ALE and EDI are the two biggest users of the IDoc interface, this interface can also be used by any two applications that need to exchange data. For example, it can be readily used to integrate SAP with Web applications.

As cross-application technologies, ALE and EDI are used in various modules of SAP such as SD (*Sales and Distribution*), MM (*Materials Management*), and FI (*Financials*). The wide-ranging application of these technologies has created an ever-increasing need for ALE, EDI, and IDoc skills. Mastery of these skills is a necessity for anyone involved in the technical or functional side of an SAP implementation.

Who Should Read this Book?

Because ALE, EDI, and IDoc are cross-application technologies, a wide audience can benefit from this book. EDI and ALE team members, support providers, data-interfacing and workflow experts, EDI and ALE programmers, aspiring EDI and ALE experts, e-commerce experts, and curious readers alike will find useful information in this book.

- ◆ **EDI team member.** This book provides you with a good foundation by explaining the concepts behind EDI and IDoc technologies. Tips throughout Part III, "Configuring the EDI Interface," show you how to tweak certain parameters to achieve a particular effect without doing an enhancement. Message control is used very widely in the EDI process. You'll learn to customize the Message control component and set up workflow for error handling. If you cannot satisfy business requirements by configuring the existing components, then you need either to enhance those components or build from ground zero. Section III, "IDocs," covers all the steps required to extend or create IDocs, along with programs to support the extensions and configuration to make these components known to the system.

- ◆ **ALE team member.** This book provides you with a good foundation by explaining the need and concepts behind ALE and IDoc technologies. You'll learn about the various configuration components involved in enabling any ALE process. Tips throughout Part VIII, "Configuring the ALE Interface," show you how to tweak certain parameters to achieve a particular effect without doing an enhancement. Master data distribution and distributed business processes are explained with real-world business scenarios. You'll learn how to set up workflow for error handling. If you cannot satisfy the business requirements by configuring the existing components, then you either need to enhance the existing components or build from ground zero. Section III, "IDocs," covers all the steps required to extend or create new IDocs, along with the programs to support the extensions and configuration to make these components known to the system.

- ◆ **Support provider.** If you are in (or anticipate being in) a support role for the ALE and EDI process, then Part IV, "Operating and Administering the EDI Interface," and Part IX, "Operating and Administering the ALE Interface," will be especially useful in understanding the various tasks and challenges that you will face in a live environment and the various kinds of problems that you can expect. These parts of the book also provide common remedies to those problems. In addition, you'll learn about utilities that will help you accomplish your everyday tasks.

◆ **Data-interfacing expert.** If you are a systems analyst and are contemplating various technologies for integrating external systems, you have several choices. Your decision does not rest simply on the capabilities of the various technologies; it also concerns ongoing support and maintenance, as well as restart and recovery options. This book helps you make an informed decision as to whether ALE and IDoc technologies are appropriate alternatives for your environment. Section III, "IDocs," is a great place to start.

◆ **Complementary software partner.** You either have a complementary product or are developing a product that will interface with SAP. Most third-party business systems (external warehouse management systems, EDI translators, production planning optimizers, and so on) interface with SAP via ALE and IDocs.

◆ **Workflow expert.** You are an expert in developing complex business workflows and have been given the task of setting up the workflow system for error handling in ALE and EDI. To understand various points in the ALE/EDI process where workflow is triggered and to familiarize yourself with various workflow tasks, turn to Chapter 9, "Configuring Workflow."

◆ **EDI/ALE programmer.** You are part of the technical team. You are responsible for writing or modifying ABAP/4 programs used by the IDoc interface. These programs have a certain structure, organization, and flow that is important to integrate seamlessly with the various components of the ALE or EDI process. You will find details about the structure of these programs in Section III, "IDocs."

◆ **Aspiring EDI and ALE expert.** You have been programming in ABAP/4 for a long time and you want to jump to the next step without forsaking your technical roots. You can easily turn yourself into an EDI/ALE programmer as long as you understand how these programs fit in the overall process; this book provides the information you need, such as locating and developing user exits in the EDI/ALE process and developing new programs from scratch.

◆ **Curious reader.** You have heard a lot about the ALE, EDI, and IDoc technologies, but you have never found any book that described them in simple language yet provided all the details. You can use this book to learn at your own pace, moving from a very high-level overview of the process into a detailed description of each component. You can select the level of detail that you are comfortable with. If you have access to the SAP system, then you can try out some of the example EDI and ALE scenarios discussed in this book.

◆ **E-commerce expert.** If you have worked on EDI projects in the past, you won't have any trouble grasping the EDI concepts in SAP. Section I of this book explains how SAP carries out the EDI process and is an excellent guide to help you build on the knowledge you've gained by working with EDI in other systems.

What This Book Covers

This book covers the full breadth and depth of ALE, EDI, and IDoc technology. You will learn the concepts behind these technologies and then configure some commonly used business ALE and EDI scenarios. You'll develop custom scenarios by either extending or developing new IDocs from scratch for different business situations. You will learn how to utilize user exits for the extended IDocs and develop new programs for custom IDocs. A brief overview of the topics covered in each part of the book follows.

Part I—EDI Basics

Part I begins with a discussion of general EDI technology and then moves on to the basics of SAP EDI architecture. The goal is to provide a high-level overview of the various components used in the EDI process, the benefits of EDI, and EDI's benefits to corporations.

Part II—The SAP EDI Interface

Part II examines the more advanced technical and functional details of the inbound and outbound SAP EDI process, including the interface with the EDI subsystem. Although this part is mainly for technical people, functional users can also benefit from this material. If you have scratched your head several times asking why SAP is behaving in a certain way, then this part should be your savior.

You will grasp the contents quickly with the aid of the flowcharts included throughout the chapters.

Part III—Configuring the EDI Interface

An SAP EDI process uses several components to generate and process EDI transactions. These components are highly configurable to meet the varying needs of several corporations. Part III provides the technical details of the concept, role, and options available for each component in the process. This material is designed for readers who are responsible for setting up the EDI interface. In a step-by-step manner, you'll learn to do the complete setup, which includes setting up the basic EDI infrastructure, building partner profiles, configuring Message control, and setting up the workflow component for error handling. The steps are illustrated with screen shots, tips, and tricks to make the learning process more fun.

Part IV—Operating and Administering the EDI Interface

Part IV covers the operational aspects of the EDI interface. After you have configured the system, you need to test your process inside and out to make sure it works as desired. You'll learn about various testing techniques and tools that you can use. After testing the interface, you can start running the process. The various monitoring tools available in the system and how to interpret the information logged in the system are also discussed. Sooner or later you will run into problems and need an efficient way to troubleshoot them, so the troubleshooting process is described in detail. A set of flowcharts has been provided to help you quickly get to the cause of a particular problem and then fix it. Finally, you'll also be involved in managing the performance and throughput of the system. The various ways to manage performance and throughput at the same time are discussed.

Part V—EDI Scenarios

In Part V, you will apply the knowledge that you have gained in the previous chapters to create actual outbound and inbound EDI transactions using real-world business scenarios. For outbound processes, you'll learn the complete setup required to send purchase orders to your vendors via EDI, and to send payment orders and remittance advice to your bank via EDI. For inbound processes, you'll learn the complete setup required to bring sales orders into the system via EDI, and sales order changes via workflow. The primary focus of this part is to present a methodology so that you can tackle any EDI transaction.

Part VI—ALE Basics

In Part VI, you are introduced to the ALE process, why it was invented, why some of the existing technologies do not suffice, its architecture, and its benefits. This is a general introduction and provides a high-level overview of the capabilities of the ALE process.

Part VII—The SAP ALE Interface

Part VII is an advanced technical and functional reference section for inbound and outbound ALE processes. You will grasp the contents quickly with the aid of several flowcharts included throughout the chapters.

Part VIII—Configuring the ALE Interface

The material in Part VIII is designed for readers who are responsible for setting up the ALE interface. First you'll learn how to set up the basic ALE infrastructure required by all ALE processes. Then you'll learn about one of the most widely used applications of ALE—the distribution of master data. You'll learn about the various distribution techniques, business issues, and strategies used by large organizations to keep master data under control. The material master data is used as an example to illustrate the various points. Another major application of ALE, the distribution of business processes, is described in complete detail using the distributed purchasing process.

Part IX—Operating and Administering the ALE Interface

Part IX covers the operational matters of the ALE interface. Once you have configured the system, you need to test your process to make sure it is working as desired. The various testing tools and techniques are discussed. Once you have tested the process, you can start executing it. The monitoring tools described in the EDI section are used for ALE processes. The monitoring tools describe how to interpret the information logged in the system. Sooner or later you will run into problems, and you'll need an efficient way to troubleshoot the problem and restart the process from the point of failure. A set of flowcharts has been provided to help you quickly get to the cause of the problem. Last but not the least, you will be involved in managing the performance and throughput of the ALE system. The possible approaches to managing performance and throughput are described.

Part X—IDoc Basics

In Part X, you will be introduced to the basics of the IDoc from an end-user perspective, and then you'll move into the more technical details required in the development and design of IDocs. The concepts cover data transfer via IDocs versus data transfer using flat files. This simple comparison will help you become an expert in a very short time.

Part XI—Customer Modifications to the IDoc Interface

A good understanding of the IDoc development process and the programming of IDocs is one of the important skills needed in a SAP implementation. In this part of the book, you will learn about the enhancement process to the IDoc interface. The enhancement process is effectively a three-step process. First, you create new IDocs or extend existing IDocs. Next, you develop programs for the new and extended IDocs. Finally, you customize the ALE/EDI interface layer to recognize the IDocs and their programs. There are three chapters in this part, devoted to each step of the enhancement process.

Part XII—Archiving in the IDoc Interface

When your system is operational and in production, the number of IDocs and workflow run-time logs can grow quickly. If your transaction volume is high, you'll need a strategy to archive IDocs. SAP provides archiving programs and deletion programs for several documents in the system, and you'll learn how to archive IDocs and delete work items and work item history.

Appendix—FAQs, User Exits, and Miscellaneous Resources

The appendix provides answers to frequently asked questions, a cross-reference chart for EDI transaction-to-SAP messages, a list of standard user exits in the system, a comparison between release 4.6 and previous versions, and other miscellaneous resources such as useful Web sites and Internet discussion groups.

Conventions Used in This Book

To comfortably absorb the information this book presents, you should be familiar with the teaching tools you'll find throughout the book.

Most notably, there are many SAP screen images, which help you to follow along with the instructions on an active SAP session of your own. Using the screen images, you can determine the pace at which you would like to progress, assuring yourself that you can clearly identify each activity being described.

Throughout the text, you'll encounter several explanatory techniques that will make the lessons easier to understand and apply. These techniques will help you quickly determine what action needs to be taken or which keyboard functions are required for the execution of each task. When you need to go through more than one menu to get where you're going, the path shows up as a series of words separated by commas.

You'll also see some special typographical devices to call your attention to certain points in the text.

 TIP

Tips present helpful information in an attention-getting format. These tips reinforce key concepts and explanations, making them easier to remember and use.

 NOTE

Notes provide additional related information, alternatives, or commentary that might help you better understand the topic under discussion or lead you to additional sources of information to make you more successful in your SAP usage.

 CAUTION

Cautions warn of potential hazards and pitfalls of which you should be aware.

These conventions will serve as your signposts throughout this text. Use them to help you identify critical elements and information about SAP. The lessons throughout this book will increase in pace and relative complexity to match your growing knowledge, and the conventions described will help you keep up.

SECTION
ONE

EDI

PART I

EDI Basics

Chapter 1

**Introduction to
the EDI Process**

EDI (*Electronic Data Interchange*) has been around for several years. The goal of this chapter is to provide a high-level overview of the EDI process, including what it is, how it started, why companies implement EDI, its benefits to corporations, and the various components used to build the EDI process. The material here is particularly important for someone who is new to EDI technology.

What Is EDI?

EDI is the electronic exchange of business documents between the computer systems of business partners, using a standard format over a communication network. EDI is also called *paperless exchange*.

This definition very nicely sums up the whole process in a few words, but the actual implementation of an effective EDI system requires considerable effort and support.

The Evolution of EDI

Consider a typical business scenario. A customer who wants to purchase an item creates a purchase order and then faxes or mails it to the vendor. The vendor receives the purchase order and manually keys in a sales order. The vendor's system generates a confirmation date that is sent back to the customer via fax or mail. The vendor then ships the goods via a carrier. The carrier delivers the products to the customer. When the goods are shipped, the vendor invoices the customer. The customer makes the payment by check, and the vendor deposits the check in the bank. Finally, funds are transferred from the customer's account to the vendor's account.

This simple scenario requires the exchange of various documents between several business partners at different times. A business process is a series of actions or functions that bring about a business result, and as such there are some inherent problems with this scenario. It:

- Is highly inefficient and laborious
- Cannot be tracked easily

◆ Gives no visibility into the process

◆ Has a very long lead time

◆ Includes redundant data entry at various points

To circumvent some of the trouble spots, business partners started exchanging data electronically via floppy disks and other storage devices, which meant that the business partners had to adopt standard formats. An ANSI committee was formed to define the standards. Ultimately, the electronic exchange of business documents in a standard format gave birth to what is now known as EDI.

EDI is not a recent invention; it has been around for more than 30 years. The transportation industry pioneered this technology and is thus responsible for its current architecture, but most industries have realized the benefits of using EDI. Today almost any industry or organization can take advantage of EDI. The retail and automotive industries are major EDI users, and the technology is also used in several other large industries, including health care and government agencies, real estate, and education. In fact, EDI can be implemented not only between organizations but also within organizations, an area that is gaining strength these days.

The Internet will undoubtedly be a major factor in the future evolution of EDI. An HTML-based specification for formatting structured data called XML (*Extensible Markup Language*), has attracted a lot of interest recently as a potential mechanism for moving EDI-like processes onto the Internet. However, as I will discuss later, many obstacles must be overcome before significant EDI is carried on using such tools. This book therefore focuses on standard EDI using the ANSI X12 and EDIFACT standards.

The Benefits of the EDI Process

Implementing EDI benefits both the sender and the receiver. It is a mutual effort, and its benefits are maximized by sharing information in a timely manner. The benefits include

◆ **Reduced data entry errors.** EDI does not involve data entry at multiple points. In the traditional process, a sender creates a purchase order on the system, prints the order, and then faxes or mails it to a trading partner. The receiver then rekeys the same information on his or her computer. The process is prone to data entry errors. This procedure is repeated when invoicing takes place. With EDI, data goes directly from one computer to another without involving a human being.

◆ **Reduced processing cycle time.** The biggest advantage is the reduced processing time of the complete cycle. As soon as orders are entered into the system, they can be processed on the receiving side in seconds. There is a considerable savings in the processing time of document transfer.

◆ **Availability of data in electronic form.** Data from EDI is in electronic form, which makes it easy to share across the organization. For example, a purchasing department can use the data to evaluate vendors, or a marketing department can use the data to analyze the trends and demands of customers.

◆ **Reduced paperwork.** The entire EDI process can be handled without using a single piece of paper. Some companies believe that they must have appropriate paperwork for audits and legal issues. In its Paperwork Reduction Act, the IRS recognizes the electronic form as a valid legal document as long as the vendor or supplier can prove the origin and show complete trails on how the data was generated. A company needs to have controlled processes to handle data flowing in and out. This ruling has created some tough auditing requirements, but complying with them is worth the effort.

◆ **Reduced cost.** Time is money. Any savings in time is directly linked to savings in money. The initial cost of an EDI setup is certainly higher compared to the paper process, but over a long period it is very cost-effective. In the long term, the overall cost of exchanging business documents in paper form can cost anywhere from $10 to $15 per transaction. If the process has to be repeated for some reason (for example, if an invoice is lost), it can cost around $45. On the flip side, the average cost of an EDI transaction is close to $2.

◆ **Reduced inventories and better planning.** Companies do not have to keep a safety stock for the time taken with order processing. Changes to planning schedules can be communicated instantaneously. MRP (*Material Requirements Planning*) can take into account a shipment in transit as soon as an Advance Ship Notice (EDI 856) transaction is received.

◆ **Standard means of communication.** Because EDI enforces standards on the contents of data, uniform naming standards and field sizes have emerged. Such consistency leads to clearer communication and less ambiguity.

◆ **Better business processes.** Compared to traditional methods of exchanging business documents, EDI is certainly a better way of communicating with your trading partners. Companies are willing to share information and participate in interorganizational issues. This environment enhances supply-chain management.

◆ **Competitive advantage.** In many cases, companies that have implemented EDI have an advantage over their competitors, especially when dealing with government agencies or large corporations. For example, potential vendors must use EDI to bid for certain government contracts. The procurement divisions in government agencies publish their RFPs (*Request for Proposal*) on the EDI network. In addition, large retailers and corporations discourage doing business with a business partner if the partner cannot send EDI transactions. The same holds true for the automotive industry. To be a certified auto-industry vendor, an organization must be able to communicate electronically. Trying to clear goods through customs is truly a nightmare if the necessary documentation is not in EDI format and has not been sent in advance.

The Business Process Using EDI

In the process of buying and selling goods, partners exchange business documents at various times. These documents record the process of creating and executing a contract for sales of goods or services. While many of these documents help to meet legal requirements, they are also all significant factors in the efficiency of processing a particular sales transaction. Well-run businesses pay a lot of attention to optimizing these business processes, and EDI frequently plays a major role in efforts to improve speed and efficiency. Many modern business process designs are feasible only because of the existence of EDI technology. Figure 1.1 depicts business documents that are commonly exchanged.

FIGURE 1.1 *Typical business documents exchanged by business partners*

Documents Exchanged with Customers

Between a customer and a supplier, it is the customer who typically drives the EDI requirements. The following are key business documents exchanged between a customer and supplier.

- ◆ The customer requests price catalogs.
- ◆ The customer requests quotes.
- ◆ The customer places blanket purchase orders.

- The customer authorizes delivery against its blanket orders.
- The customer places an order.
- The customer expects an order acknowledgment.
- The customer expects a delivery schedule.
- The customer wants to know the status of the order.
- The customer might cancel an order.
- The customer might change an order.
- The customer expects an order.
- The customer requires a shipment notification.
- The customer receives goods.
- The customer notifies the supplier that goods have been received.
- The customer wants authorization to return goods.
- The customer wants to return goods damaged in transit.
- The customer is an international customer.
- The customer receives an invoice.

Documents Exchanged with Carriers

A *carrier* is a party who undertakes the transportation of goods. The following documents are exchanged during the transportation process.

- The shipper requests a carrier pickup.
- The carrier responds with a pickup date.
- The carrier prints a bill of lading.
- The carrier informs the receiving party of the shipment.
- The receiver tells the carrier where to unload the goods.
- The shipper requests tracking for a particular shipment.
- The carrier informs the shipper of the status of the shipment.
- The carrier bills the shipper through an invoice.
- The carrier receives payment.

Documents Exchanged with Financial Institutions

Financial institutions act as agents for payers, or as guarantors or advisors in matters involving letters of credit. The following documents are exchanged in business transactions with financial institutions.

- Banks receive authorization to transfer funds from a buyer's account to a seller's account.
- The customer requests account information.
- Banks send an account summary.

Documents Exchanged with Insurance Institutions

An insurance institution writes insurance policies for freight and pays claims for items damaged in shipment. The following documents are exchanged in business transactions with insurance institutions.

- The customer establishes an insurance policy.
- The customer informs the insurer of the goods being transported.
- The insurer processes a claim for goods damaged in transit.
- The insurer settles the claim.

Documents Exchanged with Government Agencies

A government agency is a regulating agency at the federal, state, or local level that has policies regarding shipments. For example, the Customs Department is involved with shipping or receiving goods across a national boundary. The following documents are exchanged with the Customs Department in international trade.

- The shipper provides Customs with manifest data on cargo.
- The shipper obtains a cargo release and clearance information from Customs.
- The shipper obtains a rejection or approval notice from Customs.

Components Used in the EDI Process

This section describes the various components used in an EDI process (see Figure 1.2). An EDI process is a transfer of one or a sequence of electronic messages.

FIGURE 1.2 *Components of the EDI system*

Like any other communication process, it involves senders, receivers, language, content, and a medium. The components described below supply all of these basic elements. In EDI, the senders and receivers are called *trading partners*, and the X12 or EDIFACT standards supply a common language for formatting the information content of common messages. Software tools called *translators* enable trading partners to converse in a standard language, and application programs (such as SAP R/3), coupled with networking facilities such as the Internet or a commercial VAN (*Value-Added Network*), supply the messaging medium.

Trading Partners

Parties involved in a business transaction are called *trading partners*. The trading partners can be any combination of organizations or business types. For example, customers and vendors are trading partners.

Business Documents

A *business document* is a legal document that defines the transaction conducted between trading partners. The legal boundaries for these transactions are defined by trade agencies, trading partners, and the ISO (*International Standards Organization*). The trading partners are bound by the terms and conditions of these documents. Numerous business documents are in existence today. Examples of some typical business documents follow.

- Requests for quotes
- Purchase orders
- Purchase order changes
- Purchase order acknowledgments
- Invoices
- Remittance advice

EDI Messages

The transportation industry pioneered the exchange of business documents in electronic form. However, no commonly adopted standard existed among the companies involved, which resulted in multiple electronic formats for the same type of business document. The industry eventually saw a need for standardization, and a committee named ANSI ASC X12 was formed in 1975 to address this issue. The *X* signifies the committee's relevance to the computer industry, and the *12* was the next sequential number in the list of numbers assigned to each committee. The committee published its first standards in 1979. The standards defined various EDI messages that govern the rules, format, and content of data in a transaction. A one-to-one correspondence exists between the components of a paper-based document and an EDI message. The terminology may vary from one standard to another. The standards also determine the format of the transmission packet.

The formation of common standards has many advantages, some of which are detailed in the following list.

- Standardization allows representation that can be easily processed by a computer system.
- Standardization allows companies to exchange information that is independent from the application software.
- Third-party applications can provide EDI translation and thus relieve the application of having to keep up with evolving standards.

The choice of standards is mainly based on the industry and the standards used by a company's trading partner. It is common for a company to use multiple standards because its customers use a variety of standards. Two widely used standards are ANSI X12 and EDIFACT.

 NOTE

XML—an extension of HTML designed as a set of rules for formatting structured data—was introduced in 1997 and has attracted much interest as a format for EDI-like applications. A number of companies and industries have experimented with XML, and predictably, numerous candidate standards have emerged. ANSI X12 has created a task group to look into setting standards based on XML. Very little EDI is currently handled with XML-based formats, compared with ANSI X12 or EDIFACT. However, XML usage will be limited until vendors and trading partners overcome the problems hindering the use of the Internet for serious EDI, such as security and guaranteed service standards. In addition, the parties involved must accomplish the considerable task of developing and obtaining wide compliance with standards for specific business documents.

ANSI ASC X12

The ANSI ASC X12 standard is dominant in North America, New Zealand, and Australia. The committee is comprised of representatives from major organizations, government bodies, and EDI software companies. The X12 committee is divided into several subcommittees that are responsible for developing standards for a specific industry sector (see Table 1.1). The approval process is based on a consensus of all the subcommittees.

The Technical Structure of a Business Document

The structure of a business document in ANSI X12 standards can be described using a three-tier hierarchy: transactions, segments, and data elements (see Figure 1.3).

◆ **Transaction.** A *transaction* is the electronic equivalent of a business document. A transaction is usually divided into three areas: header area, detail area, and summary area. The *header area* consists of segments that apply to the entire document, and is usually mandatory. For example, in a purchase order, vendor number and vendor address are part of the

Table 1.1 The ANSI X12 Subcommittees

Subcommittee	Primary Focus
X12A	Education administration
X12C	Communications and controls
X12E	Product data
X12F	Finance
X12G	Government
X12H	Materials management
X12I	Transportation
X12J	Technical assessment
X12K	Purchasing
X12L	Industry standards transition
X12M	Distribution and warehousing
X12N	Insurance

header segments. The *detail area* contains document details. The items being ordered and their quantities are considered detail segments. The *summary area* consists of data that summarizes the entire document, and the total amount and taxes are part of the summary segments.

◆ **Segment.** A *segment* is equivalent to a record in a document. A data segment has the following attributes: a unique ID, a name, a flag indicating whether it is optional or mandatory, and a number of occurrences. A group of segments can be combined to form a loop, which can also be mandatory or optional, and can be nested as well. Segments are contained in a segment directory (X12.22). A segment consists of a sequence of logically related data elements. Data elements are separated by a data element separator and can be mandatory or optional. Some data elements are conditional, or mandatory, in certain situations.

◆ **Data Elements.** Data elements are the smallest unit of information in a transaction and are defined in the data element dictionary (X12.3). A data element is identified by a data element reference number, a data type, and a minimum and maximum length.

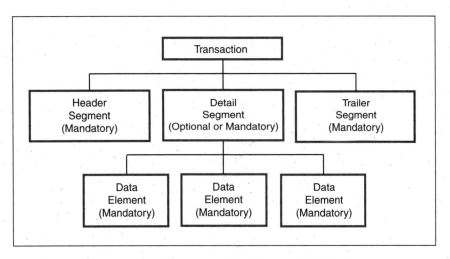

FIGURE 1.3 *The technical structure of a business document in EDI format*

The Technical Structure of a Communication Packet

It is common to bundle several EDI messages in one packet before transmitting it over the network. The communication packet as transmitted over the network has a hierarchical format, as shown in Figure 1.4.

Each message (a purchase order, for example) is wrapped in a transaction set header (ST) and a transaction set trailer (SE). Several messages of similar type can be combined into a functional group. For example, if an EDI message contains three purchase orders, they will be combined into one functional group. Each functional group is wrapped with a functional group header (GS) and a functional group trailer (GE). An EDI transmission can contain several functional groups, which are bundled together and wrapped with an EDI header and trailer—the interchange control header (ISA) and interchange control trailer (IEA), respectively. The communication network wraps yet another header and trailer on the EDI message.

UN/EDIFACT

UN/EDIFACT (*United Nations EDI for Administration, Commerce, and Transport*) was formed in 1985, using the ANSI X12 and UNTDI (*United Nations Trade Data Interchange*) as the base standards. The purpose was to develop an international

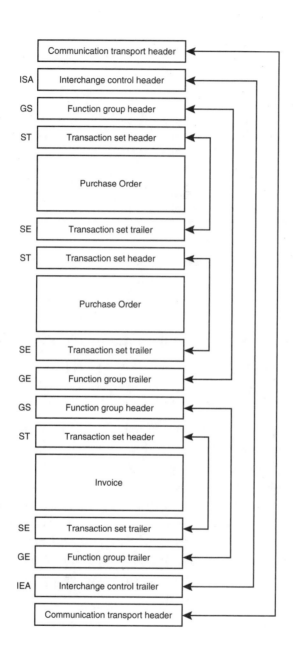

FIGURE 1.4 *The structure of an ANSI X12 message*

standard to meet the needs of a global economy. Most companies are moving toward adopting EDIFACT because of its international recognition. EDIFACT is quite similar to ANSI X12, with some minor differences in terminology and layout.

- EDIFACT calls business documents *messages* and represents them by a name such as *ORDERS* for a purchase order, whereas ANSI X12 calls them *transactions* and represents them by a number such as 850 for a purchase order.

- EDIFACT uses the same segment in multiple places, whereas ANSI has a specific use for each segment.

- EDIFACT has additional segments that apply to international trade.

- EDIFACT uses different terminology for fields. *Conditional* fields in EDIFACT are the same as *optional* fields in ANSI X12.

Application Programs

Application programs are responsible for generating and processing data in business documents. These application programs are part of the application suite commonly referred to as ERP (*Enterprise Resource Planning*). ERP systems meet a broad range of a company's business needs—SAP R/3 is an example. Most ERP vendors recognize the business needs for EDI and thus enable their software to support EDI processes. An ERP system must do the following:

- Support standard EDI transactions in the business area of interest. For example, if the focus of a company is shipping and distribution, the software must support basic shipping transactions.

- Make the data necessary for EDI messages readily available.

- Document the EDI processes and functionality.

- Be flexible enough to incorporate business requirements within the existing process.

- Provide support for enhancing existing transactions.

- Contain easily configurable and manageable systems.

- Contain a sufficient number of control points to meet business needs.

- Exhibit a disciplined approach for controlling the flow of documents within the organization, from error handling to the approval process.
- Be integrated with EDI translation software vendors.
- Provide system limits and performance measures if a company expects a large volume of EDI transactions.

SAP meets all these business requirements. Starting with Chapter 2, "Introduction to SAP EDI Architecture," you will learn about the capabilities of SAP.

Translators

The traditional approach to EDI implementation was to incorporate the conversion of application data to EDI standards as an integral part of the business application. The problem with this approach was that a separate program existed for not only each transaction, but also for each trading partner to meet its unique requirements. Keeping up with the changing standards was another problem. Programs had to be modified every time a trading partner adopted a newer version of the standards.

This approach has changed with the development of third-party translation software, which has become a key element of the EDI process chain. The translator is responsible for mapping application data to the EDI standard format, and vice versa. This technology frees the application software to concentrate on the business logic.

 NOTE

The business applications have to be *EDI-enabled*, which means that they should be capable of interfacing with the translation software, whether through a flat file or transactions.

Value-Added Networks

Communication networks, often called VANs, provide a means of transmission for EDI transactions between trading partners. The VAN provides a mailbox on the network to each trading partner. This mailbox is polled periodically for messages. The mailboxes are marked as incoming or outgoing mailboxes. The VAN picks up outgoing messages and delivers them to the incoming mailbox of the receiving trading partner. The application software does not have to be connected or running at the time of message exchange. VANs enable communication between trading partners with different internal communication networks.

The following criteria can be used in evaluating a VAN.

◆ The availability and reliability of the network

◆ The reach of the network (national versus international boundaries)

◆ Performance characteristics

◆ The flexibility of the cost structure (flat rate versus per document versus the number of characters)

◆ Retransmission of failed documents

◆ A gateway to link to other VANs

◆ The availability of audit reports and error reports

◆ The security of data transmitted over the network

The major drawbacks with VANs are the ongoing expense of network services and the cost associated with each transmission. If the volume of transactions is high, the total cost can be substantial. Some companies currently use direct links (via modems) with their trading partners to avoid the cost of a VAN. The only problem with this system is that any new partners must follow similar standards.

A new trend involves using the Internet to transmit EDI documents. The use of the Internet has some advantages: It is available and inexpensive to everyone, and it is available 24 hours a day.

Summary

In this chapter, you learned about the basic features of EDI, how it can benefit small and large organizations, and which components you use to build an EDI system. By now you should have a good understanding of the overall EDI process and its terminology. This background will enable you to understand the equivalent terminology in SAP when the SAP EDI process is introduced in the next chapter.

Chapter 2

Introduction to SAP EDI Architecture

In this chapter, you'll learn the basics of SAP EDI architecture and get a high-level overview of its various components. This chapter shows you how SAP supports the EDI process, what it means to be EDI-enabled, and what support SAP provides for creating new processes. You'll also learn the boundaries of SAP EDI in the big EDI picture.

SAP EDI Boundaries

Chapter 1, "Introduction to the EDI Process," presented a general overview of the EDI process. It is important to understand which components are supplied by SAP. Figure 2.1 illustrates the SAP EDI boundaries. SAP provides the application logic, application data, and format for the data contents. Third-party software vendors supply the other pieces.

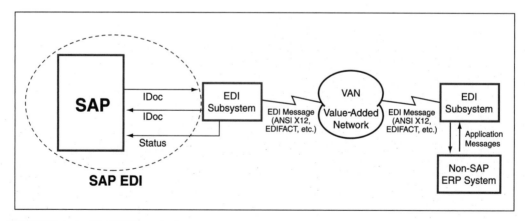

FIGURE 2.1 *SAP EDI boundaries*

EDI-Enabled Applications in SAP

EDI-enabled applications in SAP are capable of generating IDoc (*Intermediate Document*) data from an SAP document or reading IDoc data and creating application documents. The application must understand the syntax and semantics of the data in the IDoc format. In the case of outbound processes, a separate selection program reads application data and creates an IDoc, as shown in Figure 2.2. Similarly, for inbound processes, a posting program reads IDoc data to create an application document.

Chapter 1, "Introduction to the EDI Process," also introduced some of the documents commonly exchanged by business partners. You might think that SAP would support almost every EDI transaction because SAP is the enterprise system and has data in a single repository. This assumption is not completely valid.

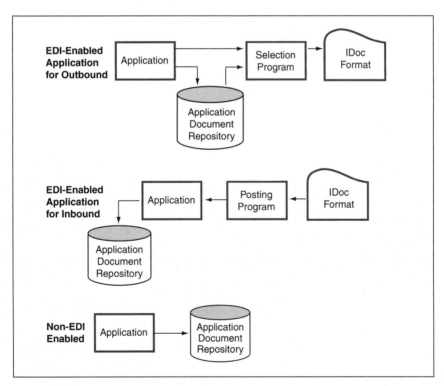

FIGURE 2.2 *An EDI-enabled application for the outbound process*

In the standard SAP system, several EDI-enabled applications in various modules are capable of generating and processing IDoc data, but all EDI documents are not supported. It is very likely that SAP supports the business process but not the creation or processing of IDocs. However, with every release of SAP, the list of supported IDocs grows considerably.

NOTE

An application that is not EDI–enabled can be enabled by developing the selection and posting programs and IDoc structures. This is an important aspect of any SAP EDI project. SAP provides a comprehensive set of tools for developing IDocs and programs. Refer to Section Three, "IDocs," for details on how to enable an application for both inbound and outbound processes.

The appendix includes a complete list of EDI documents supported in the standard process as of SAP R/3 release 4.6C.

A Process Overview

The SAP EDI process comprises two distinct processes.

- ◆ Outbound process
- ◆ Inbound process

The Outbound Process

The outbound process sends documents from the SAP system to a business partner (vendor, customer, or bank). Figure 2.3 shows the outbound process at a very high level. The outbound process consists of six steps.

1. **The application document is created**. The first step in the outbound process involves creating an application document, such as a purchase order or sales order, and saving it in the database tables. This step is no different from the way in which these documents are normally created. It is the following steps that have relevance to EDI. The document is created and leaves some hooks for the EDI process to begin.

FIGURE 2.3 *Process flow and data flow in an outbound EDI process*

2. **The IDoc is generated**. The application document just created is now formatted to an IDoc format. At this point you can think of an IDoc as yet another format in which the application document has been represented. For example, think of how a date can be stored in different formats—imagine a date as a document with three components: day, month, and year. In one case, you represent it as *MM/DD/YYYY*, a standard American way of representing a date. To make it meaningful for a German partner, you have to represent it as *DD.MM.YY*. IDocs follow a similar concept of representing information in different ways. The data in the application document format is suitable for the application modules, screens, and internal programs. A document in an IDoc format is suitable for processing by EDI components, as later sections explain in more detail.

3. **The IDoc is transferred from SAP to the operating system layer**. The IDoc created in Step 2 resides in the SAP database repository. This IDoc document must be passed down to the operating system layer for processing by the EDI subsystem. In Step 3, the IDoc is transferred to the operating system as a text file. The document is still in an IDoc format. The only difference is the medium of storage.

4. **The IDoc is converted to EDI standards**. The IDoc format is an SAP proprietary format. For EDI purposes, the document in IDoc format has to be converted into an EDI standard format. A type of third-party software called a *translator* carries out the transformation process and reports status back to the SAP system. SAP refers to these translators as *EDI subsystems*, and has certified several subsystems for connectivity to SAP. SAP takes no responsibility for translation. Thus, from SAP's perspective, after the IDoc is delivered to the subsystem, SAP does not have control over the process, but it maintains the status reported by the EDI subsystem.

 CAUTION

SAP does not restrict you to using certified systems, but doing so adds assurance of connectivity, compatibility, and support. Because there are many technical and business issues to worry about, I do not recommend exploring non-certified systems.

5. **The EDI document is transmitted to the business partner**. After the document is converted to an EDI standard format, it is transmitted to a trading partner based on the partner's EDI settings. This step is not part of the SAP EDI architecture, but is mentioned here to describe the complete process from a business perspective.

6. **The EDI subsystem reports status to SAP**. When an IDoc is under the control of the EDI subsystem, the subsystem can optionally report the state of processing at various milestones back to the SAP system. This mechanism is always recommended because it provides complete visibility of the process from within SAP, and the user does not have to be involved with the intricacies of the EDI subsystem.

The Inbound Process

The inbound process simply reverses the steps of the outbound process. The inbound process receives an EDI document (such as a purchase order response, sales order, or payment information) from a business partner (such as a vendor, a customer, or a bank) and creates SAP documents from it. Figure 2.4 shows the inbound process at a very high level. You can find complete technical and functional details in Chapter 4, "The Inbound EDI Process."

The inbound process consists of five steps.

1. **The EDI transmission is received**. EDI documents are received from a business partner via the VAN. These documents are in one of the EDI

FIGURE 2.4 *Process flow and data flow in an inbound EDI process*

standard formats. The documents are deposited in a common repository for the subsystem. This part of the process is not part of the SAP EDI architecture.

2. **The EDI document is converted into an IDoc**. The EDI-specific headers and trailers are stripped off, and the document is converted into an IDoc format suitable for SAP applications. The process is carried out at the EDI subsystem level.

3. **The IDoc is transferred to the SAP layer**. The IDoc created in Step 2 is stored in a text file at the operating system layer. The subsystem starts an inbound program in the SAP layer. This program reads the IDoc file and creates an IDoc in the SAP repository for further processing.

4. **The application document is created.** The IDoc received from the subsystem is passed to a posting program. This program creates an application document such as a sales order, purchase order acknowledgment, invoice, or shipment notice.

5. **The application document can be viewed.** The application document created via EDI is the same as any document created manually in the system: The document can be viewed using standard application transactions. For example, if an incoming sales order was created via EDI, you could view the sales order document via transaction VA03.

Exception Handling via Workflow

The preceding steps describe the path of a successful EDI transaction. Exceptions can occur at any point during either the outbound or inbound process. They are caused by technical problems (such as network connectivity failures or file system problems), data-related problems (such as data that is formatted incorrectly or missing), or a combination of both.

Workflow provides a very sophisticated method for managing the exception-handling process. Based on the type of error, workflow can be configured to identify the persons responsible for handling the problem, notify them in a timely manner, and provide a mechanism for making the necessary correction. After the problem is fixed, the process can be restarted from the point of failure. Chapter 9, "Configuring Workflow," provides complete details on how to set up workflow and manage the exception-handling process.

IDocs Explained

An *IDoc* is a container that can be used to exchange data between any two processes. The document represented in an IDoc is independent of the complex structure used in SAP to store application data. This feature enables SAP to rearrange its internal structure without affecting the existing interfaces.

The word *IDoc* is used very loosely in the IDoc interface. An IDoc represents an IDoc type and IDoc data, depending on the context in which the word *IDoc* is used. An IDoc type defines the structure and format of the data being exchanged. For example, the IDoc type INVOIC01 defines the format of an invoice document. IDoc data can be seen as an instance of an IDoc type. For example, an actual invoice received from a vendor in electronic form is converted into an IDoc.

IDoc Types

IDocs types are based on EDI standards (ANSI X12 and EDIFACT). They are closer to the EDIFACT standards than to ANSI X12. The size and format of data elements in an IDoc type are derived from these standards wherever applicable. The IDoc format is compatible with most EDI standards.

An IDoc structure consists of several segments, and segments consist of several data fields. The IDoc structure defines the syntax of the data by specifying a list of permitted segments, the arrangement of the segments, and optional versus mandatory segments. Segments define a set of fields and their formats.

IDocs

An IDoc is an instance of an IDoc type. Each IDoc is assigned a unique number for tracking and future reference. An IDoc serves as a focal object for tracking the state of the process that generated it. An IDoc consists of the following three types of records (see Figure 2.5).

- ◆ One control record
- ◆ One or many data records
- ◆ One or many status records

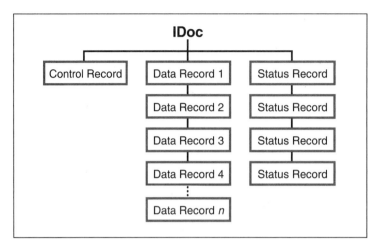

FIGURE 2.5 *The internal structure of an IDoc, showing the control record, data records, and status records*

◆ **Control record.** There is only one control record per IDoc. The control record contains all the control information about an IDoc, including the IDoc number, sender and receiver information, and other control information such as the message type it represents and the IDoc type. The structure of the control record is the same for all IDocs and is defined by SAP. The field values, of course, can be different.

◆ **Data record.** An IDoc can contain multiple data records, as defined by the IDoc structure. Segments translate into data records. Data records store application data such as purchase order header information, purchase order details lines, and other relevant information.

◆ **Status record.** Multiple status records are usually attached to an IDoc. Status records are attached to an IDoc throughout the process, as the IDoc achieves different milestones. A status code, date, and time are assigned at every milestone.

In the outbound process, after the IDoc is passed from SAP to the subsystem, the status records are generated by the subsystem and passed back to SAP. For the inbound process, SAP generates the status records because after an IDoc is generated, it stays in the system. Status records help you determine the status of the process and whether an IDoc is in error.

SAP provides tools to view the IDoc structure and IDoc data. Chapter 11, "Monitoring the Interface," provides complete details on various tools available in the system for monitoring the IDocs.

Multiple Messages per IDoc Type

A message represents a specific type of document that is transmitted between two partners. Orders, order responses, order acknowledgments, invoices, and shipment notices are examples of messages. An IDoc type in SAP can be used to represent several messages or business documents. Of course, the messages must be logically related. For example, in Figure 2.6, an IDoc type represents all possible information about an employee. This IDoc type is being used to send two separate messages to two separate applications. One message is the Employee Salary Information, the other is the Employee Security Information. The difference between the two messages is the set of segments used.

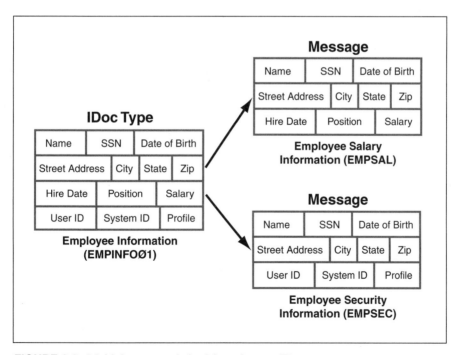

FIGURE 2.6 *Multiple messages derived from the same IDoc type*

SAP uses a single IDoc type for several logically related messages. For example, the Orders IDoc type (ORDERS02) is used for several messages, such as Order (ORDERS), Order Response (ORDRSP), and Order Change (ORDCHG).

The Independence of EDI Standards

Several EDI standards are in use today, and these standards are continuously evolving. Companies are using different versions of the standards. SAP decided not to chase the standards and instead came out with its own proprietary format, the IDoc format. The responsibility of maintaining compliance with EDI standards was left to companies that develop translators. Hence, the architecture of EDI in SAP is completely independent of the EDI standards used by any other company.

Another reason for keeping the translation and conversion out of SAP is the computing-intensive nature of the translation process. It is a logical piece that can be handled separately without affecting the process flow.

Configuration Tools

The flexible SAP EDI interface meets the varying needs of companies. The processes can be operated in real-time mode or batch mode. The components used in the interface can be customized to implement customer-specific business scenarios. For example, if one vendor accepts EDI transmissions and the other vendor accepts only faxes, the process can be configured to produce different outputs depending on the vendor. The standard scenarios are preconfigured. If you develop new EDI scenarios, the system allows you to configure the EDI interface to recognize your custom scenarios, as explained in Section Three, "IDocs."

Support Tools

Several available tools meet the everyday needs for working with the EDI interface. They can be reached through the SAP standard menu via Tools, Business Communication, IDoc. An area menu (WEDI) has been defined for EDI. You can access most of the tools from this location. The following section introduces you to the types of tools available in the system.

TIP

Under R/3 versions prior to 4.6, most EDI tools can be accessed through an area menu (transaction WEDI). This transaction can still be executed in version 4.6 (at least through 4.6B) from the SAP Easy Access screen by entering **/n** in the command box and then pressing the Enter key. This closes the Easy Access screen. You can then enter **WEDI** in the control box and press the Enter key. From version 4.6, you can also access a new EDI area menu by simply entering **WEDI** in the command box while at the SAP Easy Access screen, and then pressing the Enter key.

Documentation

IDoc structures are thoroughly documented. Using transactions listed under Documentation in the SAP WEDI area menu, you can view the documentation of IDoc structures in a report format, which can be printed and downloaded to a file. The report can be used to understand the functionality of an IDoc. The use of segments and their fields is clearly documented.

Monitoring

IDocs can be viewed using standard tools. Several tools enable you to view the IDoc information in different ways. For example, you can get a complete list of IDocs in the system, or you can limit it to IDocs that are in error. These tools are described in full detail in Chapter 11, "Monitoring the Interface" and in Chapter 12, "EDI Process Troubleshooting and Recovery."

Testing

Several tools enable you to test the inbound and outbound processes. In addition, tools that simulate the process as if the subsystem were installed enable you to test the system without having an EDI subsystem installed. Several utilities make the testing process easy by creating IDocs on-the-fly, copying existing IDocs, or simulating error conditions. These tools are described in full detail in Chapter 10, "Testing the EDI Interface."

Enhancing the Standard Processes

If the standard process does not meet your requirements, you can enhance the scenario. You can extend the standard IDocs and enhance the standard programs to meet your business needs. SAP provides user exits at strategic points in the IDoc process to add your custom code. For example, if your customer requires you to supply its engineering part number on a sales order response, you could extend the ORDERS02 IDoc to add a segment containing the engineering part number and write custom code to populate a value in the engineering part number. Enhancements are supported when you upgrade your SAP system. SAP guarantees the location of the user exit and the context in which it is invoked. Section Three, "IDocs," provides programming examples for extending IDocs.

You can also develop new scenarios from scratch. You can create new IDoc structures and programs to create or process those IDocs. After you develop the IDoc and the programs, you can configure the interface to recognize your newly created programs and IDocs. The standard monitoring and testing tools can be used for custom-defined scenarios.

Summary

SAP supports the EDI process by providing EDI-enabled applications capable of sending and receiving IDoc messages. IDocs are SAP's proprietary format for exchanging data between business applications. IDocs are based on EDI standards and have a very flexible structure to accommodate business rules for representing data. These IDocs are mapped to an EDI standard format by EDI subsystems, which are third-party tools certified by SAP for their connectivity and capability to handle IDoc messages.

One IDoc can be mapped to one or more business transactions. SAP provides a complete development and enhancement environment for extending and creating new IDocs. Various tools configure, monitor, and troubleshoot the system.

PART II

The SAP EDI Interface

Chapter 3

The outbound process uses several components. You will get a quick overview of these components and then learn how the outbound process uses them to generate an IDoc for EDI transmission. Although this chapter mainly covers technical issues, functional users can also benefit from this material. If you have scratched your head several times, asking why SAP is behaving in a certain way, this chapter will be your savior.

Components Used in the Outbound Process

The outbound process uses IDoc types, Message control, partner profiles, port definitions, selection programs, service programs, and tables to generate an IDoc. A brief description of these components follows. A detailed description and the various configuration options available within each component appear in Part III, "Configuring the EDI Interface."

The IDoc Structure

The EDI document to be generated has an equivalent message type defined in the SAP system. The message type is based on an IDoc structure. For example, if you are going to generate EDI transaction 850, which is a purchase order, the message type ORDERS is assigned in SAP to purchase orders. This message is based on IDoc type ORDERS01 and ORDERS02. A list of IDoc types and their equivalent messages in EDIFACT and ANSI X12 standards is provided in the Appendix, "FAQs, User Exits, and Miscellaneous Resources."

 TIP

The list in the appendix is valid as of release 4.6B. Because this list is evolving, check with SAP for the latest version. If you have access to SAP's online support system (OSS), see note 104606.

The IDoc is the most important component in the EDI process. A good understanding of the IDoc is necessary for working with the EDI Interface. See Chapter 29, "IDocs from the Outside," and Chapter 30, "IDocs on the Inside," for complete details on the benefits and architecture of IDocs.

Selection Programs

Selection programs, which are typically implemented as function modules, are designed to extract application data and create an IDoc. A selection program exists for each message type. The programs are generally named with the following naming convention.

```
IDOC_OUTPUT_<message type>
```

 CAUTION

The naming convention mentioned here is not a rule, but it is a common practice for naming the outbound programs. You will find certain discrepancies in the names.

These function modules have a standard interface for input and output parameters. A process code is assigned to each selection program that executes under Message control. Because process codes are flexible, you can assign any processing option to a process code. A process code can point to a function module or a workflow. In the standard system, process codes always point to a function module.

For example, the selection program for message type ORDERS is IDOC_OUTPUT_ORDERS. A four-character process code, ME10, has been assigned to this function module. You can see a list of outbound process codes and their corresponding function modules by executing the following transaction.

Transaction: WE41
Menu Path: From the area menu of EDI (WEDI): Control, Outbound Process Code

You can develop your own custom function modules. See Chapter 32, "Programming in the IDoc Interface," for details on the structure of these programs and how to write a new program.

Message Control

Message control is a cross-application technology. It is used in pricing, account determination, material determination, and output determination. The Message control component enables you to encapsulate business rules without having to write ABAP/4 programs. In the EDI process, Message control determines and processes the various outputs associated with an application document (for example, EDI, printed output, fax, confirmation, and mail). The Message control component is described in full detail in Chapter 8, "Configuring Message Control," where you'll learn how to build business rules in Message control. In a nutshell, Message control separates the logic of generating EDI documents from the logic of the application. A list of applications supporting Message control is also included in Chapter 8.

The Port Definition

A port is used in the outbound process to determine the name of the EDI subsystem program (if installed), the directory path where the IDoc file will be created at the operating system level, the IDoc file names, and the RFC destination. Port definitions are described in full detail in Chapter 6, "Configuring Basic EDI Components."

The RFC Destination

RFC (Remote Function Call) *destination* is the term used to define the characteristics of communication links to a remote system on which a function needs to be executed. In EDI, it is used to specify information required to gain access to the system on which the EDI subsystem is installed. The various parameters and options in the RFC destination definition are described in Chapter 6.

 NOTE

The function served by the RFC destination in EDI is different from the ALE process, where the RFC destination is used to specify parameters to log on to the remote SAP system.

The Partner Profile

A partner profile specifies the various components used in an outbound process (partner number, IDoc type, message type, port, process code), the mode in which it communicates with the subsystem (batch versus immediate), and the person to be notified in case of errors.

A partner profile is created for each business partner, and a record exists for each outbound message sent to a business partner. For example, if two outbound messages (purchase order and purchase order change) are being sent to vendor number VEN001, a partner profile must exist for VEN001, and two outbound records (one for each message type) must exist in the partner profile. The partner profile is an important and frequently referenced component. The various attributes of the partner profile are described in detail in Chapter 7, "Configuring Partner Profiles."

Service Programs and Configuration Tables

The asynchronous outbound process can be seen as a sequence of several processes that work together. SAP provides service programs and configuration tables to link the various components and provide customizing options for an outbound process. The process flow for the outbound process describes the role played by each service program and configuration table.

Types of Outbound Processes

By now you should be able to list the components used in the outbound process. This section describes how the components are used and explains the function performed by each component. The outbound process has two distinct paths for creating IDocs.

- ◆ With Message control
- ◆ Directly—without Message control

The Outbound Process with Message Control

Most SD (*Sales and Distribution*) and MM (*Materials Management*) applications use Message control. The FI (*Financial*) applications do not use the services of the Message control component.

The outbound process can best be described by explaining the processing that occurs at each layer, shown in Figure 3.1. The corresponding technical flow appears in Figure 3.2, to help you understand the technical components used, such as programs, table entries, and parameter values.

Processing in the Application Layer

An application document is entered via a transaction; for example, a sales order is entered via VA01. Before an application document is saved, the Message control component is invoked. An application passes several key elements of the application data to the Message control component via communication structures.

Processing in the Message Control Layer

The Message control component checks various business rules defined in the Message control configuration. Based on the business rules, Message control proposes the output type (sales order response, internal notification, and so on), timing (immediate or batch), medium (EDI, ALE, printout, mail, fax, and so on), and language of the message. Multiple outputs are possible from Message control. Each output is processed independently. A simple example of a business rule is to send a sales order response immediately via EDI for a sales order from Customer 1111 and generate an internal message for the production department.

The proposed outputs can be seen on the output control screen of the transaction. Some applications provide output control at both the line-item level and the header level. In most applications, you can reach the output control screen in one of the following ways on the application transaction screen.

- ◆ By choosing Header, Messages
- ◆ By choosing Header, Output

For example, you reach the output control screen for a purchase order by selecting Header, Messages. For a sales order, you reach the output screen at the header level by selecting Header, Output and at the item level by selecting Item, Output.

The output proposed by the Message control component can be edited. The user can delete, add, or modify any outputs proposed on the output control screen.

When the application document is saved, the outputs proposed on the output control screen are saved as a record in the NAST table. An entry in the NAST table stores the key of the application document, output type, timing, processing status, and language.

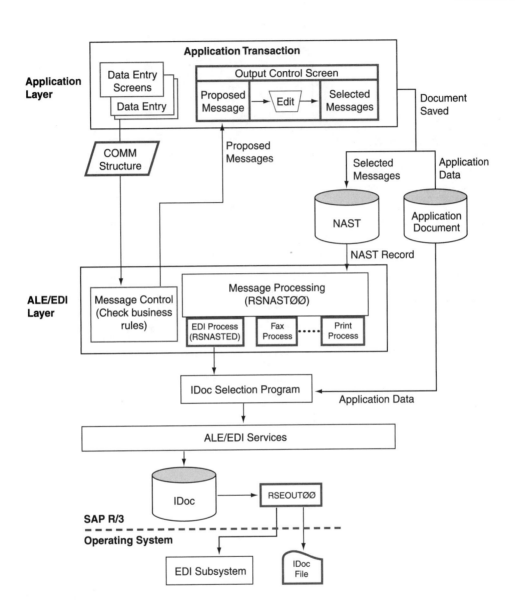

FIGURE 3.1 *Details of the outbound process with Message control*

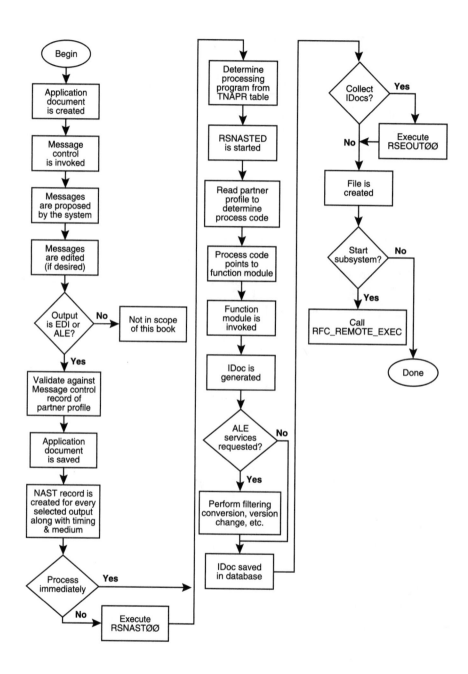

FIGURE 3.2 *The technical flow of the outbound process with Message control*

If the timing for an output is set to 4 (Immediate), the system immediately starts the processing of the output type by executing the RSNAST00 program. If the timing is set to 1 (Batch Mode), the entries are processed when the RSNAST00 program is executed explicitly. The RSNAST00 program is usually scheduled to run on a regular basis. It selects entries that can be processed based on their status and calls the appropriate program for the selected medium. Each output medium (EDI, ALE, fax, printed output, and so on) has a corresponding program to generate the output in the required medium. SAP provides standard processing programs for each output medium.

In the case of EDI, the processing program is a form routine: EDI_PROCESSING in the RSNASTED program. This program is a generic program for all EDI outputs and reads the partner profile configuration to determine the selection program for a particular message.

In ALE, the processing program is also a form routine: ALE_PROCESSING in the RSNASTED program. This program is a generic program for all ALE outputs and reads the partner profile configuration to determine the selection program for a particular message.

Processing in the Selection Program

The selection program is specified in the partner profile with a process code. The RSNASTED program calls the appropriate selection program.

One of the parameters for these function modules is the NAST entry, which contains the key of the application document. These programs extract application data, format it into an IDoc format in an internal table, and then pass control to the ALE/EDI layer.

Processing in the ALE/EDI Layer

The ALE/EDI layer is responsible for creating the IDoc in the SAP database. By now, a tangible IDoc that can be viewed using the various monitoring tools has been created in the system. The IDoc gets a status record with a status code of 01 (IDoc Created).

The IDoc, before being saved in the database, goes through a syntax check and other validations. If there are no errors, the IDoc gets a status of 30 (IDoc Ready for Dispatch to ALE Service).

Dispatching the IDoc

The next step is to pass the IDoc to the operating system layer. The settings of the Output Mode fields in the partner profile are read to determine the timing of this step, and the port definition is read to determine the directory location in which the file will be created. If the mode is set to Do Not Collect IDocs, the IDoc is immediately passed to the operating system layer automatically, using program RSEOUT00. If the field is set to Collect IDocs, the IDoc is not passed to the operating system layer until the RSEOUT00 program is executed explicitly. The RSEOUT00 program is typically scheduled to run on a regular basis. If IDocs are collected, RSEOUT00 creates a single file with all the IDocs in it. After the IDoc file is created successfully, the IDoc gets a status code of 03 (Data Passed to Port OK). The timing of this step is important from a performance point of view. For details, see Chapter 13, "Managing EDI Process Performance and Throughput."

Now the system determines whether the subsystem is to be started. This parameter is also specified in the partner profile in the Output Mode settings. If the value is set to Do Not Start the Subsystem, the process ends here. If the flag is set to Start the Subsystem, the subsystem program name is read from the port definition and the subsystem program is started. The name of the IDoc file is passed to the EDI subsystem program. If the subsystem is started successfully, the IDoc gets another status code 18 (Triggering EDI Subsystem OK).

Processing in the EDI Subsystem Layer

The control of the IDoc process has now been transferred to the subsystem layer. The subsystem takes the IDoc file as input and translates it into an EDI standard format. At various milestones, the subsystem reports the status of the process to SAP, thus providing complete visibility into the process from within SAP. The status reported by the subsystem is attached as a status record to the IDoc in the SAP database.

To report status back to the SAP system, the subsystem creates a status file at the OS level and calls the function module EDI_STATUS_INCOMING in SAP, passing the status file name as an input parameter. For this, SAP provides a standard program named startrfc at the OS level to execute any RFC-enabled function module in SAP. The layout of the status file appears in the appendix, and Chapter 6, "Configuring Basic EDI Components," describes the syntax of the startrfc command.

The Outbound Process without Message Control

The biggest advantage of the Message control component is the flexibility in proposing the outputs based on business rules and conditions, and in controlling the timing of IDoc creation.

Nevertheless, the following conditions might steer you away from Message control.

- Message control might not be available for your application document. In this case, you have no choice. Applications are programmed to make use of the Message control service, and it is not automatically available for every application. The FI applications, for example, do not use Message control. The REMADV message is generated by the Payment Run program, which does not use Message control. Most ALE processes do not use Message control.

- The Message control component is intricate because of its generic technology of building business rules without coding ABAP/4 programs. I have come across situations in which a client did not want to maintain Message control because of its complexity and decided to bypass it completely. This is not a configuration option. The client had developed custom programs to select IDoc data and pass it directly to the ALE/EDI layer.

The outbound process is best described by explaining the processing that occurs at each layer, shown in Figure 3.3. The corresponding technical flow, shown in Figure 3.4, points out the technical components that are used, such as service programs, configuration tables, and parameter values.

Processing in the Application Layer

The application document is entered by way of a transaction; for example, the Payment Run program (RFFOEDI1) is executed via SE38. The business rules for selecting objects for EDI output are established through a selection screen or a dialog box. The data-extraction logic, which is built into the application, is implemented as a separate function module but is still a part of the application logic. This concept is different compared to the outbound process with Message control, in which the data-extraction logic is not part of the application logic. The application builds the IDoc and passes control to the ALE layer. The interface to the ALE layer is through the function module MASTER_IDOC_DISTRIBUTE.

FIGURE 3.3 *Details of the outbound process without Message control*

Processing in the ALE/EDI Layer

The ALE/EDI layer checks for the sender and receiver fields. If they are not supplied, the ALE distribution model is consulted to determine the recipients. The ALE distribution model is used to model the messages exchanged between the systems. A message can have multiple recipients.

After the set of receivers is determined, the IDocs are processed for filtering, data conversion, and version change. An IDoc is generated for each partner identified

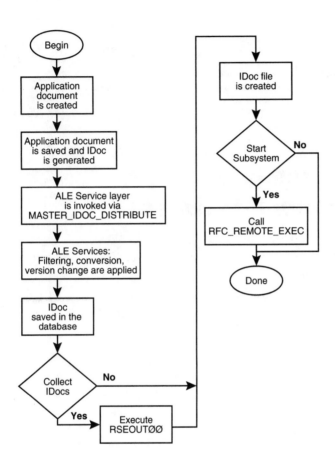

FIGURE 3.4 *The technical flow of the outbound process without Message control*

in the distribution model. These IDocs, called *communication IDocs*, are then saved in the SAP database. At this point, a tangible IDoc has been created in the system and can be viewed using the various monitoring tools. That IDoc gets a status record with a status code of 01 (IDoc Created).

The IDoc goes through a syntax check and other validations. If there are no errors, the IDoc gets a status of 30 (IDoc Ready for Dispatch to ALE Service).

NOTE

Processing in the IDoc layer is exactly the same as described for the outbound process with Message control. Processing in the EDI subsystem layer is also exactly the same as described for the outbound process with Message control.

Exception Handling in the Outbound Process

The process flows described so far in this chapter show the success path. However, the system can experience problems at any stage of the process. Workflow is integrated in the outbound process to handle exceptions. If an error occurs at any stage, a specified user is notified. Complete details on the various points of failure and how the system reports those problems are described in Chapter 12, "EDI Process Troubleshooting and Recovery."

The system uses the Post Processing: Permitted Agent Information in the partner profile to send the error notification. An error might occur when an IDoc has not yet been created, when the partner profile cannot be read, or in the subsystem. In these situations, the EDI administrator is notified. The complete details of workflow and how to set it up are discussed in Chapter 9, "Configuring Workflow."

Summary

In this chapter, you learned how an outbound process works with and without the use of the Message control component. First, an application document is created. Next, Message control provides the flexibility to propose outputs automatically, using various output media. Applications that do not use Message control provide a selection screen to limit EDI output to selected business partners. A selection program formats the application document into an IDoc format. The IDoc is then passed to the ALE layer for filtering and conversion, and is eventually passed to the operating system in a text file format. The subsystem can then be triggered to start the intended processes. If errors occur at any point in the process, a previously designated person responsible for handling the errors is notified via workflow.

Chapter 4

In Chapter 2, "Introduction to SAP EDI Architecture," you got a high-level overview of the inbound process. In this chapter, you will learn about the technical and functional details of the inbound process. Like the outbound process, the inbound process uses components such as the IDoc type, the partner profile, the port definition, posting programs, and service programs. You will learn how the inbound process uses these components to create an application document from an IDoc file. Like Chapter 2, the main focus here is on the technical aspects of the process, but functional users can also benefit from this material.

Components Used in the Inbound Process

The inbound process uses the following components to post an application document from an IDoc: IDoc type, port definition, posting programs, service programs, and configuration tables. The inbound process components are specified in the partner profile and configuration tables. The following sections give an overview of each component. For detailed descriptions and the available configuration options within these components, see Part III, "Configuring the EDI Interface."

IDoc Types

The EDI document to be posted has an equivalent message type defined in the SAP system. The message type is based on an IDoc structure. For example, if you are going to post EDI transaction 850, which is a sales order, the message type ORDERS is assigned in SAP to the document. This message type can be based on IDoc type ORDERS01 or ORDERS02. A list of IDoc types and their equivalent messages in EDIFACT and ANSI X12 standards is provided in the Appendix, "FAQs, User Exits, and Miscellaneous Resources."

> **TIP**
>
> The list in the Appendix is valid as of release 4.6. This list is evolving, so check with SAP for the latest version. If you have access to SAP's online support system (OSS), see note 104606.

The IDoc is the most important component in the EDI process. A good understanding of the IDoc is necessary for working with the EDI interface. See Chapter 29, "IDocs from the Outside," and Chapter 30, "IDocs on the Inside," for complete details on the benefits and architecture of IDocs.

Posting Programs

Posting programs are implemented in the system as function modules. A posting program exists for each message type. The programs are named with the following naming convention.

```
IDOC_INPUT_<message type>
```

These function modules have a standard interface for their input and output parameters. The function modules can handle one IDoc or multiple IDocs of the same type simultaneously.

A process code is assigned to each posting program. Because process codes are flexible, you can assign any processing type to a process code. A process code can point to a function module or a workflow. In the standard system, process codes always use the Processing by Function module processing type with the Processing with ALE Service option. Chapter 17, "Inbound via Workflow: Sales Order Changes," covers the option of assigning a workflow to a process code for inbound processing.

For example, the posting program for message type ORDERS is IDOC_INPUT_ORDERS. A four-character process code, ORDE, has been assigned to this function module. You can see a list of inbound process codes and their corresponding function modules by executing the following transaction.

Transaction: WE42
Menu Path: From the Area menu of EDI (WEDI), choose Control, Inbound process code

You can develop your own custom function modules. See Chapter 32, "Programming in the IDoc Interface," for details on the structure of these programs and how to write a new program.

The Port Definition

In the inbound process, the port definition specifies the name of the input IDoc file and the directory path where the file is located. Port definitions are described in full detail in Chapter 6, "Configuring Basic EDI Components."

 NOTE

These parameters are used only if the subsystem does not pass this information to the SAP inbound process. If the subsystem provides this information, the port definition is not used.

The SAP Business Workflow

SAP business workflow represents a sequence of customized steps (dialog and background) that are to be carried out for a process. The workflow management system is used to model the sequence, the information required to carry out the various steps, and the person responsible for the dialog steps. In workflow terminology, if there is only one step in a flow, it can be implemented using a single-step task. A single-step task is technically defined as a task described by an object method. (In SAP a method is normally implemented as a function module.) More simply put, a single-step task is a self-contained one-step process. If there are multiple steps, they are implemented as a workflow that contains multiple single-step tasks.

The Partner Profile

A partner profile specifies the various components used in an inbound process (partner number, message type, or process code), the mode in which the process communicates with the posting program (batch or immediate), and the person to be notified in case of errors.

NOTE

You might have noticed that IDoc type is not specified in the partner profile for an inbound process. This omission does not mean that IDoc type is unnecessary. The link between the IDoc type, message type, and function module for the inbound process is maintained in the EDIFCT table. This table is maintained via IMG (*Implementation Guide*). The only time you need to maintain this table is when you are developing your own customized inbound process. Chapter 33, "Customizing the Interface for New or Extended IDocs," presents details on maintaining the EDIFCT table.

A partner profile is created for each business partner, and a record exists for each inbound message received from a business partner. For example, if two inbound messages (sales order and sales order change) are received from customer number CUST001, a partner profile must exist for CUST001, and two inbound records (one for each message type) must exist in the partner profile. The partner profile is one of the most important and frequently referenced components of the EDI process. Chapter 7, "Configuring Partner Profiles," describes in full detail the various attributes of partner profiles.

Service Programs and Configuration Tables

The inbound process is asynchronous and can be regarded as a sequence of several processes that work together. To link the components and provide customizing options for an inbound process, SAP provides service programs and configuration tables. The process flow for the inbound process describes the role played by each service program.

The Inbound Process
via the Function Module

The inbound process also has two distinct paths for posting the application documents from the IDocs.

◆ Via the function module
◆ Via workflow

In this process, the IDocs are transferred from the EDI subsystem to SAP, and then they are passed to the posting function module to post an application document.

The inbound process is best explained by describing the processing that occurs at each layer, shown in Figure 4.1. The technical flow, shown in Figure 4.2, explains the technical components, such as programs, table entries, and parameter values.

Processing in the EDI Subsystem Layer

The inbound SAP EDI process begins at the subsystem layer with an EDI document converted to an IDoc format. The IDoc is stored in a text file at the operating system (OS) layer. The IDoc file can be passed to the ALE/EDI interface layer immediately via the file port using the startrfc program, or it can be processed at a later time through execution of program RSEINB00.

FIGURE 4.1 *The inbound process using a direct function module*

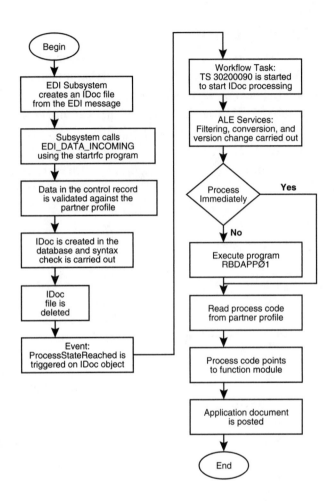

FIGURE 4.2 *The technical flow of the inbound process using a direct function module*

The startrfc program is a standard SAP program at the OS level to call any RFC-enabled function module in SAP. To trigger the inbound process, the startrfc program calls the function module EDI_DATA_INCOMING, which acts as the entry point for inbound processes. The name of the IDoc file is passed as an input parameter to this function module.

Processing in the ALE/EDI Layer

The EDI_DATA_INCOMING function module reads the IDoc file into an internal table. The IDoc is first checked for integrity by doing a syntax check. Then the standard ALE services such as version change, filtering, and conversion are applied, if necessary. The ALE/EDI layer creates an application IDoc in the database. At this point a tangible IDoc, which can be monitored via one of the monitoring transactions, is created in the system. The IDoc gets a status code of 50 (IDoc Added). If the IDoc passed the syntax check process earlier, it gets a status code of 64 (IDoc Ready to be Passed to Application), signifying that the process can continue.

 CAUTION

After the IDoc has been created in the database, the IDoc file is deleted, even if the IDoc itself has errors. If for some reason the IDoc file cannot be deleted, SAP creates an entry in the EDFI2 table with the file name to mark it for deletion. This technique prevents the same file from being processed multiple times.

Next, the processing flag and process code are read from the partner profile table. If the value of the Processing field is set to Process Immediately, the IDoc is passed to the posting program using the RBDAPP01 program. If the field is set to Background Processing, the IDocs are buffered in the system until the RBDAPP01 program is executed explicitly. RBDAPP01 is usually scheduled to run on a regular basis, or it can be started as a result of an event raised by the subsystem after the IDoc file has been loaded into the SAP system.

 NOTE

Starting with release 3.1, the process of creating IDocs in the database was disconnected from the process that posts the application document. This modification improves the efficiency of creating IDocs from the text files and logically separates the two processes. A workflow task handles the coupling of the process that creates the IDocs and the posting process. This process should not be confused with the inbound process via workflow, which is explained later. Chapter 6, "Configuring Basic EDI Components," describes the configuration of this coupling process.

Processing in the Application Layer

The posting function module either calls a standard SAP transaction, using the call transaction command for posting the document, or invokes a direct input function module.

NOTE

Direct function modules are preferred to the call transaction approach because of inherent problems of screen sequence associated with call transactions. The screen sequence might change with every release. Nevertheless, it is easier to debug inbound processes that use the call transaction method, as explained in Chapter 12, "EDI Process Troubleshooting and Recovery."

TIP

To see whether a standard inbound process uses call transaction or direct input, you can execute transaction BD51 and inspect the entries in table TBD51. Entries with a value of 1 or 2 in the Input Type column use the call transaction method, and entries with a value of 0 use the direct function module.

The results of the execution are passed back via the function module's output parameters. If posting is successful, an application document is created. The IDoc gets a status code of 53 (Application Document Posted). If errors occur, the IDoc gets a status code of 51 (Application Document Not Posted). A complete list of status codes is included in the appendix, "FAQs, User Exits, and Miscellaneous Resources."

The Inbound Process via Workflow

The inbound process via workflow is similar to the inbound process via function module, as described earlier, except for the difference in the processing that occurs in the application layer. The IDoc, instead of being processed by a posting program, is processed by a single-step task or a multi-step workflow. Pointing the process code to processing by task or process, instead of processing by function module, configures this option.

Workflow allows human intervention in the process, which is sometimes necessary. A typical example is the sales order change transaction coming in via EDI. Someone might need to review any change from a customer before the change can be accepted; if you have already begun production, you might not be able to accept a change in quantity or delivery date. This process gives you the option of reviewing the changes and taking appropriate action.

 NOTE

In the standard system, the inbound processes use function modules for posting the document. Although no process uses workflow by default, you can customize the interface to start workflow. Refer to Chapter 17, "Inbound via Workflow: Sales Order Changes," which provides an example of how to use SAP business workflow for an inbound process.

The inbound process via workflow differs from processing via function module mainly in the processing that occurs in the application layer. The processing that occurs in the EDI subsystem layer and the ALE/EDI layer is the same in the two approaches (see Figure 4.3).

Processing in the Application Layer

The posting module in this case is a workflow task. The workflow task can be designed to accommodate any customized processing, such as reviewing an incoming order change transaction followed by posting, or posting an incoming order change document followed by review.

If a complex business process is associated with an incoming document, you can use a multi-step workflow to map that process. As an example, invoices greater than $5,000 coming into the system might need an approval for payment. You might want to route the invoices to more than one person. This step can easily be accomplished via workflow. Basically, workflow is a development environment, and you can build any functionality you need. The standard EDI processes do not use this path.

FIGURE 4.3 *Details of the inbound process via workflow*

 CAUTION

Workflow might seem like a useful method for processing inbound EDI transactions, but it adds additional load to the system, especially when you have high-volume EDI transactions. It also blocks the process unless someone processes the work item, which can cause unnecessary delays.

Exception Handling in the Inbound Process

The inbound process described in this chapter shows the success path from the IDoc's creation through the final creation of the application document, but the system can experience problems at any stage during the process. Compared to the outbound process, the inbound process has more opportunity for error because data originates outside the SAP system. SAP validates the data using the same business rules as if the document were entered online.

The workflow system uses the Post Processing: Permitted Agent fields in the partner profile to send the error notification. For example, an error might occur before an IDoc is created or because the partner profile cannot be read; in any case, the EDI administrator is notified. Chapter 9, "Configuring Workflow," discusses the complete details of workflow and how to set it up.

Summary

In this chapter, you learned how an inbound process posts an application document from an IDoc file. The subsystem starts the inbound process by passing an IDoc file to the ALE/EDI interface layer. The IDoc is read by the system, and an IDoc is created in the SAP database. The new IDoc is passed to the posting module, which can be either a function module or a workflow. In the standard system, the posting module is a function module. The posting module then creates the application document using either a standard call transaction method or a direct input function module. If errors occur at any point in the process, a previously designated person responsible for handling the errors is notified via workflow.

Chapter 5

The EDI Subsystem

Although SAP does not provide the EDI subsystem, the subsystem plays a key role in the SAP EDI process. In this chapter, you will learn about the various functions carried out by the subsystem and take a quick look at typical subsystem architecture. Then you will be introduced to the mapping process, one of the key functions provided by an EDI subsystem. Finally, you will learn about the certification process that ensures the compatibility of the EDI subsystem with SAP.

An Overview of the EDI Subsystem

The EDI subsystem carries out the task of converting an EDI document in a standard EDI format to an IDoc file, and vice versa. As you might have observed, the conversion process is one of the key tasks in SAP EDI architecture. SAP does not supply the EDI subsystem because several EDI standards are in existence and each standard has multiple versions. To further complicate the process, these standards are still evolving. Hence, this task is best carried out by EDI vendors, who stay current with the standards.

EDI vendors have developed translators to help with the conversion of application-specific messages—IDocs, in the case of SAP—to standard EDI format. Any translator software product is completely independent of the SAP software and resides outside the SAP system. The translator can be installed on the same hardware as the SAP system, or it can stand alone on another computer. The operating system environment of the EDI subsystem can be different than the SAP operating system environment. If the SAP system is installed on a UNIX platform, the subsystem can reside on a separate platform that operates on, for example, Windows NT (or any other OS platform, for that matter).

SAP certifies several EDI subsystems for compatibility with the EDI interface. The IDoc interface has changed with every release (2.2 through 4.6). For this reason, the certification is applicable only for a specific release of SAP. Check with your third-party vendor for the release level of its certification. You can obtain the latest list from SAP's Web site at http://www.sap.com.

The Responsibilities of the EDI Subsystem

The subsystem has several responsibilities in the EDI process chain. The following sections describe these, in order of importance, from the SAP perspective.

Data Mapping

Within the framework of SAP EDI, the conversion of a business document in IDoc format to an EDI standard format (and vice versa) is the most important task performed by a subsystem. This process is resource intensive and, hence, is better done at the subsystem level than within SAP. The following conversions and translations are carried out by the subsystem.

◆ **Creating a control record for each inbound IDoc**. An inbound IDoc must have a control record. The EDI subsystem builds the control record using the information stored in its local repository or from the SAP repository.

◆ **Removing the control record during the outbound process**. The control record in the IDoc file is used by the subsystem for housekeeping functions, such as locating the trading partner profile. The data on the control record is not needed for translating the content of the EDI documents.

◆ **Translating data from IDoc format to EDI format.** For an outbound transaction, the EDI subsystem converts data in the IDoc format to a suitable EDI format.

◆ **Translating data from EDI format to IDoc format.** For an inbound transaction, the EDI subsystem converts data in the standard EDI format to IDoc format.

◆ **Bundling and unbundling IDocs.** If several IDocs are passed to the EDI subsystem in one file, the subsystem separates them into individual documents. Similarly, on the inbound process the subsystem can bundle multiple IDocs into a single file to improve performance.

Maintaining the Partner Profile

A *partner* is defined as the business partner with whom you conduct business and exchange EDI documents. These partners are not necessarily the same as the partners in the partner profile of SAP. However, the concept is quite similar. In SAP, the partner profile maintains parameters specific to the IDoc process, and in the subsystem the partner profile maintains parameters specific to the EDI process. Some typical attributes in a partner profile are

◆ A unique partner number

◆ The partner type (Customer, Vendor)

◆ The standard used (EDIFACT, ANSI X12, and so on)

◆ The version of the EDI standard

◆ The EDI message exchanged (850, 860, ORDERS, ORDCHG)

◆ A functional acknowledgment flag

Triggering the Inbound Process

After receiving an inbound EDI transmission and creating an IDoc file, the subsystem is often responsible for triggering the inbound process. SAP provides a program named startrfc to start any RFC-enabled function module from the operating system level. For the EDI process, the subsystem uses the startrfc program to trigger the function module EDI_DATA_INCOMING. Chapter 6, "Configuring Basic EDI Components," provides the complete details and parameters of the startrfc program.

Reporting Process Status to SAP

In an outbound process, after an IDoc has been transferred from SAP to the subsystem, SAP loses control over the process. However, SAP maintains visibility into the process by requiring the subsystem to report on the status of the process. SAP provides a file interface for the subsystem to send a status report at every milestone. Table 5.1 presents the status codes reported by the subsystem to SAP, depending on the state of the process.

When the subsystem has status information to send to SAP, it creates a status file and uses the startrfc program to trigger the SAP system. The status file contains the IDoc number, which is used to identify the IDoc to which the status record is

Table 5.1 Status Codes Reported by the EDI Subsystem to SAP

Status Code	Description
04	Error within control information of EDI subsystem
05	Error during translation
06	Translation OK
07	Error during syntax check
08	Syntax check OK
09	Error during interchange handling
10	Interchange handling OK
11	Error during dispatch
12	Dispatch OK
13	Retransmission OK
14	Interchange Acknowledgment positive
15	Interchange Acknowledgment negative
16	Functional Acknowledgment positive
17	Functional Acknowledgment negative
22	Dispatch OK, Acknowledgment still due
23	Error during retransmission
24	Control information of EDI subsystem OK
36	Electronic signature not performed (timeout)

to be attached. The startrfc program calls the EDI_STATUS_INCOMING function module to start the processing of the status file in SAP.

Handling Functional and Interchange Acknowledgments

An *interchange acknowledgment* is the message that the VAN sends to the subsystem to inform it about the transmission results. A *functional acknowledgment* (ANSI X12 transaction 997) acknowledges the receipt of data by the receiving system. This transaction verifies the successful receipt of an EDI document but does not guarantee successful data processing. The subsystems are responsible for generating this document on receipt of an EDI transmission.

For an outbound process, the status codes that the subsystem reports to SAP depend on the results of the acknowledgment. Status codes 14, 15, 16, 17, and 22 are returned to SAP. (Refer back to Table 5.1 for a description of these status codes.)

Performing a Syntax Check

The EDI standards have a rigid structure. The segments and fields have the following characteristics.

◆ Optional or mandatory

◆ Conditional or non-conditional

◆ Data format

◆ Data length

◆ Loop counts

◆ ID codes (similar to SAP IDoc qualifiers)

These characteristics form the basis for a syntax check. If any rules are violated, the document processing can fail. To avoid wasteful transmissions, the subsystem checks the documents for conformance to the standards defined by the standards committee. The results of the syntax check are sent back to SAP using status code 07 or 08 (refer to Table 5.1).

Handling Partner-Specific Processing

The subsystem also handles partner-specific processing. For example, business partner A sends all purchase orders bundled as one huge purchase order. For business partner B, you might need to break down the single purchase order by shipping location and create several smaller purchase orders.

Several data elements in the EDI transactions have not been assigned a definitive meaning. Companies can freely use those fields to mean different things. If you are a vendor, you will end up accepting whatever data your customers send you and you will send them any specific data relevant only to them. The subsystem can handle this partner-specific processing.

NOTE

Sometimes it is necessary to retransmit EDI documents because they are lost or have errors at your trading partner's end. The subsystems provide tools to retransmit a document.

Handling Errors

In the outbound process, the subsystem is responsible for reporting to SAP any errors, including translation errors, syntax errors, transmission errors, and connectivity issues.

In the inbound process, until an IDoc is created, the subsystem is responsible for reporting and managing the errors. The subsystem provides the necessary monitoring and recovery tools. Once an IDoc is inside SAP, SAP has full responsibility for handling errors.

Communicating with Business Partners

Business partners can provide a direct connection to their network or subscribe to a VAN. The subsystem is responsible for establishing and terminating connections with the business partner's network or VAN to send and receive EDI transmissions. The subsystem is also responsible for processing acknowledgments from the VAN and communicating those to SAP.

Attaching EDI Headers and Controls

EDI transmissions have several header and trailer segments that act as control information (for example, the ISA and GS headers and trailers). The subsystem is responsible for attaching these segments to the document.

Archiving

All important documents, such as payment stubs or remittance advice transmitted to the trading partners, might have to be archived for auditing purposes and liability issues. The subsystems provide data archiving and management options.

Subsystem Architecture

In one way or another, all EDI subsystems carry out the responsibilities described in the preceding section. The basic subsystem architecture does not vary much from one software vendor to another. This section does not describe the architecture of any particular subsystem; rather, the architecture presented here can be applied to any EDI subsystem product.

When you buy a subsystem, it has two major components.

- ◆ The definition component
- ◆ The execution component

The Definition Component

The definition component is where mapping definitions between EDI and IDoc formats are created. This component can run without any connection to the SAP system or its server module. The maps are platform-independent. The definition component carries out the following functions.

- ◆ Defines the source structure and destination structure.
- ◆ Maps fields in the source structure to fields in the destination structure.
- ◆ Compiles maps for other platforms.
- ◆ Tests maps.
- ◆ Provides utilities to download and upload IDoc structures, document structures, and maps. (Software vendors usually license this component on a per-user basis.)

 NOTE

The structure of standard EDI documents for commonly-used standards (ANSI X12 and EDIFACT) is shipped with most EDI subsystems.

The Execution Component

Maps created in the preceding step are executed on the server, which is known as the *execution component*. The execution component is where the complete environment for executing the maps, trading partner relationships, and other server-related functions are performed. The execution component is usually licensed on a per-installation basis. The following is a list of common tasks performed on the server and features commonly found in EDI subsystems.

◆ Execution of maps

◆ Maintenance of trading partner agreements

◆ Configuration of the environment

◆ Maintenance of log information

◆ Archiving

◆ Tools for monitoring the process

◆ Tools for restart and recovery of failed transactions

◆ Scripts for connectivity with VAN

Mapping Concepts for IDocs and EDI Document Formats

The most important function of a subsystem is data transformation, or mapping. A map is created for every message exchanged with a business partner. Thus, if you receive sales order data from 10 customers via EDI, you might have 10 maps. Even though the data format has been standardized, only the syntax is standardized. (The syntax rules are described earlier in the chapter.) The company using the data still needs to interpret the meaning of the data, and several data elements do not have a definitive meaning and are open to interpretation by a company. The result can be a document that is slightly different for each company. Mapping an IDoc to an EDI format requires the following steps.

1. **Download the SAP IDoc structure**. In this step, the IDoc structure is downloaded into the definition component. SAP provides a program named RSEIDOC3 that generates a structured report of the IDoc structure. The report is downloaded to a file and can then be copied to the PC on which the definition component is installed.

2. **Define the IDoc structure**. The output file can be imported into the definition component to make the IDoc format known to the system. To create the IDoc structure, the software vendors provide a utility program to import the file automatically. The IDoc structure has a control record structure and several data record structures.

3. **Define the EDI document structure.** Software vendors usually provide the structure of the standard EDI documents. For example, if you are interested in the sales order document of ANSI X12 version 3050, you do not have to build the structure from scratch. Vendors provide formats for various standards and versions. This information is their bread and butter.

 TIP

Most software vendors also provide special maps designed for particular companies. For example, if you are going to accept sales orders from a large corporation such as Ford or Wal-Mart, you can buy maps that define the syntax and semantics used by that company. Access to these maps can reduce your development time considerably.

4. **Define the maps.** Mapping is the process of linking source fields to destination fields. Mapping can be a simple operation (for example, one-to-one mapping, in which a field from the source structure is directly copied to the destination structure) or a complex process. In complex mapping, values from several fields of the source structure are manipulated in different ways to generate an output value for a field in the destination structure. The systems usually allow manipulation using functions, external program calls, and so on. You must check with your software vendor about the sophistication of the mapping process.

5. **Compile the maps.** Maps need to be compiled before they can be executed. The compilation process is simple. The system checks the syntax of the map, the consistency of business rules used in the map, and the source and destination data elements in the map. If compilation is successful, the map is ready to be executed.

6. **Test the compiled maps.** The maps can be tested on the definition system using some test data. An input file is processed through a map to generate the output. The output should be verified manually—the data should be in the correct location and in the correct format.

7. **Transport the maps.** The definition component can usually compile maps for use on other platforms. Thus, if the execution engine resides on

UNIX and the definition component is on a PC, the system can generate a compile map for the UNIX system. The compiled map can then be transported to the EDI server system via any file transfer techniques.

8. **Execute the maps.** The maps can then be executed on the server. During production, the system executes maps on the server.

Certification and Test Scenarios

The certification process is an endorsement by SAP regarding (1) the connectivity between the SAP system and the subsystem and (2) the capability of the two systems to exchange data in an IDoc format. The internal structure of the IDoc has changed with every major release, so SAP certifies the subsystems on a per-release basis. A subsystem certified for release 3.0 IDocs does not necessarily work with release 4.0 IDocs. Check with the subsystem vendor for certification information.

Certification requires the subsystem to pass the following tests.

◆ Connectivity

◆ The capability to process IDoc format

◆ The capability to report status to SAP

SAP has developed standard test scenarios recorded using the CATT (*Computer Automated Test Tool*) system. These tests are played and the results are verified. The following sections describe the test scenarios.

Test Scenarios for Connectivity

An outbound IDoc is created, and the shell script provided by the subsystem vendor to start the EDI subsystem is executed. If the shell script executes successfully, the test of outbound connectivity is successful.

To test inbound connectivity, the subsystem calls the startrfc program to pass an IDoc file or a status file to the SAP system. The program calls the EDI_DATA_INCOMING function module for IDoc files and EDI_STATUS_INCOMING for status files. If the function modules are started correctly, the test is considered successful.

Test Scenarios for Handling the IDoc Format

Two business scenarios are implemented in SAP to test the subsystem's capability to handle IDocs.

◆ Sending out purchase orders and receiving a purchase order acknowledgment

◆ Receiving sales orders and sending out a sales order acknowledgment

The steps are as follows.

1. SAP creates a purchase order for a vendor. This purchase order is passed to the subsystem as an IDoc file. The subsystem converts the IDoc into an EDI standard format and then reports the IDoc's status to SAP.

2. The outbound purchase order is sent to SAP as a sales order from a customer.

3. A sales order response is created in the SAP system. This sales order response is passed to the subsystem as an IDoc file. The subsystem converts the IDoc into an EDI standard format and then reports the IDoc's status to SAP.

4. The outbound sales order acknowledgment is sent to SAP as a purchase order acknowledgment for the purchase order created in Step 1.

These steps are repeated for several vendors and for different types of purchase orders (single-line item and multiple-line item). If the results are positive, the subsystem is certified. You can obtain complete details of the certification process from SAP's Web site at http://www.sap.com. Once on the Web site, execute a search using the search term **EDI AND subsystem**.

Summary

The subsystem is a key component in the SAP EDI architecture. Although not provided by SAP, it works very closely with the SAP system. The subsystem carries out the conversion from IDoc format to EDI document, and vice versa. The subsystem is also responsible for other tasks, such as providing status reports to SAP and handling IDoc structures. SAP certifies the subsystems for their connectivity to SAP and their capability to handle the IDoc format. Although it is possible to work with an EDI subsystem that is not certified, I do not recommend it because you cannot be certain about the connectivity.

PART III

Configuring the EDI Interface

Chapter 6

Configuring Basic EDI Components

To generate IDocs, you cannot use the EDI interface right out of the box. SAP cannot possibly know your business partners and the messages you want to exchange. You must set up the various components before you can get an IDoc out of or into the system. Before you start, you need a good understanding of the inbound and outbound process flow and the role of the components, especially the IDoc, used in the process.

Two types of components build and support the SAP EDI process.

◆ Components specifically designed for the ALE/EDI process (for example, the port definition, partner profiles, and process codes)

◆ Flexible cross-application technologies that are deployed in the EDI process and can be adapted across multiple applications (for example, Message control and workflow)

These components are highly flexible and can be adapted to meet a variety of customer needs and requirements. The next four chapters provide full technical details about each component in the process—including its concept, role, and available options. The material is intended for readers who are responsible for setting up the EDI interface. Although this information is meant for first-time users of the EDI interface, it is not at an introductory level. You should be conversant with the SAP system and able to navigate through it. In this chapter, you will learn about the components designed solely for use in the EDI/ALE process. You will also learn about the basic IDoc settings, which are mainly one-time settings, and about communication settings, which define the link between the EDI subsystem and the SAP system.

The Configuration Settings

The various configuration settings for the EDI process are done in the IMG (*Implementation Guide*) and in the area menu of the EDI system. Explanations of these elements follow.

◆ **Implementation Guide**. The various EDI customization settings (see Figure 6.1) are available under the following path in the IMG: Basis Components, Basis Services, IDoc Interface/Electronic Data Interchange.

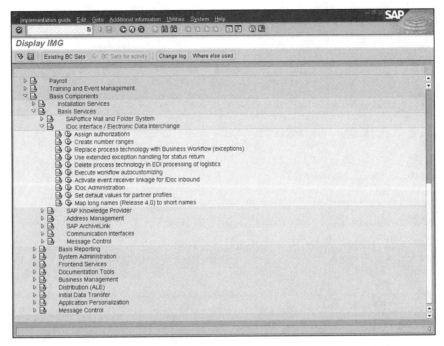

FIGURE 6.1 *The area in the IMG where you make EDI settings* (© SAP AG)

◆ **The IDoc Area menu (WEDI).** The methods to get to this area menu are as follows.

Transaction (prior to version 4.6): WEDI

Area menu (starting with 4.6): WEDI

SAP Standard Menu Path: Tools, Business Communication, IDoc, IDoc Basis

---

 NOTE

From version 4.6, you reach the area menu for IDocs by typing **WEDI** in the command box from the SAP Easy Access menu. To access the old menu in version 4.6, you type **/N** in the command box and press the Enter key to exit the SAP Easy Access menu. Then, you type **WEDI** in the command box and press the Enter key.

Basic Settings for IDocs

This section describes the basic settings required for the IDoc interface used in the EDI process. You establish these only once for the whole system. They rarely need to be changed.

Number Ranges for IDocs

Transaction: OYSN

Path: EDI settings in the IMG, Create number ranges

Every IDoc created in the system, inbound or outbound, is assigned a 16-digit number that uniquely identifies it in the system. The IDoc number range is already defined. You normally do not have to maintain this number range, but theoretically you could exhaust the number range and then have to reset it.

 CAUTION

Be careful when resetting the number range. Make sure that old IDocs with the number range to which you are resetting have been archived and deleted from the system. Otherwise, the system will not be able to create IDocs in the number range that has been initialized.

 NOTE

If you change the number range in R/3 systems prior to version 4.6, you will have to transport the number range interval manually to your production system because number range objects are not automatically recorded for transport. To manually record a number range interval for transport, select Interval, Transport from the number range maintenance screen.

Global IDoc Interface Parameters

Transaction: WE46

Path: From the Area menu of EDI, choose Control, Partner profile, IDoc administration

In transaction WE46, you assign values to the global variables used in the EDI process (see Figure 6.2).

CAUTION

In R/3 versions before 4.6, you set these parameters by entering the parameter names and values in table EDIADMIN. See the Appendix, "FAQs, User Exits, and Miscellaneous Resources," for more information. The system validates the parameter values only if the parameter name is correct. Hence, there is a chance for error if you type a parameter name incorrectly. Be extra careful when entering these values. From version 4.6, this information is stored in table EDICONFIG.

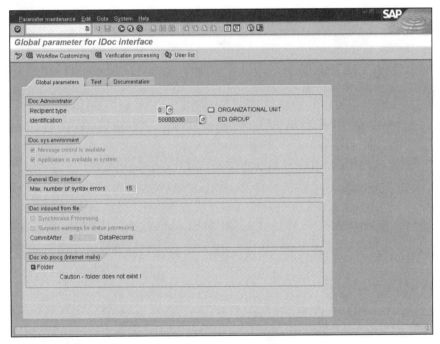

FIGURE 6.2 *Global parameters for the IDoc interface* (© SAP AG)

The settings you need to make for the global IDoc interface parameters are explained in the following list. The screen for transaction WE46 under version 4.6 has 3 tabs. The key settings described in the following list are all under the Global Parameters tab, except for the TestPort parameter, which appears under the Test tab. The Documentation tab contains settings for displaying and exporting IDoc definitions. These settings are not important for configuring the IDoc interface, and are not described here.

- ◆ **IDoc Administrator**. This parameter group specifies the administrator for the IDoc interface at run time. The IDoc Administrator group consists of two parameters, named Recipient Type and Identification, which identify the individual(s) who will be responsible for the integrity of the overall IDoc interface. You must enter the recipient type (for example, US for user ID, S for position, or O for organizational unit), along with the identification value. See Chapter 9, "Configuring Workflow," for details on all the different types of objects you can specify here. For example, if the position with position number 12345678 is assigned as the administrator, the value of the parameter in the Recipient Type field will be S, and the value for the Identification field will be 12345678. If a user with user ID AN000001 is the administrator, the value of the parameter in the Recipient Type field will be US, and the Identification field will be AN000001. This parameter is used by the workflow system in either of the following situations.

  - A technical error occurs in the EDI interface layer, for example, an error in deleting an IDoc file after successfully creating an IDoc.

  - An application error occurs in processing an IDoc. In this case, workflow first attempts to send a notification to the ID specified in the partner profile. If the error is such that the partner profile cannot be read, notification is sent to the IDoc administrator.

 NOTE

Normally, these situations should not occur because the IDoc administrator has overall responsibility for the interface and cannot handle application-specific errors. During development and testing, the IDoc administrator usually gets several work items, which are instances of workflow tasks. However, in a production system this should be extremely rare.

TIP

It's wise to avoid a user ID as the IDoc Administrator. You should use more abstract object types, such as position, job, or organizational unit. This approach saves you the headache of changing the entry when the user leaves the company or changes jobs. Compared to users, organizational objects such as positions, jobs, and organizational units tend to be more stable.

- ◆ **IDoc Sys. Environment**. These parameters should always be checked.
- ◆ **General IDoc Interface, Max. Number of Syntax Errors**. This parameter sets the maximum limit on the number of status records created for syntax errors—a good recommendation is five. If your IDoc gets more than five syntax errors in a production environment, something is terribly wrong. Setting this number higher usually does not help you debug the problem; at that point, you need to investigate the process more deeply at the source of data.
- ◆ **IDoc Inbound from File, Synchronous Processing.** The standard IDoc processing method is asynchronous, which usually provides higher throughput and allows decoupled parallel processing of individual IDocs. At times, such as when IDocs must be processed in sequence to prevent record-locking problems, synchronous processing can offer a possible solution.

CAUTION

Be careful with the Synchronous Processing parameter. It affects all inbound IDocs and can profoundly slow the throughput of IDoc processing.

- ◆ **Test Tab, Parameter Setting, TestPort**. You use this setting for testing purposes only. It defines the port name that will be used for assigning default parameters during inbound testing. The naming convention used for this port is SAP<*xxx*>, where <*xxx*> is a three-character ID assigned to your SAP instance. For example, if the System ID (SID) of your development instance is DV1, the port name will be SAPDV1. This port must be defined in the port definition.

TIP

The *instance ID* is the three-character name in the status bar that appears at the bottom portion of any SAP screen. However, if the status bar is turned off, you can also determine the instance ID by executing transaction SM51. The three characters following the first underscore under the server name are the instance ID.

Coupling IDoc Creation to IDoc Processing

Path: EDI settings in the IMG, Activate event receiver linkage for IDoc inbound

The process of creating IDocs from the input file was disconnected from the processing of the IDocs for posting for two reasons.

♦ To improve the efficiency of the process of creating IDocs from a file

♦ To separate logically the process of posting an IDoc from the process of creating an IDoc, because they are two independent processes

However, the two processes have to be coupled for EDI process flow. The workflow concept of publish and subscribe, shown in Figure 6.3, accomplishes the coupling. The link is maintained via an event-linkage table. When an IDoc is created, it raises an event, which is the publishing piece, to inform the system about the creation. The subscriber is the process that processes the IDoc. The subscriber starts automatically when the corresponding event is published. To establish the linkage, you execute the customizing step (Activate Event Receiver Linkage) in the EDI settings of the IMG or run program RSEINBEV.

NOTE

For inbound IDoc processing, the event triggered is PROCESSSTATEREACHED, and the subscriber is the workflow standard task TS30200090.

Communication Settings

This section describes the technical settings for linking the subsystem to SAP. These settings are made one time. They are independent of both the transaction and the business partner.

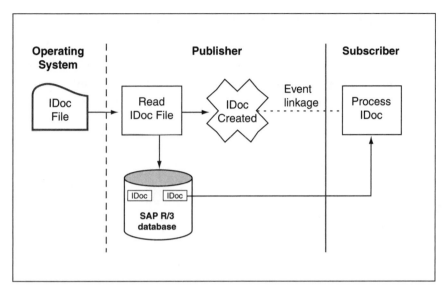

FIGURE 6.3 *Coupling IDoc creation and IDoc processing*

Setting an RFC Destination

In this section, you will learn how SAP uses an RFC destination to link to the subsystem program. If you have not yet installed a subsystem, you can skip this step and go to the next step, configuring the port definition. This will not affect the EDI functionality in SAP. By skipping this step, you lose only the automatic start of the subsystem when an outbound IDoc file is created. In fact, some companies skip this step completely and schedule the subsystem program to run periodically and process the IDoc files. However, if you are planning to implement a real-time EDI scenario, you must perform this step. The following section starts with an introduction to the RFC concept, followed by details on maintaining an RFC destination.

 NOTE

Several applications besides ALE and EDI use RFC destinations. For example, they are used to access external print programs, fax programs, tax programs, and barcode readers. In fact, an RFC destination is used to start the online help program on your computer when you select Help, R/3 library from any menu in SAP.

What Is an RFC Destination?

An *RFC destination* is a logical name used to identify a remote system on which a function has to be executed. In the RFC destination, you specify the characteristics of the remote system, such as the host name and the program containing the function to be executed. An RFC destination is used for the subsystem because the subsystem is an external system from SAP's perspective, no matter whether it resides on the same system as SAP or a separate system. The following two prerequisites apply when executing a function remotely.

◆ The systems should be accessible to each other via TCP/IP or one of the supported network protocols. An operating system-level SAP user ID should be able to start a program remotely on the destination system. This feature requires configuration at the operating system level.

◆ The program that implements the functions must use RFC protocols to communicate with SAP. RFC protocols are implemented via a set of APIs (*Application Programming Interfaces*) that both the sending and receiving programs use.

How the EDI Interface Uses an RFC Destination

The subsystem is considered a remote system because it is not an SAP program. It can be installed locally on the SAP box or on an external system. Hence, any communication between SAP and the subsystem requires the RFC destination (see Figure 6.4).

For connectivity to occur, you must meet two prerequisites.

◆ You must connect the systems via TCP/IP and maintain a "trusted user ID" on each system so that each can execute programs on the other system.

◆ The subsystem vendors must write their subsystem programs using RFC protocols. You can circumvent this problem by using the rfcexec program shipped with the standard SAP system. rfcexec is a program at the operating system level that acts as the RFC server and can respond to SAP's RFC requests. When it has to start the subsystem, SAP calls the function RFC_REMOTE_EXEC, which is implemented in the program rfcexec (refer to Figure 6.4). SAP passes the name of the shell script for the subsystem, and the RFC_REMOTE_EXEC function executes the shell script. This strategy means that the EDI subsystem program does not have to use RFC protocols.

FIGURE 6.4 *The RFC link between the SAP system and the EDI subsystem for the automatic start of the subsystem*

 NOTE

SAP uses <*SID*>adm as the ID to access the operating system files and commands, where *SID* is the instance of your SAP system.

 TIP

RFC_REMOTE_EXEC is a function in the rfcexec program and, hence, cannot be seen in the function library on the SAP system via SE37.

The trusted user setting is necessary to allow the SAP system to trigger rfcexec remotely. Assume that you have two systems, one running SAP and the other running the EDI subsystem. Assume further that the TCP/IP host names of the two systems are hostsap and hostedi.

Before you proceed with any settings, make sure that the systems are configured at the TCP/IP level to see each other. You can execute the ping command at the

OS level to verify that the two systems are connected and can see each other. After you verify the connection, you must set up the rhosts files and users on both systems. Because of the security implications of these settings, your system administrator and security specialists should participate in the design. A simplified example of this setup is as follows.

1. Set up a user ID on the hostedi system. Give that user ID the same name as the SAP user ID at the OS layer on the hostsap system, which is <*SID*>adm. Thus, if your SAP instance is DV1, the user ID will be dv1adm.

2. Create a home directory for this user on hostedi. The directory should be the same as the home directory on hostsap.

3. Create an .rhosts file in both systems. This file allows you to create trusted users. The permissions on this file should be 600, which is read and write for the user ID only. Setting permissions to any other value will cause security vulnerability.

4. In the .rhosts file on hostedi, enter **hostsap**, and in the .rhosts file on hostsap, enter **hostedi**. This step completes the configuration for trusted users.

You can verify the trusted user setup by executing the following command at the OS level.

◆ Execute remsh hostedi date from hostsap. This command should return the date from the hostedi system.

◆ Execute remsh hostsap date from hostedi. This command should return a date from the hostsap system.

How to Set Up an RFC Destination in SAP

Transaction: SM59
Path: From the SAP standard menu: Tools, Administration, Administration, Network, RFC Destination

There are several types of RFC destinations. EDI uses type TCP/IP to connect to the subsystem. A default RFC destination (SERVER_EXEC) is shipped with SAP; that RFC destination starts the rfcexec server program on the SAP application server on which the process is executing. You can change this destination to suit your needs or create a destination from scratch. The attributes relevant to EDI configuration and their meanings follow (see Figure 6.5).

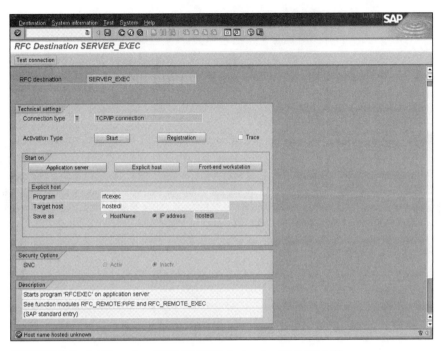

FIGURE 6.5 *Attributes in a TCP/IP RFC destination* (© SAP AG)

- ◆ **RFC Destination.** This attribute is a unique name for your RFC destination.

- ◆ **Connection Type**. Use type T to indicate TCP/IP.

TIP

Pressing Enter after you put in the type and description of your RFC destination enables the fields necessary for connection type TCP/IP.

- ◆ **Activation Type**. Click the Start button. The Registration button is used only when your EDI subsystem is registered with a gateway, a technique used only for RFC-enabled EDI subsystems. For your purposes, do not assume an RFC-enabled EDI subsystem.

- ◆ **Start On**. Select either Application Server or Explicit Host, depending on where the subsystem is installed. An application server is usually local to the SAP environment, namely the saphost itself, and Explicit Host refers to a remote server. An explicit host can also be used for locally installed EDI subsystems. Check with your Basis people for this installation. If you select Explicit Host, the system lets you enter the TCP/IP host name of the system on which your EDI subsystem is installed.

 CAUTION

If you select the Application Server and have installed multiple application servers, make sure that they share the file system through some technique. A commonly used technique is NFS (*Network File System*), which allows a file system to be shared across multiple systems.

 TIP

You can view the list of application servers running in your instance by executing transaction SM51.

◆ **Program**. Enter the RFC server program name **rfcexec** in this field.

 CAUTION

The program name and the server name are case sensitive.

 TIP

You can test the connectivity to the rfcexec program by clicking the Test button. If the result is successful, you have successfully connected to the system that has or will have the EDI subsystem.

◆ **Security Options**. If you have SNC (*Secure Network Communications*) installed, the option will be active.

Local versus Remote Subsystems

If the subsystem is installed locally on the SAP server, you will have very few problems because SAP and the subsystem operate under one environment and share a common file system. IDoc files created by the SAP system are automatically available to the subsystem. However, this configuration is not always advisable because of the additional load created on the system. Thus, it's sometimes necessary to install the subsystem on a separate box.

If the subsystem is installed on a separate server, you must make sure that IDoc files created by SAP are accessible to the EDI subsystem and vice versa. The two options are NFS mounts and remote file copy. Check whether the subsystem can NFS mount the same directory where IDocs are created by SAP. (The Basis staff can help you with NFS mounting.) If so, the IDoc files are accessible.

Companies sometimes restrict the number of mount points for a file system. In this case, the subsystem does not have visibility into the IDoc file created by SAP. If the two systems are completely separate and have only a TCP/IP connection, you need a mechanism to copy the file from the SAP system to the subsystem. Typically, a script using a remote copy command (such as an rcp command in UNIX) provides this functionality, an FTP (*File Transfer Protocol*) mechanism is put in place, or a middleware software package is used.

The Port Definition

Transaction: WE21
Path: From the Area menu of EDI, choose IDoc, Port Definition

The port defines the technical characteristics of the connection between SAP and the subsystem. It also defines the medium in which data is exchanged between the two systems.

In the EDI process, IDocs are transferred to external systems via ports. Table 6.1 presents the types of ports available in release 4.6.

The EDI process uses the file port. The type of port also depends on the receiving side. If the receiver cannot accept data in the medium used by a port, the port cannot be used. For example, the tRFC port cannot be used for EDI unless the receiving subsystem has support for tRFC. Check with your vendor for the port supported. All vendors support the file port, so don't pick up your phone unless you are interested in using another port.

Table 6.1 SAP Release 4.6 Ports

Port	Function
Transactional RFC	Used for ALE communication
File	Used by EDI
CPI-C	Used to communicate with an R/2 system
Internet	Used to connect with Internet applications
ABAP-PI	Used for custom IDoc processing via ABAP programming interface
XML	Used for processing files in IDoc/XML format

A port is a client-independent object. The following are the parameters specified in a port definition. Figure 6.6 shows an example of how to specify the various attributes in a port definition.

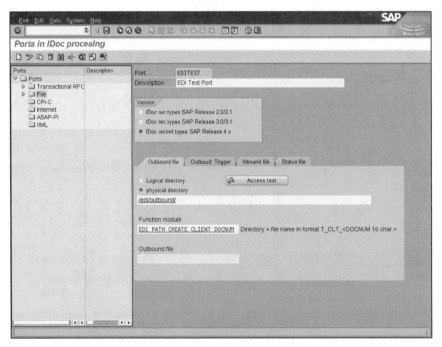

FIGURE 6.6 *Attributes in a file port definition* (© SAP AG)

- ◆ **Port**. The port name is any meaningful name that uniquely identifies the port.

- ◆ **Description**. Any meaningful description of the port will suffice. This parameter is for documentation purposes only.

- ◆ **Version**. You can control the release level of the IDoc being generated by SAP. In SAP, the internal structure of the IDoc has changed in every major release. For example, in release 4.0 and newer, the IDoc name can be as long as 30 characters. To support backward compatibility, you set the version of the IDoc to be generated. Consider a scenario in which you have upgraded to SAP release 4.6, but your subsystem is still working with IDocs of SAP release 3.0. In this field, you specify the version to be generated, using the following values for R/3 versions prior to 4.6.

  1. Format for R/3 2.2 IDocs

  2. Format for R/3 3.0 and 3.1 IDocs

  3. Format for R/3 4.0 and above IDocs

The Outbound File

This tab specifies the name and location of the IDoc file generated for an outbound process. The various fields on the Outbound File tab (see Figure 6.6) are as follows.

- ◆ **Logical Directory**. The logical directory where the IDoc file will be generated. You define the logical directory by using transaction FILE.

- ◆ **Physical Directory**. The physical directory where the IDoc file will be generated. You define the physical directory name by entering the fully qualified directory path, ending with a forward slash for UNIX systems or a backward slash for Windows systems.

 CAUTION

The directory path must be accessible to the SAP user ID *<SID>*adm. The *SID* is the system ID or the instance ID. Access to the directory path is usually not a problem for *<SID>*adm because *<SID>*adm is set up as the SAP Administrator who owns the directory and the files in it.

TIP

If you are using a port for testing and you do not know of a directory path for your IDoc files, or if you are having permission problems, use the /tmp/ path on UNIX systems. This path is always present, and any user can write to this directory.

◆ **Function Module**. With this field, SAP provides a dynamic file-naming option that generates a file name at runtime. Several function modules ensure that a unique file is created for every IDoc that uses this port. You can select the function module that fits your needs. If these standard function modules do not meet your needs, you can create your own function module for naming the files. Execute transaction WE55 to add your custom function module for naming the files.

CAUTION

If you use the Function Module option, the Outbound File field should be blank.

TIP

If you are going to write your own function module, it's easiest to copy and modify an existing function module.

◆ **Outbound File**. You can specify a fixed file name for your outbound IDocs. This file name is used for all outbound IDocs and is overwritten every time you create an outbound IDoc using this port. This option is useful during testing only—in a production environment, you leave this entry blank and use dynamic file names generated via a function module.

The Outbound Trigger

The command file parameter specifies the program SAP uses to invoke the EDI subsystem. It is defined on the Outbound Trigger screen. This program is usually in the form of a shell script or batch file provided by your subsystem vendor. The various fields on the Outbound Trigger tab (see Figure 6.7) are as follows.

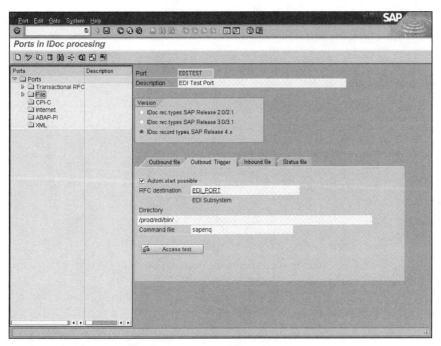

FIGURE 6.7 *Attributes of the command file used to start the subsystem* (© SAP AG)

- ◆ **Autom. Start Possible**. The flag specifying whether SAP can start the subsystem.

- ◆ **RFC Destination**. The name of the RFC destination defined in the "How to Set Up an RFC Destination in SAP" section. This field locates the system on which the subsystem is installed. If the subsystem is not installed, you can use the default RFC destination SERVER_EXEC here.

- ◆ **Directory**. The fully qualified directory path where the subsystem shell script is installed.

TIP

The directory path must end with a forward slash (/) for UNIX or a back slash (\) for PC-based systems.

◆ **Command File**. The name of the shell script supplied by the subsystem vendor. It is case sensitive for UNIX.

The Inbound File

Entries for the inbound file are optional. The entries specify the name and location of the IDoc file for an inbound process. Typically, you do not use these values because the subsystem provides a fully qualified path name and file name when it triggers the inbound process via startrfc. If the subsystem does not provide other values, these specified values are used. You also use these values during testing, so it might be worthwhile to specify this option for the test port. The various fields on the Inbound File tab (see Figure 6.8) are as follows.

◆ **Logical Directory**. This field defines the directory path where the IDoc file will be present. You define a logical directory by using transaction FILE.

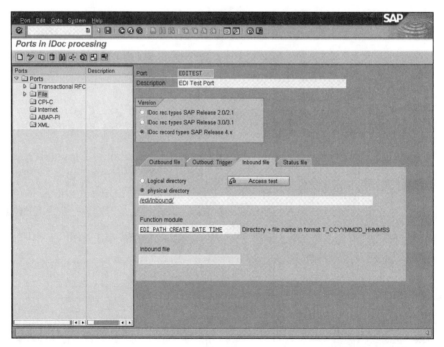

FIGURE 6.8 *Attributes of the inbound IDoc files imported into SAP* (© SAP AG)

◆ **Physical Directory**. This field defines the physical directory path where the IDoc file will be present. For the physical directory name, enter the fully qualified directory path.

 CAUTION

The directory path must be accessible to the SAP user ID specified in the startrfc command on the inbound process.

◆ **Function Module**. SAP provides a dynamic file-naming option, which ensures that every file has a unique file name.

◆ **Inbound File**. You can specify a fixed file name to be used for all your inbound IDocs. This item is useful during testing only. In a production environment, you leave this entry blank and use dynamic file names.

The Status File

Entries for the status file are optional. This setting specifies the name and location of the status file used to pass status information for an outbound IDoc. Again, the values are typically not used because the subsystem provides a fully qualified path name and file name when it triggers the process via startrfc. If the subsystem does not provide other values, these specified values are used. The various fields on the Status File tab (see Figure 6.9) are as follows.

◆ **Logical Directory**. This field defines the logical directory path where the status file will be present. You use transaction FILE to define a logical directory.

◆ **Physical Directory**. This field defines the physical directory where the status file will be present. You enter the fully qualified directory path for the physical directory name.

◆ **Function Module**. SAP provides a dynamic file-naming option, which ensures that every file has a unique file name.

◆ **Status File.** You can specify a fixed file name for your inbound status file. This item is useful during testing only. In a production environment, you leave this entry blank and use dynamic file names.

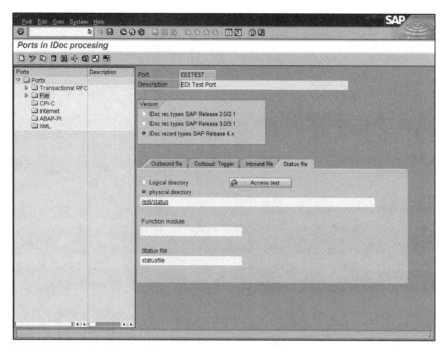

FIGURE 6.9 *Attributes of the status files imported into SAP* (© SAP AG)

 CAUTION

The directory path must be accessible to the SAP user ID specified in the startrfc command.

Strategies for Building Ports

The port is not simply a parameter that you have to complete—you can use strategies in port definitions. In the following situations, you might have to define multiple ports.

- ◆ If you need to communicate with two separate systems and they use different IDoc formats (for example, one uses 3.0 IDocs and the other uses 4.0), you have to create a separate port for each type.
- ◆ You must create a separate test port for testing the process.

◆ You might want to send the IDoc files to separate directories based on the type of EDI transaction. For example, you might want outgoing invoices to be in a separate directory from the outbound sales order response.

Triggering the Inbound Process by the Subsystem

The subsystem triggers the SAP system in two situations (see Figure 6.10).

◆ The EDI subsystem has converted an EDI document to an IDoc file format for an inbound process. This file must be passed to the SAP system to start the inbound process in SAP.

◆ An outbound IDoc was passed to the subsystem in a file format. The subsystem has converted the file into an EDI document and transmitted the EDI document to the business partner. The subsystem now must report the status of the process at every milestone to SAP, so that SAP has visibility into the process after it leaves the SAP boundaries. The subsystem creates a status file to report the status to SAP.

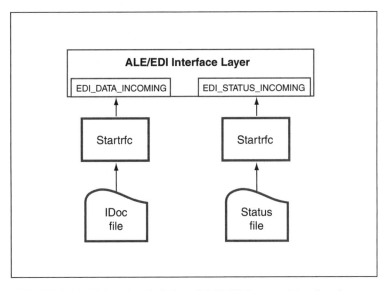

FIGURE 6.10 *Triggering the inbound SAP EDI process from the subsystem*

You carry out these two tasks by using startrfc, a generic program supplied by SAP. This program resides on the operating system and can trigger any RFC-enabled function module synchronously. SAP provides two function modules that act as entry points for an inbound process, specifically for the two tasks just described. The function modules are

- EDI_DATA_INCOMING
- EDI_STATUS_INCOMING

The syntax for the startrfc command follows. When you read the syntax, keep in mind all the information that is generally necessary for anyone to log on to the SAP system.

> startrfc -3 −d <system id> -u <userid> -p <password> -c <client>
> -l <language> -h <App. Server> -s <system number>
> -g <gateway host> -x <gateway services> -t −E <file name>
> -E <port name> -F <function module name>

- **-3**. Indicates the script is to log on to the R/3 system.
- **system id**. The three-character identifier assigned to your SAP instance. You determine this by looking at the status bar on your SAP screen. You can also execute transaction SM51 to determine the instance ID. The instance ID comprises the two characters following the underscore.
- **userid**. The ID used to log on to the SAP system. This user should be a background user or a CPI-C user. This ID has SAPALL permission.
- **password**. The password for the logon ID used to log on to the system.
- **client**. The SAP client.
- **language**. The language of the logon ID.
- **App. Server**. The server to which the user will log on in order to connect to the SAP system.
- **system number**. The two-digit system number. Use SM51 to display the application servers. The last two digits in the application server name provide the value for the system number.
- **gateway host**. The name of the host on which the gateway service programs are executing. The gateway host is used for all RFC communications that use CPI-C communications behind the scenes. In a simple installation, this entry is the name of the application server host, but you

can install the gateway services separately. Check with your Basis staff for the gateway server.

◆ **gateway services**. Gateway services as defined in the services file at the OS level. From within SAP, you execute program RSPARAM and, on the output screen, look for an entry with rdisp/sna_gw_service in the parameter name column. The value displayed in the user-defined column is the value you enter in the gateway services parameter.

◆ **-t**. The option that turns on trace. If you use this option, a trace file named dev_rfc is created in the current directory.

Summary

In this chapter, you learned about general EDI settings and communication settings used in the EDI configuration. These configuration items are one-time settings that you must do at the beginning of the project. The Basis group is likely to carry out some of the configurations because they involve setting up communication components. The parameters discussed in this chapter have a major effect on the overall performance and operation of the interface and must be set correctly before you can proceed with other EDI components.

Chapter 7

In this chapter, you will learn about the partner profile component in complete detail, including the use of partner profiles, the various views, how to define the parameters, and the significance of those parameters. A large corporation can have hundreds of partners, and therefore needs a way to maintain partner profiles (other than entering them manually online). You will also learn how to use effort-reducing techniques to streamline that process. At the end of the chapter are advanced tips and tricks that can help you address some common problems without having to write ABAP programs as workarounds. A partner profile is defined for every business partner with whom you exchange business documents. In EDI, a partner can be a customer, a vendor, a bank, or any entity with which your company does business. In ALE, a partner is a remote SAP system or legacy system with which you exchange data. A partner profile specifies the various characteristics of data that you exchange with a business partner, the mode of operation, and an organization or person responsible for handling errors for that business partner.

The Three Views of a Partner Profile

Transaction: WE20

Path: From the Area menu of EDI, choose IDoc, Partner Profile

A partner profile has three views, which maintain different parameters for the partner (see Figure 7.1).

- ◆ **The General Parameters view**. Values are stored in table EDPP1.
- ◆ **The Outbound Parameters view**. Values are stored in table EDP13, except for the Message control parameters, which are stored in table EDP12.
- ◆ **The Inbound Parameters view**. Values are stored in table EDP21.

The values are stored in tables. The partner number and partner type bind all the views together.

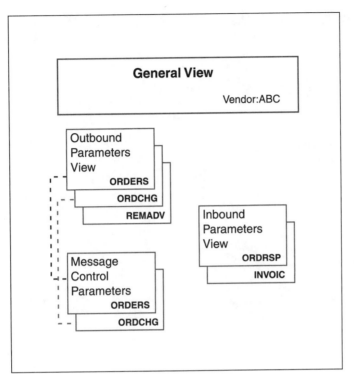

FIGURE 7.1 *The component structure of a partner profile*

The General View

The main Partner Profiles screen, shown in Figure 7.2, displays the general parameters view at the top of the right frame. The outbound and inbound views are also accessed from this screen; they appear below the general view fields. These other views will be described in detail later.

The General Parameters view contains very basic information about the partner, such as partner number, partner type, partner status, and default individual to notify in case an error occurs. These partner attributes appear at the top of the main Partner Profiles screen and under the Post Processing: Permitted Agent and Classification tabs. The entries under the Telephony tab are generally not relevant to EDI or ALE. You enter this information only once for each partner, and these values are stored in table EDPP1.

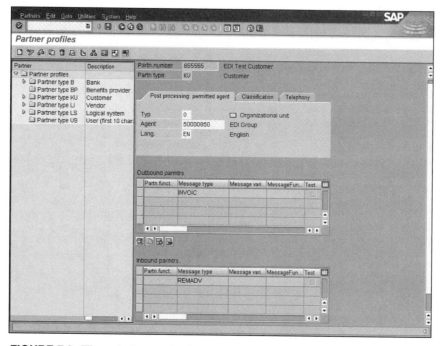

FIGURE 7.2 *The main Partner Profiles screen* (© SAP AG)

You define the following attributes in the General Parameters view.

◆ **Partn. Number**. In EDI, the partner number can be a customer number, vendor number, or bank ID. In ALE, it is the logical name assigned to the partner SAP system or legacy system. The standard system validates the partner number against the customer master, vendor master, or bank master data, depending on the type of business partner.

◆ **Partn. Type**. The partner type represents the type of your business partner. For example, in EDI it is customer (KU), vendor (LI), or bank (B). In ALE, it is the logical system (LS).

In the Post Processing: Permitted Agent tab, you define the individuals to be notified when an error occurs in IDoc processing at a point where the system has identified the partner, but not the message type. The fields on this part of the General Parameters view are

◆ **Typ**. This field identifies the workflow object type of the Agent to be notified in case of error (for example, US for user ID, S for position, or O for organization).

◆ **Agent**. This field indicates the workflow object (for example, user, position, or organizational unit) used for notification. This object is notified when a corresponding outbound or inbound record is not found for a message that is being sent to or received from this business partner. See Chapter 9, "Configuring Workflow," for details on how the system sends workflow notifications for errors. For example, if a person with position ID 12345678 is responsible for handling errors for this business partner, the value of the various fields are S for Typ, 12345678 for Agent, and E for Lang.

◆ **Lang.** This field identifies the language in use for this agent.

TIP

Avoid using a user ID in the Agent field. You should use more abstract object types, such as position, job, or organizational unit. This approach saves you the headache of changing the entry when the user leaves the company or changes jobs. Compared to users, objects such as positions, jobs, and organizational units tend to be more stable. However, during the development phase you can use your user ID for a quick start.

On the Classification tab, you define the following:

◆ **Partner Class**. This field is for documentation only and has no intelligence behind it. You use this field to classify your partners. For example, if you want to classify automotive vendors versus railroad vendors, you can enter particular codes representing automotive or railroad.

◆ **Archv.** This field is also for documentation purposes only. It indicates whether a partner agreement exists. *Partner agreement* is an EDI term for legal documents that define each partner's responsibilities in a business relationship.

◆ **Partner Status**. This field makes a partner active or inactive. If a partner is deactivated, no documents are passed to it.

TIP

If you maintain partner profiles in the production system, you can use the Partner Status field to indicate that a partner profile is under construction. After the partner profile is complete, you activate it to mark it ready for use.

The Outbound Parameters View

The outbound parameters define the characteristics of an outbound message to your business partner and how SAP transfers the IDocs to the subsystem. A record is created for every outbound message to a business partner. The main Partner Profiles screen displays the outbound parameters as a table control (labeled Outbound Parmtrs) in the middle of the right frame (refer to Figure 7.2). You can display, create, or delete the outbound parameters for individual messages by selecting a line on the table control and/or clicking one of the icons displayed just beneath it. Table EDP13 stores the outbound attributes. In the Outbound Parameters view (see Figure 7.3), you specify the message type and sets of parameters displayed under the Outbound Options, Message Control, Post-Processing: Permitted Agent, and EDI Standard tabs. The Telephony tab parameters are generally not relevant to EDI.

◆ **Partn. Number.** The same values as specified in the General Parameters view. In fact, the system automatically copies the values from the General view when you maintain the Outbound Parameters view.

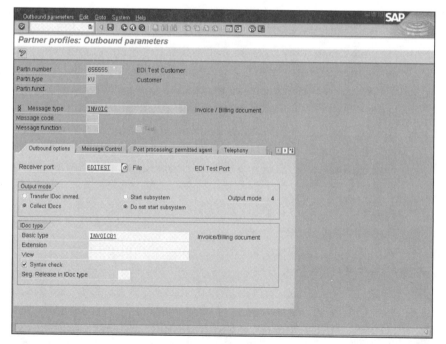

FIGURE 7.3 *Attributes in the Outbound Parameters view of a partner profile* (© SAP AG)

◆ **Partn. Type**. The same values as specified in the General Parameters view. Again, the system automatically copies the values from the General view.

◆ **Partn. Funct**. In SAP, a business partner can have multiple roles. The Partn. Funct. field describes the partner function being used for this message.

◆ **Message Type/Message Code/Message Function**. These three fields together represent the SAP message type assigned to the EDI transaction being sent to a business partner. The Message Type field is derived from the EDIFACT messages, but a one-to-one equivalence is not guaranteed. The message type is independent of the ANSI X12 or EDIFACT standards. The Message Code and Message Function fields are not commonly used. Refer to the Appendix, "FAQs, User Exits, and Miscellaneous Resources," for a cross-reference list between the SAP message type and the EDI messages.

TIP

Using the Message Code and Message Function fields, you can create a variation of the same message by assigning different values in these two fields. The "Using the Partner Profiles" section later in this chapter presents the details.

◆ **Test**. This flag indicates whether the system generates a test IDoc before generating an actual IDoc. This option is not available for all messages. It is available for certain FI-related messages, such as remittance advice and payment orders. It helps you verify the data contents before transmitting the actual message. This attribute is also a directive for the subsystem not to transmit these messages to the business partner.

CAUTION

The Test flag is part of the key. Therefore, you must create two entries (with and without the test flag) for your message type to generate a test IDoc and an actual IDoc.

The Outbound Options tab contains the outbound parameters defining the output port, the output mode, and the type of outbound IDoc used. The specific parameters are

◆ **Receiver Port**. This field contains the port your outbound process will use. In EDI this entry is the file port explained in Chapter 6, "Configuring Basic EDI Components." The port defines the directory location and file name for IDoc files, and the name of the subsystem program (if installed). In ALE the receiver port is of type tRFC, as explained in Chapter 22, "Configuring the ALE Infrastructure."

◆ **Pack Size**. This field is specific to ALE processes and is visible only when the port used in the partner profile is of type tRFC. This field defines the number of IDocs that are bundled in a packet for transmission to a partner system. The value in this field affects the performance of the system. Initially, you can select defaults proposed by the system, but read Chapter 28, "Managing ALE Process Performance and Throughput," for details on how to calculate the value to enter in this field.

◆ **Output Mode**. Output mode controls when the IDocs are transferred to the subsystem and whether the subsystem is to be started. The settings you make here affect the performance of the system. See Chapter 13, "Managing EDI Process Performance and Throughput," for details on how to set these values. The following subfields are defined in Output mode.

• **Transfer IDoc Immed**. If this flag is turned on, each IDoc is passed to the subsystem layer immediately upon creation as an IDoc file.

• **Collect IDocs**. If this flag is turned on, the IDocs are collected in the system. A program RSEOUT00 must be executed to transfer the collected IDocs to the subsystem.

• **Start Subsystem**. If this flag is turned on, the subsystem is started as soon as IDocs are transferred to the subsystem.

• **Do Not Start Subsystem**. If this flag is turned on, the subsystem is not started. This flag is useful if you do not have a subsystem installed.

◆ **IDoc Type**. The fields in this section of the Outbound Options tab define the details of the IDoc to be used for a particular outbound message.

- **Basic Type**. This field contains the basic IDoc type used in the process. A message type can be assigned to multiple IDoc types. You select the IDoc type that is relevant to your process.

- **Extension**. If you have extended a basic IDoc type, this field contains the name of the extension you are using in your IDoc.

- **View**. This field identifies a defined subset of segments of the basic IDoc type being used.

- **Syntax Check**. This flag controls how the system behaves when a syntax error is found in an IDoc. If you check this flag, the system stops the IDoc processing and sends a workflow message to a user. If you do not check this flag, the processing continues and a workflow message is sent to indicate that a syntax error has occurred. See Chapter 30, "IDocs on the Inside," for a list of syntax rules checked in an IDoc.

- **Seg. Release in IDoc Type**. A segment gets a new definition when new fields are added to it. The standard SAP segments have different versions, depending on when they were enhanced by SAP. If you want to use the latest segment definition in an IDoc, you must leave this field blank. However, if you are interested in a specific version of a segment, you must enter the version of the segment here.

For an explanation of the Message Control tab, see the next section.

On the Post Processing: Permitted Agent tab, you specify the following:

◆ **Type**. This field identifies the workflow object type of the Agent to be notified in case of error (for example, US for user ID, S for position, or O for organization).

◆ **Agent**. This field indicates the workflow object (for example, user, position, or organizational unit) used for notification when an error occurs in the outbound process for a message being sent to the business partner. See Chapter 9, "Configuring Workflow," for details on how the system sends workflow notifications for errors. For example, if a person with position ID 12345678 is responsible for handling errors for this business partner and message type, the values of the various fields are S for Typ, 12345678 for Agent, and E for Lang.

◆ **Lang.** This field indicates the language in use for this agent.

The EDI standard tab parameters define the EDI standards being used and the EDI message type or transaction number, along with the version. These values are for use by the subsystem only; SAP does not have any functionality behind these fields, and you can leave them empty. Note that this tab is not displayed on Figure 7.3. These parameters are

◆ **EDI Standard.** The standard being used for the message. Examples are E for Edifact and X for ANSI X12.

◆ **Message Type.** The message type identifier used under the standard. For example, 850 for an ANSI X12 purchase order.

◆ **Version.** The version of the standard being used for the message. For example, 3050 for ANSI X12 version 3050.

The Message Control Outbound Parameters

You maintain Message control parameters for those outbound messages that make use of the Message control component to generate IDocs (for example, a purchase order, a sales order response, or an invoice). If an outbound message (for example, a remittance advice) does not use Message control, you do not maintain this view. You enter the values for the Message control attributes under the Message Control tab in the Outbound Parameters screen. They are stored in table EDP12.

In the Message Control tab, you specify the Message control components to use in the process of generating IDocs by entering them in the table control shown in Figure 7.4. The various attributes you define for the Message control parameters are as follows.

◆ **Application.** Each Message control-enabled application is assigned a two-character ID. For example, Sales is V1, and Purchase Order is EF. This field identifies the application generating the outbound message. See Chapter 8, "Configuring Message Control," for more details on the application ID.

◆ **Message Type.** Message control assigns a four-character output type (for example, BA00 for order response, or NEU for purchase order) to the

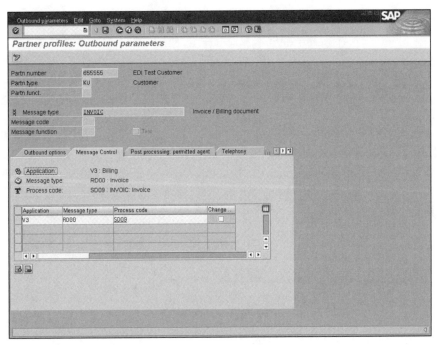

FIGURE 7.4 *The Message control outbound parameters for a partner profile* (© SAP AG)

various messages exchanged between business partners. Enter the appropriate output type in this field. See Chapter 8 for more details on the output type.

◆ **Process Code**. A process code points to a function module that reads application data and formats the data into an IDoc format. These function modules are commonly referred to as *selection programs* or *data extraction programs*. A selection program exists for each outbound message generated via Message control. Execute transaction WE41 and look under Outbound Process Codes for a list of process codes for outbound messages. You can double-click any process code to view its details.

◆ **Change**. Set this flag if the output represents changed output for a document that was sent earlier. For example, if an order change message (ORDCHG) is being sent, this flag is turned on.

The Inbound Parameters View

The inbound parameters define the characteristics of an inbound message coming from your business partner and how the IDoc is processed by SAP. A record is created for every inbound message (for example, a sales order, purchase order acknowledgment, or invoice) from a business partner. You can view or modify the values using the lower table control, labeled Inbound Parmtrs, on the right frame of the main Partner Profiles screen. The values are stored in table EDP21. In the Inbound Parameters view (see Figure 7.5), you specify the message type and sets of parameters displayed under the Inbound Options and Post-Processing: Permitted Agent tabs. The Telephony tab parameters are generally not relevant to EDI.

- ◆ **Partn. Number**. The same values as specified in the General Parameters view. The system automatically copies the values from the General view when you maintain the Inbound Parameters view.
- ◆ **Partn. Type**. The same values as specified in the General Parameters view. Again, the system automatically copies the values from the General view.

FIGURE 7.5 *Attributes in the Inbound Parameters view of a partner profile* (© SAP AG)

- **Partn. Funct**. In SAP a business partner can have multiple roles. This field describes the partner function being used for this message.

- **Message Type/Message Code/Message Function**. These three fields have the same meaning as in the Outbound Parameters view.

- **Test**. This flag indicates whether the message is a test message or real message.

On the Inbound Options tab, you specify the following:

- **Process Code**. A process code points to a posting program that is implemented as a function module. A posting program exists for each inbound message type. Execute transaction WE42 for a list of process codes for inbound messages. You can double-click any process code to view its details.

- **Syntax Check**. This flag controls how the system behaves when a syntax error is found in an IDoc. If this flag is checked, the system stops the IDoc processing and sends a workflow message to a user. If this flag is not checked, the processing continues and a workflow message is sent to indicate that a syntax error has occurred. See Chapter 30, "IDocs on the Inside," for a list of syntax rules checked in an IDoc.

- **Processing by Function Module**. The Processing field controls when the IDocs are transferred to the posting modules. The settings you make here affect the performance of the system. See Chapter 13, "Managing EDI Process Performance and Throughput," for details on how to set these values. Select one of the following settings.

  - **Trigger by Background Program**. If this flag is turned on, the IDocs are not passed to the posting module immediately. The RBDAPP01 program must be executed to process the IDocs.

  - **Trigger Immediately**. If this flag is turned on, the IDoc is immediately passed to the posting module upon creation.

On the Post Processing: Permitted Agent tab, you specify the following:

- **Type**. This field identifies the workflow object type of the Agent to be notified in case of error (for example, US for user ID, S for position, or O for organization).

- **Agent**. This field indicates the workflow object (for example, user, position, or organizational unit) used for notification when an error occurs in the inbound process for a message received from a business partner. The types of values that can be specified here are the same as described earlier in the Outbound Parameters view.

◆ **Lang**. The language in use for this agent.

Tips for Maintaining Partner Profiles

The partner profile is an important element in customizing the ALE/EDI interface. You will be frequently involved in creating, changing, and adjusting values in the partner profile. An incorrect partner profile can lead to hours of debugging and frustration. In this section, you will learn some simple techniques that make it easier to maintain partner profiles.

Checking Consistency

A standard program RSECHK07 is available in the system to carry out the following checks on the values specified in the partner profile.

◆ Process code

◆ Recipients of notifications

◆ Consistency of Message control parameters with outbound parameters

You can execute the RSECHK07 program via transaction SE38 or from the menus of the initial partner profile screen (under Partners, Check). The output is a color-coded report that details any problems.

Although a check is carried out when the partner profile is initially created, some parameters can eventually become invalid. For example, if a user ID specified in the Post Processing: Permitted Agent fields in the partner profile no longer exists, this report will flag it as an error.

Copying Partner Profiles

The copy function is very useful in maintaining partner profiles, especially if you have partners who are similar. You can create a sample partner profile with all possible messages, copy it for a new trading partner, and then delete the unwanted components. Deleting extraneous components is much easier than creating the whole partner profile from scratch.

Copying Partner Profile Views

If you've created a record (inbound or outbound) with incorrect key values, the only way to change it is to delete it and create it again. However, the copy function can be very useful in this case. Assume that you've forgotten to enter a partner function and you've created everything else correctly. Rather than delete the record, you copy it, change the key values, save the new record, and delete the original record.

Using Message Defaults for Automatic Generation

From release 4.0, the IMG contains a tool to set default parameters for each message for a partner type. Then you can build your partner profiles using these defaults. This tool quickly creates your partner profile using the defaults set for each message. See the Appendix, "FAQs, User Exits, and Miscellaneous Resources," for more details.

However, if you are still using release 3.0, you can use an ALE tool (transaction BD82) to generate partner profiles automatically for ALE partners, based on the ALE distribution model. This tool is mainly designed for ALE, but you can use it to build a basic partner profile structure with some default values for EDI. You must edit the entries to adjust certain parameters, such as ports, so this tool is for expert users only.

 CAUTION

Transaction BD82 can interfere with your existing ALE configuration, so use this tool only if your site is not using ALE or if you know exactly what you are doing.

Programming to Maintain Partner Profiles

If several-hundred partner profiles are already being used in your legacy environment, you can build an interface to create your partner profiles in the SAP system. You can use the following options to create your partner profiles.

◆ Write a BDC (*Batch Data Communication*) program
◆ Use standard function modules

Several function modules are available in the system so you can maintain partner profiles without having to go directly to the database. The function modules are present in function group EDI6.

Moving Partner Profiles to the Production System

Until release 3.0F, partner profiles were treated as configuration tables, which meant that profiles could not be created or modified in the production system. They had to be modified in the development system and then transported to the production system. This approach was unacceptable to customers who wanted to change partners in the production system and could not wait for the profile to be transported from development systems.

SAP has provided a temporary fix for this problem for customers who are still on release 3.0F or prior. Check OSS note 0049758 for details on how to fix this problem. The note essentially changes the delivery class of the table from customizing to master data. This modification allows changes to be made in the production system.

In release 3.1, the partner profile tables have been changed to class Master Data. This modification allows companies to maintain partner profiles directly in the production system.

Alternatively, you can maintain partner profiles in the development system if you maintain very few partner profiles, if they do not change frequently, or if your company prefers that method. In this case, you must manually transport the partner profiles. From the initial partner profile screen, choose Partners, Transport. The system prompts you for a change request.

From release 4.5 on, the feature allowing manual transport of partner profiles no longer exists.

Using the Partner Profiles

This section mentions some tricks I have learned to solve certain problems without writing any ABAP code or to otherwise make particular tasks a little easier.

Problems Communicating with the Subsystem

If you have set up your EDI subsystem on a system other than SAP, you already know the pain involved in getting all the links in the communications process to work correctly. You might have called your EDI subsystem vendor to come in for a day and enable that link—especially the piece where the SAP system cannot find the subsystem. You constantly see your IDocs going into status 20 (Error Triggering the EDI Subsystem). Problems in linking the two systems at the OS level cause this error. Chapter 6, "Configuring Basic EDI Components," describes the setup for RFC destinations, but the following is an alternative that does not require that complex setup.

The solution approaches the problem by first understanding what you are trying to do with this remote link. You are trying to make sure that when an IDoc file is written, the subsystem can pick up the file for processing.

The solution is to execute the two processes independently. In the partner profile, enable the Do Not Start the Subsystem flag. After the SAP EDI process creates the outbound file, SAP will not attempt to start the subsystem. Next, have the subsystem poll the outbound directory for any new files on a periodic basis. You can control the timing of this job to suit your needs. After processing the file, the EDI subsystem can report the file's status to the SAP system as usual. This trick saves you from trying to figure out why the subsystem could not be started. Because the EDI process is asynchronous, operate the SAP to EDI subsystem connection using this approach, unless you want a near real-time behavior with certain transactions.

Workflow Notifications

A typical problem in large organizations is the need to route workflow notifications in EDI to a different person, depending on the business conditions. For example, consider the following situations.

◆ You have a staff that handles errors in the processing of incoming sales orders via EDI. You want to assign different people the job of handling workflow notifications for different types of incoming sales orders (for example, customer orders and internal orders).

◆ You want to assign different people the job of handling workflow notifications for incoming sales orders for different sales organizations.

Both the Inbound Parameters view and Outbound Parameters view of the partner profile have two fields (Message Code and Message Function) that are part of the key but are usually left blank. To address these two business situations, you use these fields. Create two variants of the ORDERS message by assigning a three-digit code to the Message Code field, based on the order type or on the sales organization, respectively. The incoming IDoc originates in the EDI subsystem, so you must make sure the control record contains the appropriate codes in the Message Code and Message Function fields.

Now, with the two variants, you can create two entries in the partner profile for the same message. You should be able to assign a different workflow object type in the Post Processing: Permitted Agent fields.

Summary

In this chapter, you learned about the partner profile component, which defines the characteristics of the messages exchanged with a business partner and the mode (batch versus immediate) in which an IDoc is processed. The partner profile has three views: the General view, the Outbound Parameters view, and the Inbound Parameters view. The General view defines the basic attributes of a business partner, such as partner number and type. The Outbound Parameters view defines the components used in the outbound process, and how SAP hands over the IDocs to the subsystem. It also includes parameters to specify the Message control objects for those message types that use Message control to handle the creation of outbound IDocs. The Inbound Parameters view defines the components used in the inbound process and how IDocs are passed to the posting module for processing.

SAP provides various tools to help you maintain partner profiles. You can build an interface program for creating partner profiles, and you can use the basic copy function to speed up the process.

Chapter 8

Configuring
Message Control

In this chapter, you will learn about the Message control component used in the outbound process. It is important to note that Message control is not built specifically for the EDI process. It has applications in areas such as account determination, material determination, and pricing. Therefore, the terminology of Message control is not related to EDI terminology. You will discover several new terms that you should get accustomed to. This chapter introduces the concept of Message control—what it is, how it is used in EDI, the architecture of the whole process—and then describes the steps for using the standard Message control components. The chapter also discusses how to develop new Message control components.

An Introduction to Message Control

Message control—also referred to as *output control* or *conditioning technique*—is a cross-application component used as a service program in several areas. The biggest application is in pricing, but you also use Message control for output determination in EDI and account determination and material determination in the SD (*Sales and Distribution*) module.

The basic concept behind Message control is to generate and manage outputs from an application and control their timing and medium of exchange. For example, you can create the following outputs when a sales order is entered in the system (see Figure 8.1).

- ◆ An internal mail message to the production control staff immediately
- ◆ A sales order response to the customer via fax immediately
- ◆ Printed output for warehouse personnel when necessary
- ◆ A sales order response to the customer via EDI at night
- ◆ Workflow notification to the quality engineer at the end of the day
- ◆ A sales order to another system via ALE

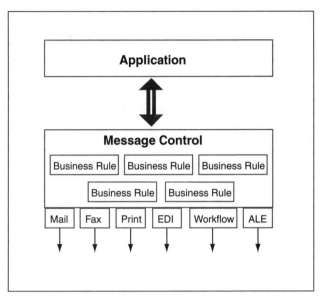

FIGURE 8.1 *Outputs managed by Message control*

 NOTE

If this is not your first encounter with Message control, skip ahead to the "Setting Up Standard Message Control" section.

The outputs can require certain business conditions to be met before they are proposed. For example, send out the EDI message only when the customer number is 3000009. Otherwise, send a printed output. Print the output in German if it is for a customer in Germany; for customers anywhere else, print the output in English. Message control encapsulates such if-then business rules without having to write ABAP/4 programs. The Message control technique has proven to be quite useful and provides a consistent way of generating outputs from several applications. Most SD and MM applications are enabled to use the Message control component.

The Benefits of Message Control

From an EDI perspective, Message control has several advantages. Some of these advantages will become more apparent when you start using the Message control component.

◆ **Disconnecting the process of creating an application document from the process of generating outputs**. For example, the sales order transaction VA01 does not have any logic in its code to generate IDocs for the EDI process. Creating application documents and generating IDocs are two separate processes. The separation helps keep errors in one process from affecting the processing of the other component.

◆ **Automatically proposing output based on business rules specified in Message control**. Rules can be very generic or very specific. After the business rules are encapsulated in Message control, the output is proposed only when the business conditions are met.

◆ **Overriding the automatic proposal**. Although you can set up the system for automatic proposal, the system allows for the outputs to be edited before they are sent. For example, an EDI message is sent to vendor 300009 for purchase orders. However, the vendor has reported some temporary problems and does not want to accept EDI for a certain time period. You can delete the proposed output, and the system will not send the EDI document.

◆ **Manually selecting an output**. Some business rules require human intelligence and, therefore, cannot be encapsulated in Message control. For example, an internal notification is to be sent to an MRP (*Material Requirements Planning*) planner when the delivery date proposed by the sales system is unacceptable to a customer and the customer is a major one. In this case, the concept of *major customer* requires human intelligence and cannot be adequately encapsulated in a business rule. Hence, the sales order clerk entering the order can manually select the output type for internal notification.

◆ **Generating multiple outputs**. The system can propose any number of desired outputs (for example, printed output and order response via EDI) at the same time.

◆ **Controlling the timing, medium, and language of the output messages**. As part of the configuration, you can specify all these parameters. For example, EDI can wait until the end of the day for transmissions, but the internal notifications can be printed immediately.

◆ **Retransmitting an output.** If a printed output is lost or if an EDI transmission fails at the subsystem level and it is necessary to retransmit the output, the system can resend the output without having to duplicate the application document.

◆ **Monitoring the results of execution.** The results of processing an output type are logged in the system, and they can be monitored from the application document.

Applications Enabled for Message Control

Most SD and MM applications use Message control for output determination. Thus, if you enter a sales order, a quote, a scheduling agreement, a purchase order, an invoice, or other business documents in the SD or MM module, you can control the EDI output using Message control. You can find a complete list of applications that currently use Message control, using transaction NACE.

Message control is a service module, and applications call the Message control services using standard function modules of Message control. A list of applications commonly used in the EDI process and enabled for Message control follows.

◆ Billing

◆ Delivery schedule

◆ Purchasing

◆ Purchasing outline agreement

◆ Request for quote

◆ Sales

◆ Shipping

◆ Transportation

The Message Control Architecture

First, I will describe the various components that make up the Message control architecture. Then you will learn how the Message control process uses these components to propose various outputs and process them.

The Message Control Components

To understand the Message control process, it is important to clarify the terminology and identify the various components. The terminology associated with Message control can be confusing because several terms can be used for the same thing, depending on the particular application area. Also, two terms that seem similar can have very different meanings. Such ambiguity can be a problem for not only beginners, but also seasoned consultants. Take note of the following terms.

◆ Output types are also called *messages*, *message types*, or *condition types*.

◆ Procedures are also called *message schemas*.

◆ *Condition type* and *condition record* are two separate things.

Figure 8.2 shows the relationship between various components that make up the Message control system and the reusability of components. Components are reusable within an application. For example, you can use a condition table in more than one access sequence. Components are related to each other via one-to-one relationships or one-to-many relationships. In a one-to-one relationship,

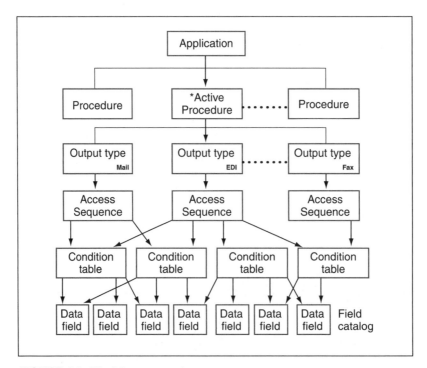

FIGURE 8.2 *The Message control components*

a component can have only one component linked to it. For example, an output type can have only one access sequence associated with it. In one-to-many relationships, a component can be associated with more than one component. For example, an application can have more than one procedure associated with it. To access the Message control components for various applications, you execute either transaction NACE or NACO.

TIP

If you are using an R/3 version older than 4.6, use transaction NACE. You might see a button labeled Expert Mode. If so, click it to see the list of Message control applications.

The Application ID

Applications capable of generating various outputs are assigned a two-character application ID in Message control. For example, the ID for the purchasing application is EF, and the ID for the sales order application is V1. Figure 8.3 (transaction NACE) shows a complete list of application IDs. Application IDs serve as the starting points to drill down into the various Message control components used by an application.

TIP

A quick shortcut to access various Message control components for the SD and MM applications is to use transactions VOK2 for SD and VOK3 for purchasing.

The Communication Structure

The *communication structure* passes application information to Message control. Thus, the communication structure acts as a container. Each application has its own application structure. The communication structure for output determination uses the naming convention KOMxByy, where x can be K or P. K means the header structure and P means the line-item structure. yy is the two-character application ID. Hence, KOMKBV1 is the communication structure for sales order header information.

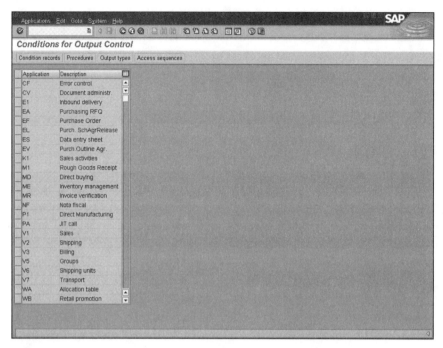

FIGURE 8.3 *A two-character application ID is assigned to applications that support Message control.* (© SAP AG)

The Procedure

A *procedure* defines a set of possible outputs for an application. A procedure is assigned a six-character name. You can define several procedures for an application, but only one can be configured as active. A list of procedures for an application can be seen via the IMG or, in transaction NACE, by selecting an application and clicking the Procedures button. To see the attributes of a procedure, select a procedure and double-click the Control folder in the Dialog Structure frame. A procedure has three main attributes that affect the proposal of an output type (see Figure 8.4).

- ◆ A list of output types
- ◆ A Requirement field
- ◆ A manual flag

The list of output types represents a set of outputs that are possible for an application. It does not mean that they will be proposed; it simply means that the

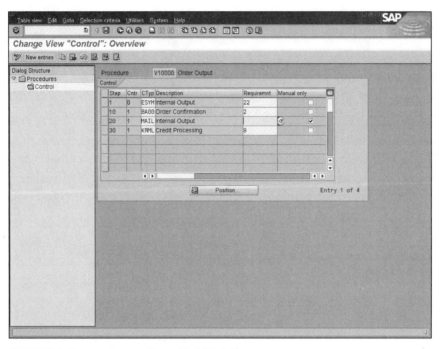

FIGURE 8.4 *Procedure attributes* (© SAP AG)

  NOTE

You can view fields in a communication structure by using transaction SE11. By using append structures, you can extend communication structures. If a communication structure is extended, the extended fields have to be populated in a user exit to pass those values to Message control. User exits are available for populating the extended fields in a communication structure.

system evaluates these outputs for proposal. An output type that does not exist in a procedure cannot be proposed. Examples of certain output types applicable for a sales order are

- ◆ A sales order response
- ◆ An internal message
- ◆ Hard copy output

For each output type, you can define preconditions. (For example, a sales order response should not be sent out unless the sales order is complete.) These preconditions are captured in the requirements. A *requirement* is implemented as an ABAP/4 program and assigned a number. You can view a list of requirements defined in the system by using transaction VOFM. A requirement is optional, but if you want, you can specify one for each output used in a procedure.

You can mark an output type as *manual* in a procedure, meaning that the system does not attempt to propose that output automatically. This output can only be selected manually by a user. This type of output can be important when you do not want an automatic proposal or when the business rules are based on human intelligence and cannot be encapsulated in an ABAP/4 routine.

 NOTE

You can create new procedures, output types, and requirements to suit your needs.

The Output Type

An *output type* defines the characteristics and attributes of the output itself, as shown in Figure 8.5. You access the output types on transaction NACE by selecting an application and clicking the Output Type button. Then double-click an output type to see its details. Examples of output types available for a sales order are BA00 (sales order response), ESYM (internal output), and MAIL (mail).

You define the following attributes for an output type, beginning with the output type name, which is a maximum of four characters long. Examples of output type names are NEU and BA00.

On the General Data tab, you define the following:

- ◆ **Access Sequence**. Basically, this is a set of business rules.
- ◆ **Access to Conditions**. If you select this flag, the values for the output medium and timing are determined from the condition records using the access sequence. For the output types used in the SD modules (sales, shipping, and billing), if this flag is not selected, the values for the output medium and timing are not determined from the condition records. Instead, those values are determined from the customer master data. In the customer master data, an output view exists in the sales area data to

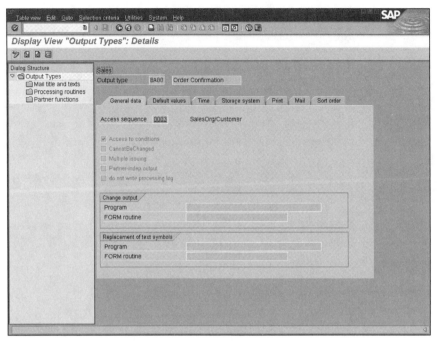

FIGURE 8.5 *Output type attributes* (© SAP AG)

specify the values for the output medium and the language. Specifying the values in the customer master is useful when you do not have any complex rules and the values for the output medium and timing are based on the customer number.

◆ **CannotBeChanged**. This determines whether the output can be edited.

◆ **Multiple Issuing**. This determines whether multiple outputs are permitted.

◆ **Change Output**. Here you can specify a program and form routine that determine whether changes made to the document are relevant for sending the output in a change mode.

On the Default Values tab, you define the following:

◆ **Transmission Medium**. Possible values include EDI, print, SAP office mail, workflow, and ALE.

◆ **Dispatch Time**. This determines whether the message is sent immediately or in batch.

This list of attributes you can assign to an output type is not complete, but it covers the most commonly used attributes for EDI.

The Access Sequence

An *access sequence* defines a sequence in which business rules are checked for proposing an output type. A business rule is checked by comparing the values passed in the application data with the values defined in the condition records of the condition table. If a match occurs, a business rule is considered satisfied. After a business rule is satisfied, the output values from the condition record are used for the output type.

You give an access sequence a four-character name, usually a number. It has the following attributes.

- A set of business rules or conditions
- A sequence in which the rules or conditions are checked
- A requirement that checks for business rules using ABAP programs
- An exclusive or inclusive strategy

To view the access sequence, select an application in transaction NACE, then click on the Access Sequences button. To see the details of an access sequence, select it and then double-click on the Accesses folder in the Dialog Structure frame. Figure 8.6 illustrates two business rules. Business rule 1 is based on Doc.Type/Sales Org./Customer. Business rule 2 is based on Sales Organization/Customer Number. Each business rule is, effectively, a set of fields defined in a condition table.

Each business rule can also have some preconditions, which are implemented in requirements. The concept is the same as in the procedure but provides a more granular control at the business-rule level. (For example, an output message is to be sent to the credit department only if there is a credit block on the sales order.) These preconditions are captured in the requirements. A requirement is implemented as an ABAP/4 program and assigned a number. You can view a list of requirements defined in the system by using transaction VOFM. A requirement is optional, but if you prefer, you can specify it for each business rule used in an access sequence.

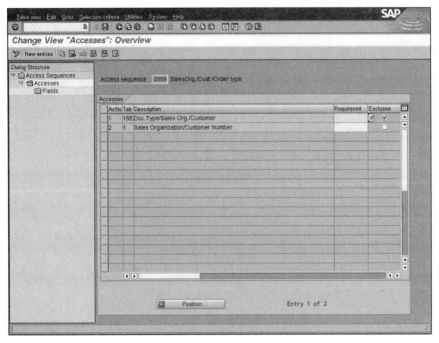

FIGURE 8.6 *Access sequence attributes* (© SAP AG)

The exclusive or inclusive strategy specifies whether the system should exit after the first match of the business rule against the condition records or should continue to process other business rules in the access sequence.

If you choose the exclusive strategy, the system exits on the first match. In the inclusive strategy, the system continues to validate the rest of the business rules. The reason for an inclusive strategy is to have an output type proposed multiple times. However, one of the attributes (partner function, partner number, or language) must be different. The system does not allow two output types to have identical values.

For example, you choose the inclusive strategy when you have to send a purchase order to your business partner via EDI and also to another SAP system via ALE. The output is the same, but the partners are different. An access sequence can define any number of business rules.

The Condition Table

The *condition table* specifies the key fields for a business rule. If a business rule requires you to send EDI based on sales organization and customer, the key for the business rule is Sales Organization (VKORG) and Customer Number (KNDNR). Thus, you formulate a business rule by specifying the fields that are to be used in decision making, as shown in Figure 8.7. (You get to this screen from the Access sequence by double-clicking on the Fields folder in the Dialog Structure frame.) You use this key to access the condition records for output values such as output medium, partner function, partner number, output language, and output time for the message.

If the standard condition tables supplied in the system do not meet your requirements, you can create new condition tables. You must derive the keys for condition tables from the field catalog, which is a subset of the communication structure. This added layer helps you to manage fields. You can select all the fields from the communication structure in your field catalog.

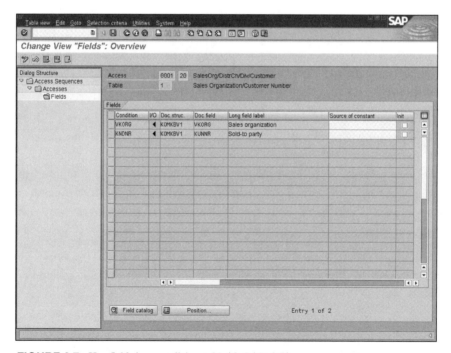

FIGURE 8.7 *Key fields in a condition table* (© SAP AG)

Condition Records

Condition records are inserted in the condition table. *Condition records* contain the actual data against which the business rules are checked to propose an output. In Figure 8.8, customer number is used as a rule to propose the output. Looking at Figure 8.8, you can see that a condition record has two pieces.

◆ Key values of the business rule by which a condition record is accessed. (In Figure 8.8, customer number is the key value.)

◆ The output values of partner function and number, and output medium, timing, and language.

Condition records are considered master data and are maintained by customers. If you are using standard pieces of Message control, the only components you need to create are condition records and Message control parameters in the partner profile.

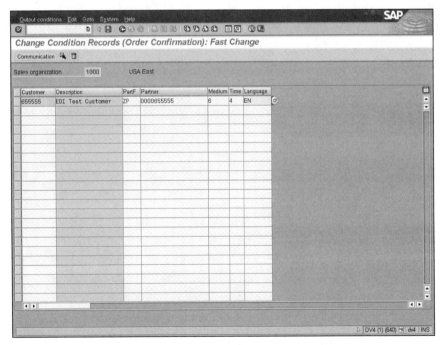

FIGURE 8.8 *Condition records for a condition table* (© SAP AG)

Processing Programs and Tables

Several programs and tables are part of Message control. For EDI, you will frequently deal with the following tables and programs.

- **NAST**. This table stores an entry for each output type created for an application document.
- **TNAPR**. This table has an entry for the processing program used for an output type.
- **RSNAST00**. This program is used to process entries in the NAST table.
- **RSNASTED**. This processing program exists for each output medium. EDI_PROCESSING is a routine in the RSNASTED program to process EDI outputs. The relationship of the output type, output medium, and processing program is established in the TNAPR table.

Understanding How Message Control Works

Message control is a three-step process.

1. **Output proposal.** Message control checks various business rules and proposes various output types.
2. **Output editing.** The user accepts or changes the proposed output types.
3. **Output processing.** The system processes the final list of output types to produce the actual outputs.

The various components used in the process appear in Figure 8.9, and Figure 8.10 describes the technical flow.

Output Proposal

The process described in Figure 8.10 begins when an application document is created or changed. The application program fills the communication structure with values from the application data entered on the screen. This communication structure is passed to Message control, along with the application ID and the procedure.

The various output types defined in a procedure are processed one at a time. They are mutually independent, so the results of one do not affect the other outputs.

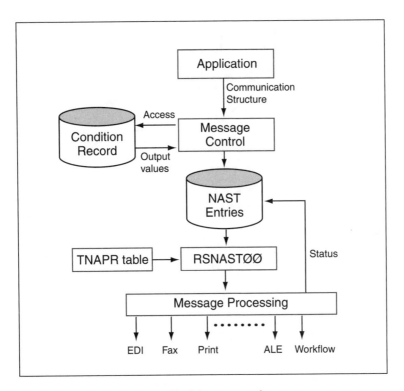

FIGURE 8.9 *Components used in Message control to propose outputs*

An output type marked as manual in a procedure is not used for an automatic proposal. Only the end user can manually select this output. This approach can be important when you do not want an automatic proposal or when business rules are based on human intelligence and cannot be encapsulated in an ABAP routine.

The processing of output types that are not marked as manual is as follows. If you specify a requirement for an output type in the procedure, the code behind the requirement is executed to see whether the output type meets the requirements or preconditions. If requirements are met, further checking continues. If the output type does not meet the requirements, the next output type in the list is processed. (For example, a sales order response should not be sent out unless the sales order is complete.) After parsing the list of output types in a procedure, the system "short lists" the output types that meet the requirements or preconditions.

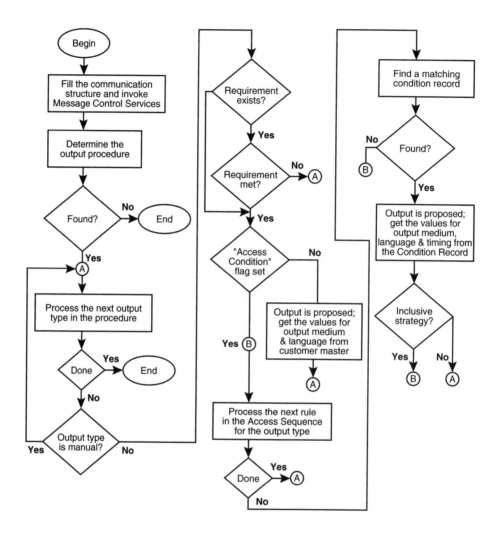

FIGURE 8.10 *The process for proposing an output*

In the case of output types for the SD modules (sales, shipping, and billing), the system checks whether the access condition flag is set for an output type. If the flag is not set, the values for the output medium and timing for the output type are determined from the customer master data. If the flag is selected, processing continues for determining the output medium and timing, as described next.

For each output type in which the access condition flag is set, the access sequence associated with the output type is used to access various business rules and determine which of these business rules are satisfied. A business rule is satisfied if the application values passed in the communication structure result in a condition record being found using the keys of the business rule. The process is as follows.

1. Validate any requirements that exist for a business rule. If the result is negative, the current business rule is skipped, and the next business rule in the sequence is checked.

2. If a business rule passes the requirement check or a requirement is not specified, the condition table for that business rule is accessed for any condition records that match the application data passed in the communication structures.

3. If a match is found, the values of the partner function, partner number, output medium, output language, and output timing are copied for that output type, and the output type is considered as proposed.

4. If the business rule uses exclusive strategy, the process ends here, and the processing starts from the very beginning for the next output type.

5. If an inclusive strategy is used, the next business rule in the access sequence is processed. The purpose of an inclusive strategy is to propose multiple outputs of the same type to different partners. Two instances of the same output type cannot have identical output parameters.

 TIP

You can display the logic used to evaluate the various outputs. From the output control screen, choose Goto, Determination Analysis from the menu.

Output Editing

After the output proposal process is complete, the list of proposed outputs displays on the output control screen of an application, as shown in Figure 8.11. The output control screen is usually available at the header level, but in some cases it is available at other levels. For example, with sales orders, it is available at the sales order header and at the sales order item level.

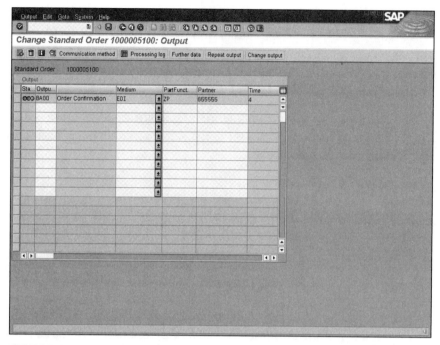

FIGURE 8.11 *The output control screen, showing the outputs proposed for an application document* (© SAP AG)

To reach the output control screen of an application, follow these steps.

1. Go to the application document with which you are working (a sales order, purchase order, delivery, or billing document).

2. Look for Extras, Output or Header, Output or Header, Messages on the menu, depending on the application area. At the line-item level, you look for Item, Output.

The initial status of these outputs is 0 (Not Processed), displayed as an icon with a yellow light. After the output has been successfully issued it is in status 1 (Successfully Processed), displayed as a green light icon

The user entering the application document can carry out the following editing operations.

◆ Delete proposed outputs.

- ◆ Change timing.
- ◆ Select new outputs from the list. The same output cannot be listed twice in status 0.
- ◆ Copy a previously processed output for reprocessing.

If the output medium is 6 (EDI) for an output, the partner number in the proposed output is validated against a partner profile entry. If an entry does not exist in the partner profile table, you cannot save the output.

Output Processing

When the final selection of the output is complete, you can save the application document. A record for each proposed output is saved in the NAST table with the following values.

- ◆ Application ID
- ◆ Application document key (prefixed with zeros if fewer than 10 characters)
- ◆ Output type
- ◆ Output medium
- ◆ Output timing
- ◆ Status code with value 0 (Not Processed)

You can view a complete list of fields in the NAST table via transaction SE11.

The RSNAST00 program processes entries in the NAST table. This program is started immediately for NAST entries whose timing is set to immediate. For other NAST entries, you must schedule this program. The selection list for this program allows you to specify various parameters.

After RSNAST00 selects a record for processing, it checks the TNAPR table for the processing program associated with an output medium. For EDI, a standard routine, EDI_PROCESSING, exists in the RSNASTED program.

The EDI_PROCESSING routine reads the Message control record in the partner profile and determines the process code. The process code points to a function module. The function module has a standard interface for its input and output parameters. One of the input parameters is the NAST record. This function module then has all the information necessary to read the application document data, and it formats the document for the message to be generated, using the IDoc format. The output parameters of the function module are the IDoc data and the control record.

The EDI_PROCESSING program creates a physical IDoc from the data passed back to it from the function module. Then the IDoc is ready for the ALE service layer, where it goes through version change, filtering, and conversion, and is subsequently sent to the operating system through a file port. Refer to Chapter 3, "The Outbound EDI Process," for details on process flow using Message control.

 TIP

The results of processing an output type are logged in the system. To view the results, select the output type from the output control screen, and click Goto, Processing Log.

Setting Up Standard Message Control

This section describes the steps for using the standard Message control component for an application document. The standard system ships with a complete suite of Message control components for each application. You can use these components as is, or you can modify them to suit your needs. If your objective is to use the standard components, all you have to do is create condition records to enable your application to use Message control. If you plan to build some of the components, such as a new condition table, you have to carry out some configuration steps, described in this section.

Creating Condition Records

Creating condition records is specific to each application. You can reach the screen to create condition records via the application menu or by using transaction NACE. The steps are as follows.

1. Execute NACE to display the various applications.
2. Choose the application in which you're interested, and click the Condition Records button.

3. Specify the output type for which you want to create the condition records.

4. Pick the business rule (condition table) for which you want to maintain the condition records.

5. Enter values for the key fields, and specify the output medium, output timing, partner number, and partner function for each record.

6. Save your entries.

Creating a New Condition Component

If the standard Message control functionality does not meet your requirements, you can build the necessary pieces in Message control. The following information explains how to create a new condition type or business rule. These steps are intended to be a guideline; you will need to use the knowledge you've gained from previous sections to carry them out.

An area presented here sends out an order response via EDI for customer group 01 and sales organization 3000. Standard components are used wherever appropriate. In the analysis of the standard system, output type BA01 is used for EDI output. It points to access sequence 0003, which lacks a business rule based on customer group and sales organization. Therefore, a new business rule will be created and added to an access sequence.

The customer group number is available on the header portion of the sales order. An analysis of the existing condition table shows that there is no condition table based on the customer group and sales organization combination. You reach the steps to build the components for the SD applications from the IMG under Logistics-General, Sales and Distribution, Basic Functions, Output Control, or from the SAP standard menu under Logistics, Sales and Distribution, Master Data, Output. You can also access the steps via transaction VOK2.

 NOTE

You don't have to extend the communication structure if it has the Customer Group field in it. If a field does not exist in the communication structure, you can extend the structure by appending user-defined fields. In such cases, the customer-defined fields have to be filled in a user exit, defined for the communication structure.

Accessing the Field Catalog

Transaction: V/86

Menu path: From transaction VOK2, choose SD Document, Sales Document, Condition Table, Field Catalog

Make sure that the Customer Group field (KDGRP) is selected in the field catalog. If it is not, insert the entry in the field catalog.

Creating a Condition Table

Transaction: V/56

Menu path: From transaction VOK2, choose SD Document, Sales Document, Condition Table, Create

You establish the key for your business rule in this step. For the scenario, the key fields are Customer Group (KDGRP) and Sales Organization (VKORG).

Use table numbers 900 and above. Numbers lower than 900 are reserved for SAP. Enter a description for your business rule, and select the Sales Organization field and the Customer Group field from the field catalog. After you create your condition table, you must generate it so that it will be available for later steps.

Defining New Requirements

You can create new requirements if necessary; the current scenario does not require this step. To create new requirements, execute transaction VOFM.

Creating an Access Sequence

Transaction: V/48

Menu path: From transaction VOK2, choose SD Document, Sales Document, Access Sequence

A new access sequence does not have to be created, because you can modify the existing access sequence 0003 being used in the condition type BA01. Because the access sequence can be used in several output types, you should build a new access sequence to avoid conflicts with other output types.

You can begin by copying an existing access sequence, or you can create a new sequence using the preceding transaction. Start your access sequence with a Z to distinguish it from the standard access sequences.

Creating an Output Type

Transaction: V/30

Menu path: From transaction VOK2, choose SD Document, Sales Document, Condition Type

You can assign the new access sequence to BA01 (order response) or create a new output type. If a new output type is to be created, the best option is to copy BA01 as ZB01 (order response). Select BA01 and click the Copy icon.

Adding the Output Type to a Procedure

Transaction: V/32

Menu path: From transaction VOK2, choose SD Document, Sales Document, Output Determination Proc.

If you created a new output type in the preceding step, you must add it to the standard procedure. You can also create a new procedure to keep your entries separate from the SAP entries. The procedure for sales order is V10000. To add an output type to this procedure, select Procedure V10000 and add an entry for the new output type.

Assigning the Procedure at the Header Level

Transaction: V/43

Menu path: From transaction VOK2, choose SD Document, Sales Document, Assign, Header

Creating a new procedure is generally unnecessary, but if you decide to do so, the new procedure has to be assigned to the application at the header level, using the preceding transaction. Select the order type and assign your newly created procedure to it.

Creating Condition Records

The last step is to maintain the condition records for your newly created condition table. The steps are the same as described earlier in the "Setting Up Standard Message Control" section.

TIP

To reach the SD Message control maintenance, you execute VOK2; to reach the MM Message control maintenance, you execute VOK3. These functions can also be reached through the IMG.

Summary

The Message control module, through its various components, provides a great deal of flexibility and enables the application to generate and manage various output types associated with it. You can use Message control to determine the timing and the medium of the output at run time. The various outputs can be generated conditionally, depending on the business rules. To meet business needs, you can encapsulate various business rules within Message control.

Each application is associated with a procedure that defines the various output types. These output types are processed one at a time to determine whether they are valid for proposal. The proposed outputs can then be edited, and the edited outputs are saved in the NAST table. A program, RSNAST00, processes each NAST entry and generates the output. The results are logged in the processing log.

In standard Message control, several condition tables have been predefined. If your intent is to use the standard components, all you have to do is create condition records for using the Message control system. If your business needs cannot be met using the standard components, you can enhance the Message control component accordingly.

Chapter 9

**Configuring
Workflow**

Workflow technology is a cross-application component used in various areas, including the ALE/EDI interface. I have found that workflow is a big mystery for most ALE and EDI users. This chapter introduces the concept of workflow—what it is, how it is used in ALE/EDI, the elements of the workflow module, and the configuration of components used by the ALE/EDI interface. At the end of this chapter, you should have a good handle on the workflow process.

The section on design tips at the end of the chapter contains tips and techniques you can use to handle everyday issues with ALE/EDI and workflow.

 NOTE

If you're interested in the bare minimum configuration required to enable the workflow for error handling in the standard system, you can go directly to the "Setting Up Workflow for Error Notification" section later in this chapter.

An Introduction to the Workflow Management System

This section provides a high-level overview of the workflow module. You will learn about the basic theme underlying workflow, why it was invented, what problems it solves, and how it's used in the ALE/EDI process.

Understanding the Workflow Management System

The workflow management system provides procedural automation of steps in a business process. A formal definition has been prepared by the WFMC (*Workflow Management Coalition*), which is a nonprofit organization devoted to the development of workflow standards to ensure compatibility between workflow software products. WFMC defines workflow as "the automation of a business process, in whole or part, during which documents, information, or tasks are passed from one participant to another for action, according to a set of procedural rules."

A business process can consist of several steps. Historically, the tasks have been coordinated manually or by some informal means of communication (sticky note, e-mail, shouting, and so on). The common problem in these approaches is inefficiency; each lacks a way to trace where a task is, who executed (or is executing) it, and how much time it required. In contrast, the workflow management system ensures that the right work is sent to the right person at the right time in the right sequence with the right information.

 CAUTION

Workflow does not add any new business functionality when coordinating business processes! If a business function is not available in the system, workflow cannot execute it. Contrary to popular belief, workflow does not fill in gaps identified in a business process.

In the early days of workflow, it was mainly viewed as document management software, but recently the popularity of off-the-shelf ERP systems has blessed the use of workflow in managing everyday business processes. SAP embraces workflow as a cross-application technology for use in all modules. SAP provides a full development environment to model and implement your business process via workflow.

You can view workflow development as a programming environment. The workflow development environment is a true object-oriented development environment. The basic component in workflow is a business object on which operations are carried out. These operations are implemented as methods. BAPIs (*Business Application Programming Interfaces*) are special methods implemented in the business objects. Events, which are part of the business object, are triggered for changes in the state of the object, which can cause other processes to begin.

Workflow uses the organization structure to determine the person responsible for executing a task. The organization structure is modeled by using the Organizational Management component of the HR (*Human Resources*) module.

The Benefits of Using Workflow

From an operational perspective, workflow provides several benefits. With workflow, you can trace and audit the entire process. Some of the key benefits of using the workflow module follow.

◆ **Business process integration**. The actual time spent executing a task is far less than the time from when it becomes available for execution to the time it is completed. When a task is ready for execution, workflow eliminates unnecessary waiting by sending it directly to the right person to execute it.

◆ **Intelligent routing**. Tasks are often routed to the wrong person because the person who originally carried out the task is no longer with the company or has moved to another division. Workflow has a built-in module to determine the right person for the job dynamically at run time. Workflow takes into account the organization's dynamics and ensures that the right person is notified.

◆ **Flexible task assignments**. Using workflow, you can set the person to be notified at a level that is more abstract than user ID. Assigning a task directly to a user has several disadvantages. The user can leave the company or change jobs. On the other hand, positions and jobs tend to be relatively stable. It is more likely that a user would leave a job than that a company would eliminate a job. Thus, if tasks are assigned to a position or a job, whoever holds that position in the company at any given time is responsible for the task.

◆ **Proactive approach**. The responsible person does not have to look constantly for problems. If a situation requires the user's attention, a work item appears in his or her SAP Inbox. This system is also called *active monitoring*.

◆ **Substitution and backup facility**. Substitution and backup are built in to the workflow system. You can assign a backup for each position on an as-needed basis. When the primary person for execution of a task is unavailable, work can be automatically routed to a backup.

◆ **Process monitoring capability**. Several tools are available in the workflow system to monitor the current state of a process and to determine workload by user, position, and so on.

◆ **Deadline monitoring**. Tasks in a business process can be assigned a time limit for completion. If the task is not completed within the time frame, someone else (such as the person's supervisor) can be notified.

◆ **Statistical analysis**. The monitoring tools also provide statistical information for fine-tuning the business process. You can identify bottlenecks in the process and take corrective measures.

Applications of Workflow in ALE/EDI

The ALE/EDI interface mainly uses workflow for exception (or error) handling. You can also use workflow for handling notifications in other areas.

Error Notification

Error notification is the primary use of workflow in the ALE/EDI interface. Figure 9.1 illustrates the process for error handling via workflow. When exceptions are raised in the outbound or inbound process, workflow is started, and a user responsible for handling the error receives a notification in his or her SAP Inbox. After the problem is analyzed and fixed, the process can be restarted from the Inbox. If the problem is severe enough to require the process to be restarted from the beginning, the process in error can be purged to avoid any further processing.

Errors are intelligently routed to the right person based on the type of error. Errors have been grouped into various categories. A person can be responsible for handling multiple types of errors, or several users can be responsible for resolving a single type of error. You can configure the system to handle errors in various ways, depending on the size of your company. Technical details of the error notification process are described in the "Understanding the Error Notification Process" section, and steps to configure workflow for error notification are described in the "Setting Up Workflow for Error Notification" section later in this chapter.

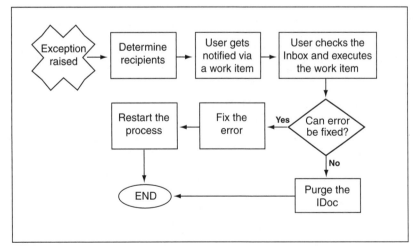

FIGURE 9.1 *The error-handling process using workflow*

Active Monitoring

Active monitoring allows you to specify threshold values for the state of the system. If the system crosses the threshold limit, a person responsible for system problems can be notified. You set a threshold on the number of IDocs in error or the time limit in which a process must complete. For example, you can have someone notified when the number of failed invoice IDocs in the system exceeds 50. The "Setting Up Active Monitoring" section later in this chapter describes a complete set of options and how to set up the system for active monitoring.

Rule-Based Inbound Flow

This application of workflow in ALE/EDI does not fall under the category of exception handling. You can set up workflow to handle processing of an inbound IDoc (see Figure 9.2). Normally, an inbound IDoc starts a function module that invokes the posting program to create an application document from the IDoc.

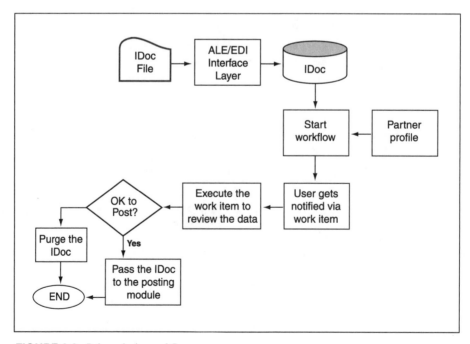

FIGURE 9.2 *Inbound via workflow*

In contrast, if you use a workflow, you can set it up to do whatever is needed for your business process. SAP does not provide standard workflows for the inbound ALE/EDI processes, but you can develop your own workflows and tie them to the ALE/EDI process. Refer to Chapter 17, "Inbound via Workflow: Sales Order Changes," if you are interested in using workflow to process an incoming IDoc.

Consider the example of an inbound order change transaction that allows a customer to modify a previous order. Whether order changes are passed to the system with or without verification is a business issue. In such a situation, it might be essential to review the changes before allowing them to be posted. You can accomplish this step via workflow. An incoming order change IDoc can be routed via workflow to a person for review. If the changes requested by the customer are acceptable, the IDoc can be posted. If the customer's changes are not acceptable, the IDoc can be rejected, and an IDoc can be generated to send a response to the customer.

As a simple example, the customer might request a change in a quantity or delivery date that is not acceptable, possibly because production has already started or because of the lead time required to procure material. You can also design the workflow system to handle complex business processes.

Successful Posting Notification

The system can notify a person of a successful IDoc posting. This feature can be useful when critical documents are posted in the system. Notification after successful posting is not used in the standard ALE/EDI processes, but the system provides hooks to achieve this functionality for custom scenarios without doing any ABAP development. Refer to the "Setting Up Notification of Successful Posting" section later in this chapter.

The Architecture of ALE/EDI Workflow

This section describes the terminology and components of the workflow module as used in the ALE/EDI interface. This material is intended for readers who want detailed knowledge of how the workflow component works in ALE/EDI.

To understand the ALE/EDI workflow process, you must learn the workflow terminology and the concept behind the various components. The components used in workflow fall into two categories: PD-ORG (organizational) objects and workflow

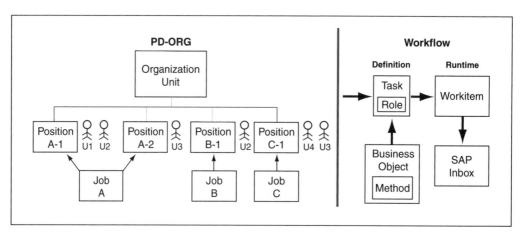

FIGURE 9.3 *Objects used in the workflow process*

objects, as shown in Figure 9.3. You can view and maintain these components by using standard transactions, which you reach via the area menu for workflow.

`Transaction (prior to Version 4.6):` SWLD

`Menu Path:` From the SAP standard menu, choose Tools, Business Workflow, Development

---

 NOTE

You can reach the new version 4.6 SWLD area menu by typing **SWLD** in the command box at the SAP Easy Access menu and pressing the Enter key. To reach the old transaction SWLD in version 4.6, go to the SAP Easy Access menu screen, enter **/N** in the command box, and press Enter. This ends the SAP Easy Access menu. Then type **SWLD** in the command box and press Enter.

PD Organizational Objects

PD-ORG objects are used to represent a company's organization structure in SAP. SAP provides several types of PD-ORG objects, such as positions, jobs, organizational units, and work centers. These objects are assigned a one-character or two-character ID to represent the object type. In the following sections, you will gain a basic understanding of these objects, their significance, and how you can use them in building your organization structure. The type of object appears in parentheses wherever applicable.

Organizational Plans

An *organizational plan* represents the complete information about a company's organization structure. The main elements of an organizational plan are as follows.

◆ **Hierarchy among various organizational units**. A company can have several organizational units broken down by function. For example, a company can have several divisions, such as engineering, manufacturing, and finance. A division can be divided further. For example, a manufacturing division can contain several plants.

◆ **Jobs performed in a company**. A job involves performing one or more business tasks. For example, purchasing clerk, sales order clerk, design engineer, programmer, secretary, and manager.

◆ **Positions held by the organization's employees in the organization and the reporting structure**. For example, purchasing clerk for plant 1000, manager of the accounting department, and secretary to the CEO. The reporting structure or chain of command might be that the accounting department manager reports to the head of the finance division, and so on.

Organizational Units (O)

An *organizational unit* is responsible for a specific function in a company. For example, an organizational unit can represent a department, physical location, division, subsidiary, or project team. An organizational unit can contain other organizational units. Organizational units are linked in a hierarchical fashion to form the entire organization structure. An EDI department is an example of an organizational unit.

Jobs (C)

From a workflow perspective, jobs represent a flexible means of identifying a user responsible for handling errors. A *job* describes a set of tasks performed by a person holding a position to which that job is assigned. Although you can assign individual tasks directly to a position, it is advisable to group tasks together in a job and to assign the job to the position. This approach helps to reduce the maintenance effort. EDI administrator, manager, secretary, and engineer are jobs. The job of an EDI administrator can be to handle all the technical errors associated with the EDI interface.

Positions (S)

From a workflow perspective, a *position* is another flexible means of finding a person responsible for handling errors. A position in a company represents a rank. For example, a level 1 manager represents the first level of management. Positions are linked in hierarchical fashion to represent the chain of command in a company. A user is assigned to a position that represents his or her rank. If an employee is promoted, that person leaves his or her current position and is assigned to another position. Positions are thus more stable entities than employees in a company. Positions are assigned jobs to represent the tasks performed by the position. Tasks can be assigned to a position directly or via jobs.

TIP

The system allows multiple users to hold a position or a single user to hold multiple positions. It is advisable to set up one person per position. Doing so eases the maintenance effort when a person changes positions or when a user is assigned to a vacant position. Sharing a position with multiple users also has a complicating effect on HR reporting of resource use.

Workcenters represent physical locations where sets of activities are carried out. In the case of workflow, you can use workcenters to represent one or more groups in the EDI department.

Users (US)

A *user* is a person who has been granted access to the SAP system to use its various functions. A user ID identifies a user in the system.

Workflow Objects

Workflow objects model a workflow process. Workflow objects are also assigned a two-character ID to represent the object type. The following sections describe the various workflow objects used in an ALE/EDI process. The object type appears in parentheses wherever applicable.

Business Objects

Transaction: SW01
Menu Path: From the Area menu of Workflow, choose Definition Tools, Business
Object Builder

A *business object* represents a business entity that has a definite state and various
properties. You can carry out various functions on the object. A business object
encapsulates the entire functionality of an object. A business object is given a
name in SAP. For instance, a standard material is assigned the name
BUS1001006; it has properties such as material number, description, and material type. These properties are represented using attributes of the business object.
The various operations that can be carried out on an object are implemented with
methods. For example, if you want to create a material, you can call that business
object's Create method. An object also has different states. It exposes its various
states by publishing events. For example, the material object has a created event
that is published whenever a new material is created.

Several business objects are defined in the system and organized in the BOR
(*Business Object Repository*). Objects are implemented as a series of inherited
objects, starting with a generic object and ending with a very specific object. The
various objects designed for the ALE/EDI process are as follows.

◆ **IDOC**. The IDOC object represents a generic IDoc. This object is not
used directly in the process, but it provides a generic implementation of
the attributes and functions associated with an IDoc.

◆ **IDOCAPPL**. The IDOCAPPL object represents a generic application
IDoc used in ALE and EDI. It is inherited from the IDOC object and
acts as the main object from which application-specific objects are inherited. Most functions and attributes used in an IDoc are implemented in
this object. Figure 9.4, the transaction SW01 display for this object,
shows the various components of the IDOCAPPL.

◆ **IDOC<message_type>**. This object is derived from the IDOCAPPL
object and represents an application-specific object. Although no
additional functionality is added after inheriting the IDOCAPPL object,
it is the application-specific object that is referenced in the configuration
tables.

◆ **IDOCPACKET**. This object represents a packet of IDocs.

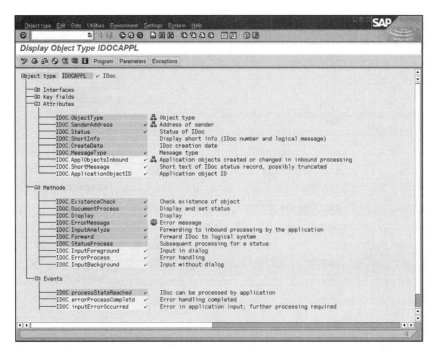

FIGURE 9.4 *The attributes, methods, and events in the application IDOC object (IDOCAPPL)* (© SAP AG)

- ◆ **IDPK<message type>.** This object represents a packet of specific types of IDocs. For example, IDPKORDERS represents a packet of IDoc orders. The IDPKORDERS object is inherited from IDOCPACKET.

Each IDoc-related object has several attributes, methods, and events. When a work item is executed, it executes one of the methods encapsulated in the object.

Tasks (T or TS)

Transaction (Prior to version 4.6): PFTCTransactions (From version 4.6): PFTC_INS (create), PFTC_CHG (change), PFTC_DIS (display), PFTC_DEL (delete)

Menu Path (From Version 4.6): From the Area menu of Workflow, choose Definition Tools, Tasks/Task Groups

A *task* defines a piece of work that can be executed and tracked in the system. Technically, a task points to a method of an object, as shown in Figure 9.5. In addition, a task defines the text describing the purpose of the task, the triggering event based on which the task is started, the terminating event that marks the

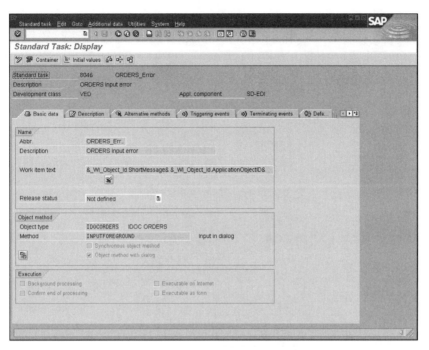

FIGURE 9.5 *Standard task ORDERS_Error* (© SAP AG)

completion of a task, and a role that contains the rules to identify the person who is responsible for executing the task. A task can be started in response to an event triggered in the system.

Tasks are categorized as standard tasks (TS) or customer tasks (T). Standard tasks are provided by SAP and are client independent, and customer tasks are client dependent and developed by customers.

In the ALE/EDI process, tasks are mainly used for error handling. A task has been defined for every standard message and for each type of error in the process. The tasks for a message are named as *<message type>*_Error. Table 9.1 shows the tasks for errors in the process.

 NOTE

Process codes EDIL, EDIN, EDIR, and EDIP were introduced in version 4.6. Also, prior to version 4.6, the task assigned to process code EDIM was TS00007988.

Table 9.1 Error Tasks in the EDI Process

Process Code	Task Number	Description
EDIM	TS30000020	No IDoc created yet.
EDII	TS00008068	Error in the inbound process.
EDIY	TS00008074	Syntax error—inbound.
EDIN	TS70008037	Display NAST record with msg. No IDoc created yet.
EDIO	TS00007989	Error in the outbound process.
EDIX	TS00008070	Syntax error—outbound.
EDIP	TS60001307	Error in the outbound process (IDoc packet processing).
EDIL	TS70008373	Error in the inbound status file.
EDIR	TS70008125	Error in the subsystem, post-processing allowed.
EDIS	TS30000078	Error in the subsystem.

Customers can change the following attributes of a task.

◆ Work item text

◆ Triggering events

Roles

Transaction (prior to version 4.6): PFAC
Transactions (from version 4.6): PFAC_INS (create), PFAC_CHG (change) PFAC_DIS
(display) PFAC_DEL (delete)
Menu Path: From the Area menu of Workflow, choose Definition Tools, Standard
Roles

Roles are workflow objects used to determine the person responsible for carrying out a specific task. Each task has a role assigned to it.

Roles for the ALE/EDI process are implemented as function modules in the system (see Figure 9.6). These function modules can read any information stored in the SAP system. SAP sets the interface for these function modules. The return parameters of this function module are the object type and object ID.

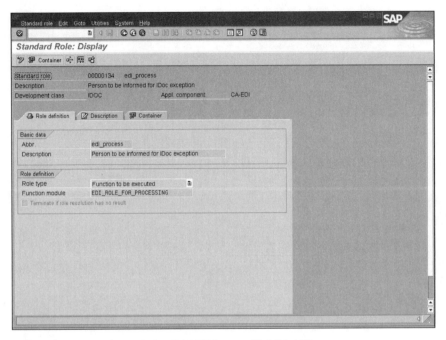

FIGURE 9.6 *Standard role for ALE/EDI errors* (© SAP AG)

Work Items

A *work item* represents an instance of a task that needs to be executed. A work item has text describing its purpose (see Figure 9.7) and can have various states that govern the operations allowed. Table 9.2 describes the various states of a work item and its effect on usability.

Table 9.2 Work Item States from Inception to Completion

Status	Description
Ready	A work item is created and is visible to all selected agents.
Reserved	A work item has been reserved by a user and disappears from the Inbox of other selected users.
In Process	A work item is being worked on and can be seen only in the Inbox of the user who started working on it.
Completed	A work item is complete and cannot be seen in the Inbox of any user.

FIGURE 9.7 *A work item describing the cause of an error in the ALE/EDI process* (© SAP AG)

The SAP Inbox

Transaction (prior to version 4.6): S001

Transaction (from version 4.6): SBWP

Menu Paths: From the SAP Easy Access menu, click on the Business Workplace icon. Or, from the SAP standard menu, choose Office, Workplace, and then expand the entry for Inbox. From the area menu for Workflow, choose Runtime Tools, Business Workplace.

The *SAP Inbox* is an interface to manage workflow work items and SAP office documents. Figure 9.8 shows a list of work items in a user's Inbox. It can be compared with the Inbox of regular e-mail systems that you use at work. The SAP Inbox contains separate buckets for office documents and workflow items. Office documents are the e-mail documents, and workflow items are work items. You can display and execute the work items from the Inbox. The Inbox interface is highly configurable.

A detailed description of the SAP Inbox appears in Chapter 11, "Monitoring the Interface," as part of the discussion on monitoring tools.

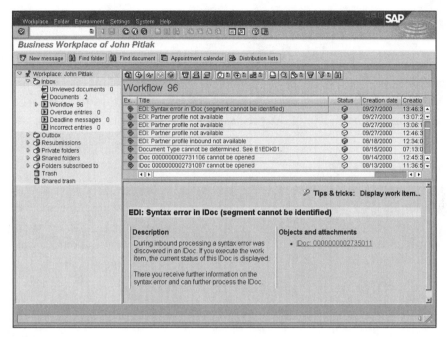

FIGURE 9.8 *A work list in the SAP Inbox* (© SAP AG)

Understanding the Error Notification Process

This section describes how to use the workflow components in the error notification process to inform the right person about an error situation, and how to get the right information to execute the process in a timely fashion. Errors can be encountered at various points in the inbound and outbound processes. Errors are routed to responsible agents (also called *selected agents*) via workflow. The selected agents find a work item in their Inboxes. The work items can be executed to examine the details of the error. After the problem is fixed, the process can be restarted from the point of failure.

The error notification process comprises the following steps.

    1. Determining the task to be started.

    2. Routing the error to a responsible agent as a work item.

    3. Processing of the work item by the responsible agent.

Determining the Task

Errors are classified into categories, depending on the type. A task is started in response to an error. The error-handling process for each type of error is unique and defined in a task via the method that is executed. A role is also defined for each task to identify the person responsible for it. The following sections describe the error categories, listing the process code and task for each.

General Errors

General errors are encountered in the process before an IDoc is created. In the inbound process, these errors are related to reading or deleting the IDoc file at the OS level, or to any internal errors in processing an incoming IDoc file. In the outbound process, these errors can be related to errors creating the output file.

No IDoc Created Yet: EDIM—TS30000020

This process code can sometimes be invoked by file-opening and reading problems when processing status files from the EDI subsystem.

The system initiates this task, and the IDoc administrator is notified.

Display NAST Record with Msg. No IDoc Created Yet: EDIN—TS70008037

If an error occurs before an IDoc is created in an outbound process using Message control, this process code is invoked. When the work item is processed, it displays the object keys of the NAST record that attempted to trigger the IDoc creation.

The system initiates this task. Using information from the NAST record, the system attempts to notify the receiver identified either in the Outbound Partner Profile view for the partner and document or in the General view. If neither can be determined, the IDoc administrator is notified.

Error in the Inbound Status File: EDIL—TS70008373

If an error occurs in the processing of an IDoc status file from the EDI subsystem before an IDoc is created, the system triggers this process code. Such errors result from problems opening the file, reading the status records, or formatting problems on a record.

The system initiates this task, and the IDoc administrator is notified.

Syntax Errors during Inbound Processing

After an inbound IDoc has been created successfully in the system, the IDoc goes through a syntax check. When syntax errors are found in an incoming IDoc, they are logged in the IDoc with a status code of 60 (Error during Syntax Check—Inbound). Syntax errors usually occur during testing; frequent syntax errors in a live system suggest a lack of testing. Refer to Chapter 30, "IDocs on the Inside," for syntax rules checked in an IDoc.

Syntax Error—Inbound: EDIY—TS00008074

If the inbound IDoc fails the syntax check, the system initiates this task, and the person identified in the partner profile for the IDoc message is notified.

Errors in the Inbound ALE/EDI Interface

Errors other than syntax errors can occur from the point at which a physical IDoc is created in the system to the point at which the IDoc is delivered to the application-posting program. These errors are mainly due to configuration problems in the partner profile or to information passed in the control record that does not find a matching partner profile. These errors are logged with a status code of 56 (IDoc with Errors Added).

Error in the Inbound Process: EDII—TS00008068

For a non-syntax error during inbound IDoc processing before calling the posting program, the system initiates this task, and the person identified in the General view of the partner profile is notified. If a partner profile cannot be read at all, the IDoc administrator is notified.

Errors in the Application Posting Program

After an IDoc is passed to the posting program, errors reported by the posting program are considered application errors. These are logged in the IDoc with a status code of 51 (Application Document Not Posted). Such errors are usually related to data in the IDoc and are among the most common errors seen on an inbound process.

A standard task exists for each incoming message. The naming convention is *<message type>*_Errors. These tasks are initiated as a result of an error event (InputErrorOccurred) triggered by the system on the application IDoc object.

The person identified in the Inbound view of the partner profile for that message is notified. For example, the task for incoming orders is ORDERS_Error (TS00008046). This task is started when the InputErrorOccurred event is raised on object IDOCORDERS. By using transaction SWE2, you can see the linkage between an event and the task in the event linkage table.

Syntax Errors during Outbound Processing

After an outbound IDoc has been created successfully in the system, the IDoc goes through a syntax check. This task is started for syntax errors found on an outbound IDoc. Errors are logged in the IDoc with a status code of 26 (Error during Syntax Check—Outbound). This error usually occurs during testing, and frequent syntax errors in a live system suggest a lack of testing.

Syntax Error—Outbound: EDIX—TS00008070

If an outbound IDoc fails the syntax check, the system initiates this task. The person identified in the partner profile for the IDoc message is notified.

Errors in the Outbound ALE/EDI Interface

Errors other than syntax errors can occur from the point at which a physical IDoc is created in the system to the point at which the IDoc is delivered to the EDI subsystem. These errors are mainly due to configuration problems in the partner profile, but they can also occur when receivers for a message cannot be determined. These errors are logged with a status code of 29 (Error in ALE Service).

Error in the Outbound Process: EDIO—TS00007989

For non-syntax errors when processing outbound IDocs the system initiates this task, and the person identified in the General view of the partner profile is notified. If a partner profile cannot be read at all, the IDoc administrator is notified.

Errors in the Outbound ALE/EDI Interface (IDoc Packet Processing)

When outbound IDocs are processed in groups, errors other than syntax errors can occur from the point at which a physical IDoc is created in the system to the point at which the IDoc is delivered to the EDI subsystem. These errors are mainly due to configuration problems in the partner profile, but can also occur when receivers for a message cannot be determined. These errors are logged with a status code of 29 (Error in ALE Service).

Error in the Outbound Process (IDoc Packet Processing): EDIP—TS60001307

For non-syntax errors when processing outbound IDocs in packets, the system initiates this task and the IDoc administrator is notified.

Errors in the Subsystem

These errors are relevant only for outbound IDocs. When an IDoc leaves the SAP system and is transferred to the subsystem, errors encountered in the subsystem or processes thereafter are reported to SAP. These errors start a workflow that sends a notification to the EDI administrator. This task allows the administrator to initiate immediate reprocessing of the IDoc, if desired, when executing the work item.

Error in the Subsystem, Post-Processing Allowed: EDIR—TS70008125

When the subsystem sends a status record reporting a processing error, the system starts this task and the IDoc administrator is notified.

Error in the Subsystem: EDIS—TS30000078

This error is also relevant only for outbound IDocs and is triggered by situations similar to those that trigger EDIR. EDIS was the standard process code up to version 4.6A, when EDIR replaced it. It can still be triggered as a fallback when configuration does not result in EDIR being called.

If triggered, the system starts this task and the IDoc administrator is notified.

Routing to a Responsible Agent as a Work Item

After an error has been classified into one of the preceding categories, the task associated with the error is started. The user responsible for the task is determined via the role defined at the task level. A work item is created for the task and sent to the person identified using the role.

The workflow concept behind resolving a person responsible for an error is interesting. The system defines various types of agents, and each type has a specific objective. When you work in the workflow module, you might have trouble at first figuring out who gets notified, why work items seem to disappear automatically, why sometimes everyone in the SAP system receives a work item in his or her Inbox, what happens if a person does not exist, and so on.

Possible Agents versus Selected Agents versus Actual Agents

A task has three types of agents: possible agents, selected agents, and the actual agent (see Figure 9.9). *Possible agents* represent persons who can execute a task. Not all the possible agents get a work item when a task is started.

Possible agents are configured in the system by assigning a task to several HR objects (job, position, organizational unit, and so on). A task can be set to General Task, which means that it can be executed by anyone. If you define a task as a General Task, you do not have to assign a task specifically to an HR object.

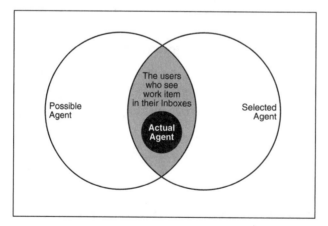

FIGURE 9.9 *The agents applicable to a work item in workflow*

CAUTION

Setting a task as a General Task is useful if the possible agents cannot be identified any other way. The only drawback is that workflow sends a work item to possible agents if it cannot determine selected agents, meaning that everyone in the SAP system will get a work item in his or her Inbox. Such a situation indicates that the IDoc administrator is not set up correctly.

Selected agents are the users who get a work item in their Inbox. They are determined by the role resolution logic. Selected agents must be a subset of possible agents. If they are not a subset of possible agents, the status of the work item is set to Error, and the work item is routed to the workflow administrator.

If the selected agents cannot be found, the work item is sent to all possible agents. In the ALE/EDI process, the selected agents are configured in the partner profile and the IDoc Administrator settings in transaction WE46.

The *actual agent* is the person who executes the work item from the Inbox. A work item can have several selected agents but only one actual agent. When a selected agent executes a work item, the actual agent for the work item is established, and the work item immediately disappears from the Inbox of other selected agents. However, if an actual agent realizes that he or she cannot resolve the problem, the user can replace the work item, causing it to reappear in the selected agents' Inboxes.

Agents in the ALE/EDI Process

In Chapter 6, "Configuring Basic EDI Components," and Chapter 7, "Configuring Partner Profiles," you were introduced to four places (the IDoc administrator and the General parameters, and the Inbound and Outbound parameters views of the partner profile) where you can specify the agent responsible for handling errors in the ALE/EDI process. This section summarizes what happens when a specific agent is notified. The agent for each type of task is described in the task categories earlier. The EDIM, EDIP, EDIL, EDIR, and EDIS categories of errors are reported directly to the EDI administrator. The remaining errors,

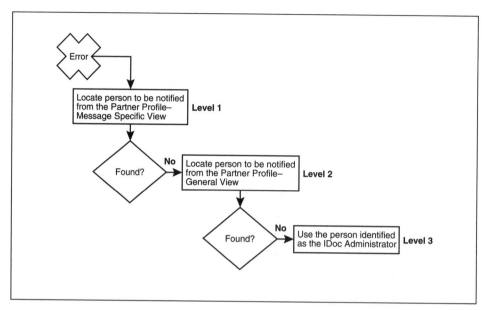

FIGURE 9.10 *Levels of agents in the ALE/EDI process*

EDIX, EDIY, EDIO, EDIN, and EDII, have three levels of support for reporting the error (see Figure 9.10).

- ◆ **Level 1**. If a partner profile is located for that problem, the organizational object specified at the message level (inbound or outbound) in the partner profile is notified.

- ◆ **Level 2**. If level 1 cannot be identified because of a problem locating the record, the level-2 organizational object specified in the General view of the partner profile is read.

- ◆ **Level 3**. If neither level 1 nor level 2 can be identified, the system reads the EDICONFIG table for the IDoc administrator and sends a notification.

Processing by the Responsible Agent

A selected agent can access the work items from the Inbox. Executing a work item establishes the actual agent of the work item and causes it to disappear from the view of other selected agents. After the work item has been processed completely, it also disappears from the actual agent's Inbox. The steps necessary to fix an error for which a work item is generated are as follows.

1. Execute work item to display the error. Examples of errors include problems in the control record, errors in the IDoc data, and incorrect configuration.

2. The cause of the problem can usually be determined from the error message. If applicable, additional error information is also available for certain types of errors (for example, application errors).

3. After the cause of the problem has been determined, it must be fixed outside workflow (or in some cases, within workflow). The recovery procedure depends on the nature of the problem.

   - If the error is in the IDoc data, the IDoc can be edited and then reprocessed from workflow.

   - If the error requires restarting the process from the beginning, the IDoc has to be marked for deletion to stop it from further processing and to clear the work item from the Inbox.

   - If the error involves an IDoc that has not been created yet, the work item merely informs the person about the error. The work item is deleted when the user exits the display screen. Sometimes the user is prompted to acknowledge that he or she has completed the processing. For such cases, the work item stays in the user's Inbox until the user acknowledges that processing is complete.

Setting Up Workflow for Error Notification

Although the workflow component seems very intricate and involves several components, don't worry. Most of the components and configuration for the standard components have already been done in the standard system. You do need to carry out steps that SAP cannot supply, for example, the organization structure and the identification of the users responsible for error handling. The workflow settings you need to be aware of are described next.

Basic Workflow Settings

Transaction: SWU3

Menu Path: From the IMG, choose Basis Components, Business Management, SAP Business Workflow, Maintain standard settings for SAP Business Workflow

TIP

You can also reach transaction SWU3 by pressing the Workflow Customizing button in transaction WE46.

Before any workflow configuration can begin, a set of basic workflow settings must be maintained in the system. If you have a workflow team, these settings are probably already done for you; otherwise, the Basis team can help you with them. If an application is using the workflow module for the first time, these settings will most likely be missing. The steps to carry out the Basic workflow settings are not in the scope of ALE/EDI settings, but you will have to verify that these settings are maintained. These settings establish a basic infrastructure for the various workflow components.

At the bottom of the screen are two sets of lights: one for the definition components and one for the runtime components of workflow. A green light indicates that all the necessary settings are correct. However, a red light does not necessarily mean that workflow will not work; that depends on the item that is not configured correctly. You can use the Automatic Customizing button, but you must be logged on with the highest authorization level. A Basis person is usually the best person to execute Automatic Customizing because his or her ID should have all possible authorizations.

Setting Up the EDI Organizational Unit

As a person responsible for ALE/EDI customizing, you are responsible for either maintaining the organizational unit for the ALE/EDI department or providing your input to the HR group that maintains the PD-ORG. You must first develop a strategy for your ALE/EDI organization and then carry out the steps to enter the information into the system.

Developing a Strategy

Your objective is to design the organization structure so that the right person is notified and the workload can be managed efficiently. The following steps will help you build a strategy.

- Develop a list of messages being used in the ALE/EDI process. Identify the tasks associated with each message.

- Develop a list of users who will handle application errors for each of the identified messages. When selecting a user, make sure that you select a business person and not a technical person, because most errors that occur during production are data-related, and business people are the best equipped to fix data errors.

- Identify a key technical person who will handle technical problems with the interface. This person becomes the IDoc administrator; he or she does not need detailed functional knowledge.

- Identify the number of positions that will be required to handle the ALE/EDI process. This number depends on the organization's complexity, the number of EDI messages, and the volume of EDI transactions. It is usually best to define a position for each business function. For example, one position can handle all messages related to the purchasing cycle, and another position can handle messages related to invoicing. Your organization might require one person per message type.

- Identify backups for each user.

After the various objects such as positions, tasks, and users are identified, you can start building the PD-ORG for the EDI group.

Building an Organizational Unit

Transaction: PPOC

Menu Path: From the Area menu of Workflow, choose Organizational Management, Organizational Plan, Create

The organization and staffing maintenance transactions in version 4.6 are quite different from previous versions. They employ multiple frames within the transaction window and use some drag-and-drop functions. There is an Expert mode, which is faster to use after you become familiar with the process. You can reach it from the Organizational Plan node on the SAP standard menu or with the following transactions.

- ◆ PO10 Organizational unit
- ◆ PO03 Job
- ◆ PO13 Position
- ◆ PO01 Workcenter
- ◆ PFCT Task catalog
- ◆ PP01 General

For SAP versions prior to version 4.6, the organizational unit can be maintained via the Simple Maintenance tool or the Detail Maintenance transactions. The Simple Maintenance tool was specifically designed for workflow users. It's easy to use and provides a visual perspective of the organization structure in a tree format. The various objects are color-coded to differentiate one from another. Although the Simple Maintenance tool is easy to use and intuitive, it doesn't provide all the functions available in the PD-ORG. Therefore, you might have to maintain certain components and relationships via the regular maintenance transactions. You can still use the Simple Maintenance tool under version 4.6 by calling the following transactions.

- ◆ PPOC_OLD Create
- ◆ PPOM_OLD Change
- ◆ PPOS_OLD Display

To build an organizational unit, follow these steps.

1. Start by using transaction PPOCE. Accept the default validity dates on the Create Root Organizational Object pop-up dialog.

2. The main maintenance screen, shown in Figure 9.11, has four windows. Clockwise from the upper-left corner, these are the Object Selection window, the Overview window, the Details window, and the Search Result window. Enter an abbreviation and name for your organizational unit in the Details window and click the Save icon.

3. To create and assign positions to your organization, click the far-left icon in the Overview window to display a list of views (see Figure 9.12). Select the Staff Assignments (List) view. At this point, you can change the view to a workflow-specific one by selecting Goto, Switch Settings from the drop-down menu. Select the Organization and Staffing

FIGURE 9.11 *The organization and staffing maintenance screen* (© SAP AG)

(Workflow) view. This will add several workflow-specific object icons in the Object Selection window.

4. Create the various positions as required by clicking the Create Position icon in the Overview window (see Figure 9.13). You can leave the job description blank for now. Assign an abbreviation to the position, and give it a meaningful name. Repeat this step for all positions identified earlier.

5. Assign users to these positions. Click the User icon in the Search window and select a group of users. The Search Result window will display the users selected. Drag each user to the Overview window and drop it into the appropriate position. Figure 9.14 shows the result. Repeat this step for all positions.

Your organizational unit is now complete. Figure 9.15 shows how an organizational unit consisting of a position for the EDI administrator and several positions for the application areas can look. Remember, though, that your organization structure might be totally different.

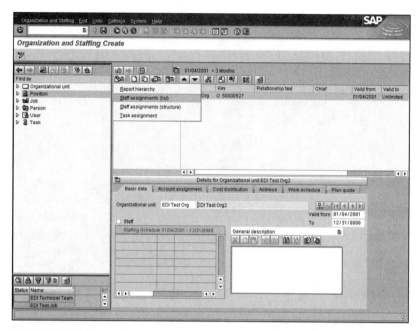

FIGURE 9.12 *Preparing to add staff assignments to a new organization* (© SAP AG)

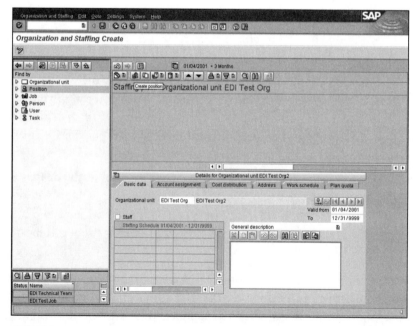

FIGURE 9.13 *Preparing to create a position* (© SAP AG)

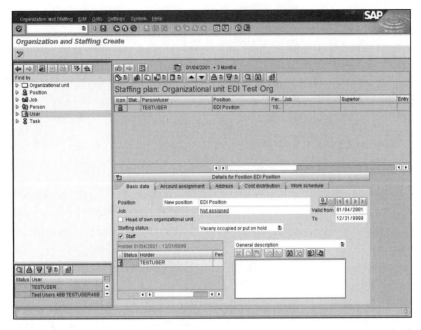

FIGURE 9.14 *The position has now been created, and a person has been assigned to it.* (© SAP AG)

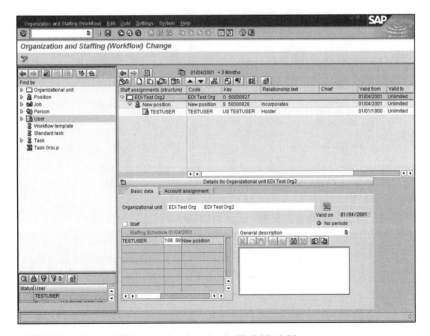

FIGURE 9.15 *An EDI organizational unit* (© SAP AG)

Assigning a Task Profile

As discussed in the preceding section, it is important to define the possible agents for each error task that will be used in the ALE/EDI process. To do so, you have to assign the task to various positions that can possibly execute it. Keep in mind that the possible agents are not necessarily the selected agents. You can adopt either of the following strategies for assigning the possible agents to a task.

◆ Possible agents = Everyone

◆ Possible agents = Certain positions only

In the first case, you simply have to specify the task as a General Task, which means that anyone can execute it. You can use this technique for ALE/EDI messages. The only drawback is that if the workflow system cannot determine selected agents for a task, it will send the work item to all possible agents. Then, every user of the system sees this work item in his or her Inbox until one person elects to execute it. However, the chances of this particular situation occurring in the production system are slim, because it implies an incorrect ALE/EDI configuration or that a user has been deleted from his or her position. Therefore, usually the General Task assignment is the best approach. The steps are as follows.

Transaction: PFTC or PFTC_DIS (from version 4.6)
Menu Path: From the Area menu of Workflow, choose Definition Tools, Tasks/Task Groups, Display

1. Enter the task number. Click Display.
2. From the menu, choose Additional Data, Agent Assignment, Maintain. Click the task, and click the General Task button. Check the General Task check box and save the values.

In the second strategy for assigning agents, you specifically assign each task to a set of positions you have identified. The steps, again from transaction PFTC or PFTC_DIS, are as follows.

1. Enter the task number. Click Display.
2. From the menu, choose Additional Data, Agent Assignment, Maintain.
3. Click the task, and click the Create Agent Assignment icon. Select the Position radio button and then enter the position number. You can repeat this step for all positions that are to be assigned to this task.

> **NOTE**
>
> You can also use the organization and staffing maintenance transaction to create the task profile. To use this method, you start at the position level and assign all the tasks for a position.

Setting Up Active Monitoring

Active monitoring sends a work item when the state of the system exceeds a predefined threshold state. For example, if the number of error IDocs for invoices exceeds 100, you can have the system send a work item to a user or position.

SAP provides a report program RSEIDOCM that you can schedule to run at regular intervals or execute online. The selection parameters for this report allow you to specify the threshold values and the person to be notified (see Figure 9.16). You can restrict the report by IDoc type, groups of messages, and several other parameters. The system starts a single-step task (TS30200088) when it exceeds the defined threshold.

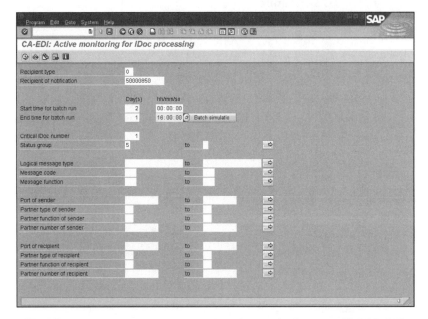

FIGURE 9.16 *Selection parameters for the active monitoring report* (© SAP AG)

Follow these steps to run the report online.

1. Create a task profile. Like any other task, you have to define the possible agents for the task (TS30200088). You can use the two strategies discussed in the preceding section: Make the task a General Task, or specifically assign the task to certain positions, jobs, or organizational units.

2. Execute the report (RSEIDOCM) by using transaction SE38. Refer to Figure 9.16 for the selection parameters.

3. Specify the responsible PD-ORG object on the selection screen. This object can be a user, a position, a job, or an organizational unit.

4. Define threshold values. The selection parameters allow you to specify threshold values. Most of the parameters on the selection list are self-explanatory. The following parameters might need some explanation.

   - **Start Time for Batch Run**. From the current date and time, specify the number of days, hours, minutes, and seconds in the past from which the run should be executed.

   - **End Time for Batch Run**. From the current date and time, specify the number of days, hours, minutes, and seconds up to which the run should be executed. This value should be less than the start date.

   - **Critical IDoc Number**. The value in this field specifies the threshold value that is checked for sending a work item. If the state of the system exceeds this value, a work item is sent.

   - **Status Group**. The various status codes associated with an IDoc have been categorized in status groups. This arrangement allows you to monitor the state based on a status group. For example, group 5 represents errors in the IDoc interface for outbound IDocs. The various status codes in this group are 02, 20, 21, 26, 27, 29, and 34. You can see the grouping in table TEDS3.

Click the Execute button to start the report. If the system state exceeds the threshold, the person specified in the report will receive a work item. Executing the work item generates the IDoc statistics report, and you can drill down to see a list of IDocs that were selected.

Setting Up an Inbound Process via Workflow

Transaction: WE42
Menu Path: From the Area menu of EDI, choose Control, Inbound Process Code

In the standard system, the inbound process is implemented as a function module that calls a posting program for an IDoc. The standard system can be configured to start a workflow or a single-step task for an incoming IDoc. This approach of using a workflow or a single-step task can be useful when you want someone to review the IDoc data before it's posted in the system. For example, you can use this approach for incoming sales order change transactions to review changes to quantity and delivery dates before they are applied.

The steps to process an incoming IDoc via a single-step task or workflow are as follows.

1. Identify a standard task, customer task, or workflow that needs to be started. In the standard system, none of the processes are configured for starting a task or workflow for inbound. You have to develop a custom workflow to implement your business process.
2. Create a new process code, and point the process code to the new workflow using transaction WE42.
3. In the partner profile for the inbound message, make sure that the inbound message uses the new process code.

Setting Up Notification of Successful Posting

The ALE/EDI interface can be set up to raise an event when an IDoc posts successfully. This option is provided in the settings for an inbound process code. You can attach a single-step task or a workflow to be started when the event is raised.

Follow these steps to set up notification of successful posting.

1. Identify the application object created by the IDoc. You can view the setting in table EDIFCT or execute transaction WE57. A link is defined between a message, a business object, and the function module.
2. Identify the event in the application object that needs to be raised.

3. Execute transaction BD67, select the process code used for the inbound process, and go to the details. In the application object, enter values for the Object Type and Start Event fields, as identified in Step 2.

4. Identify an existing task, or create a new task or workflow that should be started based on the event.

5. Define the event linkage between the event and the workflow. You can also perform this step from the task itself by activating the triggering event.

Setting Up Advanced Workflow

This simple organizational unit will get you started, and you will soon see the workflow system sending each error notification to the right person. In the long run, though, you will need to understand some advanced workflow concepts. This section addresses some common issues faced with the workflow process and proposes some techniques and solutions to address resulting problems.

Setting Up Backups

From a security point of view, workflow acts very much like an e-mail system. If a work item is not meant for you, you cannot see or execute it. In the real world, you need some way of assigning the responsibility of fixing errors to multiple people or an ability to define backups, for the following reasons.

- ◆ The workload is too much for a single person.
- ◆ The person who normally handles the problem has called in sick.
- ◆ The person who normally handles the problem is on vacation.

Multiple Users to a Position

The first solution is to use a position as the organizational object to which errors are directed. You can assign multiple users to a position so that all users assigned to the specified position receive a work item in their Inbox. The users can examine the work item by looking at the description and decide whether to start processing. As soon as someone starts processing a work item, it disappears from all other Inboxes. This step automatically resolves the second and third issues in the preceding list.

Assigning multiple users usually works, but some organizations have rules requiring one user to each position. Also, you simply might not want to assign multiple users to a position because doing so doesn't enforce any rules for a specific user to process the work items. Then you can use the substitution capability.

Substitution by User

Substitution is the capability to designate another position as a backup to execute your work items. The person who wants to assign someone else as his or her substitute has to initiate the process.

Assume that John and Mary are in the EDI department. When John is away, Mary will handle all the EDI problems that are normally routed to John. To define a substitute, John has to initiate the process from his Inbox. The steps are as follows (assuming that you are John).

1. Go to Business Workplace.
2. Choose Settings, Workflow Settings, Maintain Substitute.
3. Click the Create Substitute button.
4. Enter the user ID of the person who will substitute for you, and enter the date(s) on which you will be gone in the validation period.

If John sets the substitute option correctly, Mary can log on to the system with her ID and select John's work item as follows.

1. Go to Business Workplace.
2. Select Settings, Workflow Settings, Adopt Substitution.
3. From the list of users who have assigned you as the backup, click John. Mary should see John's work items.

The right-most column in the worklist has the name of the person for whom you are substituting.

Substitution by the System Administrator

What if John has to leave town on very short notice and does not get a chance to set the substitute? Then the system administrator can set a substitute in the HR module. Typically, the manager of the EDI department can be given authorization to execute this transaction. The steps are as follows.

1. Execute transaction PO13.
2. Enter the position of the person who needs a substitute. Click the Relationship Infotype under the Active tab. Click the Create button.
3. Use B311 in the Type of Relationship field. Enter S for the Type of Related Object, and enter the position of the user who will be the substitute in the ID of the Related Object field. Save your entry to define the substitute.

Executing Subordinate and Peer Work Items

The ability to see and execute work items of subordinates and peers can be useful for managers and peers. Sometimes a manager wants to view the work items of his or her subordinates, or a person needs to share the load of his or her peers and should be allowed to process specific peers' work items on an as-needed basis.

This setup requires some detailed knowledge of evaluation paths in the HR module. An *evaluation path* defines an access path to navigate from one organizational object to another.

The setup consists of the following steps.

1. Define an evaluation path that starts at the user level and ends in a position or a user ID. Use transaction OOAW.

2. Create a view using transaction SWLV, and assign it the evaluation path created in Step 1.

3. Go to Business Workplace, Select Settings, Workflow Settings, Adopt View. The name of the view you created in the last step is displayed. At the prompt, select the organizational object whose work items you want to see. Click the Select button to see the worklist in your Inbox.

Connecting the SAP Inbox to a MAPI-Based E-Mail Client

When using workflow, you might want to receive work items through your company's regular e-mail system. The ability to do so is useful to infrequent users of the system who don't want to log on to the SAP system and view their work items on a daily basis. These users can view their work items via their regular e-mail system if the e-mail system is MAPI-compliant.

SAP Labs, a subsidiary of SAP AG, has developed a MAPI connector to link the SAP Inbox to a MAPI-based client such as Microsoft Outlook or Exchange. You can download the free connector from the SAP Labs Web site (http://www.saplabs.com). Instructions on how to install the product are included.

During the installation process, the system records the SAP server name, client number, user ID, and password for the SAP system. This information is used to automatically log on to the system to retrieve work items for the e-mail client on a periodic basis.

After the software is installed, a new folder for SAP is created in the e-mail client Inbox. You can click this folder to view the work items. No settings have to be made on the SAP system. Work items continue to reside in the SAP system as well. When a work item is executed, the system automatically logs on to the SAP system and takes you to the screen you normally use when you execute a work item from the SAP Inbox.

TIP

In large organizations, it's a huge undertaking to install and maintain new software on every PC. Therefore, these organizations are often reluctant to use this tool. As an alternative, corporations use the SAP server to e-mail server connections. At present, an Exchange connector is available from SAP to link Microsoft Exchange server with the SAP server. This enables you to receive an e-mail in your regular e-mail system, telling you that you have a work item in SAP. You must apply note number 131795 for this process to work.

NOTE

Use of this system does not prohibit you from executing the work items directly from the SAP Inbox.

Using Tips and Techniques

The following tricks and tips can help you in certain situations.

Changing Work Item Text

The work item text that appears in the user's Inbox can be customized to the needs of your users. This modification is considered a customizing change and will be supported on upgrade. You can change the text as follows.

1. Using transaction PFTC_CHG, go to the task for which the text needs to be modified.
2. Choose the Change button.

3. Change the work item text to suit your needs. The text can include substitution parameters from the workflow container fields. Put an ampersand in the text, and click the Insert Variables button to select parameters from the container.

Using Workcenters instead of Organizational Units

Using workcenters instead of organizational units is an interesting business scenario. For example, a client was implementing the HR module and enforced the following rules.

◆ Single user to a single position.

◆ EDI functional users were already assigned to a position in their respective organizational units.

The problem was that the EDI group was not allowed to create additional organizational units, but they wanted multiple users to be able to receive the same notification.

The solution was to create a workcenter for each functional area. For example, workcenters were created for the purchasing group, sales group, and FI group. The positions held by users in their respective organizations were each assigned to a workcenter. The workcenter was used in the partner profile as the party to be notified. This technique provided a clean solution without interfering with the required HR functionality.

Summary

In this chapter, you saw the various applications of the workflow module in the ALE/EDI process. The biggest application of the workflow module is exception handling. Errors are intelligently routed to a user, a job, a position, or an organizational unit. The workflow module uses the PD-ORG component of the HR module to determine users from positions or jobs. Within the ALE/EDI process, the workflow module has several other applications, for example, processing incoming IDocs and actively monitoring the state of the system.

Solutions to some everyday problems of backups and substitutes are designed into the workflow module. Work items can be transferred to your company's e-mail system as long as it is MAPI-compliant.

PART IV

Operating and Administering the EDI Interface

Chapter 10

After you have completed all the necessary steps to configure the EDI interface, you need to test each component to verify that the configuration settings work. This chapter introduces the utilities and techniques used in testing an inbound and an outbound EDI process. The standard system provides several utilities and tools, and every release includes both new tools and enhancements to existing tools. If you are working with a release older than 3.1G, some of the inbound tools mentioned here might not be available to you.

 TIP

In designing the test utilities, SAP assumes that a subsystem might not be installed at the time of testing. Therefore, the tools can be used whether or not the subsystem is connected to the test environment.

You want to make sure that all the EDI configuration steps have been carried out correctly. If you developed some of the EDI interface components from scratch to meet your business needs (for example, Message control, the IDoc structure, or IDoc programs), testing each individual piece thoroughly before deploying it in production is especially important.

This chapter describes the various tests for the outbound and the inbound processes. The following items are mentioned for each test wherever appropriate.

- ◆ Steps to carry out the task
- ◆ Places to look for problems
- ◆ Possible causes of the problem(s) (for debugging)
- ◆ Ways to verify the successful execution of the test

The focus of this chapter is on the testing methods and techniques. On several occasions, you will need to refer to Chapter 11, "Monitoring the Interface," for details on the monitoring tools and to Chapter 12, "EDI Process Troubleshooting and Recovery," for details on the troubleshooting process.

Testing the Outbound Process

The outbound process is relatively simple to test, and requires the least simulation because the process originates in SAP and all the major components reside in SAP. The best approach for testing an outbound process is to first test each component, and then test the whole process. Descriptions of the utilities available for testing and complete details of testing each component follow.

Types of Test Utilities

SAP provides two types of test utilities.

- ◆ Utilities for a sanity test
- ◆ Utilities to test the process

The first type performs a basic sanity test on the configuration of EDI objects such as the partner profile, port definition, and RFC destination parameters. A sanity test enables you to test a component without executing the actual process. For example, you do not have to execute the purchase order process to test the accuracy of settings in the partner profile. You can access these utilities from within the maintenance screens of the objects.

You can test the outbound process using the actual components involved in the process. The only piece that can be missing is the subsystem. A utility in the standard system simulates the functionality of the subsystem, which is to report the process status to the SAP system. This utility will be described later in this chapter.

Prerequisites for Testing an Outbound Process

The outbound process is composed of programs that are linked to run one after another. To test each component separately, you have to make the following settings to ensure that the components are disconnected from each other and do not start the next process immediately.

- ◆ If your application uses Message control, the timing of the output type should be set to 1 (Run with the Next Selection of RSNAST00) in the condition records. This setting causes the RSNAST00 program not to run immediately after creating an entry in the NAST table.

◆ In the partner profile, set the Collect IDocs flag and the Do Not Start the Subsystem flag. These settings cause the RSEOUT00 program not to run immediately after an IDoc is created in the system.

Performing a Configuration Sanity Test

This section describes the basic sanity tests available for individual objects such as the partner profile, RFC destination, and port definition. Sanity tests check for the validity of attributes in the objects without executing the process. Although you might have carried out some of these tests while configuring the various components, I will explain the tests here with complete details.

Testing the Partner Profile

You can test partner profiles to make sure that the parameters specified are still correct. The following checks are carried out.

◆ The process code

◆ The user to be notified

◆ Message control consistency with outbound parameters

To check the consistency of partner profiles, you execute the program RSECHK07. You can do this via transaction SE38 or from the menus of the initial partner profile screen. The output is a color-coded report that shows the details of any problems that were found.

Although a check is carried out when the partners are created, some parameters can become invalid over time. For example, if a user ID specified in the partner profile no longer exists, this report flags the invalid user ID as an error.

Testing the RFC Destination

This test confirms the connectivity between the computer system on which SAP is running and the system on which the subsystem is or will be installed.

Execute transaction SM59. Click the RFC destination being used in the process. The destination is typically SERVER_EXEC, but confirm your RFC destination by viewing the details of the port definition that will be used for outbound processes. Click the Test button. If the results are positive, the connectivity is working correctly.

If the test connection returns negative results, the message should indicate the problem. If the message is not self-explanatory, you can turn on RFC trace to log every step of the RFC test. This log is cryptic. Knowledge of CPI-C (*Common Programming Interface Communication*) is necessary to understand the trace information.

The problem is basically the connectivity between the two systems. The possible causes of errors are

◆ The RFC destination is using an explicit host name to reach the destination system, and this name is misspelled.

TIP

If the problem persists, you can try to use the IP address of the host on which the EDI subsystem is or will be installed. If this test works, the problem lies in the TCP/IP configuration. Check with your Basis staff.

◆ The RFC server program (typically rfcexec) is unreachable; perhaps this program does not exist on the destination server, or the path is unreachable or inaccessible. Keep in mind that the path name and program name are case sensitive. The ID used to access the files is <*SID*>*adm*, where *SID* is the system ID. If you are using separate systems for SAP and the subsystem, refer to Chapter 6, "Configuring Basic EDI Components."

◆ Although the network is rarely at fault, check that the physical links and network links are working. You can execute the ping command at the OS level to ensure that the link is up.

Testing the Port Definition

This test confirms access to the directory location where the IDoc files will be stored for the inbound and outbound processes.

Execute transaction WE21. Select your port definition, and then click the Outbound File button to view the directory location where IDoc files will be stored. Click the Check button on this screen to test accessibility to the directory. If the check is successful, the port definition is correct. Perform a similar operation for the inbound process and the Command file.

If the test connection returns negative results, the message should indicate the problem.

◆ The problem involves access to the directory location. Check that the path name is spelled correctly. It is case sensitive, and the directory name must end with a slash.

◆ If access to the file system is via NFS (*Network File System*), the NFS mounts should be verified from the application server to which you are logged on.

Testing the Outbound Process Steps

The outbound process is essentially a sequence of subprocesses that link together to form the total process. Five subprocesses are tested in the outbound process (see Figure 10.1).

◆ The successful creation of an application document

◆ The proposal of output by Message control

◆ The generation of IDocs

◆ The connection between the SAP system and the subsystem

◆ Status reporting by the subsystem

FIGURE 10.1 *Testing outbound components*

Verifying the Successful Creation of an Application Document

In this test, you want to ensure that your application document can be created successfully. Here are the steps to execute the test and verify the results.

Execute your application transaction (for example, VA01) to create a sales order or ME21 to create a purchase order. Check that the application document is created successfully. This step usually works without any problem. However, this step can fail completely (in which case, a document is not created) or fail partially (in which case, the document is marked incomplete).

 CAUTION

In certain situations, the system reports that the document was created successfully, but when you go into the display mode, you do not see a document. The problem lies in the IDoc selection program. Check that the timing in the condition record is set to 1, as described in the prerequisites.

The system reports any problems to you immediately on the application status bar. You click the problem reported in the status bar to get additional details. You can also use extended help (if available) to view the online help in that context.

The application configuration can have a variety of problems. For example, pricing has not been maintained, a credit block is on the customer, or the vendor has not been maintained in the desired company code. You must work closely with the business team to resolve this type of problem.

If this step is successful, you should have an application document in the system. Verify it by going into the display transaction and making sure that you see the document and that it is complete.

Verifying the Proposal of Output by Message Control

If your output (EDI, ALE, or fax) will be proposed automatically via Message control, you must ensure that all the desired outputs are proposed with correct values.

You test this component by executing the application transaction. No tool is available to test the Message control component by itself. The only option is to create an application document and go to the output control screen. In some cases (for example, order change), you must go to the Change Document transaction instead of the Create Document transaction.

Verify the following on the output control screen.

◆ The existence of an output record (if output is to be proposed automatically). If output is to be entered manually, display the list of output types and select your output.

◆ The accuracy of the output medium, timing, and language.

If your desired outputs (such as EDI, ALE, fax, and print) are not proposed, go to the menu bar on the output control screen and choose Goto, Determination Analysis to view the output log, which is shown in Figure 10.2.

TIP

Press Enter on the output control screen to validate the values.

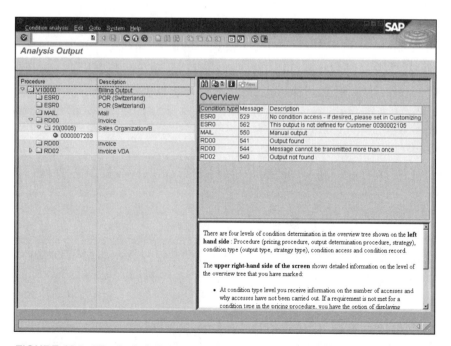

FIGURE 10.2 *The Analysis Output screen, showing the steps used in proposing an output type*

The output log displays the reason for the problem. This log is cryptic, but it is the only alternative. If you understand the Message control concept, you should have no problem reading the log. For example, the next-to-last line in the Overview window (refer to Figure 10.2) indicates that the RD00 output has already been processed once and that a subsequent automatic proposal is not allowed.

The following list identifies common problems that can prevent the output record from being proposed. This list is not complete, but it will help you resolve some of the common problems.

♦ The condition record is missing.

♦ The Message control record of the partner profile is missing.

♦ The output type is set to manual.

♦ One of the prerequisites for the conditions was not satisfied in the requirement logic of the Message control.

If the output proposal is working correctly, you must make sure that a NAST entry is created for each of the outputs. To see the NAST entries, execute transaction SE16 or SE17, and enter **NAST** in the table name. Enter your application document number in the Object Key field, click the Execute button, and verify that a record exists for each output proposed on the output control screen.

 TIP

If the application document number is fewer than 10 characters, you must prefix it with leading zeros; otherwise, the record will not be located.

Verifying the Generation of IDocs

In this step, you verify the process of generating IDocs from the application document. If you have extended the IDoc selection program via user exits, modified it, or created a new one, this step allows you to debug your program logic.

Transaction: WE15
Path: From the Area menu of EDI, choose Test, Outbound from MC

You test this step by executing the RSNAST00 program via transaction SE38 or by directly executing transaction WE15. Figure 10.3 shows the selection screen for this program. This step processes the NAST entries you created in the

FIGURE 10.3 *The selection screen for the RSNAST00 program* (© SAP AG)

preceding step and calls the selection program for that message. For example, IDOC_OUTPUT_ORDERS will be called for message type ORDERS.

TIP

After a NAST record has been processed successfully, the record can be re-sent either by selecting the Send Again check box without creating a new document or by going into the application document again. You must make sure that the timing of the output is set to 1 or 2, as mentioned in the prerequisites.

If an error occurs during the execution of RSNAST00, it creates an output log that is displayed on the screen. You can also find extended help on each record of the log by clicking the Documentation button.

Another possibility is that syntax errors have been found in the IDoc. The IDoc will be in status 26 (Error during Syntax Check of IDoc). You use transaction WE02 to display IDocs in the system. The status record in the IDoc tells you whether syntax errors were generated for the IDoc.

If you are testing a standard SAP-supplied program, errors at this stage are rarely due to program logic. The possible causes of the errors are

◆ The partner profile has an incorrect process code. You can perform a syntax check on the partner profile.

◆ The application document has been deleted. Display the application document to confirm that the document exists.

◆ The application document contains an inconsistency. For example, partner functions might not have been defined.

◆ The program logic has errors. If you have developed your own selection program or extended the standard program via user exits, check the program logic for errors.

If this step works correctly, a success message should appear in the output log window. You can then use transaction WE02 to display the IDoc. It must be in status 30 (IDoc Ready for Dispatch).

TIP

If you cannot figure out the problem, try debugging the program. Set a breakpoint at the start of the function module. You can set additional breakpoints, depending on the problem. For example, if you are getting an error message, set a breakpoint on the keyword *message* to navigate quickly to the code where the error is being generated.

Click the Documentation button in the output log window to view the IDoc number.

Verifying the Connection between the SAP System and the Subsystem

The connection between the SAP system and the subsystem is one of the major culprits in the process. This connection is responsible for the greatest number of problems because it crosses the boundary from SAP to the OS layer. If you successfully tested the components, you should not experience any problems here.

Transaction: WE14
Path: From the Area menu of EDI, choose Test, Outbound Processing from IDoc

If the sanity tests were successful, there is very little chance of error in transferring IDocs from the SAP system to the operating system. The IDoc must be in status 30 (IDoc Ready for Dispatch) to be passed to the subsystem. Execute program

RSEOUT00 via transaction SE38, or execute WE14 to transfer IDocs to the sub-system. The selection screen allows you to select an IDoc based on various criteria (see Figure 10.4). You can enter the IDoc number as generated in the preceding section, "Verifying the Generation of IDocs."

If this step does not execute successfully, you have a problem, so check the last status record of the IDoc. Refer to the list of errors explained in the sanity test in the "Testing the Port Definition" section earlier in this chapter. This step is verified by checking the status of the IDoc. If the RSEOUT00 program executes successfully, the status of the IDoc will change to 03 (Data Passed to Port OK). An IDoc file will also be created at the OS level with a name specified in the port definition.

TIP

If you do not have an account at the OS layer, you can execute transaction AL11 to view the IDoc file.

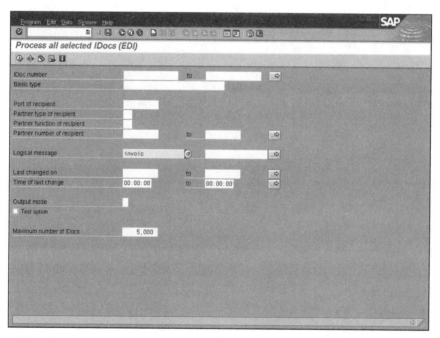

FIGURE 10.4 *The selection screen for the RSEOUT00 program* (© SAP AG)

Verifying Status Reporting by the Subsystem

In this step, you test the process of status reporting by the subsystem, but the subsystem is not required. SAP provides a utility to test this step.

Status codes can be of type success or failure. In either case, a status record is attached to the IDoc. If a status code represents an error, a workflow is also started (indicated by a Yes in the Workflow column in Table 10.1).

Transaction: WE17
Path: From the Area menu of EDI, choose Test, Process Status File

Table 10.1 Status Codes Passed to SAP by the Subsystem

Status Code	Workflow	Description
04	Yes	Error within control information of EDI subsystem
05	Yes	Error during translation
06	No	Translation OK
07	Yes	Error during syntax check
08	No	Syntax check OK
09	Yes	Error during interchange handling
10	No	Interchange handling OK
11	Yes	Error during dispatch
12	No	Dispatch OK
13	No	Retransmission OK
10	No	Interchange Acknowledgment positive
15	Yes	Interchange Acknowledgment negative
16	No	Functional Acknowledgment positive
17	Yes	Functional Acknowledgment negative
22	No	Dispatch OK, acknowledgment still due
23	Yes	Error during retransmission
24	No	Control information of EDI subsystem OK
36	No	Electronic signature not performed (timeout)

You can use a standard system tool to test the process without having a subsystem installed. First, you use this tool to import a status file with any success status code from Table 10.1. You do not have to test every success status code. Then, you can test each individual error status code from the subsystem by importing a separate file each time. Figure 10.5 shows the selection screen of this test tool, where you can specify the input file name. A sample file for testing inbound status processing appears in Listing 10.1. The second line gives you a reference for the position and is not part of the file. This file adds a status record with a status code 16 to an IDoc number 1184 with a date of December 16, 1998, and a time of 10:10:03. This record contains the minimum amount of information required to append a status record. You can certainly include additional information (for example, a message and message text).

Listing 10.1 Sample Inbound Status File

```
EDI_DS40        0000000000001184199812161010030316

12345678901234567890123456789012345678901234567890
```

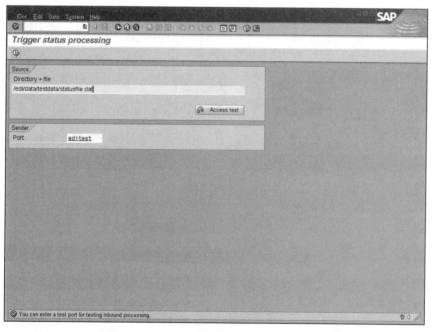

FIGURE 10.5 *Processing inbound status* (© SAP AG)

In addition, if you are deleting a large number of work items, it is a good idea to schedule the job to run when the system is less busy than normal.

The screen itself displays the results. This process does not experience many problems. The main reason for failure is that the format of the status file is imported into the system or that the IDoc number specified in the file is incorrect.

 NOTE

Because the file format has changed with every major release of SAP, the file should conform to the revision in use.

You verify the results by viewing the last status record in the IDoc. To view the IDoc, use transaction WE02 (Display IDocs). If the status code represents an error, the IDoc administrator will also be notified via workflow. The IDoc Administrator's Inbox should be checked for an error message.

Testing the Inbound Process

The inbound process is different from the outbound process because the inbound originates outside the SAP system. If the subsystem is not installed, you have to use the inbound utilities to start the inbound process. Several utilities simulate the start of the inbound process; the actual processing is carried out by the real components. The best strategy for testing an inbound process is to test each component separately.

SAP provides two types of test utilities.

- ◆ Utilities for the sanity test
- ◆ Utilities to test the process

The first type performs a basic sanity test on the configuration of the EDI objects (for example, partner profiles and process codes). You access these utilities from within the objects' maintenance screens or through special programs.

The second type tests the process. The inbound process can be tested using the components involved in the process. The only piece that can be missing is the subsystem. The standard system includes several utilities to simulate the functions of a subsystem, including creating an IDoc and simulating the start of the inbound process.

Performing a Sanity Test on the Configuration

You test the configuration components defined for the inbound process with tools provided in the standard system. These tools help perform a basic sanity test of the configuration settings without executing the process.

Partner profiles can be checked to make sure that the parameters specified are still correct. The process is the same as the one defined for the outbound process in the "Testing the Partner Profile" section earlier in this chapter.

The ALE system provides a tool to test the consistency of inbound parameters for error handling. You can use this tool to test all the process codes together or one process code at a time. The output is a color-coded report that displays the possible cause of any problem.

You run this report for all process codes by using program RBDMOINF via transaction SE38. Alternatively, you run program RBDMOINC to test an individual code.

The output screen displays the results. The report is a color-coded report showing various problems. For additional details, you double-click a problem.

- The link between the process code and the function module is not defined.
- The object type for this message's IDoc is missing. If the object is present, it checks for the presence of a triggering event (INPUTERROROCCURED) and a terminating event (INPUTFINISHED). This error is more likely to occur for custom processes.
- The object type for this message's IDoc packets is missing. If the object is present, it checks for a terminating event named MASSINPUTFINISHED.
- The task for error handling has not been defined.
- The linkage between the task and the triggering events is inactive or undefined.
- The linkage for the terminating events is undefined or inactive.
- The roles for the task are undefined.

Most of these settings are related to workflow settings for a new process. SAP already provides these objects for standard messages. The test for inbound settings is useful for custom processes. See Chapter 33, "Customizing the Interface for New and Extended IDocs," for details on the settings required for new inbound processes.

The Utilities to Start the Inbound Process

One of the major components for the inbound process is the IDoc itself. If a subsystem is not available, you need a way to create an IDoc and start the inbound process. Several utilities are available to address this problem.

Utility 1: Start the Inbound Process by Copying an Outbound IDoc as Inbound

Transaction: WE12

Path: From the Area menu of EDI, choose Test, Inbound procg of modified outb.file

The SAP IDoc architecture does not differentiate between the structures of an inbound IDoc and an outbound IDoc. Utility 1, which is also called the *turn-around utility*, uses that principle to copy an outbound IDoc file as an inbound IDoc file and start the inbound process. This utility is useful if you already have an outbound process that is generating an IDoc type you want to use for your inbound testing. For example, if you want to test the inbound sales order process and you are already generating outbound purchase orders, you know that the IDoc type for purchase orders (ORDERS02) is the same as the IDoc type for sales orders (ORDERS02). You can use the turnaround utility to make the outbound purchase order file come in as a sales order and start the inbound process.

You start this utility via transaction WE12. The selection parameters allow you to change the sender and receiver fields, as well as the message type (see Figure 10.6). However, this utility does not allow you to change the actual data contents. You must make sure that data in the outbound IDoc can be used for an inbound process. After you enter the parameters, click the Execute button. The system displays the following message.

Transfer to ALE carried out.

TIP

The default parameters for this utility are built from the port definition specified in the TestPort parameter in the IDoc administration settings.

FIGURE 10.6 *The turnaround utility to copy an outbound IDoc file as inbound*
(© SAP AG)

● CAUTION

You must check that the outbound IDoc file you are using has the correct IDoc type. I have seen a static outbound file name for the test port many times, which means that the file is overwritten every time an outbound process is executed. The tester thinks that he has the correct file, but someone else might have executed an outbound process using the same port and overwritten the file with his own IDoc type. For example, consider that you are using a test port in which the outbound file name is static. Assume that the name of the file is *outfile* and that you want to test the inbound process for sales orders. You have been generating purchase orders using this port. Now someone else on the team generates an outbound invoice using the same port, and the invoice IDoc overwrites the IDoc containing the purchase order. If you are unaware of this situation, you can waste a lot of time wondering why your process is failing. Using a dynamic file name based on your user ID prevents accidental overwriting by another team member.

Utility 2: Start the Inbound Process from an Inbound Text File

Transaction: WE16

Path: From the Area menu of EDI, choose Test, Inbound procg of.orig.inb.file

If you have not configured any outbound process, you cannot use the turnaround utility. Also, you might have noticed that there is no facility to save a variant for the utility. If you are involved in testing an inbound process again and again, using the same data, specifying the parameters repeatedly becomes a nuisance.

You can use utility 2 to start the inbound process from an inbound file, but first, you must build an inbound file. You can build an IDoc file in several ways, depending on your needs, the situation, and the amount of effort you want to expend. The options are listed from easiest to hardest.

- ◆ Copy an existing inbound IDoc in the system, and save the IDoc to a file via transaction WE19, by selecting an existing IDoc number and clicking the Create icon. On the next screen, you can change the values. Then, click the Inbound File button, enter the file name, and deselect the Start IDoc Inbound Processing of File Immediately flag. Click the Continue button, and an IDoc file is created for you.

- ◆ Copy an outbound file and modify it to look like an inbound file. Alternatively, if you have an outbound file, you can set a breakpoint while executing the turnaround utility. Set the breakpoint where it has copied an outbound file, has modified it to look like an inbound file, and is ready to start the inbound process. At that point, you can end the session. Now you have an IDoc file you can use for your inbound process.

If you copy an outbound IDoc file manually, you must change certain fields in the control record. Table 10.2 lists these fields. Refer to the structure of the control record (structure EDI_DC40) for the position and data length of these variables.

- ◆ Use WE19 to create an IDoc on-the-fly, based on IDoc type or message type. Before you click the final Execute button, save the IDoc to a file as described earlier.

- ◆ This option should be your last resort, but you can use a text editor to create an IDoc from scratch. Refer to the EDI_DC40 and EDI_DD40 structures for the position and length of each required field. Good luck!

Table 10.2 Required Fields in the Control Record of an Inbound IDoc File

Field	Value
outmod	Spaces
docrel	Spaces
docnum	Spaces
mandt	Client in which you are going to test
direct	2
rcvpor	Your test port or any valid file port
rcvprt	Receiver partner type
rcvpfc	Receiver partner function
rcvprn	Receiver partner number
sndpor	Sender port: any valid file port
sndprt	Sender partner type
sndpfc	Sender partner function
sndprn	Sender partner number
mestyp	Message type
mescod	Message code
mesfct	Message function
test	Test flag

 CAUTION

After the system successfully reads a file, the file is deleted. If you plan to use the file again, you must make a copy of it before you execute this process.

After you create the IDoc file, you are ready to start inbound processing using utility 2. The selection parameters of this program allow you to specify the file

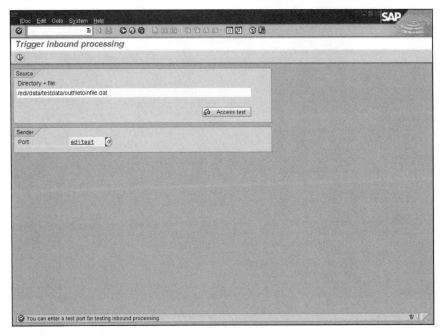

FIGURE 10.7 *Start inbound processing from a file* (© SAP AG)

name for the inbound IDoc file, as shown in Figure 10.7. Then, click the Execute button to start the inbound processing.

Utility 3: Start the Inbound Process with the Inbound Test Tool

Transaction: WE19

Path: From the Area menu of EDI, choose Test, Test Tool

This tool is a two-step process. In the first step, you create an IDoc using one of the five methods (see Figure 10.8). These methods include copying an existing IDoc, creating an IDoc based on the IDoc type, creating an IDoc based on a message type, creating an IDoc using an existing IDoc file as a template, or creating an IDoc with no template. You will modify the IDoc data as needed (see Figure 10.9).

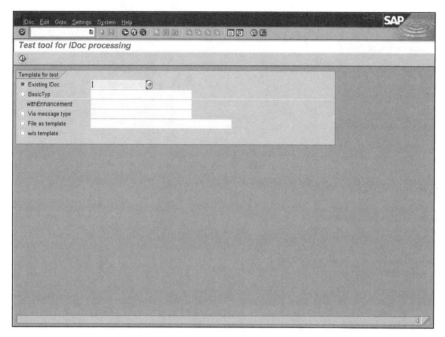

FIGURE 10.8 *The options for creating an IDoc* (© SAP AG)

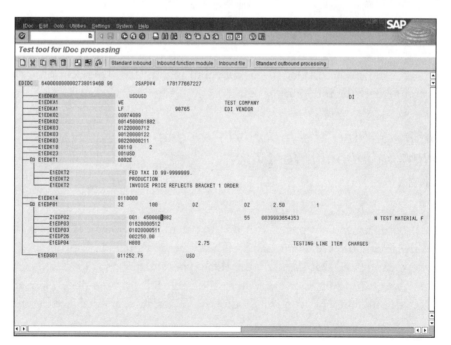

FIGURE 10.9 *The data entry screen to modify the IDoc before it is saved in the system* (© SAP AG)

> **NOTE**
>
> Prior to version 4.6, IDocs generated by transaction WE19 for outbound testing were assigned a status of 01, and IDocs generated for inbound were assigned a status of 50. From version 4.6 on, SAP assigns outbound IDocs created with the test tool a status of 42 and inbound IDocs a status of 74. The benefit of this is to differentiate between IDocs created via normal process and those created by the test tool.

In the second step, you process your newly created IDoc. You can call the inbound process using the normal path by clicking the Standard Inbound button, in which case the process goes through the checks as if it had been sent in by the subsystem. Alternatively, you can pass the process to a function module directly, by clicking the Inbound Function Module button. In this case, the system bypasses the checks for partner profile and hands the IDoc data to your inbound function module directly (see Figure 10.10). This approach is useful for testing an inbound process without

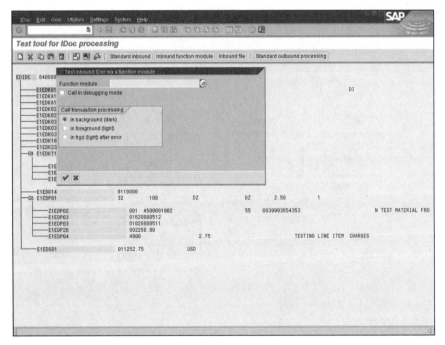

FIGURE 10.10 *The dialog box for testing an inbound IDoc via a function module* (© SAP AG)

having to maintain any inbound configuration. You can also start the function module in debug mode and select the processing option for your posting module. Finally, you can choose to save the IDoc in a file, as described in utility 2.

Testing the Inbound Process Steps

Now that you have selected a method to start the inbound process and have met the prerequisites, you need to understand the various components you will test on the inbound process (see Figure 10.11).

◆ The inbound triggering process

◆ The successful creation of IDocs in the database

◆ The posting of the application document

Verifying the Inbound Triggering Process

This step tests the connectivity between the subsystem and the SAP system. Although you might not have a subsystem, you can start the startrfc program from the command line. The subsystem uses the same technique to start the SAP system.

FIGURE 10.11 *The testing of inbound components*

This test requires the process to begin at the OS layer using an IDoc file. Use one of the utilities described earlier to create an IDoc file for the inbound process. At the OS level, execute the startrfc command, using the syntax described in Chapter 6, "Configuring Basic EDI Components."

The results of executing the startrfc command are displayed at the command line where you started the program. The errors are usually from message class E0. If you see a message with E0, you can use transaction SE91 to look up the details of the message. If the error message is unclear, you can turn on the trace when executing startrfc to view detailed information.

Problems are very common in this test. Use the following list to troubleshoot problems.

- **Permission problems in executing the startrfc command**. You must have proper authorization to execute operating system commands.
- **Problems with input parameters**. The parameters must be specified according to the syntax. Typically, the user ID and passwords have problems. You can use your logon ID to test the process.
- **Problems with the gateway services**. You can use transaction SMGW to check the status of your gateway services. Gateway services are used for every CPI-C communication, and RFC is implemented using CPI-C protocols. Check with your Basis staff for appropriate gateway service values.
- **Problems accessing the inbound file**. The file system, if NFS mounted, might not be available, or SAP does not have authorization to read the file.

If this step is successful, an IDoc should be created in the SAP database. You should not be concerned about errors in the IDoc at this stage. The scope of this test is limited to ensuring that the triggering process works.

Verifying the Creation of Successful IDocs

In this step, you use the information in the IDoc's control record to verify that a partner profile is found and that the IDoc is created without any structural errors. This step is useful for custom IDocs when you want to make sure that the incoming IDocs are structurally correct.

Start the inbound process with one of the utilities described earlier. This time, the process does not have to start from a file.

The results are logged in the IDoc's status records. You can display the status records by using the IDoc display utilities. If an error occurs, the IDoc gets a status code of 56 (IDoc with Errors Added), and an error workflow is started. The person notified in this case depends on whether a partner profile could be read. If a partner profile was found, workflow is sent to the person specified in the partner profile. If a partner profile entry could not be read, the message is sent to the IDoc administrator.

Common problems in this step are related to data in the control record and to syntax errors in the IDoc. The parameters in the control record must match the key of the partner profile record for that inbound message. The various causes of syntax errors are described in Chapter 30, "IDocs on the Inside." The status records should give you the specific details. If this step is successful, you will see an IDoc that has a status code of 64 (IDoc Ready to Be Passed to Application).

 TIP

If you are seeing some strange segment names that you think do not exist in the IDoc, the problem lies in the process that created the IDoc. Remember that SAP treats the incoming file as a stream of data. It parses the data by position, so if any field is off by even one position, you will see these problems. For example, you might have accidentally deleted a character in the data records.

Verifying the Posting of Application Documents

Transaction: BD87

The logic for posting an application document is coded in inbound function modules. Verifying the logic of the inbound function module is the most important step for custom function modules. You verify not only that the posting function module is working correctly, but also that the logic and interface of the function module are correct. If problems exist, you might also want to debug the process one step at a time.

The IDoc created in the "Verifying the Creation of Successful IDocs" section is used to test this process. To start, execute program RBDAPP01 via SE38, or execute BD87. Then, enter your IDoc number and start the process. The selection screen for the RBDAPP01 program appears in Figure 10.12.

Errors in this step are mainly related to data errors and are logged in the status records of the IDoc. You can display the status records by using the IDoc display utilities. The IDoc gets a status code of 51 (IDoc with Errors Added). A multitude of errors can be related to data errors. Detailed information about a specific error is also logged in the status record, and an error workflow is started to notify the person responsible for handling the error. If your posting program uses the call transaction to post the document, you can step through every screen to determine the exact location of the error.

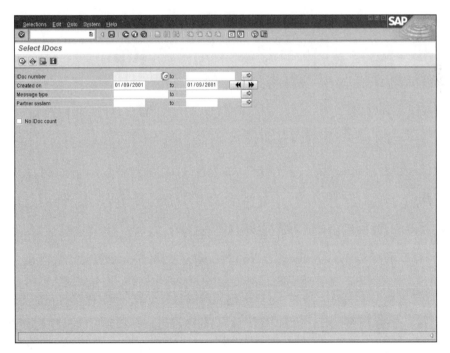

FIGURE 10.12 *The selection screen for passing an IDoc to the posting program* (© SAP AG)

The common problems in this step are either data related or in the application configuration, so you must make sure that the data values are correct in the data record fields. Check your program logic for any errors.

If this step is successful, an application document is created, and the IDoc gets a status code of 53 (Application Document Posted). The document number is logged in the status record. For example, if an incoming IDoc creates a sales order number 10000, this number appears in the last status record.

Testing the Workflow Exception Process

After you have tested the inbound and outbound processes, you can specifically test the workflow component's exception-handling process. One obvious method is to create an error in the process and check for a work item in the Inbox of the responsible user. However, this approach requires you to build error data, which can be difficult at times. You can test the workflow component itself by using the simple procedure listed here. This procedure applies to all error workflows for the outbound and inbound processes.

Transaction: SWUS

Menu Path: From the Area menu of Workflow, choose Runtime Tools, Start Workflow (Test Environment)

In this step, your aim is to test the exception-handling process and to make sure that the correct person is notified when an error occurs. You start the error process manually, using transaction SWUS. In an actual process, the system starts the error process based on the type of error. The steps are as follows.

1. Identify the workflow task that is started for a particular exception. Refer to Chapter 9, "Configuring Workflow," for a list of error tasks.

2. On the selection screen (see Figure 10.13), enter the task number in the Task field and click the Input Data button. On the next screen, press F4 and enter an IDoc number.

3. Click the back arrow and click the Start button. This step should start a workflow process.

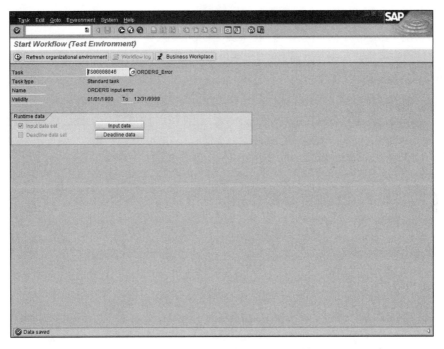

FIGURE 10.13 *Starting an error task manually* (© SAP AG)

Errors in this step are communicated in the status bar. You click the message to get additional details. The common problem in this step is related to workflow configuration. If the system reports that you are not one of the possible agents, either the task profile has not been maintained, or there is a problem with your PD-ORG setup. To create a task profile, refer to Chapter 9. If this step is successful, the person responsible for the task should receive a work item in his or her Inbox.

Summary

In this chapter, you learned about tools and techniques for testing an outbound and an inbound process. An outbound process uses the same components during testing that a real process does, except that the test does not require the subsystem. A test utility simulates the logic of the subsystem, passing status records to SAP. The outbound process is split into five steps to test each component separately.

Several utilities enable the inbound process to generate an IDoc in the database or an IDoc at the OS level in the form of a text file. You generate an IDoc by using one already in the system or by building one on-the-fly. After you create an IDoc, you perform a three-step test for each component of the inbound process. You verify the results of each step before proceeding to the next step.

Chapter 11

Monitoring
the Interface

Monitoring tools are used in two situations: to display errors and to get an overview of the state of the system. For example, you might want to know why an IDoc was not generated for a purchase order, how many EDI orders were received in a certain time, or how the ALE data transfers are progressing. In this chapter, you will learn to operate monitoring tools used in the ALE/EDI process. You will learn about the significance of error logs, where to look for key information that will help you debug problems, and how to interpret the information displayed in the logs.

SAP provides extensive logging features at different milestones in the ALE/EDI process. The main component used for logging information is an IDoc. However, processing occurs before an IDoc is created, which means that you must monitor the process at other points. Errors not directly related to the IDoc are logged in places other than the IDoc. At times, the system can experience severe errors, such as system dumps, and it has no opportunity to log an error. Monitoring the process at several points is important. This chapter outlines all the areas where SAP logs information for ALE/EDI processes.

The first section of this chapter describes how to operate the SAP Workplace Inbox (known prior to version 4.6 as the *SAP Inbox*, which is the term I use here) and process various work items. Over time, you will become adept at working with these tools. The troubleshooting guide in Chapter 12, "EDI Process Troubleshooting and Recovery," helps you decide which log to review for a given problem or situation in EDI. The troubleshooting guide in Chapter 27, "ALE Process Troubleshooting and Recovery," helps you decide which log to review for a given problem or situation in ALE.

The tools that you use depend on your role in the company. If you are an end user, you will probably be interested in looking at the application log and IDocs, but if you are a system administrator for the ALE/EDI interface, you will use system-level tools such as the tRFC (*Transitional RFC*) log or update log. For each tool, you will find a mention of the user group that uses the tool. It is best to experiment with these tools to get a feel for how and where they display the required information.

NOTE

The tools described in this chapter are applicable to both the ALE and EDI processes. However, sometimes a tool is used specifically in the ALE or EDI process, so you will find some mention of the tool's specific use.

Monitoring Errors via the SAP Inbox

Workflow is useful for detecting errors that are infrequent, unpredictable in timing, and meant for a specific group of people.

For example, assume that you are in charge of handling errors with purchase orders going out to your vendors via EDI. Several purchasing clerks can create purchase orders in the system. You could try to stay up-to-date with the problems by displaying a list of purchase orders created in the system every hour, looking for purchase orders that go via EDI and then checking the status of each output to make sure that the EDI part is correct. You could devote your entire day to monitoring the system manually and not find a problem, or you could be busy doing something else and end up being accountable for an unresolved error.

The SAP ALE/EDI interface handles most of the errors via workflow. When an error occurs, an event is raised that causes workflow to be started. If you are responsible for handling errors, you receive a work item in your SAP Inbox. The SAP Inbox is a common interface for all messages sent to you by any ALE/EDI process via workflow. Thus, you can monitor errors from one place.

Understanding the SAP Inbox

Transaction (from version 4.6): SO01
Transaction (from version 4.6): SBWP
Path: From SAP Easy Access menu, click on Business Workplace icon

The SAP Inbox is an interface to view and process work items and SAP office documents (see Figure 11.1). It is similar to the inbox of any e-mail system and contains separate folders for the office documents and work items. The office documents are e-mail documents, and the work items are workflow items. It is almost

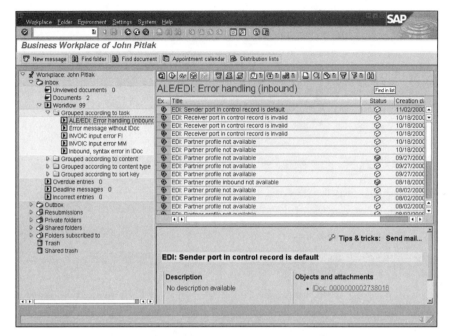

FIGURE 11.1 *The SAP Inbox interface* (© SAP AG)

an offense to call a work item an *e-mail message* because the workflow system was specifically designed to circumvent the inherent problems of communicating via e-mail.

The number next to each folder indicates the number of items in the folder. Workflow items are accessible in any of four folders within the overall Workflow folder. Each folder displays the work items in a different order according to task, content, content type, or sort key.

 NOTE

The work item highlighted in the worklist is displayed in the preview window below the worklist. You can customize this preview window through the use of a user exit. To see some of the options this user exit provides, execute the workflow template, Demo for User Exit on WI Preview (WS70000640). The menu path to this is Tools, Business Workflow, Development, Environment, Start Demo Workflow.

Understanding Work Items

A *work item* represents an instance of a task that needs to be executed. For example, a workflow task (ORDERS_Error) handles application errors in the orders IDoc. When a sales order IDoc has application errors in posting, a work item representing this task is instantiated. A work item has brief text describing its purpose (but you can also specify long text separately when necessary). A work item is executed from the Inbox to carry out the task, and can have more than one status governing the operations allowed on it. Table 11.1 describes the statuses you most commonly see in a work item.

Table 11.1 Work Item Statuses

Status	Description
Ready	The work item is visible to all selected agents.
Reserved	The work item has been reserved by a user and disappears from other selected users' Inboxes.
In Process	The work item is currently being worked on and can be seen only in the Inbox of the user who started working on it.
Executed	The work item has been executed at least once.
Completed	The work item is complete and cannot be seen in any user's Inbox.
Error	The work item itself has gone into error status because of an internal problem with workflow. (This is a very rare occurrence.)

As part of the ALE/EDI interface, the following items can appear in the SAP Inbox. Because work items are intelligently routed to the person responsible for them, the work item's type determines who is notified. You can expect to see work items for the following items.

- ◆ Errors in the outbound ALE/EDI interface.
- ◆ Errors in the inbound ALE/EDI interface.
- ◆ Syntax errors in an IDoc for the outbound process.
- ◆ Syntax errors in an IDoc for the inbound process.
- ◆ Application errors in posting an IDoc on the inbound process.
- ◆ Errors reported by the EDI subsystem.

◆ Technical errors in the EDI interface with reading and deleting IDoc files for the inbound process.

◆ A predefined threshold state exceeded by the number of IDocs. For example, someone is notified when at least 10 sales order IDocs are not posted because of application errors.

◆ Inbound EDI processes routed via workflow. For example, someone needs to review an order change IDoc before it is posted.

◆ Successful posting of an application document. For example, you want to view invoices whenever they are successfully posted in the system via EDI.

These scenarios are part of the standard SAP ALE/EDI functionality; refer to Chapter 9, "Configuring Workflow," for details on setting them up. The last three scenarios mentioned above are available in the system, but are turned off or require additional configuration before you see their work items.

Viewing a Worklist

A *worklist* is a list of work items sent to your SAP Inbox. Click the Workflow node to see a list of all the work items for which you have been selected as the responsible person. The default list has nine columns (see Figure 11.2).

◆ **Column 1.** Displays an icon indicating that the work item is executable.

◆ **Column 2.** Gives a short description of the work item.

◆ **Column 3.** Displays an icon indicating the work item's status.

◆ **Column 4.** Displays the work item's creation date.

◆ **Column 5.** Displays the work item's creation time.

◆ **Column 6.** Indicates the work item's priority.

◆ **Column 7.** Indicates whether an attachment is associated with this work item. An attachment can be a file, a note, a business document, or any other object the system supports.

◆ **Column 8.** Indicates that the user must confirm the end of processing.

◆ **Column 9.** Indicates whether the work item is overdue.

The worklist includes a short description of the work item. To see additional details (such as status, long text, terminating event, selected agents, or IDoc number), double-click a work item's Description entry or select the work item and click the Display icon (see Figure 11.3).

FIGURE 11.2 *A list of work items in a user's SAP Inbox* (© SAP AG)

FIGURE 11.3 *Details of a work item* (© SAP AG)

The Description box on the Basic Data tab is usually blank. As part of workflow customizing, you can change the text that appears in this box. From the menu options on this screen, you can obtain additional information about a work item. For example, to find out who else received this work item, choose Goto, Agent, Selected Agents. You can also find a work item's technical data, such as the task number. Another important piece of information is the IDoc number, which you find by clicking the Available Objects tab and choosing the Process Objects folder.

Processing a Work Item

There is a standard procedure for execution of any work item. On the worklist window, you can double-click the work item, or you can click the Execute button on the work item detail screen. When you click the Execute button, you are automatically established as the owner of this work item, and it disappears from the Inboxes of other selected agents.

Executing a work item starts the task behind it. You do not have to know the transaction or the underlying data. Executing a task automatically takes you to a screen with all the information filled in. From this screen you execute the task steps. This screen is different for every task, but the concept behind executing any work item is the same.

The work item in Figure 11.4 represents an application error in an incoming invoice. From this screen, which displays the IDoc's last status record, you can analyze the error. After you fix the error, you restart the failed process by clicking the Process button.

 NOTE

If a work item is sent to multiple users, each user can see an entry in his or her Inbox. As soon as one user reserves or executes the work item, its status is changed to reserved, and it disappears from the other Inboxes.

 TIP

If the user who first looks at the work item decides not to work on it, he or she can replace the work item in the pool by executing the Replace function from the Inbox. This step returns the work item to the original Inboxes.

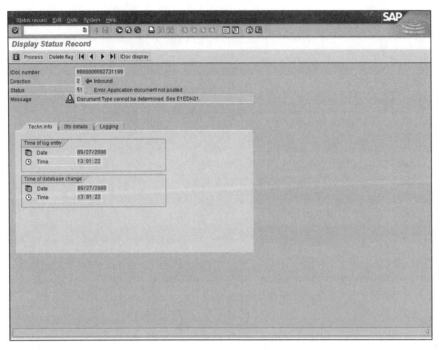

FIGURE 11.4 *The results of executing a work item for an invoice error* (© SAP AG)

Marking a Work Item as Complete

Work items are automatically removed from the Inbox when the task they represent is completed. They can be classified into two categories.

- ◆ Work items requiring a terminating event
- ◆ Work items not requiring a terminating event

Terminating events are raised from within applications. The workflow management system then automatically removes the work item from your Inbox. For example, work items for application errors associated with an IDoc are completed by the terminating event ErrorProcessCompleted. After you fix the error and restart the process and the document posts successfully, the work item automatically disappears. The advantage of this method is that the task can be executed outside the workflow system and the work item disappears from the Inbox. However, such work items cannot be deleted from the Inbox unless a terminating event is raised.

TIP

To find out whether a work item requires a terminating event, display the work item details by selecting the work item and clicking on the Display icon. On the resulting screen, select Goto, Technical Work Item Display. This screen has a check box, labeled Processing End by User Confirmation, to indicate whether the work item requires a terminating event. This box will be empty if the work item requires a terminating event.

Work items of the second type are completed when a user's explicit input indicates that the task is complete. SAP uses this approach for tasks for which it cannot determine the completion. For example, if the task is to write a letter, the system cannot know when you are done. In the SAP ALE/EDI process, tasks that are for information only—for example, technical errors in the IDoc interface—use this approach. The system displays the error. Upon exiting, the system asks whether you want to complete the task. If you click the Complete Processing of Step button, the work item is considered complete and disappears from the Inbox. Note that the system cannot validate what you have done to complete the task logically outside workflow. If you click Cancel, the work item stays in your Inbox, and you can reprocess the work item later.

Executing Additional Operations on a Work Item

Besides executing a work item, you can carry out several other operations on it. Following are some common operations.

- ◆ **Forwarding.** You can forward a work item to another person to work on it, as long as that person is one of the possible agents. See Chapter 9, "Configuring Workflow," for configuring possible agents.

- ◆ **Reserving.** By reserving a work item, you can take ownership of the work item task without executing it. This step makes the work item disappear from other Inboxes.

- ◆ **Replacing**. If you start working on a work item that was sent to multiple agents, it disappears from other Inboxes. If, however, you decide that the work item is not for you, you can replace it in the pool. It will then be available to you, as well as the other original recipients.

- ◆ **Setting an item to done**. Any work item that does not have a terminating event can be completed by setting it to *done*. This step removes the work item from your Inbox.

- ◆ **Resubmitting**. If a work item does not require your immediate attention, you can make it disappear temporarily. It will reappear in your Inbox upon expiration of the specified time. For example, if you receive a work item and decide that you will work on it two days later, you can use the Resubmit option to make the work item disappear from your Inbox for two days.

Displaying the Processing Log for the Output Type

The processing log is maintained in the Message control component to provide details of an output type's processing. This log is available only for applications that use Message control to send an output. It is helpful for end users who create application documents and want to know the status of the output. For example, an accounts receivable clerk who created a billing document for a vendor might want to find out whether a message was successfully processed.

Follow these steps to view and interpret the output log.

1. Go to the output control screen of the application document. You can usually reach this screen by choosing the menu options Header, Messages or Header, Output. The output list in Figure 11.5 shows the various output types for this document. The list is sorted by time, so if you have multiple output types of the same kind, the latest output type is at the top.

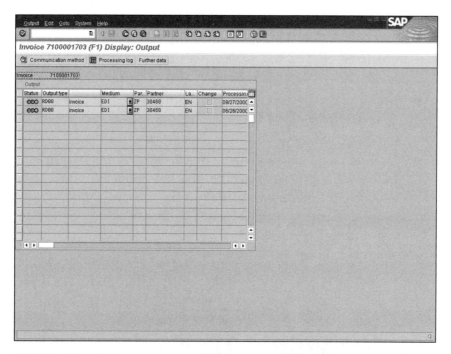

FIGURE 11.5 *Various outputs proposed by the system, visible on the output control screen* (© SAP AG)

2. Look at the Status column (column 1) for your output type. The various values are as follows.

- **Yellow.** The processing has not started yet. The timing of the output was not set for immediate processing; it's waiting for the next run of the RSNAST00 program. If you want to start the processing immediately, you click the Further Data button, set the timing in the Send Time field to 4, and save your document. This starts the processing.

- **Green.** The output was successfully processed. You can find additional details, such as the IDoc number generated for the output, by selecting your output type and then choosing Goto, Processing Log from the menu (see Figure 11.6).

- **Red.** Errors occurred in processing the output type. You can find additional details about the errors by selecting the output type in error and then choosing Goto, Processing Log from the menu. The log will display the error message. To view the long text for the

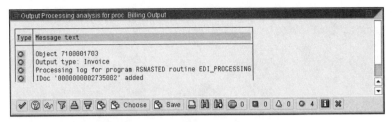

FIGURE 11.6 *The processing log for an output type* (© SAP AG)

message, click the Message Long Text icon (the second icon from the left at the bottom).

Displaying Information in the IDoc Tables

The tools described in this section provide three ways to retrieve the IDoc data stored in the tables, but the information is the same. Each tool has a purpose, so you will end up using all these IDoc display tools according to your needs at a given moment.

IDoc Display

Transaction: WE02
Menu Path: From the Area menu of EDI, choose IDoc, Display IDoc

The IDoc Display tool is one of the most commonly used tools for viewing the status of an ALE/EDI process. This tool generates a list of IDocs that match your selection criteria. As mentioned earlier, after an IDoc is created in the system, all the status information at various milestones is recorded in the IDoc's status records. Everyone who works with the ALE/EDI interface uses this tool. This tool's selection parameters (see Figure 11.7) allow you to restrict the number of IDocs that are selected.

The output is a list of IDocs sorted by date and time, as shown in Figure 11.8. You can double-click any line to display the specific IDoc. If the selection results in exactly one IDoc, the system displays the IDoc directly, without going through the intermediate step of listing the IDoc.

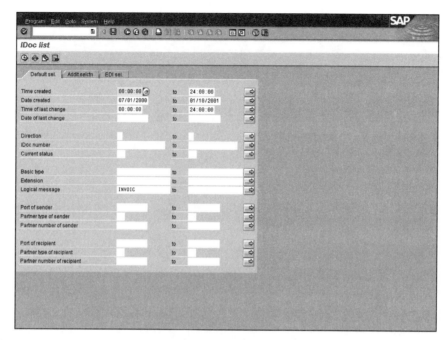

FIGURE 11.7 *Selection parameters for the IDoc Display program* (© SAP AG)

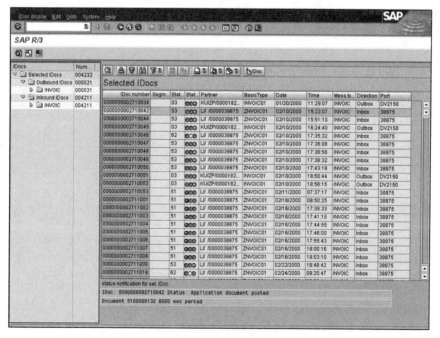

FIGURE 11.8 *A list of IDocs sorted by date and time* (© SAP AG)

TIP

The transaction WE02 uses program RSEIDOC2. You can call this program in your custom programs to display a specific IDoc.

The IDoc Display screen, shown in Figure 11.9, lists the IDoc components, including the control record, data records, and status records.

The Control Record screen (see Figure 11.10) displays commonly used information about a control record. You can obtain additional details—such as technical details, EDI details, and address information—by selecting the appropriate tab.

The data records portion of the IDoc (refer to Figure 11.9) displays the data records sequentially. You can view detailed information for a record by selecting the record on the tree display. The field contents then appear in the Content of Selected Segment window. For a more comprehensive display of the segment, click the page icon to the left of the segment name in the tree display. This takes

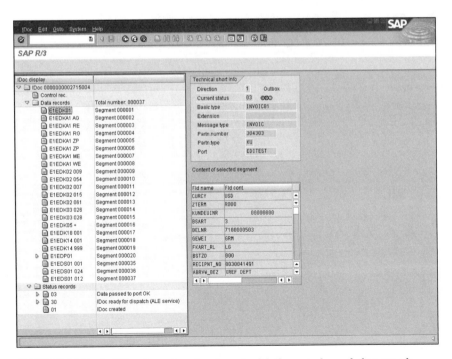

FIGURE 11.9 *An IDoc shown in a tree format with the control record, data records, and status records* (© SAP AG)

FIGURE 11.10 *IDoc control record details* (© SAP AG)

you to the screen shown in Figure 11.11. This view's major advantage is that it gives access to value help for many fields via function key F4. This enables you, for instance, to display a list of possible values for a qualifier field, as shown in Figure 11.11.

NOTE

If a data element is blank in the IDoc, it does not show up on the screen.

The status records portion of the IDoc (refer to Figure 11.9) displays the status records sequentially. An arrow icon in front of a status record indicates that a message is available in the status record. You can double-click the message to view its long text. Double-clicking the record displays additional details of the status record, such as the date and time (see Figure 11.12). If a status record contains application error information, you can also see a segment number and a field that

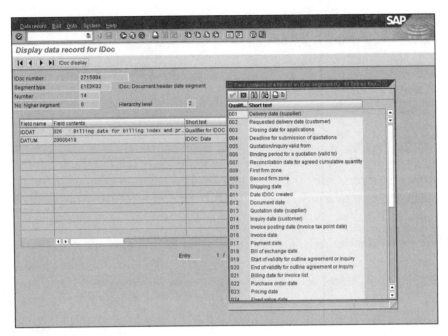

FIGURE 11.11 *IDoc data record details, showing the value list for the qualifier field IDDAT* (© SAP AG)

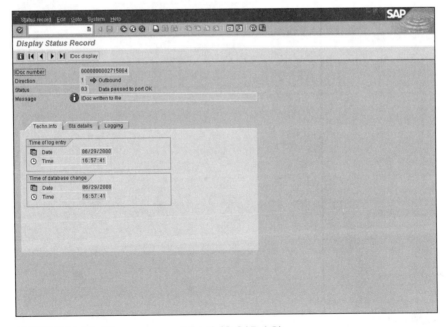

FIGURE 11.12 *IDoc status record details* (© SAP AG)

is in error. This information is displayed only if the application that processes the IDoc has logged this information.

IDoc List

Transaction: WE05

Menu Path: From the Area menu of EDI, choose IDoc, IDoc List.

The IDoc List program is another commonly used ALE/EDI interface tool for viewing the status of an ALE/EDI process. This program generates a list of IDocs that match your selection criteria. The selection parameters of this program (see Figure 11.13) allow you to restrict the number of IDocs that are selected.

The output is a tree structure of IDocs sorted first by direction (inbound or outbound) and then by status codes (see Figure 11.14). IDocs in error are displayed with red icons, IDocs with a warning are yellow, and successful IDocs are green. You can double-click any line to display the IDocs with that status code. A list of

FIGURE 11.13 *The IDoc List program selection screen (© SAP AG)*

FIGURE 11.14 *The IDoc List program output* (© SAP AG)

IDocs for the currently selected tree node appears in the list window to the right of the tree display.

IDoc Statistics

Transaction: WE07

Menu Path: From the Area menu of EDI, choose IDoc, IDoc Statistics

The IDoc Statistics program provides an excellent report on the overall status of all the IDocs in the ALE/EDI interface. This program generates an output of IDocs that match your selection criteria. The selection parameters of this program (see Figure 11.15) allow you to restrict the number of IDocs that are selected. The default is all IDocs.

The output is a report of all the IDocs by status groups. A *status group* is a number that represents a list of status codes that have been grouped together to represent a particular type of error. For example, status group 6 represents errors in

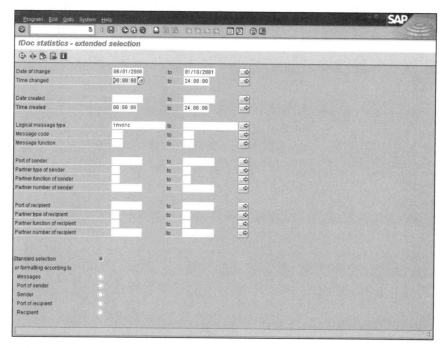

FIGURE 11.15 *The extended selection parameter list for the IDoc Statistics program*
(© SAP AG)

the subsystem. In table TEDS3, you can see a list of various status groups and the status code included in each group.

By looking at the output of this report (see Figure 11.16), you can tell how many IDocs are in the EDI subsystem, how many are in error, how many are awaiting dispatch, and so on. You double-click any box to display the list of IDocs in a particular status group. From the list, you can drill down to a specific IDoc.

Displaying the Workflow Log

The workflow management system maintains an extensive log of all the activities carried out in the workflow system. From the time a work item is created to when it's completed, it goes through several steps. A log documents each step, along with any vital information. The two tools described next help you retrieve the logged information in a useful and presentable format. The tools are mainly used

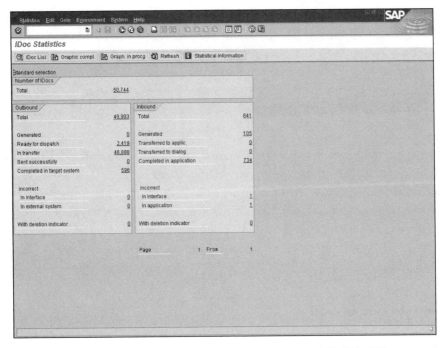

FIGURE 11.16 *The output screen of the IDoc Statistics program* (© SAP AG)

by the EDI administrator to view the state of work items and the duration of the process (how long it took to resolve the problem). This report can help you identify bottlenecks and the source of any major problems.

Work Item Analysis

Transaction (prior to version 4.6): SWI2
Transactions (from version 4.6): SWI2_FREQ, SWI2_DEAD, SWI2_DURA
Menu Path: From the Area menu of workflow (SWLD), choose Reporting, Work Item
Analysis

The work item analysis reports are comprehensive reports for determining the state of work items in the system. You can execute these reports for the following information.

◆ The number of work items created in the system and their statuses
◆ The time it took to resolve the problems

If you're interested in an overview of the ALE/EDI processes that have errored out in the past, you can use the work item analysis reports in place of the IDoc reports. Compared to IDoc reports, work item analysis provides better information because the IDoc reports are based on the current status of the IDocs. For example, if you want to analyze the cause of problems in the ALE/EDI interface, you need to know which processes have errored out in the past. The IDoc report does not show this information unless you drill down into each individual IDoc.

The selection parameters list (see Figure 11.17) allows you to restrict the number of entries returned to you. You can restrict them by time or process type. For example, if you're interested only in invoice IDocs that have failed in the past month, you use the task number for invoice IDoc as the restricting criteria. You press the F4 key on the task field and enter the task abbreviation (**Invoic_MM_er**). The system will return the task number.

You will be mainly interested in the frequency (SWI2_FREQ) and process duration (SWI2_DURA) reports. The other report is mostly used for SAP business workflow processes.

FIGURE 11.17 *Selection parameters for the work item analysis reports* (© SAP AG)

The *frequency report* output is a summary of work items by task. You can drill down from this display to a list of work items that have been generated in the system based on your selection criteria. You can drill down to display the status of these work items, as shown in Figure 11.18. Further, you can drill down to each work item to get the details, such as the person who has it and the IDoc number associated with the work item.

The output of the *process duration report* is a time analysis of the completed work items for the selected period. You can toggle between average values and threshold values on the output report. The *threshold values report* provides a breakdown by percentage (10 percent, 50 percent, and 90 percent) of items completed in the given time period, as shown in Figure 11.19. A value of zero means that the IDoc was processed in a negligible time period. This report gives you an idea of how long it took to fix an error, from the time the user saw the error until it was finally resolved.

The *average values report* provides a breakdown by wait time and process time, as shown in Figure 11.20. Wait time is the elapsed time from when the work item

FIGURE 11.18 *Details of the frequency report* (© SAP AG)

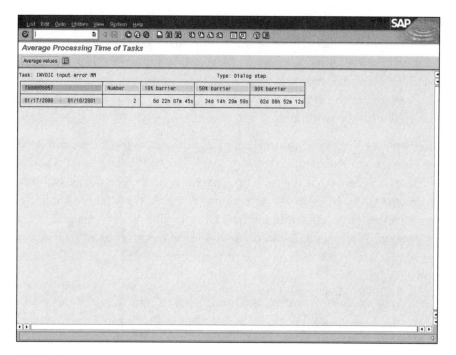

FIGURE 11.19 *The work item report, showing the percentage of items completed at various milestones* (© SAP AG)

was created in the system by workflow to when a user actually looked at the work item. Process time is the elapsed time from when the user looked at the error until it was finally resolved.

The process duration report also draws comparisons with work items from a previous interval of the same value. Thus, if you select the output for the last week, the system will draw a comparison with values from a week before that and show you the change in processing times.

Workload Analysis

Transaction: SWI5

Menu Path: From the Area menu of workflow (SWLD), choose Reporting, Workload Analysis

The *workload analysis report* monitors load on an organizational object such as a user, position, job, or workcenter. The only restriction is that work items have to

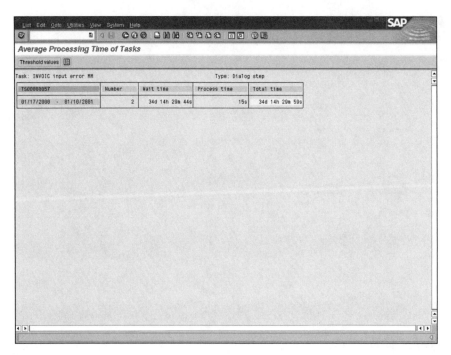

FIGURE 11.20 *The work item report, showing average values for wait time and process time* (© SAP AG)

be executed and completed from within the workflow. If they are completed outside the workflow, the system does not have visibility into the person who carried out the task. The selection parameters of this report allow you to restrict the output by type of organizational object, completion date, and task (see Figure 11.21). The output is a report showing the work items that have been completed by the user (see Figure 11.22).

Displaying System-Level Logs

The system maintains log information for critical errors related to technical problems, such as problems with the network or the file system. A functional user is not involved in analyzing or resolving these errors. The main users are the system administrators responsible for maintaining the system. The EDI administrator will most likely be involved with these tools at some point. The ALE/EDI programmers also interact with these tools during the development and testing phase.

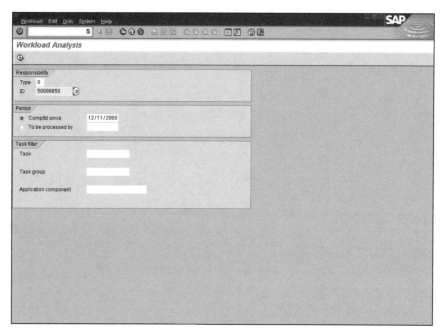

FIGURE 11.21 *The selection parameters list for the workload analysis report* (© SAP AG)

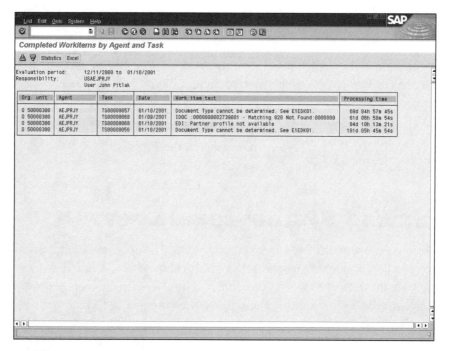

FIGURE 11.22 *A workload analysis report showing work items completed by a user* (© SAP AG)

The Input File Log

Transaction: WE08

Menu Path: From the Area menu of EDI, choose IDoc, Display Status, File
Interface

A file log is maintained in the EDI process to log any problems in reading or
deleting IDoc files on the inbound process. The inbound process maintains this
log, stored as table EDFI2, to avoid processing the same file twice in case of an
error. The EDI administrator is notified when entries are created in the file log.

The system maintains the file name and the last record read successfully from the
IDoc file. The system also records the last IDoc number generated from the file.
The EDI administrator has to edit the incoming file manually, by looking for
problems near the record number recorded in the log, copying into another file
the records that have not been processed yet, and then starting the process again.

The Asynchronous Update Log

Transaction: SM13

Menu Path: From the SAP standard menu, choose Tools, Administration, Monitor,
Update

Most applications use an asynchronous update method to speed the response time
for end users. When an application document is saved, the data is stored in intermediate storage and then transferred to the database by asynchronous update
processes.

For outbound ALE/EDI processes, the IDoc selection program in many cases is
started in the update routine. Syntax errors in the selection program or other hard
errors can cause the update process to fail and result in a dump. In this event, the
system maintains an update log (shown in Figure 11.23). Usually, the Basis group
or a programmer who is testing an IDoc selection program monitors this log. For
detailed information, you double-click the error line.

An express mail is also sent to the user, informing him or her about the error. If
you have written IDoc selection programs for the ALE/EDI interface, you probably remember receiving an express mail saying that the update was terminated
when an error occurred in your selection program.

FIGURE 11.23 *Sample entries in the asynchronous update log* (© SAP AG)

Dump Analysis

Transaction: ST22
Menu Path: From the SAP standard menu, choose Tools, Administration, Monitor, Dump Analysis

This log maintains a list of *dumps* (that is, a log of program crashes). You can view this log to resolve any dumps described in the preceding section. The dump report is highly technical and is used mainly by a programmer developing IDoc programs. I tend to use it when the system behaves mysteriously and everything looks fine. The reason for the mysterious behavior is obvious: The program crashed and did not have a chance to log any information. The dump analysis report in the SAP system is far superior to similar reports in any other system I've used. The report provides several leads to help you determine the cause of the problem, and also shows you the line of code where the failure occurred. Figure 11.24 shows the typical options available in the dump report.

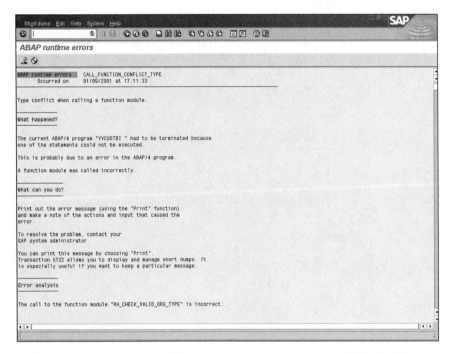

FIGURE 11.24 *Options available to analyze a dump analysis report* (© SAP AG)

The System Log

Transaction: SM21

Menu Path: From the main menu, choose Tools, Administration, Monitor, System Log

The system log is a very comprehensive log maintained on each application server and possibly copied to a central log. This log records all system events, such as system startup, shutdown, process terminations, system errors, and communication problems. This universal log is used by all the application modules and is typically monitored by the Basis administrators. Because of the universal nature of this log, the entries can be cryptic and are best analyzed by a Basis person in conjunction with the application person.

If you experience any unexplainable behavior in the ALE/EDI system, there is a good chance that something has gone wrong and is logged in the system log. Figure 11.25 shows an example of entries in the system log.

FIGURE 11.25 *A sample entry in the system log report* (© SAP AG)

Displaying the Transactional RFC Log

Transaction: SM58

Menu Path: From the Area menu of ALE (BALE), choose Services, Communication, Transactional RFC, Display Incorrect Calls

tRFC (*transactional RFC*) is SAP's enhanced asynchronous communication concept in which delivery of data is guaranteed. If network problems or any other conditions prevent data from being transferred, SAP holds the data and information about the remote system in the tRFC tables and attempts to deliver the data based on the configuration settings in the tRFC destination. This tool is used mainly in the ALE process. Chapter 22, "Configuring the ALE Infrastructure," discusses the tRFC settings. A standard program, RSARFCRD (transaction SM58), is provided to display entries in the tRFC log. On the selection screen, the User Name field defaults to your user ID, but you can clear it to see tRFC entries for all users. The output report (see Figure 11.26) shows entries that are in error. The following columns should be of interest to you.

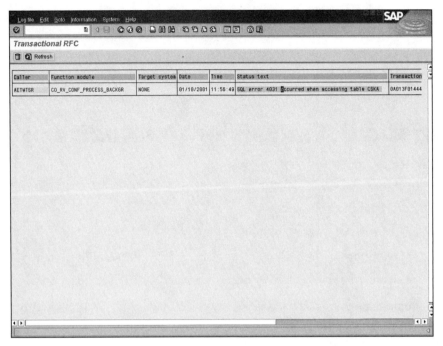

FIGURE 11.26 *Entries in the transactional RFC log* (© SAP AG)

 TIP

Transactional RFC is a general technology, and, therefore, you can see entries from other applications (such as workflow) if they have failed. Entries that have INBOUND_IDOC_PROCESS in column 2 are ALE-related errors.

- ◆ **Column 1 (Caller).** The user who initiates the ALE process.
- ◆ **Column 2 (Function Module).** The RFC function module that is to be invoked on the destination system. The RFC function module for ALE processes is INBOUND_IDOC_PROCESS.
- ◆ **Column 3 (Target System).** The name of the destination system.
- ◆ **Column 4 (Status Text).** A short description of the problem. You can double-click this text for extended information. In most cases, the problem is due to an incorrect user ID or network connection. Check your tRFC destination.

Some additional fields are not visible on the screen; you have to scroll to the right to see them. These display administrative information such as date, time, and the calling program's name. This information is useful only for identifying the process that made the tRFC call. It does not have any value in debugging the problem.

Statistical Analysis of the Audit Log

Transaction: BDM7
Menu Path: From the Area menu of ALE, choose Monitoring, ALE Audit, Evaluate Audit Statistics

The audit analysis for a destination system allows you to

◆ Monitor the processing state of IDocs from the sending system
◆ Monitor IDocs currently being processed on the sending system

A standard program, RBDAUD01 (transaction BDM7), is provided to display entries in the audit log. On the selection screen of this program, you can choose the logical system name of the destination system, message type, and creation date of IDocs. The output shows IDocs in process on the current system for the destination system and IDocs in process on the receiving system. You double-click any line to display detailed statistics.

To Use or Not to Use the SAP Inbox

You will notice that when you execute a work item, it takes you to a log that you can also view without using workflow. For example, if you have a work item for an application error in the IDoc, it takes you to the IDoc display screen where you can look at the error. By now, you're probably wondering why you use workflow when you can get to the IDoc display directly using transaction WE02 or WE05.

Workflow notifications are useful for error situations that can be predefined, but where the timing of errors is unpredictable. For example, the problem with the file log is very rare, so the system administrator will not be monitoring the log on a regular basis. Workflow monitoring is also suited for people who are not frequent users of the system. The advantages of using workflow are timeliness and accountability for resolving the problems.

System administrators are interested in the overall state of the system and are more tuned to using the tools directly for everyday repetitive tasks. For example, the EDI administrator will most likely be monitoring the IDoc list for errors to get a global view of the problems in the system. The information that administrators need cannot be defined concisely. Also, they have to monitor a wide range of errors.

Summary

The ALE/EDI interface provides several tools to monitor the overall health of the system, display IDocs, process work items in the Inbox, and display Message control logs, system-level logs, and workflow logs. IDoc monitoring tools (WE02, WE05, and WE07) are the most commonly used tools because the IDoc is the main component in an ALE/EDI process. An IDoc's status records provide details of the process at various milestones. Errors in the ALE/EDI process are reported via workflow whenever possible. The SAP Inbox serves as the interface to view work items sent to a user as part of the error-handling process via workflow. Workflow is best suited for infrequent, predefined problems addressed to a specific group of people. System administrators use the system-level tools to monitor update logs, file logs, and system logs. You can glean statistical information from the workflow logs to help you analyze trends in the types of errors that occur in your environment. A wealth of information is available in the system, as well as a wealth of tools to view that information.

Chapter 12

**EDI Process
Troubleshooting
and Recovery**

Even if you carry out all the configuration steps detailed in Chapters 6 through 9 and test all the components thoroughly, the system will experience problems at some point. Now you will learn how to identify a successful process execution, to troubleshoot the system when it fails, and to restart the system from the point of failure. This chapter extends the coverage of Chapter 11, "Monitoring the Interface," and shows you how and when to use the various system-monitoring tools introduced there. In the following section, you will learn how to navigate logically to the location of an error or a problem so that you can correct it quickly.

The best approach to troubleshooting any process is to understand the process, learn the points of failure, and then determine how the system reports problems. (This chapter assumes that you already understand the outbound and inbound processes.)

Follow this simple approach to troubleshooting.

1. Determine whether a failure has occurred.

2. For a given symptom, use the troubleshooting chart (Figures 12.1 to 12.16) as your guide to get to the root of the problem quickly.

3. Use the appropriate monitoring tools, as described in Chapter 11, to read and interpret the appropriate log. Use the information in the log to help you analyze the problem.

4. Fix the cause of the problem.

5. Determine the point of restart as suggested in the troubleshooting chart. Depending on the problem, you restart the process from the point of failure or from the very beginning.

6. Use the technique most suitable for restarting the process. You can restart it from within workflow (if applicable) or use one of the ALE/EDI tools for restarting the process.

Troubleshooting the Outbound Process

In this section, you will learn how to troubleshoot an outbound process—find the cause of a problem, fix it as necessary, and restart the process using an appropriate technique.

Points of Failure in the Outbound Process

The outbound process is a sequence of asynchronous processes, and failure can occur within any process. The points of failure on an outbound process are as follows.

- An error in creating the application document
- An error in the output type proposal
- An error in the NAST processing
- An error in the output type processing
- An error in the ALE/EDI interface layer
- An error in the IDoc (syntax errors, conversion, and so on)
- An error in sending the IDoc to the EDI subsystem
- An error in triggering the subsystem
- An error in the subsystem
- Unknown errors or mysterious errors

Reporting Problems

When problems occur in the outbound process, the system uses the technique most suitable at that point to report the problem. The main technique used is the workflow component, but workflow is not started until you are interacting with the system in a dialog mode. After control is passed to the SAP system for processing, the system logs the problems and reports them via workflow. The mechanism used to report problems at different points of failure is as follows.

- When an application document is created, the output control screen displays the proposed outputs. For any problems at this point, use the Determination Analysis option from the menu to identify the cause of the problem. No workflow is necessary.
- After the document is saved, control passes to the SAP system, and the processing of the output types starts asynchronously. The NAST table is processed for output types. Errors in managing the NAST entries are logged in the Message control table, but no workflow is started. Errors in managing the NAST table are very rare.

 TIP

With release 4.5, a workflow is created for errors with the processing of NAST.

◆ The output type for EDI messages is processed by calling the IDoc selection program. Until an IDoc is created, the system cannot log the problems in the IDoc, so problems at this point are logged in the Message control tables. For applications that use Message control, you view this log from the output control screen. If an error occurs in the IDoc selection program before an IDoc is created, the system sends a workflow message to the EDI administrator.

◆ After an IDoc is created, the system logs every problem in the IDoc's status records and then uses the workflow component to send a work item to the responsible person (as identified in the partner profile).

◆ The system performs some basic integrity checks on the IDoc, as well as a syntax check. If an error is found, the IDoc gets a status code of 26 (Error during Syntax Check of IDoc Outbound). A workflow message is sent to the responsible person (as identified in the partner profile). Up to this point, any errors discovered in the system are categorized as ALE/EDI interface errors.

◆ The IDoc is then passed to the OS. Errors can occur for several reasons and are reported with a status code of 02 (Error Passing Data to Port). A workflow message is generated for the responsible person (as identified in the partner profile).

◆ After an IDoc is passed to the OS and the subsystem is installed, the system tries to start the subsystem. Errors can occur for several reasons and are reported with a status code of 20 (Error Triggering the Subsystem). A workflow message is generated for the responsible person (as identified in the partner profile).

Determining Whether an Outbound Process Is Successful

Problems can occur at any point in the process, as noted earlier in the chapter. Your objective is to receive a success message. Knowing what is considered successful will help you achieve your goal. If everything works as desired, there is no need to dig into the troubleshooting process. The final success milestone depends on whether the subsystem is installed.

◆ **Subsystem not installed**. If the subsystem is not installed, the process is considered a success when the IDoc generated for your process gets a status code of 03 (Data Passed to Port OK).

◆ **Subsystem installed.** If the subsystem is installed, the final status code depends on the various status codes reported by your subsystem. The subsystem can be set up to send one final confirmation at the end or to report status at every milestone, in which case there can be several status codes in an IDoc. The milestones are based on typical EDI translator processing. When the IDoc is initially received by the subsystem, the subsystem checks for critical control information, such as the partner and type of message. If these are valid, they tell the subsystem which translation procedure, or "map," to use. The subsystem then translates the IDoc into a standard EDI document. It then checks the syntax of the document. If all is well, the document is wrapped in an interchange envelope, usually with other documents of the same type for the same trading partner, and dispatched through a network. When the interchange is received by the trading partner, the trading partner's EDI translator returns an acknowledgment confirming receipt. From SAP's perspective, the process is successful if you get a status code of 18 (Triggering EDI Subsystem OK). If the subsystem reports any of the status codes listed in Table 12.1, the process is considered a failure on the subsystem.

Table 12.1 Subsystem Error Codes

Status Code	Description
04	Error within control information of EDI subsystem
05	Error during translation
07	Error during syntax check
09	Error during interchange handling
11	Error during dispatch
15	Interchange Acknowledgment negative
17	Functional Acknowledgment negative
23	Error during retransmission

The Troubleshooting Guide for Outbound Errors

The best way to troubleshoot an outbound process is to check the output control log for errors first and then check the IDoc or the SAP Inbox.

The flowcharts shown in Figures 12.1 through 12.9 depict the logical sequence of the troubleshooting process. They also tell you which log to monitor, and they identify the point of restart.

You always start at the top of the flowchart in Figure 12.1 and then navigate to the cause of the problem, using the decision boxes. Figure 12.1 shows the troubleshooting process when your desired output type is not proposed correctly on the output control screen. Figure 12.2 walks you through the troubleshooting process when your output types have been proposed correctly, but an IDoc is not generated. Figure 12.3 guides you to look for severe errors in the system if the sys-

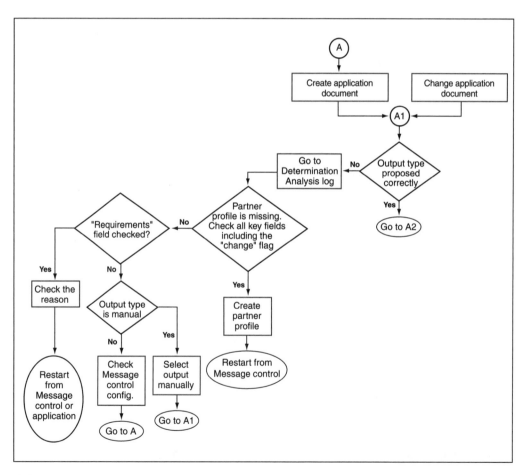

FIGURE 12.1 *The troubleshooting chart for outbound errors—error in proposing the correct output type*

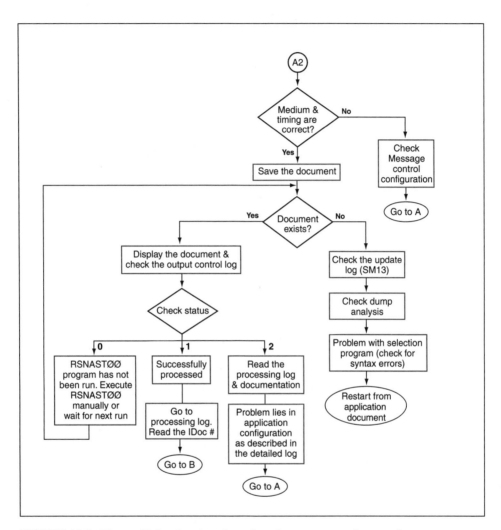

FIGURE 12.2 *The troubleshooting chart for outbound errors—errors in processing an output type*

tem confirms that an IDoc was generated, but an actual IDoc does not exist. If an IDoc exists, depending on the IDoc status, you navigate to the respective diagrams as described.

Refer to Figure 12.4 for IDoc status 02 (Error Passing Data to Port). The cause of the problem is probably the port settings. Refer to Figure 12.5 for IDoc status 03 (Data Passed to Port OK). This status usually indicates success unless you have

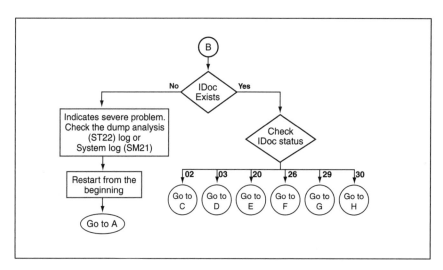

FIGURE 12.3 *The troubleshooting chart for outbound errors—locating errors based on the IDoc status*

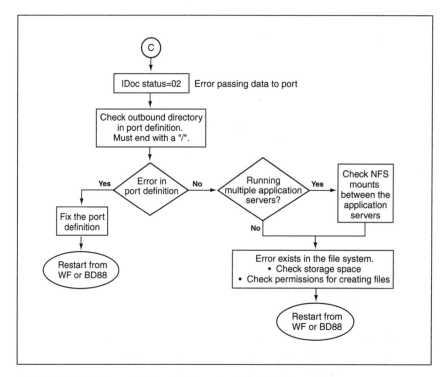

FIGURE 12.4 *The troubleshooting chart for outbound errors—IDoc status 02*

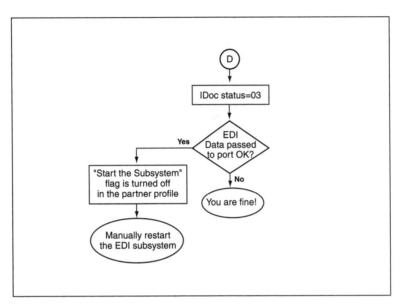

FIGURE 12.5 *The troubleshooting chart for outbound errors—IDoc status 03*

a subsystem installed and the subsystem was not started. Figure 12.6 describes the troubleshooting process when the IDoc goes into status 20 (Error Triggering the Subsystem). This is mainly caused by connectivity errors between SAP and the EDI subsystem.

Figure 12.7 helps you locate the cause of syntax errors in an IDoc (status 26, Errors during a Syntax Check). Figure 12.8 helps you analyze errors in the ALE service layer (status 29, Error in ALE Service). In most cases, it is a problem with partner profiles. Figure 12.9 describes a situation in which an IDoc is stuck in status 30. It can be related to a configuration error or it can be some other severe error.

 NOTE

The set of Figures 12.1 through 12.9 should be viewed as one logical figure. Like any other flowcharting technique, you will find suitable connectors that allow you to navigate from one chart to another.

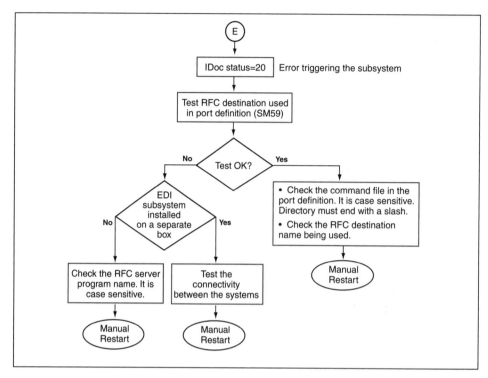

FIGURE 12.6 *The troubleshooting chart for outbound errors—IDoc status 20*

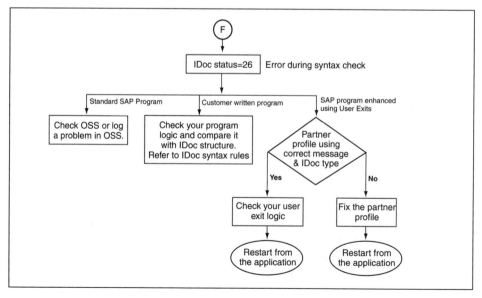

FIGURE 12.7 *The troubleshooting chart for outbound errors—IDoc status 26*

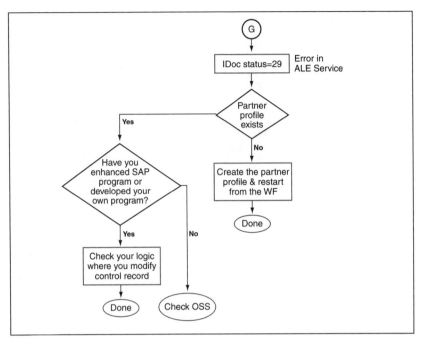

FIGURE 12.8 *The troubleshooting chart for outbound errors—IDoc status 29*

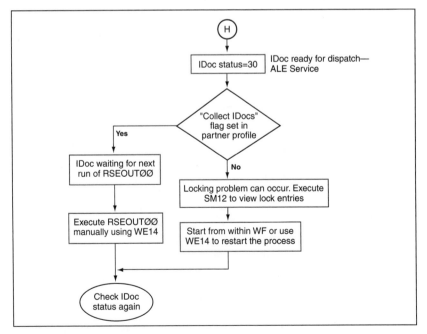

FIGURE 12.9 *The troubleshooting chart for outbound errors—IDoc status 30*

Restart Points for Outbound Errors

The restart can be carried out from the very beginning or from the point of failure (refer to Figures 12.1 through 12.9). The following sections explain the steps for restarting from various points.

Restarting from the Application Document

Following the same steps you used the first time, you must recreate the application document. This time the error should be gone. If you run into problems again, follow the troubleshooting guide to find the cause of the problem.

Restarting from Message Control

The restart from within Message control can be carried out for applications that use Message control. The following sections describe three techniques for this type of restart, depending on the configuration of the Message control component and your preference.

Automatically

You can restart the outbound process from within the application document by going to the output control screen. You go into the document in change mode. Some output types are configured to be proposed every time you enter the document this way. A new entry will exist with a current status of yellow, or 0, indicating that the entry has not been processed yet. The document can then be saved. The timing of the output type determines when processing will start.

 TIP

To see whether an output type is proposed every time you change a document, go to the settings of the output type. If the Condition Access and Multiple Issuing flags are checked, the output type is configured for proposal every time. However, the output still might not be proposed if condition records and requirements are not satisfied. Refer to Chapter 8, "Configuring Message Control" for details on output type, requirements, and condition records.

Repeat Output

If your output is not proposed automatically, you can manually repeat the output from the output control screen by selecting the previously failed output and then clicking the Repeat Output button on the toolbar.

This step will create a new entry in the output type list. After you save the document, the timing of the output determines when the processing will start.

Output from NAST

You can also start the process from a NAST entry. This approach is possible only for entries that were once successful and were sent with a timing of 1 or 2 in the output type. This technique is useful when you have to send an output because it was lost or when you have to repeatedly test an output type. In this case, if you use the output control screen, it fills up very quickly and looks quite messy. This is a personal choice; if you feel comfortable with the first technique, you can ignore this option.

To start the processing, you execute the RSNAST00 program via SE38 or directly by executing transaction WE15. Enter the object key, which is your document number (prefixed with zeros if it is fewer than 10 characters), and select the Send Again check box. Click the Execute button to restart the outbound process.

Restarting from the SAP Inbox

If a workflow message was generated for the error, you have the option of restarting the process from within workflow. However, for some errors, the workflow message is merely an FYI message, so you cannot restart the process from workflow. Such processes are restarted either manually or from outside the SAP system. You can easily tell whether a work item allows restart by executing it. If the resulting screen has a Process button, restart is possible from within workflow.

Restarting from the SAP Inbox saves you the trouble of remembering the application transaction and data values. Remember, workflow brings the right task with the right information to the right person at the right time in the right sequence. You can simply execute the work item to start the process.

TIP

If the error was such that several IDocs failed for the same reason, it is convenient to use one of the ALE/EDI tools to start the process, as described in the next section.

Restarting Using ALE Tools

Transaction (prior to version 4.6): BD88
Transaction (from version 4.6): BD87
Menu Path: From the area menu for ALE Administration (BALE), choose Monitoring, Process IDocs

This method is an alternative to restarting the process from the SAP Inbox and is commonly deployed for mass errors, but you can also use this approach for single errors. Using this tool instead of the workflow tool has merit in certain cases. Consider the following situation: If the file system has some problem—say that it's full or inaccessible—the dispatch program will fail in passing the IDocs from the SAP system to the EDI subsystem. A work item will be generated for every IDoc that fails. The number of such work items can be enormous, considering the number of IDocs typically exchanged in a company. After you fix the problem, you can use the outbound ALE tool to restart all the failed IDocs in one step, without having to execute a work item for each failed IDoc in the SAP Inbox. You use transaction BD87 to bail out IDocs that are in error. It works for IDocs that are in the status codes shown in Table 12.2.

Table 12.2 Outbound Status Codes Processed by the ALE IDoc Processing Tool

Status	Status Code	Status Text
IDocs in ALE/EDI error	02	Error passing data to port
	04	Error within control information of EDI
	05	Error during translation
	25	Processing despite syntax error (outbound)
	29	Error in ALE service
IDocs with syntax error	26	Error during syntax check of IDoc (outbound)
IDocs ready for dispatch	30	IDoc ready for dispatch (ALE service)
IDocs that have been edited	32	IDoc was edited

This tool allows you to process the IDocs from the point of failure without having to restart the process from the beginning. The steps are as follows.

1. Execute transaction BD87.

2. From the screen displayed (see Figure 12.10), fill in the selection criteria.

3. On the next screen (see Figure 12.11), you can select a summary line and click the Process button to reprocess all IDocs represented by the line. By clicking the Restrict and Process button, you are shown another selection screen to further restrict the number of IDocs to be processed.

Manual Restart

This technique is useful when an error has occurred outside the SAP system or a strange error occurs in the SAP system. If the error occurs in the EDI subsystem, the SAP system can resend the IDoc only for the following status codes.

◆ 04 (Error within Control Information of EDI Subsystem)

◆ 05 (Error during Translation)

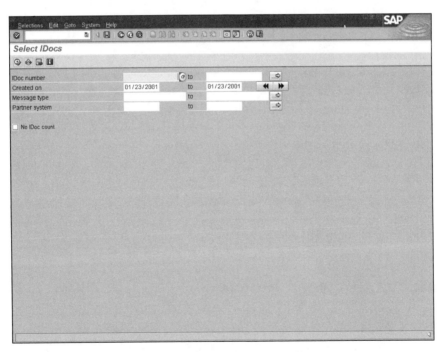

FIGURE 12.10 *The selection screen for manually restarting IDocs* (© SAP AG)

FIGURE 12.11 *The summary screen for manually restarting IDocs* (© SAP AG)

In other cases, you have to fix the problem within the subsystem. For unexplained errors within the SAP system, it is best to restart from the application document. For example, if you created an application document for which an output type is proposed with a timing of 1, the system would wait for the RSNAST00 program to execute and process the output type. However, in the meantime, someone could delete the application document, and the RSNAST00 program would be thoroughly confused. I call this type of event a "strange error," or an error the system cannot handle. You will get a work item, but SAP cannot restart the process. In such a situation, you must find the cause of the problem and manually fix it. You will most likely end up restarting the process from the very beginning.

Purging the Outbound Process

The recovery process doesn't always mean getting the IDoc to the final success milestone. In certain situations, corrupt data can prevent you from fixing a problem and force you to start the process from scratch. If the process in error has created an IDoc, you don't want to leave the IDoc in limbo. You must make it impossible to reprocess the IDoc accidentally.

You can purge the IDoc that is not going to be used. An erroneous IDoc can be purged from the work item generated as a result of this error or from one of the ALE tools discussed earlier. The only other means of getting rid of an IDoc is via the archiving process.

The steps to purge an IDoc from a work item are straightforward. First, you need to identify the work item that was sent to you for the error situation you want to purge. Execute the work item and look for the Delete button. After you click the Delete button, the IDoc is marked for deletion and gets a status code of 31 (Error—No Further Processing). This step prevents the EDI or ALE tools from accidentally reprocessing the IDoc.

Troubleshooting the Inbound Process

In this section you will learn how to troubleshoot an inbound process—find the cause of the problem, fix it as necessary, and restart the process using an appropriate technique.

Failures in the Inbound Process

The inbound process is a sequence of asynchronous processes, and failure can occur within any process. The points of failure on an inbound process are as follows.

◆ An error in triggering the SAP system from the EDI subsystem

◆ An error in creating the IDoc

◆ An error in the ALE/EDI interface layer

◆ An error in the posting function module

◆ Unknown or mysterious errors

Reporting Problems

When problems occur in the inbound process, the system uses the technique most suitable at that point to report the problem. The main technique used is the workflow component, but workflow is not started until an IDoc file is passed to the

SAP system. After control is passed to the SAP system for processing, the system logs the problems and reports them via workflow.

The EDI subsystem handles problems encountered in processing an inbound EDI document on the EDI subsystem. You will have to check with the subsystem vendor for a troubleshooting guide. However, you can design your EDI subsystem to send a TXTRAW message to the SAP system to report problems. This message can be directed to the EDI administrator.

The following mechanism is used to report problems at different points of failure.

◆ Errors that occur in triggering the SAP system from the EDI subsystem are logged in the system log and are reported to the subsystem as RFC errors. No workflow is started until this point. Thus, errors up to this point have to be monitored at the EDI subsystem level.

◆ From the point when an IDoc has been passed to the SAP system to the point when it is created in the database, errors are logged in the EDFI2 table (file log). A workflow message is also generated to inform the EDI administrator.

◆ After an IDoc is created, errors are logged in the IDoc's status record, and problems are reported via workflow.

◆ The system performs some basic integrity checks on the IDoc. After the basic checks, the control information is matched against a partner profile. If a partner profile is not found, the IDoc gets a status code of 56 (IDoc with Errors Added), and a workflow message is sent to the EDI administrator.

◆ After an IDoc is created, a syntax check is done, the IDoc goes through version change, and conversion occurs. If an error is found, the IDoc gets a status code of 60 (Error during Syntax Check of IDoc Inbound). A workflow message is sent to the responsible person (as identified in the partner profile).

◆ Up to this point, any errors discovered in the system are categorized as ALE/EDI interface errors.

◆ The IDoc is then passed to the posting module. If the posting module returns an error, the IDoc gets a status code of 51 (Application Document Not Posted). A workflow message is sent to the responsible person (as identified in the partner profile). There are several reasons for failure of an application document, but in most cases, the problem is with the data.

Determining the Success of an Inbound Process

Errors can occur at several points in the inbound process, as noted earlier in the chapter. Your objective is to receive a success message; knowing the measure of success will help you achieve that objective.

When an incoming IDoc is successfully posted, it gets a status code of 53 (Application Document Posted).

The Troubleshooting Guide for Inbound Errors

The best approach for troubleshooting an inbound process is to check the SAP Inbox first. If there is no error message, check the IDoc list for any problems.

The flowcharts in Figures 12.12 through 12.18 will help you with the troubleshooting process. The charts depict the process in logical sequence, tell you which log to monitor, and help you determine the correct point of restart.

You always start at the top of the flowchart in Figure 12.12 and then navigate quickly to the cause of problem, using the decision boxes. Figure 12.12 shows you the steps for locating problems when the inbound process is started, but an IDoc is not present. If an IDoc was created, use Figure 12.13 to branch to the next figure that corresponds to the IDoc status. Figure 12.14 helps you resolve IDocs stuck in status 50. This is mainly due to a configuration error.

Figure 12.15 describes the troubleshooting process for the most common errors found in inbound IDocs—the application errors. Refer to the next section, "Resolving Application Errors," for details on how to resolve the errors. Figure 12.16 shows you the possible cause of errors in the ALE/EDI layer, which results in an IDoc becoming stuck in status 56. Figure 12.17 helps you debug the cause for syntax errors in an incoming IDoc. Figure 12.18 helps you locate the reason for the IDoc in status 64. This is usually a configuration error in the partner profile, but if the partner profile configuration is correct, it indicates a severe error or another problem that might have been fixed by SAP. You need to consult OSS, the SAP online service system, in this case.

 NOTE

The set of Figures 12.12 through 12.18 should be viewed as one logical figure.

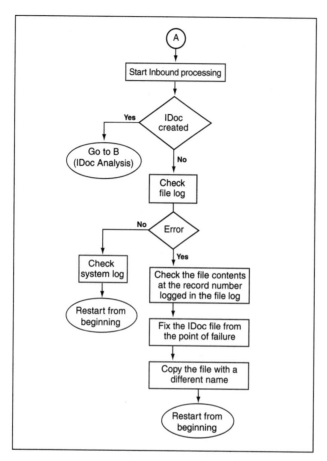

FIGURE 12.12 *Troubleshooting inbound errors—errors in triggering the inbound process*

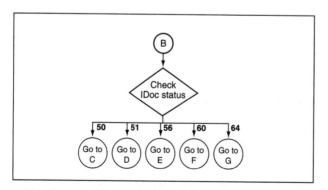

FIGURE 12.13 *Troubleshooting inbound errors—branching to the troubleshooting chart based on IDoc status*

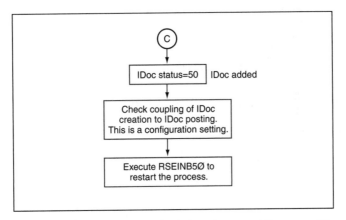

FIGURE 12.14 *Troubleshooting inbound errors—IDoc status 50*

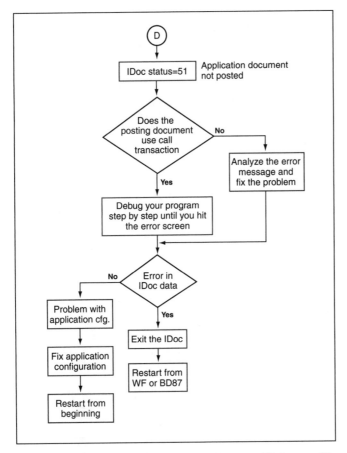

FIGURE 12.15 *Troubleshooting inbound errors—IDoc status 51*

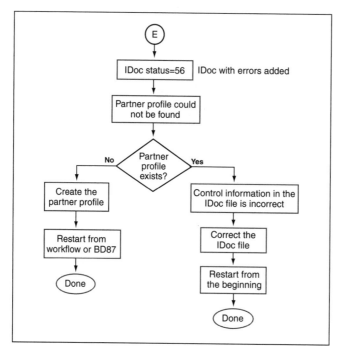

FIGURE 12.16 *Troubleshooting inbound errors—IDoc status 56*

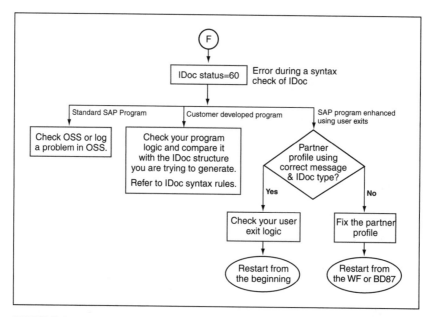

FIGURE 12.17 *Troubleshooting inbound errors—IDoc status 60*

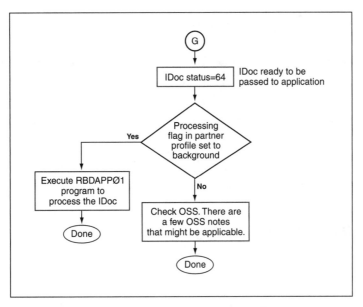

FIGURE 12.18 *Troubleshooting inbound errors—IDoc status 64*

Resolving Application Errors

Application errors are by far the most common errors in an inbound process. Because data originates outside the system, you might always have data-related problems to resolve. Problems within SAP will eventually cease as you find fixes or make appropriate changes. The following tips can help you resolve application errors.

◆ **Execute failed processes in foreground mode**. If the posting program in SAP uses call transaction, you can restart the process in foreground mode and step through each screen until you find the problem. To see whether your posting program uses call transaction, execute transaction BD51. Entries with a value of 1 or 2 use call transaction.

◆ **Edit failed IDocs**. Editing a failed IDoc is a quick fix for data-related problems. For example, if your vendor sends in a wrong material number, you can change the value in the IDoc. You can then restart the process, and the document should post. SAP makes a backup copy of the original IDoc and assigns it a status of 70 (Original of an IDoc that was Edited). You should not use this technique as a permanent fix, however, because doing so addresses only the symptoms, not the cause of the problem.

Restart Points for Inbound Errors

Restart can be carried out from the very beginning or from the point of failure. The restart point should be determined from the troubleshooting chart. The following sections explain the steps for restarting from various points.

Restarting from the EDI Subsystem

In this case, you resend the IDoc file from the EDI subsystem to the SAP system. You can use the startrfc command or one of the inbound utilities. Refer to Chapter 10, "Testing the EDI Interface," for a review.

Restarting from the SAP Inbox

If a workflow message was generated for the error, you have the option of restarting the process from within workflow. However, for some errors, the workflow message is merely an FYI message, as with an error in reading or deleting the inbound file. Such processes are meant to be restarted manually or from outside the SAP system.

 TIP

You can easily tell whether a work item allows restart by executing it. If the resulting screen has a Process button, restart is possible from within workflow.

Restarting from the SAP Inbox saves you the trouble of remembering the application transaction and data values. You can simply execute the work item to restart the process.

If the error caused several IDocs to fail for the same reason, it's convenient to use one of the ALE tools to start the process, as explained in the next section.

Restarting Using ALE Tools

Transaction: BD87

Menu Path: From the area menu for ALE Administration (BALE), choose Monitoring, Process IDocs

This method is commonly deployed for mass errors, but you can use it for single errors. Using this tool instead of the workflow tool is advantageous in certain cases. For example, if several orders are received from a customer and a small glitch occurs in the customer master record, the orders will not post successfully. These IDocs are now in status 51 (Application Document Not Posted), and the system sends a workflow message. You could certainly go into the SAP Inbox, execute the work items one at a time, and fix the problem, but it is more convenient to use the ALE tools to restart the failed IDocs in one step.

You can use transaction BD87 to bail out IDocs that are in error. This technique works for IDocs with the status codes in Table 12.3.

Table 12.3 Inbound Status Codes Processed by the ALE IDoc Processing Tool

Status	Status Code	Status Text
IDocs in application error	51	Error: Application document not posted
Error in the ALE/EDI interface layer	56	IDoc with errors added
	61	Processing despite syntax error
	66	IDoc is waiting for predecessor IDoc (serialization)
	62	IDoc passed to application
	63	Error passing IDoc to application
	65	Error in ALE service
IDocs with syntax errors	60	Error during syntax check of IDoc (inbound)
IDocs ready for posting	64	IDoc ready to be passed to application
IDocs that have been edited	69	IDoc was edited

This tool allows you to process the IDocs from the point of failure without having to restart the process from the beginning. The steps are as follows.

1. Execute transaction BD87.
2. From the screen displayed (refer to Figure 12.10), fill in the selection criteria.

3. On the next screen (refer to Figure 12.11), you can select a summary line and click the Process button to reprocess all IDocs represented by the line. By clicking the Restrict and Process button, you will be shown another selection screen to further restrict the number of IDocs to be processed.

Purging the Inbound Process

Just like in the outbound process, you can purge the IDoc that's not going to be used. An erroneous IDoc can be purged from the work item that was generated because of this error or from one of the ALE tools discussed earlier. The only other means of eliminating an IDoc is via the archiving process.

To purge an IDoc from a work item, you have to identify the work item that was sent to you. Execute the work item and look for the Delete button. After you click the Delete button, the IDoc is marked for deletion and gets a status code of 68 (Error—No Further Processing). This step prevents the EDI or ALE tools from accidentally reprocessing the IDoc.

Summary

Errors can occur at various steps in the outbound and inbound processes, and SAP provides extensive log information at various points. Until an IDoc is generated, SAP logs the error in the application initiating the process. After an IDoc is generated, the IDoc becomes the main vehicle for any log information, and errors are routed via workflow to the right person.

Because errors are possible at various points, knowing where to look can reduce the time required to fix them. The troubleshooting process follows a simple approach: Determine whether an error has occurred, and then use the troubleshooting flow-chart to track down the problem. After you find the cause of the problem, fix it; then restart the process from the point of failure if the system permits a restart. If not, you must restart the process from the very beginning. In some cases, you can restart the process, but you will opt to start from the beginning because data is corrupted. Then, you must ensure that the items in error are purged.

Chapter 13

**Managing EDI
Process
Performance
and Throughput**

In this chapter, you will learn how to manage the performance of your EDI interface so that it provides the necessary throughput without causing the other processes to slow down. This chapter focuses on ways to manage performance at the application level by controlling the execution of processes. The focus is not on performance-tuning procedures used for program and database tuning. The latter procedures are part of an overall performance-tuning strategy that applies to all modules.

Performance is a relative term. A system that is executing fast enough for one user might not be fast enough for another. Luckily, you don't have this problem because the EDI process is inherently *asynchronous*, meaning that the user does not have to wait for the process to complete. For example, if you create a purchase order document, you do not have to wait for a response from your business partner. After you create a document, the system carries out the EDI process behind the scenes.

EDI processes consume a lot of system cycles, which can hamper system performance for other users. Each time an outbound IDoc is created, the system extracts application data, creates an IDoc, extracts the IDoc data, and creates an outbound file. On the inbound, an application document is created from an IDoc. If the inbound transaction uses call transaction, the process is very much like a user entering data online. A huge EDI transaction volume can slow down system performance considerably.

You need to manage your EDI processes so that outbound IDocs are created when the system is not heavily loaded; the same applies to application documents for incoming IDocs. This guideline is not a suggestion to run everything at night. Some transactions, such as advance shipment notices and delivery schedules, are designed to support a JIT (*Just In Time*) environment. You can configure the interface to run these immediately, as described in the following section.

Managing Outbound Process Performance

The outbound interface can be run in near-real-time mode or in batch mode. The benefits and drawbacks of each approach are discussed next.

Outbound in Near-Real-Time Mode

The EDI process in SAP is implemented as a series of application programs. An asynchronous process can be operated in a near-real-time mode by executing the various programs in a coordinated fashion, so that as soon as one program completes, the next program starts instantaneously.

In near-real-time mode, as soon as the application document is created, the IDoc is generated and passed to the subsystem, and the subsystem is started. This sequence gives a real-time feel, which is useful for critical EDI transactions. *Criticality* is a relative term and has a different meaning for each organization. In some businesses, outgoing invoices are critical; for JIT partners, advance shipment notices are critical transactions. This option should not be used for high-volume and non-critical transactions because it will cause performance problems.

The configuration option enables you to control the output at a very granular level. You can have a partner enabled for all messages to go in real-time mode or for only specific messages to go in real-time mode. The outbound interface can be thought of as a link of the following programs.

- **Application Transaction**. Creates the application document, for example, VA01—Create Sales Order, ME21—Create Purchase Order.
- **RSNAST00**. Starts the process of generating IDocs from the application document.
- **RSEOUT00**. Transfers IDocs from the SAP database to the OS, and starts the subsystem.

The following settings are necessary to achieve near-real-time behavior (see Figures 13.1 and 13.2).

- In Message control, the dispatch time of the output type should be set to 4 (Immediate). On the output control screen, you can reach this setting by clicking the Further Data button.

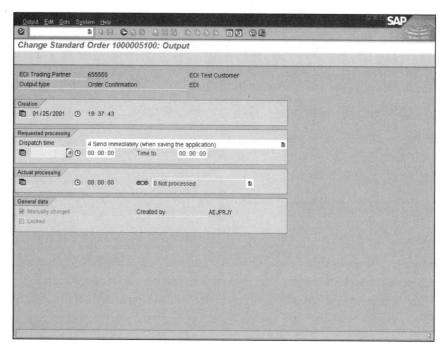

FIGURE 13.1 *Output type settings for immediate processing* (© SAP AG)

♦ In the partner profile for the outbound message, the output mode should be Transfer IDoc Immediately and Start Subsystem (refer to Figure 13.2).

Outbound in Batch Mode

Batch mode is appropriate for non-critical and high-volume transactions. This mode is useful from a performance perspective because output is not generated immediately upon the creation of the application document.

You can control the process at two stages, depending on your company's needs. The first point of control is at the Message control level. When an application document is created, you can set up the process to start creating the IDocs as a batch process by setting the dispatch time in the Message control output screen to 1, as shown in Figure 13.3. In this case, a record is created in the NAST table with the application document number. Buffering IDocs at this stage provides the highest performance benefits because there is no load on the system from an EDI perspective. You can schedule the process to run when the system is not loaded,

FIGURE 13.2 *Partner profile settings for immediate processing* (© SAP AG)

FIGURE 13.3 *Output type settings for batch processing* (© SAP AG) such as at night. The only drawback with this approach is that any outbound process errors will not be discovered until the process is executed. At this stage, you use the RSNAST00 program to start the process of generating IDocs. Several instances of this program can be scheduled with different variants to achieve the desired results.

As an example, suppose that outbound purchase orders and invoices are buffered. A decision has been made to send purchase orders once every day at night, and invoices must go out within four hours of their creation. You can schedule two instances of RSNAST00: one to run every night at 11:00 p.m. to process the purchase order documents, and the other to run every four hours to process the invoices.

The second point of control is when IDocs are transferred to the OS layer. You control this feature as well, by setting the output mode in the partner profile to Collect IDocs, as shown in Figure 13.4. There are two advantages to buffering IDocs at this stage. First, the IDocs have been generated, and any errors in the outbound process should have been discovered. Second, performance is improved by collecting IDocs and thus creating a single file bundled with several IDocs.

FIGURE 13.4 *Partner profile settings for collecting IDocs* (© SAP AG)

The RSEOUT00 program transfers buffered IDocs in the database to the OS. You must schedule this program on an as-needed basis. Several instances of this program can also be scheduled to send the buffered IDocs to the OS layer.

Outbound with and without ALE Services

When IDocs are created from the application document, they are passed to the ALE/EDI interface layer. The ALE interface layer handles any formatting, filtering, and data conversion applicable to the IDoc. In an EDI process, these functions can be better handled in the subsystem layer, and thus an IDoc does not have to go through the ALE services layer. This approach also improves performance to a certain extent. In the standard system, the IDocs generated in the EDI process go through the ALE services layer.

To prevent the process from using the ALE services, the process code must be moved from its current location (with ALE services) to a new location (without ALE services), as shown in Figure 13.5.

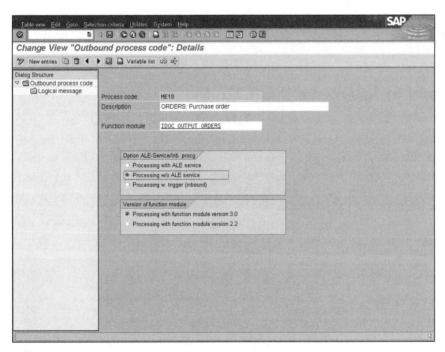

FIGURE 13.5 *Process code settings for EDI processes without the ALE service layer* (© SAP AG)

The steps are as follows.

Transaction: WE41

Menu Path: From the Area menu of EDI, select Control, Outbound process code

1. Click the Change icon to enter change mode. Select the process code to be changed, and click the Details icon.

2. Select the Processing w/o ALE Service radio button, and then save.

 CAUTION

This procedure is not supported on upgrade, so make a note of it in your to-do list for upgrade items.

Managing Inbound Process Performance

The inbound interface can be run in near-real-time mode or in batch mode. The following sections describe the benefits and drawbacks of each approach.

Inbound in Near-Real-Time Mode

In near-real-time mode, when an IDoc is passed to the EDI interface layer, an application document is created almost immediately. Although the process is asynchronous, the system gives the feel of a real-time system. This mode is useful for critical EDI processes, such as order changes and advance shipment notices, but should not be used for high-volume and non-critical transactions.

The execution of the following programs is controlled for achieving near-real-time behavior.

- **Startrfc**. This program is at the OS layer and starts the inbound process, which creates an IDoc.

- **RBDAPP01**. This program passes the IDoc to the posting program, which creates the application document.

The settings shown in Figure 13.6 are necessary to achieve near-real-time behavior.

FIGURE 13.6 *Partner profile settings for immediate processing* (© SAP AG)

NOTE

Keep in mind that startrfc should be started as soon as an IDoc file is created and that in the inbound record of the partner profile message, you should set the processing option to Trigger Immediately.

Inbound in Batch Mode

The batch mode is used for non-critical and high-volume transactions, and is beneficial from a performance perspective. The application document is not created as soon as an IDoc is created, but it is batched to support mass processing.

The process can be controlled at the subsystem layer and within SAP. The subsystem can bundle several IDocs into one file to improve the performance of creating IDocs in the database. In the SAP system, the IDocs can be batched until the system is not busy (at night, for example), to pass the IDocs to the posting programs.

The processing option field (Processing by Function Module) in the partner profile's inbound record should be set to Trigger by Background Program, as shown in Figure 13.7.

The RBDAPP01 program passes buffered IDocs in the database to the posting program. You must schedule this program on an as-needed basis. Also, you can schedule several instances of this program to send the buffered IDocs to the posting program based on the IDoc type. Each instance can be scheduled with a different variant.

By way of example, suppose that inbound sales orders and invoices are buffered. A decision has been made to process sales orders once every hour, but the invoices can wait until the end of the day. Two instances of RBDAPP01 can be scheduled: one to run every hour to process sales orders, and the other to run at 10:00 p.m. to process the invoices.

The RBDAPP01 program can pass the buffered IDocs in a single-threaded or multithreaded (parallel posting) mode. In single-threaded mode, the program

FIGURE 13.7 *Partner profile settings for batch processing* (© SAP AG)

passes one IDoc packet and waits for the process to finish before the next IDoc packet is sent. You set the packet size in the selection list of the RBDAPP01 program. A general rule cannot be established for the packet size because the value varies depending on the memory, processor size, and load on the application server. You will have to experiment with various values; it's an iterative exercise to determine the optimal packet size.

In multithreaded mode, the IDoc packets are passed to the inbound process simultaneously. If there are several IDoc packets, the system keeps dispatching until it runs out of packets or the number of processes is exhausted.

Improving Performance

In addition to the preceding methods suggested for improving performance, you can adopt the following strategies for both inbound and outbound processes.

The EDI Subsystem on a Separate Server

Placing the EDI subsystem on a separate server is an easy way to achieve high-performance benefits. The EDI subsystem is not part of the SAP system and can be installed to run stand-alone on a separate server. Depending on the EDI transaction volume, you can house the EDI subsystem on a UNIX-based or PC-based system. The systems can be configured to share a file system to avoid complications with file sharing.

A Dedicated Application Server for EDI Processes

If you run the inbound IDoc processes in a parallel mode, the programs have a tendency to take up as many sessions as are available on the application server. On a large inbound set, such behavior can cripple the system and bring it to a halt. However, you do want the parallel processing to achieve the throughput you need. It is advisable to have a server group established for EDI processing, to limit the number of processes allocated to a server group. The server group is also a parameter that can be specified on the RBDAPP01 program for inbound IDocs. For outbound processes, you can schedule the RSNAST00 and RSEOUT00 programs to run on the dedicated application server.

ABAP Program Performance

IDoc programs contain a large amount of executable code. Some sections of the code are not necessarily optimized for batch input, which results in a long processing time. To improve the efficiency of individual programs, several patches are available in the OSS (*Online Service System*).

Tuning the Database

Database access can be improved by creating an index of table fields that are frequently used to access the table. Adding an index improves the performance considerably, especially if a table has numerous entries. As part of the overall strategy to improve system performance, your Basis group performs this exercise.

Summary

A system's performance is usually measured by the response time of a user transaction. When a user creates a document or runs a report, the time it takes for the process to complete is used as a starting measure to improve the performance. The asynchronous EDI process does not have this problem because users are not waiting for the process to complete. Nevertheless, the EDI processes can take up a major chunk of system cycles. The best way to improve performance is to install the EDI subsystem on a separate server. Another approach, useful for high-volume transactions, is to batch the generation of IDocs and to perform parallel processing. You must schedule the processing programs, such as RSNAST00, RSEOUT00, and RBDAPP01, with appropriate variants to process the buffered IDocs. Low-volume and critical transactions can be set up to run in near-real-time mode.

PART V

EDI Scenarios

Chapter 14

In the next four chapters, you will apply the knowledge you've gained in the previous chapters to create some outbound and inbound transactions. This chapter explains the steps you must follow to build an EDI transaction. In Section Three, "IDocs," you will learn about ways to modify the process, such as extending the IDocs and programs that create or receive the IDocs.

The technical details are not repeated here, so for any technical matters, please refer to Part III, "Configuring the EDI Interface."

In the case of outbound transactions, there are two paths to create an outbound IDoc: via Message control and without Message control. This chapter uses an outbound purchase order transaction to illustrate the methodology for creating an outbound transaction using Message control. The next chapter provides an example of an outbound process without using Message control. The purchase order transaction was chosen because you're probably familiar with this process and because it's the most commonly deployed transaction in a company. The concept applies to all outbound EDI transactions that use Message control. Therefore, what you learn about purchase orders is also applicable to, say, outbound advance shipment notices or outbound invoices, because they also use Message control. The values and parameters vary from transaction to transaction, but the concept remains the same.

An Overview of the Purchase Order

The purchase order transaction is a business document sent by a customer to a vendor to procure materials or services. The purchase order document has been assigned number 850 in the ANSI ASC X12 standards.

The formal definition of the ANSI ASC X12 850 transaction is as follows: "This transaction set provides for customary and established business and industry practice relative to the placement of purchase orders for goods and services."

In this example, you are using EDI to order 200 units of 800-MHz processors from Computer Mart Corporation (the vendor). The methodology to create an IDoc for an outbound process uses a simple approach. First, you analyze the business requirements and compare them with what SAP provides (analysis phase). Then, you identify various parameters used in the process (preparation phase). Next, you configure the EDI components and build the necessary master data (setup phase), test the setup (testing phase), execute the process (execution phase), verify the results (verification phase), and celebrate if they look good! In the following sections, you will learn the objectives and tasks involved in each phase (see Figure 14.1).

The Analysis Phase

The analysis phase consists of analyzing business requirements and comparing them with the standard functionality of SAP. It's useful to have a good understanding of the SAP business process because, in several cases, you can fill gaps by customizing the system. If gaps cannot be filled via customizing, you should explore the use of user exits to meet your business needs (before you decide to build the process from scratch). The tasks in the analysis phase are described next.

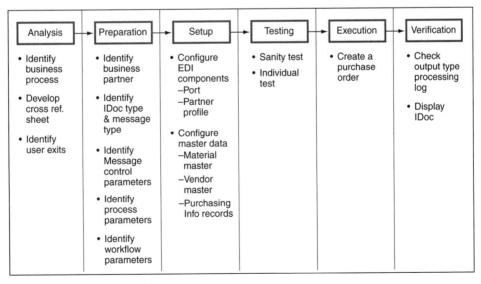

FIGURE 14.1 *Phases for an outbound EDI process*

Identifying Business Processes

Identify the SAP business process that supports the EDI transaction in which you are interested. Sometimes the lingo in SAP can be different from what you are accustomed to. The online help is very useful at this stage. You will have to identify the SAP transaction from which you can initiate the process. For example, the purchase order transaction is part of the Materials Management module. The transaction is ME21 for creating new purchase orders. This information, although not tricky, helps you understand which business process will be used and at which stage you initiate the process. For example, if you are going to send out an advance shipment notice transaction, you can carry it out at the time of creating a delivery or after a goods issue process. Thus, identifying a business process helps you understand your company's business rules.

Developing a Cross-Reference Sheet and Performing a Gap Analysis

In the analysis phase, you identify the gaps between the SAP-provided functionality and your business needs. Customers develop a cross-reference spreadsheet that maps the IDoc data fields to the SAP data elements and the EDI standards. A template is provided for reference (see Figure 14.2). This cross-reference list helps to identify gaps between your business needs and the standard system. Every company develops the cross-reference sheet in one form or another for each transaction.

 TIP

Helpful resources in this area are user groups, such as the EDI user group under ASUG *(America's SAP User Group)* at http://www.asug.com. You can consult with member companies for this information. A cross-reference sheet is also provided as part of the EDI configuration guide when you attend the SAP EDI course CA210 at SAP.

You can develop this cross-reference sheet from the documentation of the IDocs. The fields in the IDocs derive from the data dictionary and use the same data elements as the application whenever and wherever possible. The only time the application data field is not used is when the internal SAP format is not character-based. The fields in the IDocs are always character-based. Several unused

									Business Partner Requirements			

Name of the transaction:_____

Description: _____

IDoc Type: _____

Message Type: _____

EDI Standard: _____ Version: _____

Segment Description: _____

IDoc segment name	IDoc field name	Field length	Qualifier	Qualifier description	IDoc field description	EDI segment field	SAP table field	Screen field	Partner A	Partner B	Partner C	Notes & Gaps

FIGURE 14.2 *The template for developing a cross-reference list between IDoc fields, SAP application fields, and EDI segment fields*

IDoc fields are available for your own purposes, but it is possible that SAP will use those fields in the future.

Identifying Available User Exits

As a result of the gap analysis, you discover gaps between your business needs and the standard SAP functionality. If the gaps cannot be filled using one of the customizing options, you can use one of the user exits. User exits allow you to add customized code formally to an existing SAP process. They have been provided at strategic points in the process and are supported during an upgrade. You can browse the list of user exits by using the CMOD/SMOD transactions. Refer to Chapter 32, "Programming in the IDoc Interface," for details on locating user exits for the IDoc processes.

The user exit for the outbound purchase order transaction is MM06E001. To view a list of all user exits and their purposes, execute transaction SMOD, enter the enhancement name **MM06E001**, click the Components button, and select Display. Refer to the Appendix, "FAQs, User Exits, and Miscellaneous Resources," for a reference list of the user exits for the commonly used EDI transactions.

The Preparation Phase

In this phase, you do all the groundwork and identify all the parameters necessary for your transaction. Identify the business partner (vendor) to whom you are going to send the business document. The business partner will be an entry from your vendor master data.

Identifying the IDoc Type and Message Type

Identify the IDoc type and the message type to support the process: ORDERS02 and ORDERS (from the reference chart). You might wonder why there are multiple IDocs—ORDERS01 through ORDERS05 in version 4.6B—and which one to choose. The last two digits represent the version. ORDERS05 is a newer version, which means that it still has all the segments of the original version, ORDERS01. ORDERS02 and higher support configurable materials. Always use the latest version of an IDoc type unless you specifically need the older version. Each IDoc type is thoroughly documented. To look up the IDoc documentation, execute transaction WE60.

Identifying the Message Control Parameters

The next step is to identify the Message control parameters. For each application there is an application ID from which you can drill down to other components of the Message control. You must determine the application ID and output type used in the process. Refer to Chapter 8, "Configuring Message Control," for complete details on the significance of each of these components and how to locate the list in the SAP system. For the purchase order transaction, the values are as follows.

```
Application ID: EF
Output Type: NEU
```

Identifying the Process Parameters

In this step, you determine the process code for your IDoc type and message type combination. Execute transaction WE41 for a list of process codes available in the system. The process code for generating the ORDERS message using the ORDERS02 IDoc is ME10.

Identifying the Workflow Parameters

In this step, you identify the organizational object (user ID, position, workcenter, and so on) responsible for handling errors associated with this EDI transaction.

You can choose from several types of organizational objects. Refer to Chapter 9, "Configuring Workflow," for details on the various types of objects. To begin with, you can use your user ID for this step.

The Setup Phase

After you identify the parameters, you verify the one-time settings, set up the EDI components required for each transaction, and set up the master data necessary from an EDI perspective.

The EDI Configuration Components

You should have already carried out the one-time EDI settings required by all EDI transactions. The settings include

- ◆ Basic settings for IDocs
- ◆ Communication settings

You will find the information in Chapter 6, "Configuring Basic EDI Components," helpful in performing the setup.

The Partner Profile: Creating Message Control and the Outbound View

Transaction: WE20

A partner profile is created for every business partner that sends or receives EDI documents. In the partner profile, a Message control record and an outbound record are created for each outbound message, as shown in Figures 14.3 and 14.4.

Create a partner profile if it does not exist. Add the Message control data and outbound data for your message. The necessary parameters were identified earlier, in the section, "The Preparation Phase."

FIGURE 14.3 *Message control parameters in the partner profile* (© SAP AG)

FIGURE 14.4 *Outbound parameters in the partner profile* (© SAP AG)

Message Control: Creating Condition Records

Transaction: MN04

Create a condition record for the output type identified in the preparation phase. The condition records are used to define the conditions under which the output type should be proposed. When you create a condition record, you choose the business rule on which you want to create your condition records, as shown in Figure 14.5. To start, you can be very specific, so choose a business rule that has vendor number as one of the fields. Specify the values for the medium as 6 (EDI) and the timing to suit your needs. Initially, you can specify the timing as 4 to indicate immediate (see Figure 14.6).

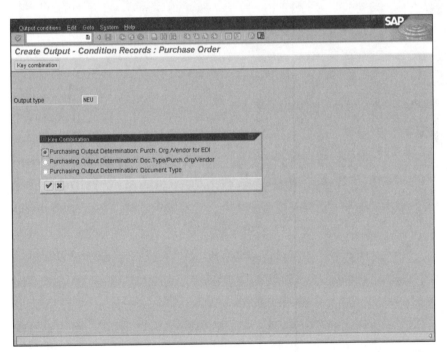

FIGURE 14.5 *Selecting a business rule when you create condition records* (© SAP AG)

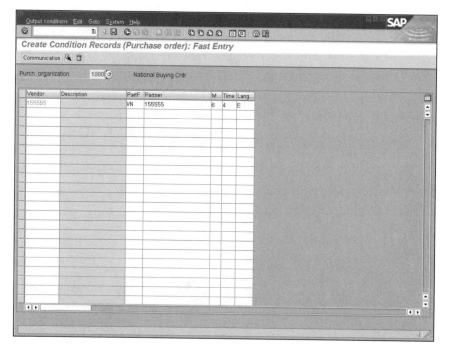

FIGURE 14.6 *Entering output values when you create condition records* (© SAP AG)

The Workflow Settings: Creating the Task Profile

This section assumes that the workflow configuration has already been done. Please refer to Chapter 9, "Configuring Workflow," for details.

Outbound messages require the following actions on workflow settings.

- ◆ Verify the basic workflow settings.
- ◆ Set up the organizational unit.
- ◆ Create a task profile for the error tasks.

TIP

To get started quickly, you can make the error task a General task. Doing so fulfills the requirement for the task profile. You can use your user ID as the person responsible in the partner profile, in which case you do not have to set up the organizational unit.

Master Data Requirements

The type of master data and the required fields from an EDI perspective in the master data vary for each transaction. Your task is not necessarily to maintain the entire master data, but you should be aware of the fields that are required from an EDI perspective. These fields might not be required fields otherwise in the master data. The values in these fields are used to populate critical information in the IDoc, or they are absolutely required fields in the EDI standards. For example, the Account at Vendor field in the vendor master data populates the Sender field in the control record of the IDoc. The cross-reference sheet will be helpful in identifying the fields that must be filled for your business needs.

The following section covers the basics of the master data concept in SAP. You can skip this review if you are familiar with the concept of master data in SAP. The master data required for the purchase order transaction is described after the introductory material.

Master Data Basics

This section is meant for those who are not familiar with the concept of how master data is implemented in the SAP system. It is an introduction to the concept of master data as implemented in SAP, not an introduction to any specific master data.

The master data in the SAP system represents the characteristics of the business entities or the business objects used in the system, for example, material, customer, and vendor. These are stored in Material Master, Customer Master, and Vendor Master tables. SAP also has SAP organizational objects that represent the various organization entities. These entities have a defined business responsibility and are used to represent the company's structure in different forms, such as the purchasing organization, sales organization, and company code.

 NOTE

A distinction exists between an organizational object and an SAP organizational object. Organizational objects are entities such as users, positions, and jobs. SAP organizational objects are company codes and sales organizations. They were named *SAP organizational objects* because of their relevance to the SAP system.

When master data is created in the system, you define views for each SAP organizational object, depending on the master data. For example, when you create a vendor, you create a separate view for each company code and purchasing organization that deals with the vendor, as shown in Figure 14.7. A view holds information specific to the respective SAP organizational object. Similarly, if you are creating a customer master, you have a separate view for each sales area, which consists of a sales organization, distribution channel, and division. For the material master, you have views that are based on plants, storage locations, sales organizations, and so on.

This concept is important to understand when you are creating transactional data, such as purchase orders and sales orders. You cannot create a purchase order for a vendor that has not been defined for your purchasing organization. You cannot order a material for a plant if the material has not been created for that plant. This setup can take a long time. As an EDI person, you aren't responsible for maintaining it, but you must be aware of your company's structure and materials before you can create a purchase order or sales order.

The Material Master Data

Transaction: MM01, MM02
Menu Path: Logistics, Materials Management, Material Master, Material, Create (general), Immediately

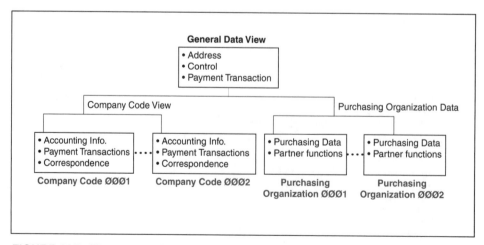

FIGURE 14.7 *The structure of master data for a vendor*

A material master is created for materials you procure from a vendor. You must create a view for the plant to which the materials will be delivered. Although these are not EDI requirements, you cannot create a purchase order without this information.

The Vendor Master Data

Transaction: XK01 and XK02

Menu Path: Logistics, Materials Management, Purchasing, Master Data, Vendor, Central, Create

A vendor master is created for vendors from whom you procure material. Maintain the vendor for each purchasing organization that can procure from this vendor. The following fields must be entered in the vendor master for EDI in their respective views. The various views to be selected appear in Figure 14.8.

◆ **General Data, Address.** The address information must be filled out. Figure 14.9 shows an example of address information fields filled out for the vendor Computer Mart Corporation.

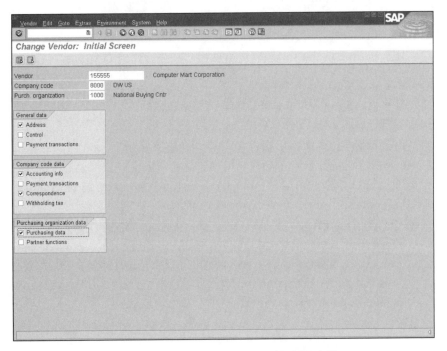

FIGURE 14.8 *Vendor master views required for EDI* (© SAP AG)

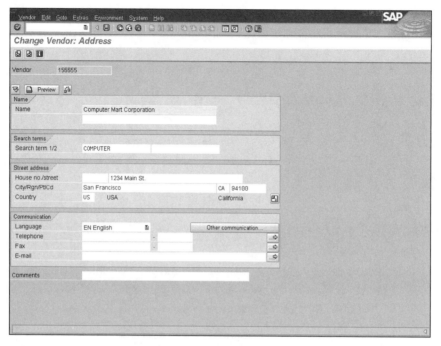

FIGURE 14.9 *Vendor master address information* (© SAP AG)

- ◆ **Company Code Data, Accounting Information**. The reconciliation account must be filled out. Figure 14.10 shows an example of accounting information for Computer Mart Corporation.

- ◆ **Company Code Data, Correspondence**. In this view you fill in the Account at Vendor field. This field is used in the Sender field of the control record and defines how the vendor recognizes your company in its system. Figure 14.11 shows an example of correspondence information for Computer Mart Corporation.

- ◆ **Purchasing Organization Data, Purchasing Data**. Order Currency, Terms of Payment, and Incoterms must be filled. Incoterms define the commonly used trading terms established by the International Chambers of Commerce. If they are not filled, they need to be filled when creating a purchase order (see Figure 14.12).

FIGURE 14.10 *Vendor master accounting information* (© SAP AG)

FIGURE 14.11 *Vendor master correspondence information* (© SAP AG)

FIGURE 14.12 *Vendor master purchasing data* (© SAP AG)

The Purchasing Information Records

Transaction: ME11

Menu Path: Logistics, Materials Management, Purchasing, Master Data, Info Record, Create

A vendor material information record contains vendor-specific information about a material. For example, if you procure a particular material from three vendors, each vendor might call it a different name, the delivery times can be different, and the prices can vary. You store the vendor-specific information about a material in this table. Figure 14.13 shows that material DPC1020 in your system is identified as VEN1000 at your vendor, Computer Mart Corporation. The fields in this table

FIGURE 14.13 *Purchasing information record details, showing the relationship between your material and vendor material* (© SAP AG)

are required. You are not required to send the vendor's part number on an EDI transaction. It is the vendor's responsibility to convert the customer part number to the vendor's internal number.

The Testing Phase

After you configure the system, it is ready for testing. Follow the unit testing technique discussed in Chapter 10, "Testing the EDI Interface." To begin, you can only carry out the sanity tests to make sure that the configuration is correct. You can execute the process as described in the next section.

Executing the Process

Starting an outbound process via Message control is standard. You create the application document from its respective application process and then go to the output control screen to verify the outputs proposed by the system.

Create a purchase order using your vendor number, the material, and a suitable quantity. Figure 14.14 shows an example of a purchase order entered for vendor Computer Mart Corporation to order 200 pieces of 800-MHz processors.

Transaction: ME21

Menu Path: Logistics, Materials Management, Purchasing, Purchase Order, Create

To see the proposed output types, go to Header, Messages. Check your output type and make sure that the medium and timing are correct, as shown in Figure 14.15. Save your document. IDoc processing should start.

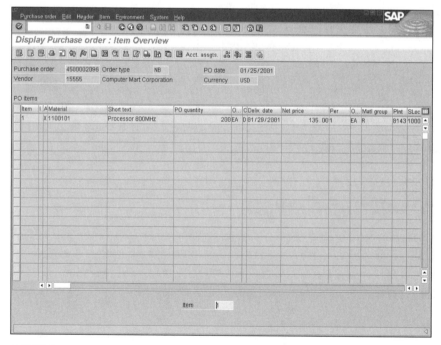

FIGURE 14.14 *The purchase order detail screen for entering items to be ordered*
(© SAP AG)

Verifying the Output

The procedure for verifying the output for messages generated via Message control is straightforward. Go to the output control screen and check the status of your output type. For a detailed log, check the processing log for the output type. The IDoc number generated for the output is logged in the processing log (refer to Figure 14.15). You can use one of the IDoc display tools to see the data in the IDoc, as shown in Figure 14.16.

For the purchase order, go to the output control screen, using Header, Messages, and check the status. Get the IDoc number from the processing log. Display the IDoc using WE02 and verify the data values.

If you experience problems in the process, use the troubleshooting guide in Chapter 12, "EDI Process Troubleshooting and Recovery," to determine the cause of the problem, and restart the process.

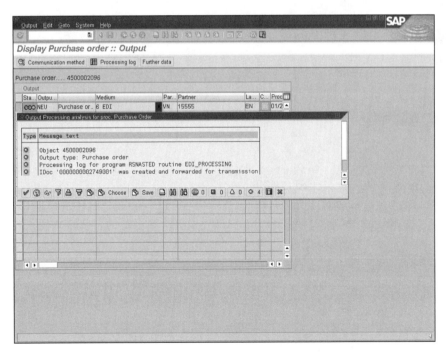

FIGURE 14.15 *The output control screen, showing the EDI output proposed for a purchase order* (© SAP AG)

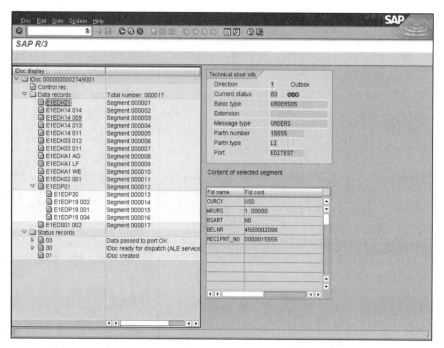

FIGURE 14.16 *The IDoc created for the purchase order document* (© SAP AG)

Summary

The steps to configure an outbound process via Message control require a preparatory phase in which you gather the necessary data for the transaction. In the next stage, you set up various components, including the EDI components and master data necessary for the transaction. The setup phase is followed by a unit-testing phase in which all the components are given a sanity test. Next, the process is executed to generate an IDoc. In the verification phase, the output is verified to ensure that all the fields are being generated as desired. These steps can be applied to any outbound EDI process that uses Message control.

Chapter 15

This chapter uses an outbound remittance advice and payment order transaction to illustrate how an outbound process works without using Message control. The remittance advice and payment order transactions are chosen because these are commonly deployed transactions in the FI module and are standard transactions in the system. These two transactions are generated from the same payment program.

This chapter describes how the process works from an EDI perspective and explains the steps you need to perform. You must have a basic understanding of the accounts payable process to be able to carry out this transaction, but the configuration of the accounts payable process is not the focus of this chapter. The concepts discussed here apply to all outbound EDI transactions that do not use Message control.

An Overview of Remittance Advice/Payment Order

The remittance advice/payment order (820 in ANSI X12, PAYADV in EDIFACT) is a transaction that can be used for three purposes.

- ◆ To advise a financial institution (a bank) to make payment to a payee on your behalf (the payer)
- ◆ To report the completion of payment to a payee by a financial institution (a bank)
- ◆ To advise a payee about a payment that has been made to the payee's account either by a payment order or through other means (inbound)

When sent to a bank, this transaction contains financial instructions (clearing information) that the bank uses to process the payment data. This information has no significance for a payee.

In the SAP system, this transaction is implemented in the FI module. Figure 15.1 shows the business partners involved in the process and the messages exchanged

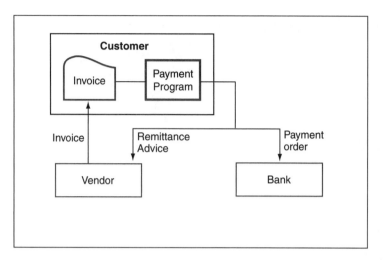

FIGURE 15.1 *EDI messages exchanged in the remittance advice/payment order process*

between them. The process begins with an invoice received in the system from a vendor, for goods or services procured from the vendor. The invoice can be entered manually in the system or can be input via EDI. When the invoice is due, payment must be made.

In the SAP system, the payment is generated through a payment run program that is scheduled periodically to process outstanding invoices. This process selects entries that are due and creates a payment proposal. The payment proposal allows you to view and edit payments that will be made. After the proposal has been verified and changed (if necessary), the actual payment run can be scheduled. The payment run will create the necessary payment documents, such as checks or payment advice, to be sent to a bank and/or a vendor.

The methodology to create an IDoc from an outbound process without Message control has six phases (the analysis phase, preparation phase, setup phase, test phase, execution phase, and verification phase), as described in Chapter 14, "Outbound with Message Control: Purchase Orders." The objectives of each phase are the same, but the tasks under each phase vary in some cases. In the following sections, you will find details specific to the remittance advice/payment order process only.

The Analysis Phase

The analysis phase consists of analyzing business requirements and comparing them with the standard functionality of SAP. The tasks in the analysis phase are described next.

Identifying Business Processes

The remittance advice transaction is part of the Accounts Payable application under the FI module. The transaction is F110 for starting the payment run program.

The payment run program is a two-step process. In the first step, called a *proposal run*, you create a proposal that allows you to view and edit the payments that will be generated. The proposal run can also create test IDocs that can be analyzed and verified before the actual IDocs are generated. The test IDocs are not transmitted to the bank or the vendor. In the second step, the actual payment run program is executed. At this time, the program generates the output that is sent to your vendors and banks. Thus, identifying a business process helps you understand your company's business rules and the SAP process.

 NOTE

To develop cross-reference sheets, refer to Chapter 14, "Outbound with Message Control: Purchase Orders," for details.

Identifying User Exits Available in the Process

The user exits for the outbound remittance advice process are FEDI0003 and FEDI0004. To see a list of all user exits and their purposes, execute transaction SMOD, enter the enhancement name (FEDI0003 or FEDI0004), click the Documentation button, and select Display.

The Preparation Phase

In this phase you do all the groundwork and identify all the parameters necessary for your transaction.

Identifying Business Partners

You must identify the business partner (vendor or bank) to whom you are sending the business document. The vendor number is an entry from your vendor master data (transaction XK02). The partner number for the bank is stored under the EDI partner profiles section in the DME (*Data Medium*) view of the house bank master entry (transaction FI12). Consult with your accounts payable team for the setup of bank master information. As an EDI person, you are responsible for making sure that there is a valid entry in the EDI partner number field. If a value does not exist, you will not be able to create a partner profile.

Identifying IDoc and Message Types

You identify the IDoc type and the message type to support the process— PEXR2001 (IDoc) and PAYEXT and REMADV (message)—from the reference chart in the Appendix, "FAQs, User Exits, and Miscellaneous Resources."

 NOTE

Use the latest version of the IDoc type unless you specifically need an older version. The version is identified by the last two characters of the IDoc type. Thus, if your system has IDoc type PEXR2002, use it instead of PEXR2001. Each IDoc type is thoroughly documented. Execute transaction WE60 to display the documentation for an IDoc type.

Identifying Workflow Parameters

In this step, you identify the organizational object (user ID, position, workcenter, and so on) responsible for handling errors associated with this EDI transaction. You can choose from several types of organizational objects. Refer to Chapter 9, "Configuring Workflow," for details on the types of objects. To begin, you can use your user ID for this step.

The Setup Phase

After you identify the parameters, you set up the EDI components required for each transaction and the master data necessary from an EDI perspective. The master data is required before you can do some of the EDI settings. For example, you cannot create a partner profile before you create the vendor master.

Master Data Requirements

The type of master data and the required fields from an EDI perspective in the master data vary for each transaction. Your task is not necessarily to maintain the entire master data, but you should be aware of the fields required from an EDI perspective. These fields might not be required fields otherwise in the master data.

The values in these fields populate critical information in the IDoc or are absolutely required fields in the EDI standards. For example, an Account at Vendor field in the vendor master populates the Sender field in the IDoc's control record. The cross-reference sheet will help you identify the fields that must be filled for your business needs. The master data required for the remittance advice transaction to a bank and a vendor is described next.

TIP

A detailed description of the master data setup required is available in the documentation for the RFFOEDI1 and RFFOEDI2 programs. To view the documentation, execute transaction SE38, click the Documentation button, and enter the program name.

Partner Settings for the House Bank

Transaction: FI12
Menu Path: From the IMG, choose Financial Accounting, Bank Accounting, Bank Accounts, Define House Banks

A bank ID is created at a company code level for every bank with which you have an account. This ID uniquely identifies the bank and contains general information such as the contact person and bank address, as shown in Figure 15.2. The

FIGURE 15.2 *General information about your bank* (© SAP AG)

DME view in the bank master contains information about the data medium used to transfer funds. In the DME view, the EDI partner profile section identifies the partner number assigned to the bank for EDI purposes. This entry must be filled with a value that uniquely identifies the bank as an EDI business partner.

TIP

If this entry does not exist and you want to add a value in this field, you must also click the Partner Profile button to create the partner profile record. The system will not let you exit without a partner profile entry.

Make sure that an account exists in the bank and that details such as the G/L account and bank account number are filled in, as shown in Figure 15.3.

FIGURE 15.3 *Bank account details from which payments are made* (© SAP AG)

The EDI Accompanying Sheet for the Paying Company

Transaction: FBZP

Menu Path: From the IMG, choose Financial Accounting, Accounts Receivables and Accounts Payables, Business Transactions, Outgoing Payments, Automatic Outgoing Payments, Payment Method/Bank Selection, Configure Payment Program

Under Paying Company Codes, select the company code and view the details. You need to verify the settings in the EDI Accompanying Sheet Form field. A standard form, F110_EDI_01, is supplied in the standard system. This sheet prints the totals. The Form for the Payment Advice field should also be set appropriately.

Vendor Master Data

Transaction: XK01 and XK02

Menu Path: Logistics, Materials Management, Purchasing, Master Data, Vendor, Central, Create or Change

A vendor master is created for vendors from whom you procure material. You must maintain the vendor for each purchasing organization that can procure from this vendor. Required fields for EDI are listed in Chapter 14, "Outbound with Message Control: Purchase Orders." You now need some additional Company Code data fields in the vendor master record, as shown in Figure 15.4. The payment run program uses the following payment transaction fields.

◆ Payment Terms

◆ Payment Methods

◆ House Bank

◆ Pmt Adv. by EDI

EDI Configuration Components

The EDI components you must set up are discussed in the next three sections.

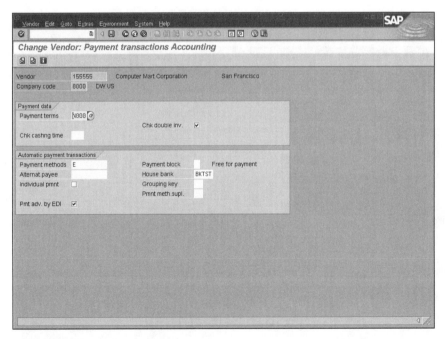

FIGURE 15.4 *The vendor master—details of payment terms for paying invoices* (© SAP AG)

Basic One-Time EDI Settings

This chapter assumes that you have already carried out the one-time EDI setting required by all EDI transactions (for details, see Chapter 6, "Configuring Basic EDI Components"). The settings include basic IDoc settings and communication settings.

The Partner Profile: Creating the Outbound View

A partner profile is created for every business partner that sends or receives EDI documents. In the partner profile, an outbound record is created for each outbound message.

Create a partner profile for your vendor and your bank. Add an outbound record for the outbound messages: REMADV and PAYEXT, as shown in Figure 15.5 and Figure 15.6, respectively. The REMADV message is created for the vendor, and the PAYEXT message is created for the bank. Both messages use the IDoc type PEXR2002. Note that the partner function field is blank.

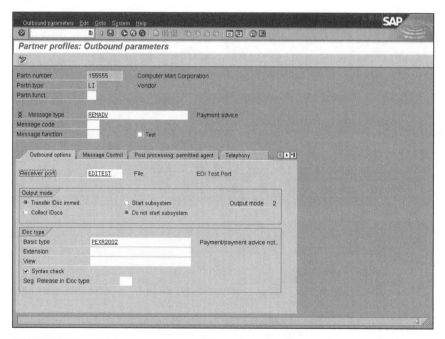

FIGURE 15.5 *The vendor's partner profile—the outbound record for the remittance advice message* (© SAP AG)

FIGURE 15.6 *The bank's partner profile—the outbound record for the payment order message* (© SAP AG)

The payment process allows you to create a test IDoc message at the time of the proposal run. To enable this text, you must create an additional entry for the test message in the partner profile. This entry looks exactly like the entry for the REMADV and the PAYEXT messages except that the test flag should be turned on. In the initial stage, I recommend this optional step to test the process.

Workflow Settings: Creating a Task Profile

This chapter assumes that the workflow configuration is complete. For details, please refer to Chapter 9, "Configuring Workflow." Outbound messages require the following workflow settings.

◆ The basic workflow settings

◆ The organizational unit setup

◆ A task profile for the error tasks

The Testing Phase

After you configure the system, you're ready for the testing phase. Follow the unit-testing technique discussed in Chapter 14, "Outbound with Message Control: Purchase Orders." To begin, you can only carry out the sanity tests to make sure that the configuration is correct. You execute the process as described in the next section.

Executing the Process

In the execution phase, you generate payments for outstanding invoices. You can view a list of open invoices using transaction FBL1. If no invoices are outstanding, the payment run will not produce any output.

As mentioned earlier, the payment run process is a two-step process: proposal run and payment run. After you complete the proposal run, you can execute the IDoc generation program, RFFOEDI1. This step generates the test IDocs for verification. After you verify the proposal run, you execute the payment run. After the payment run is finished, you execute the RFFOEDI1 program again to generate the actual IDocs to be sent to the bank and the vendor.

Another program, RFFOEDI2, resets the status of the outbound EDI process. This program is useful if you have to retransmit an IDoc. RFFOEDI1 does not allow you to retransmit unless the status has been set by RFFOEDI2.

Entering Invoices

Transaction: F-43 (Vendor Invoice), MRHR (Any Invoice)
Menu Path: Logistics, Materials Management, Invoice Verification, Invoice Verification, Document Entry, Enter Invoice

This step creates an invoice online. An invoice can also be created via EDI. In the invoice, enter the vendor line item for charges from the vendor, as shown in Figure 15.7. Balance the payment by creating an entry for the G/L account against which the document will be posted. You can enter the same G/L account as entered in the bank account.

FIGURE 15.7 *Entering an invoice for the vendor* (© SAP AG)

The Payment Proposal Run

Transaction: F110

Menu Path: Accounting, Financial Accounting, Accounts Payable, Periodic Processing, Payments

The proposal run creates the payment proposal. Each run is given a unique ID, which is entered on the first screen. The proposal run entails several steps.

Maintaining Parameters

You must specify the selection parameters for invoices that need to be paid, as shown in Figure 15.8. You can select the vendors, payment method, posting date, and so on. You should also specify the Additional Log parameters to log detailed information about the run, as shown in Figure 15.9.

FIGURE 15.8 *The selection screen to specify parameters for the payment run program* (© SAP AG)

FIGURE 15.9 *Specifying parameters for an additional log from the payment run program* (© SAP AG)

After you save the parameters, the screen displays the current status, as shown in Figure 15.10, indicating that parameters have been maintained.

Scheduling the Proposal Run

You can schedule the proposal program to run immediately, or you can set a time. The system automatically creates the background job. For testing purposes, you can elect to run the program immediately. The status is updated when you press Enter.

Viewing the Log

After the proposal program is complete, you can view the proposal log, which shows you the invoices selected by the proposal program and their statuses, as shown in Figure 15.11. At the end, a total of all the invoices is shown. If problems occur in the run, the log contains comprehensive debugging details.

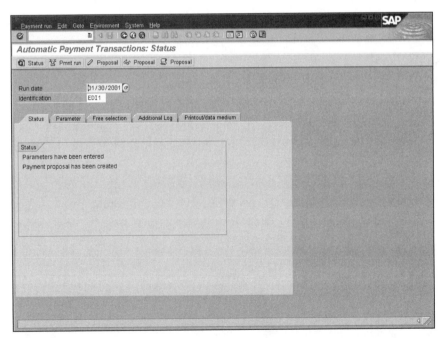

FIGURE 15.10 *The status screen for the payment proposal run program* (© SAP AG)

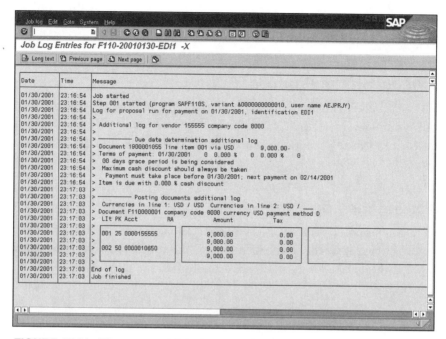

FIGURE 15.11 *The output log for the payment proposal run program* (© SAP AG)

Starting the IDoc Generation

If you are satisfied with the invoices selected in the proposal run and they have no errors, you can create the IDocs from the output of the proposal run.

Execute program RFFOEDI1 to start the generation of IDocs. Select the proposal run using the ID that was used to start the proposal run. Click the Proposal Run Only check box and any additional selection criteria you want to select, as shown in Figure 15.12. Click the Execute button, and the proposal run program should create the test IDocs. The IDoc number is displayed on the screen. If there are errors, you can double-click to view the log.

TIP

If you get a message that no records were selected, you should check the selection parameters. If everything looks fine, execute the RFFOEDI2 program to reset the status of the transmission.

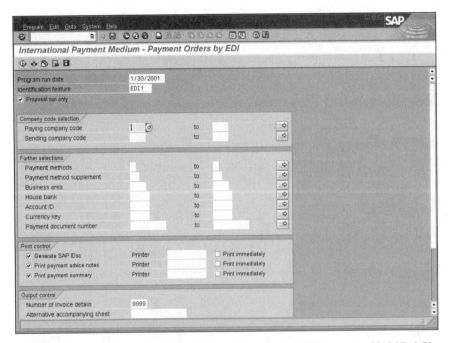

FIGURE 15.12 *The selection parameter list for the RFFOEDI1 program* (© SAP AG)

Verifying the Output

You verify the results of processing by displaying the IDoc, using any of the IDoc display tools. Verify the data fields and values. The IDoc generated in this step is a test IDoc for verification purposes only. The system generates a test IDoc for the remittance advice and payment order.

If you experience problems in the process, use the troubleshooting guide in Chapter 12, "EDI Process Troubleshooting and Recovery," to determine the cause of the problem, and then restart the process as necessary.

The Payment Run

Transaction: F110
Menu Path: Accounting, Financial Accounting, Accounts Payable, Periodic Processing, Payment

The payment run is executed after you have edited the proposal run (if necessary) and are satisfied with the output. The payment run creates the actual payments that are sent to your business partner. This consists of the following several steps.

Scheduling the Payment Run

You can schedule the payment program to run immediately, or you can set a start time. The system automatically creates a background job for you. When you press Enter, the status is updated on the screen.

Viewing the Log

After the payment run is complete, you can view the payment log. The log displays the invoices selected by the payment program, their status, and a total of all the invoices, as shown in Figure 15.13.

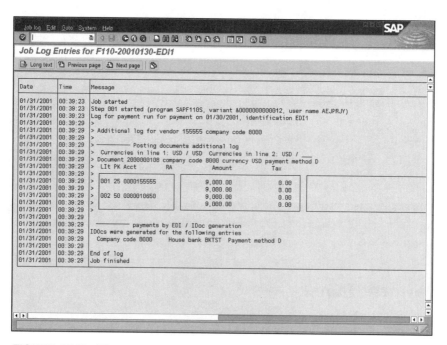

FIGURE 15.13 *The output log for the payment run program* (© SAP AG)

Starting the IDoc Generation

If you're satisfied with the invoices selected in the payment run and they have no errors, you can create the IDocs from the payment run output.

Execute program RFFOEDI1 to start the generation of IDocs. Select the payment run using the ID that was used to start the payment program. Select any field combination. Do not select the Proposal Run Only check box, as shown in Figure 15.14. Click the Execute button, and the proposal run program should create the final IDocs. The IDoc number is displayed on the screen. If there are errors, you can double-click to view the log.

Verifying the Output

You can verify the results of processing (including data fields and values) by using any of the IDoc display tools to display the IDoc. An IDoc should be generated for the remittance advice and payment order (see Figure 15.15).

FIGURE 15.14 *The selection parameter list for the RFFOEDI1 program* (© SAP AG)

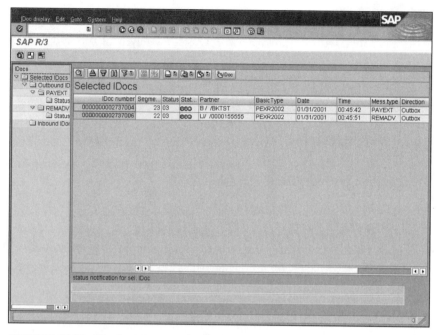

FIGURE 15.15 *The final IDocs—the payment order to the bank and remittance advice to the vendor* (© SAP AG)

Summary

Configuring an outbound process without Message control requires moving most of the selection criteria and business rules that were part of the Message control component to the selection screen for the payment program and the RFOEDI1 program. The partner profile is also slightly different without Message control than it is with it. There is no entry for the Message control view. The processing program is now part of the core application logic itself; in contrast, with Message control the processing program is disconnected from the application logic. The last difference is in the verification stage. In this case, the output log is temporary, whereas with Message control, the output processing log is permanently maintained for each output type, so you can view the results at any time.

Chapter 16

**Inbound with
Function Module:
Sales Orders**

This chapter uses an inbound sales order transaction to illustrate how an inbound process works using a direct path via a function module. The sales order process serves as a good example because you are probably familiar with sales documents, and this transaction is commonly deployed for the inbound process. You should view this chapter as a guide to help you get your transaction up and running, not as a tutorial. It points out the important steps and issues you must consider in building this transaction.

This chapter describes the phases in developing an inbound transaction and the tasks in each phase. To carry out this transaction, you need a good understanding of the sales order process, but its configuration is not the focus of this chapter. The concepts covered here apply to all inbound EDI transactions that use direct posting via a function module.

An Overview of the Sales Order Process

The *sales order* (850 in ANSI ASC X12, ORDER in EDIFACT) is a document that is received from a customer by a vendor to supply goods or services. From the customer's point of view, the 850 transaction is a purchase order, while the same document when received by the vendor is loaded into SAP as a sales order.

 NOTE

The formal definition of the ANSI X12 850 transaction is as follows: "This transaction set provides for customary and established business and industry practice relative to the placement of purchase orders for goods and services."

In the SAP system, this transaction is implemented in the Sales and Distribution module. The process begins with a sales order transaction received from a customer. The EDI document is converted to an IDoc, which is then used to post a sales order in the system (see Figure 16.1).

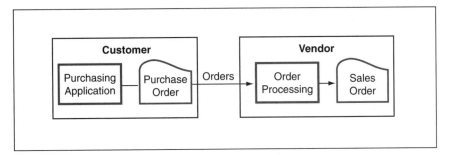

FIGURE 16.1 *Messages exchanged in the sales order process*

The methodology for creating an application document from an incoming EDI document is simple. First, you analyze the business requirements and compare them with what SAP provides (the analysis phase). Then, you identify various parameters used in the process (the preparation phase). Next, you configure the EDI components and build the necessary master data (the setup phase), test the setup (the test phase), execute the process (the execution phase), verify the results (the verification phase), and celebrate if they look good! In the following sections you will learn the objectives of each phase and the tasks involved.

The Analysis Phase

The analysis phase consists of analyzing business requirements and comparing them with the standard functionality of SAP. A good understanding of the SAP business process can help you fill the gaps by customizing the system. If gaps cannot be filled via customizing, you should explore the use of user exits to meet your business needs. Tasks in the analysis phase are described next.

Identifying Business Processes

You must identify the SAP business process that supports the EDI transaction in which you're interested. In some cases, the lingo in SAP is different from what you are used to. You can use online help to identify the SAP document created in this process.

In the case of inbound sales orders via EDI, a sales document is created. The EDI process uses the call transaction method to post an incoming sales order IDoc.

Thus, a sales document created via EDI goes through checks similar to a regular sales order entered online. Knowledge of the sales order process—how it works, what causes a sales order to fail, how pricing is carried out, how you support multiple ship-to locations, how the system performs ATP (*Available to Promise*) checks, and so on—will help you design your EDI process to meet your business needs. Work closely with the functional team to understand the process better.

Developing a Cross-Reference Sheet

Customers develop a cross-reference spreadsheet that maps the received EDI fields to the SAP data elements via IDoc data fields. The idea behind developing a cross-reference sheet is the same as with the outbound process. For details, refer to Chapter 14, "Outbound with Message Control: Purchase Orders."

Identifying User Exits Available in the Process

As in the outbound process, user exits have been provided at strategic points in the inbound process. Refer to Chapter 32, "Programming in the IDoc Interface," for details on locating user exits for the IDoc processes.

The enhancement for the inbound sales order transaction is VEDA0001. To see a list of all the user exits in this enhancement and their purposes, execute transaction SMOD, enter the enhancement name **VEDA0001**, click the Documentation button, and click Display. For instance, you see that user exit 001 (EXIT_SAPLVEDA_001) is called for each segment on the incoming IDoc. There are many reasons this could be of use, such as when you convert a non-standard customer-supplied material number to your SAP equivalent.

Developing Conversion Lists

A tricky situation occurs with inbound processes. The SAP system has its own terminology for organizational objects such as sales organizations, company codes, and purchasing organizations. These are used when you create documents in the SAP system. For example, a company code is required when you create an invoice, and a sales area is required when you create sales documents. There is no industry standard for these objects. Therefore, when an EDI document is received, it does not have these values. You need a lookup table that can provide a translation based on values from some field in the EDI document, or the values can be hard-coded in the EDI map if they are constant. For example, if you receive a sales order, the Vendor Number field on the incoming data can be used to deduce the sales area in SAP.

For the incoming sales order process, carry out the following conversions.

♦ When you create a sales order document, you are required to provide sales area information (sales organization, distribution channel, and division). This information is not available on an incoming EDI transmission. SAP provides a lookup table, EDSDC, to determine the sales area. The sales area can also be determined in a user exit of the IDoc process. If none of these techniques are acceptable, the conversion can be done in the EDI subsystem. As part of the analysis phase, you make a decision about the best place to carry out such conversions. Although the general rule is to carry out most conversions on the EDI subsystem, some situations can be better accommodated in SAP, owing to instant availability and the fact that the most recent data resides in the SAP system.

♦ Another common issue with inbound documents is the conversion of external representation to internal representation. For example, a customer generally sends you its generic customer number, which does not map to a customer number in the SAP system. You must design a solution in the EDI subsystem to do this conversion, because SAP has no standard way of handling this problem. Conversion of the customer's material number to an SAP material number is also required.

By identifying such information, you become aware of the issues you must address in processing an incoming document.

TIP

The best strategy is to offload conversions to the EDI subsystem, but this method might not always be acceptable to your EDI subsystem team.

The Preparation Phase

In the preparation phase, you do all the groundwork and identify the parameters necessary for your transaction.

Identifying Business Partners

You must identify the business partner (the customer) who is sending you the EDI document. An entry for that customer must exist in your customer master data. You can locate a customer in the system using transaction XD02.

Identifying IDoc and Message Types

Just as you identify an IDoc type and a message type for an outbound process, you identify the IDoc type and message type to support the inbound process.

For a sales order, the IDoc type can be ORDERS01 through ORDERS05, and the message type is ORDERS (from the reference chart in the Appendix, "FAQs, User Exits, and Miscellaneous Resources").

 NOTE

Notice that the IDoc types for the outbound purchase order and inbound sales order are the same. In fact, it is common for single IDoc type to be used for several logical message types.

Identifying Conversion Tables to Be Maintained

As mentioned in the analysis phase, you might have to convert some of the data in an incoming document. These conversions are best carried out in the EDI sub-system, except for conversions pointing to data that is continuously changing, such as customer numbers and material numbers.

However, sometimes the responsibility falls on the shoulders of the SAP EDI team. Then you have to collect the data for your conversion tables. For example, in the sales order, you might decide to maintain the determination of the sales area (sales organization, distribution channel, and division) for an incoming sales order in the SAP system. If so, you need data values you can use to deduce the sales area in SAP.

SAP provides the following conversion capabilities in the sales documents.

- ◆ Determination of the sales area
- ◆ An external number for a partner function (for example, a customer's ship-to locations to internal SAP ship-to customer numbers)
- ◆ A customer's material number to the material number in the SAP system

Identifying Process Codes

A *process code* represents the function module that is used for the inbound process. You can see the link between any process code and its corresponding function module by using transaction WE42. The process code for incoming sales order documents is ORDE.

   TIP

An easy way to determine the process code is to locate the function module. Function module names are based on message type.

Identifying Workflow Parameters

You must identify two elements: the organizational object and the workflow task. This step is slightly different from an outbound process, in which you do not have a workflow task specific to a message type.

The organizational object (user ID, position, workcenter, and so on) is responsible for handling errors associated with the EDI transaction. You can choose from several types of organizational objects. Refer to Chapter 9, "Configuring Workflow," for details on the various types of objects. To begin, you can use your user ID for this step.

The workflow task handles application errors. The tasks for standard SAP messages are named *<message type>*_Error. For sales orders, the task is ORDERS_Error (TS00008046).

The Setup Phase

After you identify the parameters, you set up the master data needed from an EDI perspective, conversion tables, and the EDI components required for each transaction. The master data is required before you can make some of the EDI settings. For example, you cannot create a partner profile before you create the customer master. The components to be set up vary with each transaction.

The Master Data Requirements

The type of master data and the required fields (from an EDI perspective) in the master data vary for each transaction. Your task is not necessarily to maintain the entire master data, but you should be aware of the fields that are required from an EDI perspective and how the master data is used in EDI. These fields might not otherwise be required fields in the master data.

The cross-reference sheet can help you identify the fields that must be filled in the IDoc for your business needs. A discussion of the master data for an incoming sales order document follows.

The Customer Master Data

Transaction: XD02
Menu Path: Logistics, Sales and Distribution, Master Data, Business Partners, Customer, Change, Complete

A customer master is needed for each customer with whom you exchange business documents via EDI. A customer can be of several kinds: sold-to, ship-to, bill-to, and so on. The sold-to customer is used for incoming sales orders. In SAP, a ship-to customer can be different from the sold-to customer. For example, if Wal-Mart (the sold-to customer) orders computers from IBM, it requests that the shipment be sent to SAM'S Club (the ship-to customer).

A sales area view is necessary for each sales organization that deals with the customer. For example, if a sales area (sales organization: 3000, distribution channel: 01, and division: 05) will be accepting sales orders from a customer, you must make sure that the customer is defined in the sales area.

The Material Master Data

Transaction: MM02
Menu Path: Logistics, Materials Management, Material Master, Material, Change, Immediately

A material master is needed for materials you sell to your customers. Like any other master data, the material must also be defined for the sales organization and distribution channel that will accept the sales orders.

Maintaining Conversion Tables

The conversion tables convert an external representation to an internal representation or provide a lookup mechanism to deduce information that is not supplied by your business partner.

Some conversions can be done in the EDI subsystem or the SAP system. Based on your decision in the analysis phase, you can choose to use any of the optional conversions in the SAP system, as discussed in the following sections.

Customer Material Information Records

Transaction: VD51

Menu Path: Logistics, Sales and Distribution, Master Data, Agreements, Cust-Material Information, Create

The system uses a customer material information record to convert the customer's material number to a material number in the SAP system. For example, in Figure 16.2, the customer material number CUST-MAT-01 is converted to your material number 1100005 in the SAP system.

FIGURE 16.2 *The material information record* (© SAP AG)

The Partner Conversion Table (EDPAR)

Transaction (versions prior to 4.5): VOED (Partner, Application, Conversion)
Transaction (from version 4.5): VOE4 (table EDPAR)
Menu Path: From the IMG, choose Sales and Distribution, Electronic Data Interchange, EDI Messages, Configure EDI Partners, Convert External to Internal Partner Numbers

The partner conversion table is used to convert an external representation of a partner function number (ship-to, bill-to, and so on) to an internal representation. This table can be used for all incoming and outgoing SD transactions via EDI and for entries in the E1EDKA1 segment of the IDoc.

For example, you can accept a sales order from a customer (say, 655555) and ship the products to the customer's warehouse location A or warehouse location B. These two warehouses are represented by two ship-to customers in SAP (say, 20655555 and 20655556) and are tied to the customer master in the partner functions screen. When you accept a sales order via EDI, the customer does not send you the ship-to numbers as represented in the SAP system. The customer sends its terminology (say, WH-A for warehouse A and WH-B for warehouse B). The partner conversion table converts the WH-A to your SAP number 20655555 and WH-B to your SAP number 20655556, as shown in Figure 16.3.

The first column (Customer) contains the customer number. The second column (Ext. Function) is the partner function you want to convert. The fourth column (External Partner) is the external representation of your partner. The fifth column (Int. No.) is the internal representation of the business partner in SAP.

CAUTION

Some customers have tweaked the system into using this table to convert external representation of the sold-to to an internal sold-to number by maintaining the table directly via SM31. This approach is not recommended; SAP does not officially document this feature, and you could be in trouble down the road.

TIP

If the external representation is a number, you have to prefix it with leading zeros if the number in the IDoc is prefixed with leading zeros.

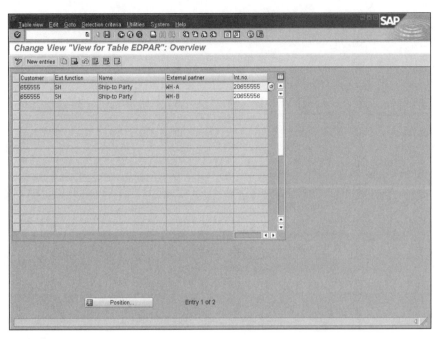

FIGURE 16.3 *The conversion of an external partner function number to an internal number* (© SAP AG)

Determining the Sales Area for the Sales Order

Transaction (versions prior to 4.5): VOED (Partner, Application, Customer/Supplier)

Transaction (from version 4.5): VOE2 (table EDSDC)

Menu Path: From the IMG, choose Sales and Distribution, Electronic Data Interchange, EDI Messages, Configure EDI Partners, Assign Customer/Vendor to Sales Organization Data

A sales area is required when you enter a sales order in the system. The system first checks the E1EDK14 segment for the sales area values. If the system doesn't find the data, it uses the sales area lookup table (EDSDC) to deduce the sales area information. Entries in the EDSDC table map a vendor number supplied in the E1EDKA1 segment to a sales area in SAP, as shown in Figure 16.4. In the example, when a customer who recognizes you as VENDOR-01 orders goods, the sales area (sales organization: 3000, distribution channel: 20, and division: 20) is used for the sales order.

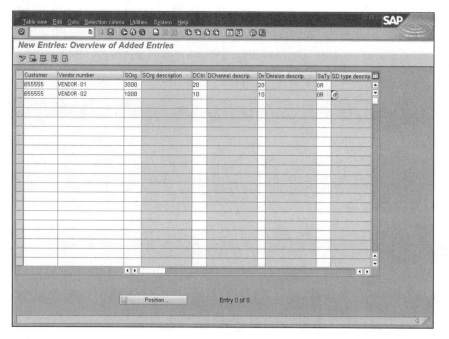

FIGURE 16.4 *Determining the sales area for an order* (© SAP AG)

The first column (Customer) is the customer number for the customer sending the order. The second column (Vendor Number) is the vendor number from the LIFNR field of the E1EDKA1 segment. The three columns titled SOrg., DChl, and Dv represent the sales area.

CAUTION

If the LIFNR field in the E1EDKA1 segment has leading zeros, the values entered in the Vendor Number field must also have leading zeros.

TIP

You can write a BDC (*Batch Data Communication*) program to load this table if you already have this information in a legacy system.

TIP

You can also use the user exit number 07 from the enhancement VEDA0001 to deduce the sales area. If you use the user exit, you do not have to maintain this table. However, you will have to design your program logic to return the appropriate values.

Maintaining Pricing

Transaction: V/08

Menu Path: From the IMG, choose Sales and Distribution, Basic Functions, Pricing, Pricing Control, Define and Assign Pricing Procedures

If an order entry clerk enters a sales order online, pricing is not a major issue. The order entry clerk can communicate any price variance between the customer's expected price and the price calculated by the system. However, the pricing issue is always important when incoming documents are being entered automatically in the system, as in the case of EDI. The system provides two condition types for incoming EDI orders: EDI1 and EDI2. These must be included in the pricing procedure adopted by your organization, as shown in Figure 16.5.

The condition type EDI1 represents the customer-expected price. The customer-requested price from the E1EDP01-VPREI field in the IDoc is used to calculate the customer-expected price. This value is compared with the actual price calculated by the system. You can specify any formula for comparing the price when including this condition type in the pricing procedure. In the standard system, the system provides a formula 9 to check the difference of a single unit of the currency. For example, if the price difference in the United States is greater than $1, the order is flagged as incomplete because of pricing issues.

The condition type EDI2 represents the customer-expected value. The customer-requested value from the E1EDP01-NETWR field in the IDoc is used to calculate the customer-expected value. This value is compared with the actual value calculated by the system. You can specify any formula for comparing the value when including this condition type in the pricing procedure. In the standard system, the system provides a formula 8 to check a difference of greater than five percent. If the value difference is greater than five percent, the order is flagged as incomplete because of pricing issues.

FIGURE 16.5 *Including pricing conditions in the pricing procedure* (© SAP AG)

Your responsibility as an EDI member is to make sure that the pricing procedures include these two conditions. The configuration of the pricing module is another issue. For more information on pricing conditions, consult the SAP Library.

EDI Configuration Components

You should have already carried out the one-time EDI settings required by all EDI transactions. The settings include

◆ The basic IDoc settings

◆ The communication settings

Refer to Chapter 6, "Configuring Basic EDI Components," for step-by-step details on performing the setup.

The Partner Profile: Creating the Inbound View

A partner profile is created for every business partner with whom you exchange business documents via EDI. In the partner profile, an inbound record is created for each inbound message.

You must create a partner profile for your customer if one doesn't already exist. Add an inbound record for the sales order message, using the values identified in the preparation phase (see Figure 16.6).

Workflow Settings: Creating a Task Profile

In this step, you verify the one-time setting of workflow components for EDI and create a task profile for the incoming EDI message. This section assumes that the workflow configuration has been done. For details, please refer to Chapter 9, "Configuring Workflow." The following workflow settings are necessary.

- ◆ The basic workflow settings
- ◆ The organizational unit setup
- ◆ A task profile for the error tasks

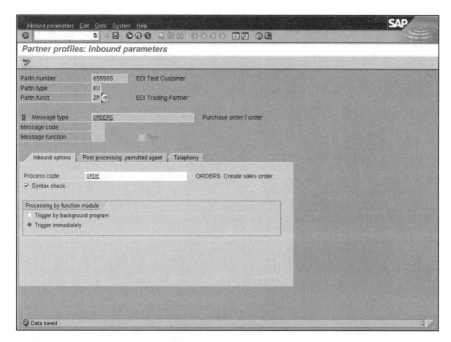

FIGURE 16.6 *The partner profile inbound record for a sales order* (© SAP AG)

In addition to the one-time settings, you must assign a task profile to the ORDERS_Error task. To begin, you can also make the task a General task, which allows everyone to handle it.

The Testing Phase

After you configure the system, you're ready for the testing phase. Follow the unit-testing technique described in Chapter 10, "Testing the EDI Interface." To begin, you can only carry out the sanity tests to make sure that the configuration is correct. You execute the process as described in the next section.

Executing Processes

To execute the process, you first create an IDoc and then pass it to the ALE/EDI interface layer for processing. To create an IDoc for the inbound process, use any of the tools for creating IDocs, discussed in Chapter 10. Figure 16.7 shows the

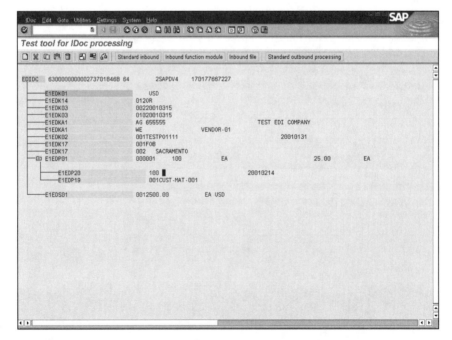

FIGURE 16.7 *Copying an existing IDoc to create a new IDoc* (© SAP AG)

most common tool (transaction WE19) used to copy an existing IDoc and start the inbound process.

Verifying Output

The process of verifying an inbound process via a function module is straightforward. First, you verify the results of processing by displaying the IDoc, using any of the IDoc display tools. The status record with a status code of 53 indicates success and logs the application document number generated using the IDoc. You can then display the application document.

For the sales order, go to the IDoc display and check the status records in the IDoc. Get the sales order number from the status record with a status code of 53, as shown in Figure 16.8. Display the sales order using VA03, confirm the values, and make sure that the document is complete. You can check for incompleteness by selecting Edit, Incomplete Log from the sales order display screen.

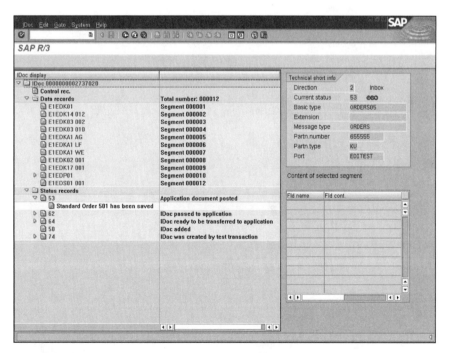

FIGURE 16.8 *An IDoc status record, showing the sales order number created from an incoming IDoc* (© SAP AG)

If you experience problems in the process, use the troubleshooting guide in Chapter 12, "EDI Process Troubleshooting and Recovery," to determine the cause of the problem, and then restart the process as necessary.

Summary

The steps to configure an inbound process via a function module are divided into phases. In the analysis phase, you develop an understanding of the SAP business process that supports the EDI transaction and then develop a cross-reference sheet to identify gaps between your business needs and standard SAP functionality. The inbound process requires several conversions. These can be done in the EDI subsystem or in the SAP system by using standard conversion tables provided for the process or through user exits. In the preparation phase, you identify the parameters used in the setup phase to configure the system. Next comes the testing phase, followed by the execution phase, in which you run the process. Finally, the results are verified in the IDoc and in the application document created in the process.

Chapter 17

Inbound via Workflow: Sales Order Changes

This chapter uses an inbound sales order change transaction to illustrate how an inbound process works using a workflow task. It points out the important steps and issues you need to consider in building this transaction. The sales order change was chosen because it makes the most sense if you are going to implement an inbound via workflow. The concepts covered here apply to all inbound EDI transactions that use workflow. You should view this chapter as a guide to help you get your process up and running, not as a tutorial.

 CAUTION

This type of transaction is not a standard scenario in the system.

An Overview of the Sales Order Change

The *sales order change* (860 in ANSI X12) is a document that a customer sends to inform a vendor of changes to a previous sales order (refer to Figure 16.1 in the preceding chapter).

 NOTE

The formal definition of the ANSI X12 860 transaction is: "This transaction set provides the information required for the customary and established business and industry practice relative to the purchase order change."

In the SAP system, this transaction is implemented in the Sales and Distribution module. The process begins with a sales order change transaction that the vendor receives from a customer. The default processing is to create an IDoc and post the order change IDoc directly into the system without any human intervention, but this approach can be a problem for many companies. You really shouldn't process an order change without knowing what will be changed. The scenario in this chapter uses workflow to notify a person of the changes being requested.

The methodology is slightly different from that described in the preceding chapter. A new development and design phase has been introduced. The steps in the setup phase are also different because of the nature of the process.

The Analysis Phase

The analysis phase consists of analyzing business requirements and comparing them with the standard functionality of SAP. In a sales order change process, a sales document created as part of an incoming sales order transaction is changed. This process does not restrict the type of changes being made to the sales order. Thus, if an original order is for 1,700 pieces and production has already started, you might receive a sales order change that reduces the quantity to five pieces.

The Design and Development Phase

The gaps identified in the process can require you to enhance the existing process or develop the process from scratch. The "SAP rule" is to use standard components whenever and wherever possible. In this phase, you design and develop the enhancements.

The scenario described in this chapter assumes that automatic changes are unacceptable and that you want to involve a person to review the changes being requested, as shown in Figure 17.1. In fact, the change scenario is a good example precisely because it is so much more complicated to implement in an automated fashion than creating a new document. One must account for numerous potential events that can alter the status of an order after it has been created. Refer

FIGURE 17.1 *An enhanced sales order change process via workflow*

to Figure 4.3 in Chapter 4, "The Inbound EDI Process," for details on the processing by workflow process flow.

The inbound sales order change process can be implemented to simulate the following process.

1. An incoming EDI document is converted to an IDoc. (This step is the same as the corresponding step in the standard scenario.)

2. The IDoc is routed to a person responsible for verifying the changes. (This step is different from the normal process of posting the IDoc.)

3. The responsible person gets a work item in his or her SAP Inbox, informing him or her of the order change IDoc. This person executes the work item, which automatically displays the IDoc.

4. If the changes are acceptable, they are manually implemented in the sales order document.

5. If the changes are not acceptable, the IDoc is not posted.

The enhanced scenario is implemented as a simple process that explains the concept very clearly. It uses existing workflow components and does not involve any programming. Your business scenario might require additional development. You can use a multi-step workflow instead of a single-step task. Workflow development and design skills are essential for a sophisticated workflow to be used in the process.

A standard task, named Display (TS30200088), exists in the system to display any IDoc. It will be used to display the sales order change IDoc data. The name for the process code chosen is ZOCH.

The Preparation Phase

In the preparation phase, you do all the groundwork and identify the parameters necessary for your transaction.

Identifying IDoc and Message Types

You must identify the IDoc type and the message type to support the process. For a sales order change, the IDoc type is ORDERS05, and the message type is

ORDCHG (from the reference chart in the Appendix, "FAQs, User Exits, and Miscellaneous Resources").

Identifying Workflow Tasks and Process Codes for Inbound Processes

The workflow task to be started is represented by a process code. You have to identify that task and establish a process code for it. The process code should start with the letter Z. In this scenario, you can use a standard system task to display an IDoc. The task name is Display (TS30200088), and the name chosen for the process code is ZOCH.

The Setup Phase

After you identify the parameters, you set up the master data needed from an EDI perspective, the necessary conversion tables, and the EDI components required for each transaction. The master data is required before you can enter some of the EDI settings. For example, you cannot create a partner profile before you create the customer master. The components to be set up depend on the transaction.

The EDI Configuration Components

You should have already carried out the one-time EDI settings required by all EDI transactions. The settings include

- The basic IDoc settings
- The communication settings

Refer to Chapter 6, "Configuring Basic EDI Components," for step-by-step details on performing the setup.

The Process Code Settings

Transaction: WE42
Menu Path: From the Area menu of EDI, choose Control, Inbound Process Code

In this step you link the process code to the single-step task. Create an entry with process code ZOCH and task TS30200088, as shown in Figure 17.2.

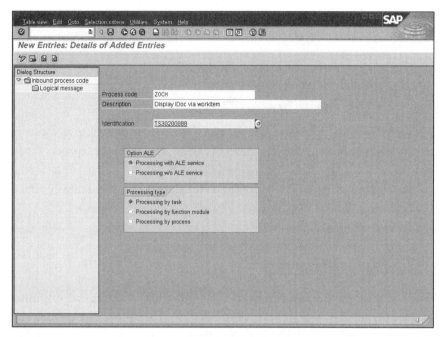

FIGURE 17.2 *Process code pointing to a single-step task for an inbound process*
(© SAP AG)

The Partner Profile: Creating the Inbound View

A partner profile is created for every business partner with whom you exchange business documents via EDI. In the partner profile, an inbound record is created for each inbound message.

Add an inbound record for the sales order change message, using the values identified in the preparation phase (see Figure 17.3).

The Workflow Settings

In this step, you verify the one-time settings of workflow components for EDI and create a task profile for the incoming EDI message. This section assumes that the workflow configuration is complete. For details, please refer to Chapter 9, "Configuring Workflow." The following workflow settings are necessary.

- ◆ The basic workflow settings
- ◆ The organizational unit setup
- ◆ A task profile for the error tasks

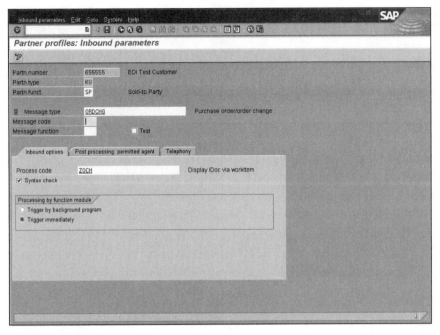

FIGURE 17.3 *The partner profile inbound record for the sales order change message* (© SAP AG)

 NOTE

Identifying the workflow parameters for error handling is identical to the step discussed in Chapter 16, "Inbound with Function Module: Sales Orders."

The Testing Phase

After you configure the system, you're ready for testing. Follow the unit-testing technique discussed in Chapter 10, "Testing the EDI Interface." To begin, you can only carry out the sanity tests to make sure that the configuration is correct. You execute the process as described in the next section.

Executing the Process

To execute the process, you first create an IDoc and then pass it to the ALE/EDI interface layer for processing. To do so, follow these steps.

1. To create an IDoc for the inbound process, use any of the tools for creating IDocs that were discussed in Chapter 10. The most common tool (transaction WE19) used to copy an existing IDoc and start the inbound process is shown in Figure 17.4.

2. When the inbound process is started, a work item is placed in your SAP Inbox (see Figure 17.5).

3. Execute the work item. This step should display the sales order change IDoc using the same screens as transaction WE02. The IDoc's last status record indicates that the IDoc was passed to a task and the work item was generated, as shown in Figure 17.6. You can view the data fields. Click on the E1EDK01 segment and look at the P.O. number in the BELNR field.

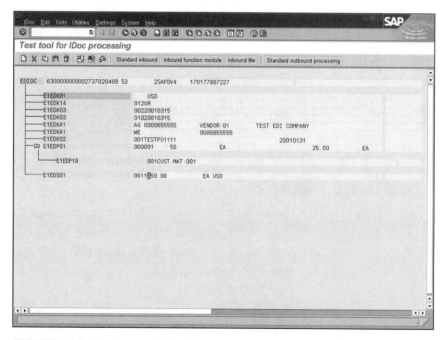

FIGURE 17.4 *Copying an existing IDoc to create a new IDoc and start the inbound process* (© SAP AG)

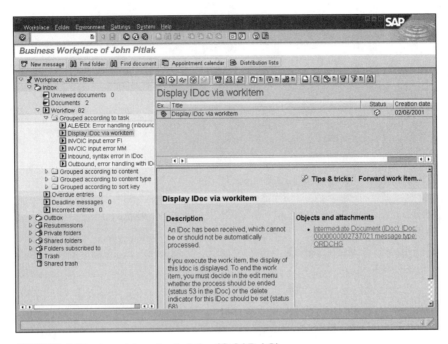

FIGURE 17.5 *A work item in the Inbox* (© SAP AG)

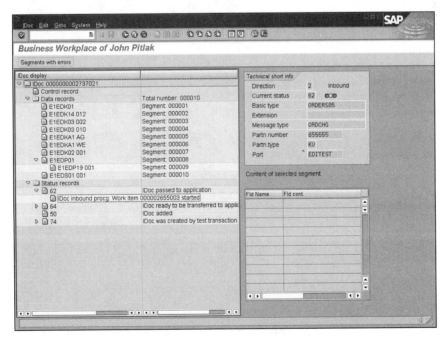

FIGURE 17.6 *An IDoc displayed via the work item* (© SAP AG)

4. Use this P.O. number to locate the sales order created in the system.

5. For each sales order item, compare the quantity field in the sales order to the value in the MENGE field in the E1EDP09 segment. If the values are acceptable, go to the sales order change transaction and manually apply those changes.

6. If any changes are unacceptable, delete the IDoc, as shown in Figure 17.7.

Verifying the Output

Verifying an inbound process via workflow occurs when a work item appears in the Inbox of the responsible user. You can additionally verify the IDoc contents by using any of the IDoc display tools. The status record with a status code of 62 indicates success. If you experience problems in the process, use the troubleshooting guide in Chapter 12, "EDI Process Troubleshooting and Recovery," to determine the cause of the problem, and then restart the process as necessary.

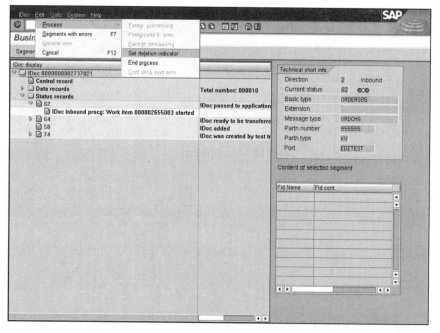

FIGURE 17.7 *Rejecting an inbound sales order change IDoc for further processing* (© SAP AG)

Summary

An inbound process via workflow incorporates human intervention. This approach is useful for incoming transactions that can negatively affect your business logistics.

Implementation of the process via workflow requires the same methodology as other transactions. Additionally, this type of inbound process involves a design and development phase in which you develop a single-step task or a multi-step workflow that replaces the posting module. The inbound IDoc is transferred to the workflow. This step creates a work item that is transferred to a responsible agent, who then executes it and displays the results. If satisfied, the agent can continue with the processing; if not satisfied, the agent can purge the process.

SAP does not provide standard workflows for the inbound EDI process. To model yours, however, you can use some of the tasks that exist for other processes. The workflow environment is like a programming environment, and you can develop very sophisticated workflow processes for your incoming IDocs.

SECTION TWO

ALE

PART VI

ALE Basics

Chapter 18

Introduction to Distributed Systems

ALE (*Application Linking and Enabling*) is SAP's technology to support distributed yet integrated processes across several SAP systems. In this chapter, you will learn what a distributed process is, why there is a need for distributed processing, why some of the existing technologies do not suffice, and how SAP provides a distributed environment. Distributed systems is a highly technical topic in computer science, but this chapter covers the concept from a business standpoint.

An Introduction to the Distributed Process

A *distributed process* is one in which part of a business process is carried out on one system and part on another. For example, consider the sales and distribution process in SAP. The sales process that performs all the sales-related activities—such as storing a sales order, calculating delivery dates, checking for availability, performing credit checks, and calculating price—could be carried out on one SAP system. The shipping process that performs shipping-related activities—such as determining the shipping point, creating deliveries, picking goods, calculating the shortest route, determining the cheapest mode of transportation, and performing goods issue—could be carried out on another SAP system.

The two systems would exchange data with each other at appropriate points to stay synchronized. SAP provides several tools to keep the systems synchronized at the technical level. In addition, business procedures are often required to keep the systems synchronized.

Reasons for Distributing Processes

Why not stay with an integrated system? Distributing a process does not enhance any application functionality; in fact, it often reduces functionality. So, why distribute?

Geographic Location

The first wave of companies to implement SAP consisted of large corporations with operations in several parts of the world. Typically, manufacturing units are strategically located to take advantage of cheap labor or to provide local distribution. These units tend to operate autonomously and don't like to depend on a distant central system. Time differences and cultural differences intensify the problems. If a manufacturing unit is located in Japan, the time difference requires round-the-clock support from the United States. In the real world, cultural and language differences are also issues.

In addition to business issues, technical considerations such as network availability and bandwidth play a major role in distributing SAP systems. High network availability, which is no longer an issue for developed countries, cannot be guaranteed in developing countries, where network outages are frequent. It is not uncommon for a dedicated link to be down for half a day. The bandwidth required to support an enterprise application over a wide area network is also a concern. Because several applications use the same network, the response time for a simple transaction can be slow. Therefore, it becomes necessary to have a dedicated system for each geographical area in which a company does business.

Consolidation

A company can have several business units that share some common resources. For example, a company with several sales operations could share a common warehouse and shipping system. In such a case, the warehouse and distribution application could reside on one SAP system and sales applications could reside on another.

System Capacity

System capacity—such as database size, memory requirements, the number of concurrent users, and network bandwidth—can force you to split a system regardless of geography. Although major improvements in speed and database capacity have been achieved, system capacity remains an issue for large corporations that have very high transaction volumes.

Mission-Critical Applications

Mission-critical applications, such as those for manufacturing and distribution, cannot afford frequent downtime due to system maintenance activities. If all business functions reside on one system, the number of such outages and activities can increase. In these situations, deploying such mission-critical applications on a separate system becomes necessary.

Separate Upgrade of Modules

With SAP delivering new modules and enhanced functionality in every release, some business units require the latest release of the SAP system, and others continue to work with an older release. For example, assume that a company has gone live with all modules in release 3.1G. The sales and marketing division is interested in the customer service module available in release 4.0. However, that division cannot use the functionality until the next implementation, when the entire company moves to release 4.0, which requires complete verification and testing of the system before it can be deployed. In such situations, the ability to upgrade a module without worrying about compatibility issues with other modules is highly desirable.

Data Security

If your organization is involved in a sensitive project for the government, you can be required to separate the classified information from the unclassified. Companies often choose to create a separate instance that is linked to the unclassified instance via ALE.

Political and Business

Other reasons—such as the autonomy of a business unit and subsidiaries, completely different business models, corporate culture, and politics—can cause a company to split a system. Such non-technical factors are the most common reasons for businesses to deploy distributed systems.

Existing Technologies for Data Distribution

By now you should be convinced that businesses have legitimate non-technical needs for distributing processes. In this section, you will learn about some of the data distribution capabilities offered by major database vendors, and why they might not be sufficient. The various technologies or techniques offered by database vendors are based on the structure of data, not the business meaning or semantics of the data. The following sections describe common data-replication techniques.

Disk Mirroring

Disk mirroring is like a disk copy. Changes occurring in a database are simultaneously propagated to another disk, which maintains a mirror image of the main disk's contents. This purely technical copy can be used for creating a repository for a DSS (*Decision Support System*), which requires the most recent data for evaluation. This technique has a severe effect on the OLTP (*Online Transaction Processing*) system and cannot encapsulate business rules for copying only specific data for an organization.

Online Distribution Using the Two-Phase-Commit Protocol

Online distribution enables you to maintain a distributed database in which enterprise data is managed across multiple database servers connected via a network. The database design dictates where a table resides, and the database management system manages queries and updates these tables. The two-phase-commit protocol guarantees that related tables across systems are updated in one logical unit of work. This process is useful to circumvent problems with database size. However, the technique cannot be used to split tables. For example, you cannot specify that a material master for your Asian subsidiary should be created on system B, but a material master for the U.S. unit should be created on system A. Segregation based on the semantics of data is not possible.

Distributed Updates to Replicas

In this technique, the system enables you to maintain redundant data across multiple systems. An owner of the data is defined, and the owner or the holder of a copy can update the data. If changes are made to a copy, changes are first propagated to the owner, from whence they again flow down to the replicas. Conflicts can occur because of simultaneous updates to the owner and replica copies. Other issues can arise—including the need for a homogeneous data model (the database structure is required to be the same), network load, managing deadlocks, synchronization in case of network failure, and long query-processing times. This technique also requires the same version of database and operating system components on the systems involved in the process.

Distributed SAP Systems

Now you're convinced that it's important to have distributed systems, and you know that the techniques offered by database management systems have limitations. What's next? In this section, you will learn how SAP faced the challenge of developing a distributed environment and what solutions the SAP environment provides.

SAP's Challenge for a Distributed Environment

The challenge was to develop a solution to meet the following requirements.

◆ A system that understands the syntax and semantics of the data. It was important from the very beginning to base the distribution of data on business rules, not on database replication techniques.

◆ Distributed systems that can maintain their autonomy while being integrated as one logical SAP system. The systems should be able to operate independently and support local processing of transactions and data.

◆ Distributed systems that can handle different data models. A local implementation should be able to customize the system to meet its local needs.

◆ Receiving systems that can handle their own problems and not tie up the sending system, and vice versa.

◆ Systems that can maintain continued operation in spite of network failure. Changes made to either system should be synchronized after the network connection is restored.

◆ A sound technology and methodology that can be used in all distribution scenarios.

SAP's Answer for a Distributed Environment

SAP introduced ALE as its initiative to support a distributed yet integrated environment. ALE allows for efficient and reliable communication between distributed processes across physically separate SAP systems to achieve a distributed, yet integrated, logical SAP system.

ALE is not based on any database replication techniques. It is based on application-to-application integration using messaging architecture; a message defines data that is exchanged between two processes. IDocs are containers that hold data exchanged between the two systems. IDocs constitute a major component of the ALE process. ALE provides a distributed environment with the benefits described in the following sections.

Integration with Non-SAP Systems

ALE architecture is independent of the participating systems, allowing SAP to use the techniques used for SAP-to-SAP communication to communicate with non-SAP systems. This breakthrough is a major advantage for ALE. In fact, you will find more third-party applications integrated with SAP using ALE than distributed SAP systems.

Reliable Distribution

The ALE technology supports guaranteed delivery, which means that an application sending a message does not have to worry about network problems or connection failures. The application can concentrate on the business logic. After the application generates a message and a correct receiver is determined, the message is delivered to the recipient. If there are network problems, the message is buffered, and when the network is restored, buffered messages are delivered. The system also guarantees that a message is not delivered twice.

Release Upgrade

Any of the distributed systems can be upgraded to a newer release of the SAP system without affecting the existing functionality. The ALE layer ensures backward compatibility of messages exchanged between systems. Thus, in the sample scenario mentioned earlier, the sales system could be upgraded without requiring an upgrade of the shipping system.

Autonomy

SAP systems connected via ALE are loosely coupled, but they provide a high level of business integration. The systems can operate independently if network problems or maintenance on one of the systems disrupts the connection. Each system maintains its own data and applications. The systems are administered separately, and various maintenance tasks can be carried out on an independent basis without affecting the partner system.

 CAUTION

It is important to understand that keeping the systems synchronized is not an easy task. It's a challenge, and companies have developed numerous procedures to keep the systems synchronized. Maintaining a poorly designed distributed system can be a nightmare.

The Provisions of the Standard System

Out of the box, the standard system provides several preconfigured distribution scenarios and master data that are enabled for distribution. You can find a list and details of these scenarios in the SAP R/3 Library, and further information is available on the SAP Labs Web site at http://www.saplabs.com.

Preconfigured Distributed Process Scenarios

In the various application modules, SAP provides preconfigured scenarios, based on the most commonly deployed distributed applications. SAP has already identified process boundaries, optimized these scenarios, and defined various IDocs that must be exchanged to keep the distributed systems integrated. Examples of these include a distributed sales and shipping system, central contracts and distributed purchasing, distributed accounting, distributed cost center accounting, and profit center accounting.

Preconfigured Distributed Application Scenarios

When it comes to distributed applications, SAP also permits third-party applications to be integrated with SAP, using ALE and IDocs. SAP provides a predefined IDoc interface that defines "what" and "when" for the IDocs exchanged between the applications. Several standard interfaces exist in the system; for example, the PP-POI (*Production Planning–Production Optimization Interface*) is used to interface with third-party production-planning optimization software products.

Preconfigured Master Data Scenarios

To support various scenarios, several master data objects in the SAP system have been enabled for ALE, including the customer master, the vendor master, the material master, profit centers, cost centers, and G/L accounts. Master data is critical information that is shared across several applications in a company. Companies deploy different strategies for the maintenance and distribution of such information.

Summary

Businesses need a distributed environment for a variety of business and technical reasons, such as autonomy of business, geographic location, and network availability. Database vendors provide a means for distributing data across several systems. The drawback to these solutions is that they understand the structure of the data but not the semantics. ALE was designed to provide a distributed yet integrated environment that does not suffer from the problems associated with database distribution.

SAP ALE provides standard scenarios for distributing processes across multiple SAP systems, distributed application scenarios to interface with third-party products, and distributed master data scenarios to support distributed processes and distributed applications.

Chapter 19

**Introduction to
ALE Technology**

In the previous chapter, you learned about distributed systems and how ALE is the basis for distributing processes in SAP. ALE technology supports all technical aspects of distributed processes, from the generation of IDocs in the sending system to the posting of IDocs in the destination system. This chapter looks at ALE technology and its architecture and components. It also provides a brief overview of IDocs and examines system tools that support distributed processing.

ALE Architecture

First, you will examine the process flow used to exchange data between distributed systems in ALE architecture. It consists of an outbound process, an inbound process, and an exception-handling process.

The Outbound Process

The outbound ALE process in SAP (see Figure 19.1) sends data to one or more SAP systems. At a very high level, an outbound process involves four steps.

1. **Identify the need for sending an IDoc**. This step can occur immediately upon creating an application document, can relate to a change to a master data object, can be user initiated, or can simply be a point in a process that necessitates the exchange of data. The outbound ALE process for the IDoc data is started. For example, when a material master is created, it consults the ALE layer to determine whether any system is interested in the data. If so, the ALE layer starts the process to send material master data to the interested party.

2. **Generate the master IDoc**. The document or master data to be sent is read from the database and formatted into an IDoc format. This IDoc is called a *master IDoc*. At this point, think of IDoc as yet another format in which a document can be represented. You know how a date can be stored in different formats, so imagine the date as a document with three components: day, month, and year. You can represent the date as MM/DD/YYYY, the standard American way. To make the information meaningful to a German business partner, though, you have to represent

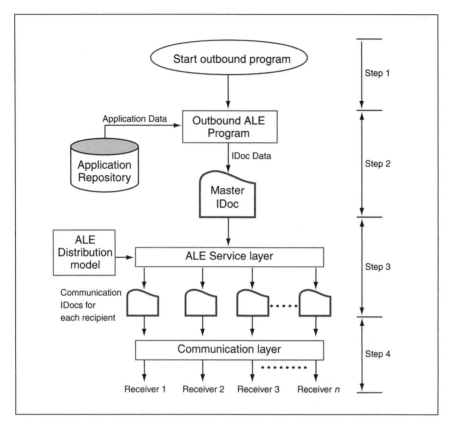

FIGURE 19.1 *The process flow for an outbound ALE process*

the date as DD.MM.YY. IDocs are based on a similar concept of representing one set of data in various ways. The data in the application document format is suitable for application modules, screens, and internal programs. The same data in an IDoc format is suitable for exchange with external systems.

3. **Generate the communication IDoc**. The ALE service layer generates a separate IDoc from the master IDoc for each recipient who is interested in the data. Separate IDocs are generated because each recipient might demand a different version or a subset of the master IDoc. These recipient-specific IDocs are called *communication IDocs* and are stored in the database. The recipients are determined from a customer distribution model that maintains a list of messages exchanged between two systems and their direction of flow.

NOTE

Communication IDocs are stored in the database, but the master IDoc is not. The master IDoc is kept in memory buffers until communication IDocs are generated.

4. **Deliver the communication IDoc**. This step delivers IDocs to the appropriate recipients using an asynchronous communication method. This allows the sending system to continue its processing without having to wait for the destination system to receive or process the IDoc.

The Inbound Process

The inbound process receives an IDoc and creates a document in the system. At a very high level, the inbound process can be seen as a sequence of steps (see Figure 19.2).

1. **Store the IDoc in the database**. First, an IDoc is received in the system and stored in the database. Then, the IDoc goes through a basic integrity check and syntax check. If everything is fine, the next step is performed.

2. **Invoke the posting module**. The control information in the IDoc and configuration tables are read to determine the posting program. The IDoc is then transferred to its posting program.

3. **Create the document**. The posting program reads the IDoc data and then creates a document in the system. The results are logged in the IDoc.

Exception Handling via Workflow

The preceding steps describe a success path. However, exceptions can occur at any point in the outbound or the inbound process. Depending on where they occur, these exceptions can be of different types, such as network problems or data problems. The type of error determines who is responsible for handling it. Workflow provides the flexibility to determine the correct person(s) at run time and to inform them in a timely manner.

Each person responsible receives a work item that can be executed to display the error and diagnose the problem. Errors are fixed outside workflow, and then the process can be restarted from the point of failure.

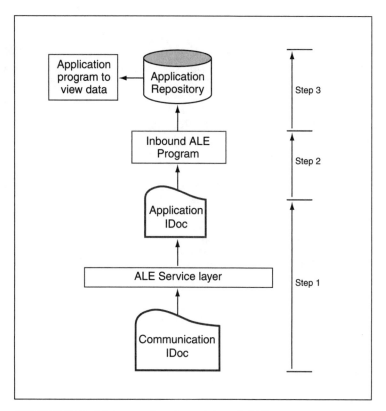

FIGURE 19.2 *The process flow for an inbound ALE process*

An Overview of IDocs

An *IDoc* is a container that is used to exchange data between any two processes. The document represented in an IDoc is independent of the complex structure SAP uses to store application data. This type of flexibility enables SAP to rearrange its internal structure without affecting the existing interfaces.

The word *IDoc* is used very loosely in the IDoc interface. It represents an IDoc type and/or IDoc data, depending on the context in which the word is used. An IDoc type represents the IDoc's definition component, which defines the structure and the format of the data being exchanged. IDoc data can be seen as an instance of an IDoc type.

IDoc Types

IDocs were originally designed for the EDI interface, but now they are used in several applications, including ALE. An IDoc type structure can consist of several segments, and each segment can consist of several data fields. The IDoc structure defines the syntax of the data by specifying a list of permitted segments, an arrangement of the segments, and any mandatory segments. Segments define a set of fields and their format.

Instantiated IDocs

An IDoc is an instance of an IDoc type and consists of three types of records (see Figure 19.3).

♦ **One control record**. Each IDoc has only one control record. The control record contains all the control information about an IDoc, including the IDoc number, the sender and recipient information, and information such as the message type it represents and IDoc type. The control record

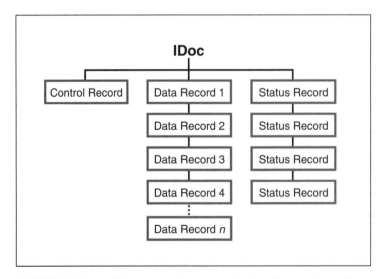

FIGURE 19.3 *An IDoc's internal structure, showing the control record, data records, and status records*

structure is the same for all IDocs and is defined by SAP. The field values can vary.

♦ **One or many data records**. An IDoc can have multiple data records, as defined by the IDoc structure. Segments translate into data records, which store application data, such as purchase order header information and purchase order detail lines.

♦ **One or many status records**. In most cases, multiple status records exist in an IDoc. When status records are processed, they are attached to an IDoc as the IDoc achieves different milestones. At every milestone, a status code, date, and time are assigned. Status records help you determine whether an IDoc is in error. Several tools are available to view the IDocs and their status records.

 NOTE

For more on IDocs, see Chapter 29, "IDocs from the Outside," and Chapter 30, "IDocs on the Inside."

Multiple Messages per IDoc Type

A *message* represents a specific type of document transmitted between two partners. Orders, order response, material master, and customer master are examples of messages. In SAP, an IDoc can be used to represent several messages or business documents. Of course, the messages must be logically related. For example, the orders IDoc (ORDERS05) is used for several messages, including orders (ORDERS), order response (ORDRSP), and order change (ORDCHG).

Also, consider an example in which an IDoc type represents all possible information about an employee, as shown in Figure 19.4. This IDoc is being used to send separate messages to two separate applications. One message is Employee Salary Information, and the other message is Employee Security Information. The difference between the messages is the set of segments used.

FIGURE 19.4 *Multiple messages per IDoc*

Special Features of Data Distribution

ALE technology includes special features for managing data exchanged between two systems. These features provide a functionally rich interface for distributing data, and include

- ◆ **Reduced IDocs.** In standard scenarios, a data object such as a material master is exchanged between two systems to its full extent. In your implementation, you might not be interested in distributing the full set. You can reduce an IDoc so that it contains only the desired information. This process is called *reducing an IDoc type*. For example, the material master IDoc (MATMAS02) is delivered with information on all possible views of a material master. If one of the business units in your company does not implement production planning, at definition time you can create a subset of the IDoc type to eliminate the production-planning information. This step helps to reduce the size of the IDoc.

◆ **Filtering**. The filtering technique creates a subset of data at run time. Filtering can remove certain segments from an IDoc or a complete IDoc for distribution to a specific system.

◆ **Conversion**. The conversion technique converts data in certain fields of the IDoc (for example, Company Code) from their local meaning to a global meaning for distribution.

◆ **Version change**. IDocs and segments are version-controlled. The system can be configured to distribute a specific version of an IDoc or a segment to a destination system. For example, if you've upgraded the sales system from version 30A to 31G, but the shipping system continues to operate on 30A, you can configure the system to generate version 30A segments for the shipping system.

NOTE

The filtering, conversion, and version changes can also be done by a receiving system. See Chapter 23, "Distributing Master Data," for more details.

Tools

To support a distributed environment, SAP provides several tools to configure, test, and monitor distributed systems. Also, SAP provides development tools to enhance a scenario or create a new scenario from scratch. You can find these tools in several places.

◆ **The ALE area of the SAP Reference IMG**. Located under Basis Components, Distribution (ALE). The ALE configuration tools are located here. You can also reach them through transaction SALE. In versions prior to 4.6, the ALE configuration tools are located under Cross-Application Components.

◆ **The ALE main menu**. Located in the SAP standard menu under Tools, ALE. All administrative and operational tools are located here. The various tools are also grouped under submenus, which you reach by entering their names in the command box while you are at the SAP standard menu. These submenus are

- **BALE**. Administrative and monitoring tools
- **BALD**. Development tools
- **BALA**. Distribution in applications
- **BALM**. Master data distribution

 NOTE

Prior to SAP version 4.6, you reach the ALE tools via transactions BALE, BALD, BALA, and BALM, and configuration through SALE. However, the organization and content of these has been changed to varying degrees in version 4.6.

Configuration Tools

Configuration tools are provided to set up communication links and to model distribution scenarios between the distributed systems. See Part VIII, "Configuring the ALE Interface," for complete details on the options and how to carry out the configuration process.

◆ **Modeling a distribution scenario**. A distribution scenario is represented in a customer distribution model. It identifies the systems involved, the list of messages exchanged between the systems, and the owner of specific data.

◆ **Communication link**. A communication link and the mode in which data will be exchanged must be established between the systems involved in the process. You accomplish this communication link by creating RFC (*Remote Function Call*) destinations, port definitions, and partner profiles. Configuration tools are also used for custom scenarios, to make the components known to the system.

Testing Tools

Several tools are available to test individual component processes such as creating and posting IDocs, checking the validity of communication links, and handling exceptions. These are discussed in Chapter 26, "Testing the ALE Interface."

Monitoring Tools

When you start executing any ALE process, IDocs are generated in the system. They serve as a focal point for the logging of information. Several tools enable you to view IDocs in different ways and to display the logged information. The status of processing in the receiving system can also be monitored from the sending system. For a discussion of these tools, refer to Chapter 11, "Monitoring the Interface."

Development Tools

If you decide to create custom ALE scenarios, you will need several tools at different stages of your development.

- ◆ **A business analysis tool**. SAP provides the business navigator tool for analyzing existing business processes in SAP. You can use this business analysis tool to study the process flow or component view of a process.
- ◆ **An IDoc development tool**. Soon after you finish your analysis and identify data that is to be exchanged, you will create IDocs for custom scenarios. SAP provides the IDoc editor, which you can use to extend existing IDocs or develop new IDocs.
- ◆ **Process extension function modules**. To enable your process for ALE, you must program it using ALE services. The ALE service layer provides several function modules that act as an interface for using the ALE services. For a discussion of these tools, refer to Section Three, "IDocs."

Documentation Tools

IDoc structures are thoroughly documented. You can view their documentation in a report format, which can be printed or downloaded to a file. These reports can help you understand an IDoc's functionality. The use of segments and their fields is clearly documented. Refer to Chapter 30, "IDocs on the Inside," for a discussion of these tools.

Summary

ALE technology is at the heart of distributed processing in SAP. ALE technology encapsulates all the tools and components required to support distributed processing. IDocs are a major component of ALE technology, and they define the structure and format of the data exchanged between two systems. Several tools are available for administrative and development functions in a distributed environment.

An IDoc generally has two programs associated with it: the IDoc generation program and the IDoc processing program. These programs are written to understand the syntax and semantics of data in IDocs.

PART VII

The SAP ALE Interface

Chapter 20

The Outbound ALE Process

This chapter describes the functional and technical details of the process flow for outbound processes, beginning with an overview of the components used in the outbound process. Distributed SAP systems exchange three types of data for achieving a distributed yet integrated environment.

◆ **Transactional data.** Sales orders, purchase orders, contracts, invoices, and G/L postings

◆ **Master data.** The material master, customer master, vendor master, and employee master

◆ **Control data.** Company codes, business areas, plants, sales organizations, distribution channels, and divisions

Transactional and master data are distributed using the ALE interface layer. Control data is transferred using the regular CTS (*Correction and Transport System*) process. For more information on CTS, a good reference is *Basis Administration for SAP* (Prima Tech, 1999).

An Overview of the Outbound Process Components

An outbound process uses the following components to generate an IDoc: a customer model, an IDoc structure, selection programs, filter objects, conversion rules, a port definition, an RFC destination, a partner profile, service programs, and configuration tables. Some of these components—for example, filter objects and conversion rules—are optional, and some of the components—for example, the RFC destination and partner profile—are configurable. For a detailed description of the configuration options within these components, refer to Part VIII, "Configuring the ALE Interface." This chapter focuses on the process flow and its components.

The Customer Model

A customer model is used to model a distribution scenario. In a customer model, you identify the systems involved in a distribution scenario and the messages exchanged between the systems. See Chapter 23, "Distributing Master Data," for details on how to set up a model.

Message Control

Message control is a cross-application technology used in pricing, account determination, material determination, and output determination. The output determination technique of Message control triggers the ALE and EDI outputs for a business document. Message control separates the logic of generating IDocs from the application logic. Refer to Chapter 8, "Configuring Message Control," for complete details on Message control.

Change Pointers

The change pointers technique is based on the change document technique, which tracks changes made to key documents in SAP, such as the material master, customer master, and sales orders. Changes made to a document are recorded in the change document header table CDHDR, and additional change pointers are written in the BDCP table for changes relevant to ALE. See Chapter 23 for details on how to set up change pointers.

IDoc Structure

A message is defined for data that is exchanged between two systems. The message type is based on one or more IDoc structures. For example, if you're going to send material master information to another system, a message type MATMAS is already defined in the system. This message is based on MATMAS01, MATMAS02, and MATMAS03. IDocs form a major component of the ALE and EDI interfaces.

NOTE

A basic overview of IDocs is presented in Chapter 19, "Introduction to ALE Technology." Complete details about IDocs are provided in Section Three, "IDocs." For lists of message types and IDoc types, see the Appendix, "FAQs, User Exits, and Miscellaneous Resources."

Selection Programs

Selection programs, typically implemented as function modules, are designed to extract application data and create a master IDoc. A selection program exists for each message type. A selection program's design depends on the triggering mechanism used in the process. See Chapter 32, "Programming in the IDoc Interface," for complete details on the structure and flow of these programs.

Filter Objects

In a distributed environment, each recipient of data can have different requirements for the data being distributed. Filter objects remove unwanted data for each recipient of data.

The Port Definition

A port is used in an outbound process to define the medium in which documents are transferred to the destination system. ALE uses a tRFC (*Transactional Remote Function Call*) port, which transfers data in memory buffers.

NOTE

The EDI process uses file ports to transfer data to the subsystem in a standard text file format.

The RFC Destination

The RFC (*Remote Function Call*) destination is a logical name used to define the characteristics of a communication link to a remote system on which a function needs to be executed. In ALE, the RFC specifies information required to log on to the remote SAP system to which an IDoc is being sent.

NOTE

The EDI process uses an RFC destination to specify parameters for the communication link to an EDI subsystem. For more information, refer to Chapter 6, "Configuring Basic EDI Components."

The Partner Profile

A partner profile specifies the components used in an outbound process (logical name of the remote SAP system, IDoc type, message type, and tRFC port), an IDoc's packet size, the mode in which the process sends an IDoc (batch versus immediate), and the person to be notified in case of errors.

A partner profile is created for each SAP system with which you communicate, and a record exists for each message sent and received from a system. For example, if you are sending two outbound messages—purchase order (ORDERS) and material master (MATMAS)—to the SHIPPING system, a partner profile will exist for the SHIPPING system. Two outbound records—one for each message type (ORDERS and MATMAS)—will exist in the partner profile.

Service Programs and Configuration Tables

The outbound process, being asynchronous, is essentially a sequence of several processes that work together. SAP provides service programs and configuration tables to link these programs and provide customizing options for an outbound process.

The Process Flow for Distributing Transactional Data

Transactional data is distributed using two techniques: with Message control and without Message control. The technique that a process uses greatly depends on the application area, but the core logic of the selection programs remains the same. The SD (*Sales and Distribution*) and MM (*Materials Management*) applications use Message control to trigger the ALE process. For example, programs for generating IDocs for sales order responses or purchase orders start via Message control. Applications in other areas, such as FI (*Financials*), PP (*Production Planning*), and

HR (*Human Resources*), do not use Message control for transactional data. The core logic of generating IDocs is part of the application logic itself.

NOTE

There is no documented reason to explain why these applications do not use Message control. The informal reason is that Message control technology is very complex, yet generic by nature.

The EDI process is used to exchange business documents such as purchase orders, invoices, and remittance advice with a business partner. It uses both techniques (Message control or no Message control) to send data. ALE uses the same process. In the case of ALE, the remote SAP system is configured as a business partner. The architecture of ALE/EDI processes allows them to be shared. The application logic is separate from the distribution and communication logic.

NOTE

Refer to Chapter 3, "The Outbound EDI Process," for complete details on the process flow for transactional data.

The difference between ALE and EDI process flows occurs at the communication level. The EDI process transmits IDocs to an EDI subsystem using flat file format. The ALE process transmits IDocs to an SAP system via memory, using asynchronous communication. There is no need for an intermediate EDI subsystem because both the sending and receiving SAP systems understand the IDoc format. These minor differences at the communication layer can be understood by referencing the master data distribution, described next. The core program logic for generating IDocs for transactional data and master data is the same.

The Process Flow for Distributing Master Data

Master data between SAP systems is distributed using two techniques: standalone programs and change pointers. The process flows are the same for these two

processes, except for the triggering mechanism that starts the IDoc selection programs. Figure 20.1 shows what occurs at each layer in the process. The technical
flow, shown in Figure 20.2, will help you understand the technical components,
such as service programs, table entries, and parameter values, that are used.

 NOTE

The ALE process flow has certain similarities to EDI processes used for distributing
transactional data without the Message control technique.

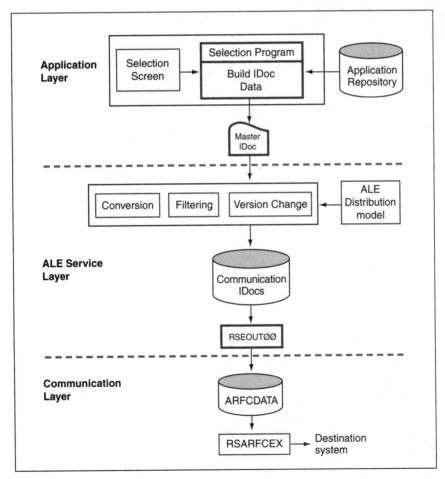

FIGURE 20.1 *The process flow for an outbound process for master data*

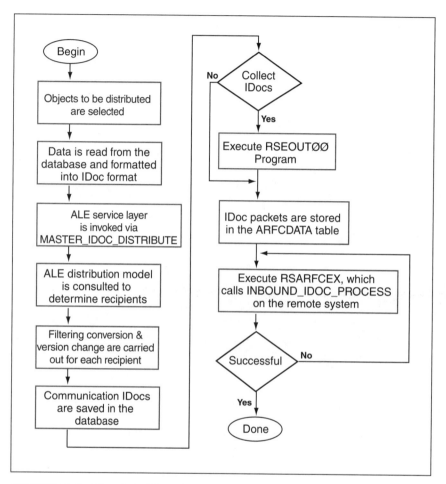

FIGURE 20.2 *The technical flow of an outbound process for master data*

Triggering the Outbound Process via Stand-Alone Programs

Stand-alone programs are started explicitly by a user to transmit data from one SAP system to another. Standard programs for several master data objects exist in SAP. For example, the material master data can be transferred using the RBDSEMAT program or transaction BD10.

NOTE

Stand-alone programs for the master data objects are grouped under the Master Data Distribution area menu (BALM). Prior to version 4.6, they can be reached by using transaction BALE.

The stand-alone programs provide a selection screen to specify the objects to be transferred and the receiving system. The selection screen for the material master object appears in Figure 20.3. After the stand-alone program is executed, it calls the IDoc selection program with the specified parameters. The call to the IDoc selection program is hard-coded in the stand-alone programs. The IDoc selection program can be implemented as a separate function module, but is still physically embedded in the stand-alone program.

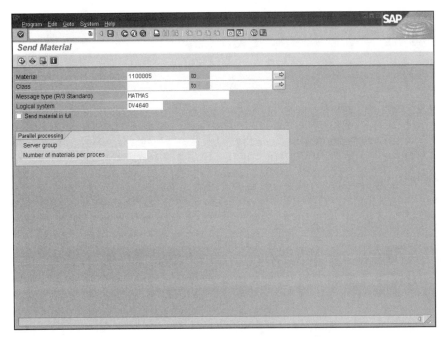

FIGURE 20.3 *The selection screen for distributing material master data* (© SAP AG)

Triggering the Outbound Process via Change Pointers

The change pointer technique is used to initiate the outbound process automatically when master data is created or changed. For example, if a user changes the basic description of a material master or creates a new material, the system automatically generates an IDoc for the material and sends it to the destination system.

A standard program, RBDMIDOC, is scheduled to run on a periodic basis to evaluate the change pointers for a message type and start the ALE process for distributing the master data to the appropriate destination. The RBDMIDOC program reads the TBDME table to determine the IDoc selection program for a message type. Entries in this table also link a message type to the change pointer table. The IDoc selection program is started.

NOTE

Entries in the TBDME table are maintained using transaction BD60.

Processing in the Application Layer

The customer distribution model is consulted to make sure that a receiver has been defined for the message to be transmitted. If not, processing ends. If at least one receiver exists, the IDoc selection program reads the master data object from the database and creates a master IDoc from it. The master IDoc is stored in memory. The program then calls the ALE service layer by using function module MASTER_IDOC_DISTRIBUTE, passing it the master IDoc and the receiver information, if known.

NOTE

The program structure and the logic of IDoc selection programs for the two triggering mechanisms are described using sample programs in Section Three, "IDocs."

Processing in the ALE Interface Layer

Processing in the ALE layer consists of the following steps.

◆ **Receiver determination**. If the receivers are not known, they are determined from the customer distribution model. If a receiver is not found, processing ends. For each receiver identified in this step, the following steps are executed.

1. **IDoc filtering**. If an IDoc filter is specified in the distribution model for a receiver, values in the filter are compared against the values in the IDoc data records. If a data record does not meet the filter criteria, it is dropped.

2. **Segment filtering**. For each sender and receiver combination, a set of segments that are not required can be filtered out.

3. **Field conversion**. Field values in data records are converted by using the conversion rules specified for the segment. Values can be converted to global values or converted to specific values for the receiver. For example, storage location 0001 can correspond to storage location 1000 in the receiving system. The rules specified here are also available in the EIS (*Executive Information System*) module.

4. **Version change for segments**. Segments are version-controlled. A new version of a segment always contains fields from the preceding version and fields added for the new version. Thus, the segment can communicate with a back-level system by blanking out the new fields. Read the version specified in the Seg. Release in IDoc Type field of the partner profile to determine the version of the segment to be generated.

5. **Version change for IDocs**. IDocs, like the segments, are also version-controlled. A new version of an IDoc always contains segments of the preceding version and segments added in the new version. Thus, the IDoc can communicate with a back-level system by deleting segments that do not exist in the version specified. The version is determined from the Basic Type field of the partner profile.

6. **Communication IDocs generated**. The final IDoc generated for a receiver after all the conversions and filtering operations is the communication IDoc. One master IDoc can have multiple communication IDocs, depending on the number of receivers identified and the filter operations performed. Communication IDocs are saved in the SAP database. At this point, a tangible IDoc that can be viewed by using monitoring tools has been created in the system. The IDoc gets a status record with a status code of 01 (IDoc Created).

7. **Syntax check performed**. The IDoc goes through a syntax check and data integrity validation. If errors are found, the IDoc gets a status code of 26 (Error during Syntax Check of IDoc—Outbound); if no errors are found, the IDoc gets a status code of 30 (IDoc Ready for Dispatch—ALE Service).

8. **IDocs dispatched to the communication layer**. In the ALE process, IDocs are dispatched using the asynchronous RFC method, which means that the sending system does not wait for data to be received or processed on the destination system. You read the setting in the Output Mode field of the partner profile to determine the timing of the dispatch. If the mode is set to Transfer IDoc Immed., IDocs are immediately transferred to the communication layer; if not, they are buffered until the next run of dispatch program RSEOUT00. After IDocs have been transferred to the communication layer, they get a status code of 03 (Data Passed to Port OK). This status does not necessarily mean that IDocs have been dispatched to the destination system.

 NOTE

The dispatch timing of IDocs to the communication layer is important from a performance standpoint. Refer to Chapter 28, "Managing ALE Process Performance and Throughput," for details.

Processing in the Communication Layer

To dispatch an IDoc to a destination system, the system reads the port definition specified in the partner profile to determine the destination system, which is then used to read the RFC destination. The RFC destination contains communication settings to log on to the remote SAP system. The sending system calls the INBOUND_IDOC_PROCESS function module asynchronously on the destination system and passes the IDoc data via the memory buffers.

Asynchronous communication means that data to be transferred (IDocs, in this case) and function modules to be invoked are temporarily stored in tables ARFCSSTATE and ARFCSDATA. A separate function module, ARFC_DEST_SHIP, transports the data to the target system, and function module ARFC_EXECUTE executes the stored function module. If a communication problem occurs, the program RSARFCSE is automatically scheduled to run on a periodic basis to process the specific entry. You can turn this automatic option on and off in the tRFC parameters in the RFC destination. If transmission is successful, entries from the ARFCSSTATE and ARFCSDATA tables are deleted. This strategy helps decouple the application from the communication process and assures delivery. If the automatic option is turned off, you can process failed entries on a mass basis using program RSARFCEX.

Exception Handling in the Outbound Process

The process flow described previously represents the success path, but the process can experience problems at any stage. Workflow is integrated in the outbound process to handle exceptions. If an error occurs at any stage, a designated user is notified.

The system uses the Person to Be Notified field in the partner profile to send the error notification. If an error occurs before an IDoc has been created or because the partner profile cannot be read, the EDI administrator is notified. You can find a complete description of workflow in Chapter 9, "Configuring Workflow."

Summary

The outbound process flow for distributing master data is similar to the outbound process for messages dispatched without Message control (see Chapter 3, "The Outbound EDI Process"). The first step is to identify a master data object to be transferred. The master data object to be transferred is made from an explicit request from a user to transfer an object, or from changes made to an object for which change pointers have been configured. The IDoc selection program formats the object into an IDoc format, called a *master IDoc*. The IDoc is then passed to the ALE service layer for filtering, conversion, and version change, which creates a communication IDoc for each recipient identified in the customer distribution model. The communication IDocs are then dispatched to the remote SAP system via an RFC. If errors occur at any point in the process, a person responsible for handling the errors is notified via workflow.

Chapter 21

This chapter describes the functional and technical details of the process flow for inbound processes. Like the outbound process, the inbound process must handle three types of data: transactional data, master data, and control data. Transactional and master data are received via the ALE interface layer. Control data is received via the CTS process. The inbound process for any kind of transactional or master data has two distinct paths for posting the documents from the IDocs.

◆ Via a function module
◆ Via workflow

An Overview of the Inbound Process Components

An inbound process uses IDoc structure, posting programs, filter objects, conversion rules, a partner profile, service programs, and configuration tables to post an application document from an IDoc. The concept behind some of these components is the same as for the outbound process, discussed in Chapter 20, "The Outbound ALE Process."

Posting Programs

Posting programs, which are implemented as function modules, read data from an IDoc and create an application document from it. A posting program exists for each message.

Each posting program is assigned a process code. You have the flexibility of assigning two processing options to a process code. A process code can point to a function module or a workflow. In the standard system, process codes always point to a function module. The option of assigning a workflow to a process code is discussed in Chapter 9, "Configuring Workflow."

For example, the posting program for message type MATMAS is IDOC_INPUT_MATMAS. A four-character process code, MATM, has been assigned to this function module.

Workflow

A workflow represents a sequence of customized steps (dialog and background) to be carried out for a process. The workflow management system is used to model the sequence, identify information required to carry out the steps, and identify the person responsible for the dialog steps.

The Partner Profile

A partner profile specifies the components used in an inbound process (partner number, message type, and process code), the mode in which IDocs are processed (batch versus immediate), and the person to be notified in case of errors.

A partner profile is created for each SAP system with which you communicate, and a record exists for each inbound message received from a remote SAP system. For example, if two inbound messages, a purchase order (ORDERS) and material master (MATMAS), are received from the SALES system, a partner profile exists for the SALES system, and two inbound records—one for each message type (ORDERS and MATMAS)—exist in the partner profile.

Process Flow for the Inbound Process via a Function Module

In this process, IDocs are received from another system and passed to the posting function modules directly. Figure 21.1 shows the processing that occurs in each layer of the inbound process. The technical flow, shown, in Figure 21.2 explains the technical components, such as programs, table entries, and parameter values, used.

 NOTE

The process flow in this case is very similar to the inbound process for EDI, except for the mode in which IDoc data is transferred to the ALE/EDI layer. In EDI, IDoc data is transferred using files, whereas in ALE the IDoc is transferred using memory.

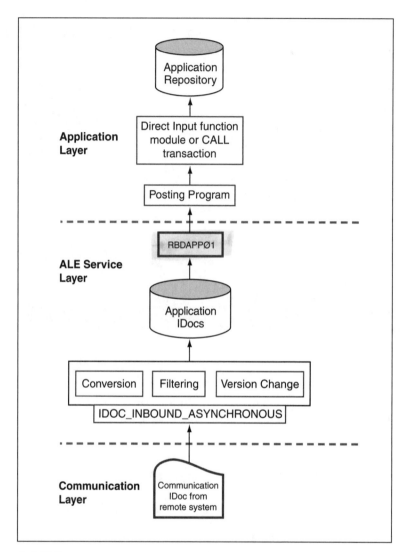

FIGURE 21.1 *The inbound process using a direct function module*

 NOTE

The function module IDOC_INBOUND_ASYNCHRONOUS is used to process version 4.x IDocs. For version 3.x IDocs, use function module INBOUND_IDOC_PROCESS.

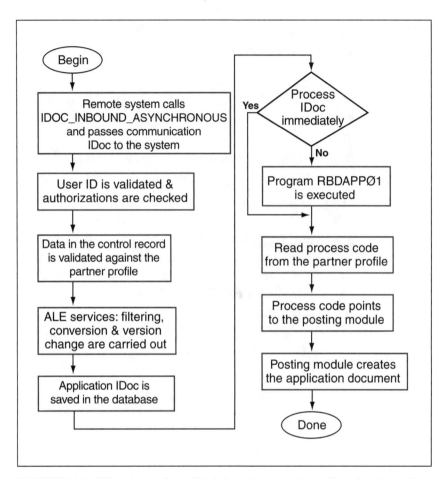

FIGURE 21.2 *The technical flow of the inbound process using a direct function module*

Processing in the Communication Layer

The IDOC_INBOUND_ASYCHRONOUS program, triggered as a result of an RFC from the sending system, acts as the entry point for all inbound ALE processes. The IDoc to be processed is passed as an input parameter. Control is transferred to the ALE/EDI layer.

Processing in the ALE/EDI Interface Layer

The processing in this layer is as follows.

1. **Basic integrity check**. First, a basic integrity check is performed on the control record, such as direction, message type, and IDoc type. The user ID used to start the process is validated to make sure that it has appropriate authorizations.

2. **Segment filtering and conversion**. Next, you can filter out unwanted segments and carry out any required conversion of field values.

3. **The application IDoc is created**. The application IDoc is stored in the database, and a syntax check is performed on it. If the IDoc fails the syntax check, it gets a status code of 60 (Error during Syntax Check of IDoc—Inbound). At this point, a tangible IDoc, which can be monitored via one of the monitoring transactions, is created in the system. The IDoc gets a status code of 50 (IDoc Added).

4. **The IDoc is marked ready for dispatch**. After some housekeeping in SAP, the IDoc is marked ready for processing. It gets a status code of 64 (IDoc Ready to Be Passed to Application), signifying that the follow-on process can continue.

5. **The IDoc is passed to the posting program**. The partner profile table is read. If the value of the Processing field is set to Process Immediately, the IDoc is passed to the posting program immediately, using the program RBDAPP01. If the field is set to Background Processing, the IDoc is buffered in the system until RBDAPP01 is executed explicitly. RBDAPP01 is usually scheduled to run on a regular basis when IDocs are buffered.

Processing in the Posting Module

The process code in the partner profile points to a posting module for the specific message in the IDoc. The posting program, implemented as a function module, either calls a standard SAP transaction by using the Call Transaction command for posting the document or invokes a direct input function module.

The results of execution are passed back via the function module's output parameters. If the posting is successful, an application document is created. The IDoc gets a status code of 53 (Application Document Posted), as shown in Figure 21.3. If the IDoc contains errors, it gets a status of 51 (Error: Application Document Not Posted).

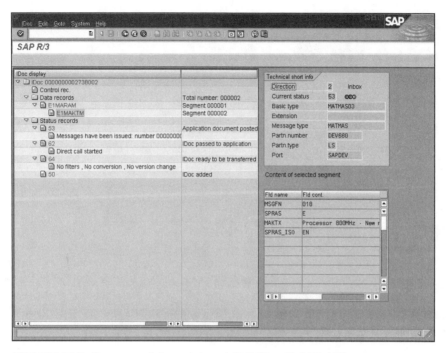

FIGURE 21.3 *Status records for an inbound ALE IDoc* (© SAP AG)

 NOTE

Direct input function modules are preferable to the call transaction approach because of the inherent problems of screen sequence associated with call transaction. (The screen sequence can change with every release.) In Chapter 27, "ALE Process Troubleshooting and Recovery," you will see, however, that it's easier to debug inbound processes that use the call transaction approach.

 TIP

To see whether a standard inbound process uses call transaction or direct input, you execute transaction BD51 and inspect the entries in table TBD51. Entries with a value of 1 or 2 in the Input Type column use the call transaction method, and entries with a value of 0 use a direct input function module.

Process Flow for the Inbound Process via Workflow

In the inbound process using workflow, the IDocs are passed to a single-step task or a multi-step workflow, rather than to a posting function module.

Workflow allows human intervention in the process, to review data before posting it in the system. In ALE, processing an incoming IDoc via workflow doesn't offer much value; doing so in EDI processes can be useful because data comes from an outside source.

 NOTE

In the standard system, the inbound processes use the function module method for posting documents. No process uses workflow. However, you can customize the interface to start workflow. For example, using workflow would facilitate triggering multiple transactions from one inbound IDoc, such as generating an inbound delivery and using it to fulfill a third party order.

The process flow in this case is very similar to the inbound process described in the EDI section, except for the mode in which IDoc data is transferred to the ALE/EDI layer. In EDI, data is transferred using files, whereas in ALE it is transferred using memory. Refer to Chapter 4, "The Inbound EDI Process," for more information on the process flow.

Exception Handling in the Inbound Process

The process flows described previously represent the success path, but the system can experience problems at any stage of the process. The inbound process is more vulnerable to error than the outbound process because the data originates outside the SAP system. Therefore, SAP validates the data by using the same business rules as if the data were entered online.

The workflow system uses the Person to Be Notified field in the partner profile to send the error notification. If an error occurs before an IDoc has been created or because the partner profile cannot be read, the EDI Administrator is notified. See Chapter 9, "Configuring Workflow," for more details on workflow.

Summary

In this chapter, you learned how an inbound process posts an application document from an IDoc. The inbound process is triggered from the remote system via an RFC. The IDoc data is transferred to the receiving system in memory buffers. It goes through basic checks, filtering, and conversion to create an application IDoc. The IDoc is then passed to the posting module, which can be a function module or workflow.

In the standard system, the posting module is always a function module. The posting module then creates the application document, using either the standard call transaction method or a direct input function module. If errors occur at any point in the process, a person responsible for handling the errors is notified via workflow.

PART VII

Configuring the ALE Interface

Chapter 22

Configuring the ALE Infrastructure

A LE-enabled processes and master data objects have to be configured to implement a distributed system. SAP doesn't know how you want to distribute your processes and data, how many systems are involved, and what data you want to exchange between systems. The first task in configuring any ALE scenario is to put the basic ALE infrastructure in place, which is like building a bridge. You must connect the ends before traffic can move over it. The bridge is built once and remains the same, regardless of the type of traffic. You are simply providing the basic infrastructure for two systems to recognize each other and communicate with each other, including logical system names, an RFC destination, and a port definition.

In this chapter, you will learn how to establish ALE communication links between two SAP systems. You will start with some basic settings for IDocs used for housekeeping and administrative purposes, and then you will learn about the communication components. The end of the chapter covers two advanced settings for monitoring the system.

 NOTE

Some of these settings are common with the EDI process because the ALE and EDI processes share the IDoc interface. Therefore, you will notice some repetition as you read.

Making the Configuration Settings

The configuration settings for ALE processes are made in the IMG (*Implementation Guide*) under Basis Components, Distribution (ALE). When describing the configuration options, the following text refers to this path as ALE customizing in the IMG.

TIP

You can also reach the ALE settings directly by executing transaction SALE. This method saves you several keystrokes. You will be spending quite a bit of time in this area, so it's a good idea to explore the options and read the IMG help.

ALE processes also require the basic settings of the IDoc interface, which are carried out from the IMG under Basis Components, Basis Services, IDoc Interface/Electronic Data Interchange. The following text refers to this path as basic settings for IDocs in the IMG when describing the configuration options.

TIP

In versions earlier than 4.6, you'll find the ALE and IDoc IMG settings under Cross-Application Components rather than under Basis Components.

Basic Settings for IDocs

The basic settings for the IDoc interface must be maintained once on each system involved in distributed processing that is not subject to frequent changes. If you have already maintained these settings for the EDI process, you can skip this material.

NOTE

The ALE process uses fewer settings in IDoc customizing than the EDI process does.

IDoc Administration

`Transaction: WE46`

`Path: From the basic settings for IDocs in the IMG, choose IDoc Administration`

In transaction WE46, you assign values to the global variables used in the EDI process, as shown in Figure 22.1.

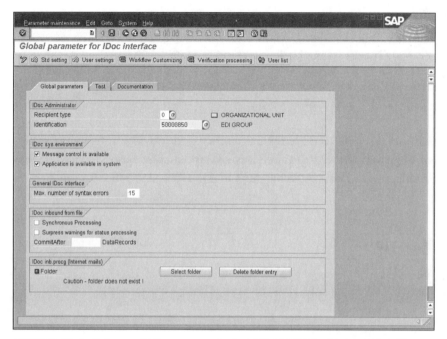

FIGURE 22.1 *Relevant ALE parameters in the EDICONFIG table* (© SAP AG)

The IDoc Administrator parameter specifies the administrator for the IDoc interface at run time. This person or organization is responsible for the integrity of the overall IDoc interface. The workflow system uses this parameter when a technical error occurs in the ALE interface layer, such as an error in reading the partner profile for an incoming IDoc.

You must enter the recipient type (for example, US for user ID, S for position, or O for organizational unit), along with the identification value. See Chapter 9, "Configuring Workflow," for details on all the types of objects you can specify here. For example, if the position with position number 12345678 is assigned as the administrator, the value of the parameter in the Recipient Type field is S, and the value for Identification is 12345678. If a user with user ID AN000001 is the administrator, the value of the parameter in the Recipient Type field is US, and the Identification is AN000001.

TIP

Avoid using a user ID for the IDoc administrator. You should use a more abstract object type, such as position, job, or organizational unit. Doing so will save you the headache of changing the entry whenever a user leaves the company or changes jobs. Positions, jobs, and organizational units tend to be more stable than users.

The General IDoc Interface, Max. Number of Syntax Errors parameter sets the maximum limit on the number of status records created for syntax errors—a good recommendation is five. If your IDoc gets more than five syntax errors in a production environment, something is terribly wrong. Setting this number higher usually does not help you debug the problem; you have to investigate the process more deeply at the source of data.

Communication Settings

This section describes the ALE settings for linking two SAP systems involved in distributed processing. These settings are done once for each system and are independent of the distribution scenario.

NOTE

A separate system does not have to be physically separate. Two clients on the same physical box can be set up to use ALE processes to exchange data.

Maintaining a Logical System

Path: From the ALE customizing in IMG, choose Sending and Receiving Systems, Logical Systems, Define Logical Systems

The systems involved in distributed processing are assigned logical names, which uniquely identify systems in a distributed environment, as shown in Figure 22.2.

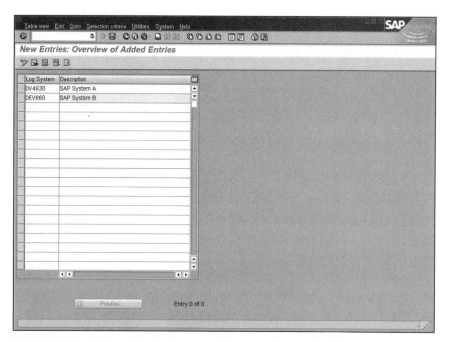

FIGURE 22.2 *Maintaining logical names for systems involved in the ALE process*
(© SAP AG)

The name can have up to 10 alphanumeric characters and must be known to all the systems in the distributed network.

Adopt a naming standard for the logical names of the systems so that they are easily identifiable. Some common naming standards used by companies are

- ◆ **The simple approach**. You can concatenate the SAP instance name with the client number. This simple yet elegant approach uniquely identifies a logical system.

- ◆ **The functional approach**. You can choose names based on the functions carried out on a system, such as SALES or SHIPPING.

- ◆ **The fancy convention**. You can choose names that identify the type of system (legacy or SAP), owning geography (US, ASIA, EUROPE), and function. This naming standard is a hybrid of the simple and functional approaches.

Allocating Logical Systems to the Client

Path: From the ALE customizing in IMG, choose Sending and Receiving Systems, Logical Systems, Assign Client to Logical System

In this step, the logical name of the local system is linked to a client of the SAP system, as shown in Figure 22.3. The link basically establishes a logical name for an SAP client in the distribution process. A one-to-one relationship exists between a logical system and a client. Again, this setting is required on every system involved in the process.

 CAUTION

> Only one person should have the authority to maintain this setting. Because some of the documents created in the FI module record the name of the logical system on which they are created, *this setting should never be changed.* When you retrieve those documents, the system checks for the logical system name.

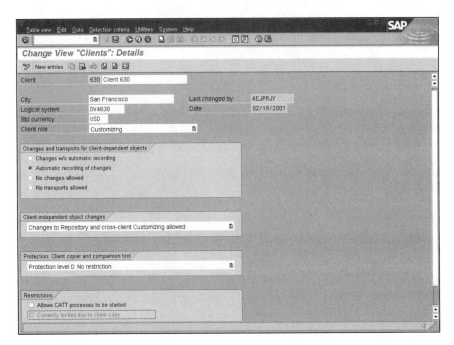

FIGURE 22.3 *Assigning a logical system to a client* (© SAP AG)

Setting Up an RFC Destination

Transaction: SM59

Path: From the ALE customizing in IMG, choose Communication, Define RFC
Destination

In this step, you create an RFC destination on the local system for each remote
SAP system with which you want to communicate. In the RFC destination, you
specify all the information necessary to log on to the remote system to execute
functions remotely, including the host name, the user ID, the password, the client,
the system number, and additional communication settings. Figure 22.4 shows
the RFC settings made in SAP System A (DV4630) to log on to SAP System B
(DEV660). A similar RFC setting will exist on SAP System B with SAP System
A as the RFC destination. A basic prerequisite for the RFC destination is that the
systems should be accessible to each other via TCP/IP or one of the supported
network protocols.

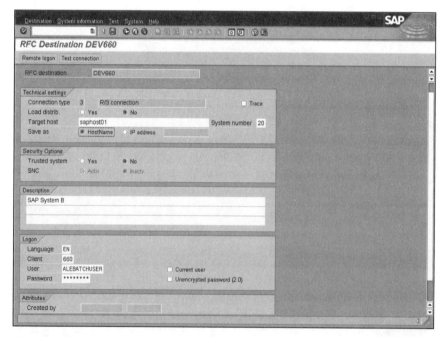

FIGURE 22.4 *RFC destination settings to log on to the remote SAP system* (© SAP AG)

Several types of RFC destinations are available. ALE uses type R/3 connections for communicating with a remote SAP system. Click the Create button to enter attributes for a new RFC destination. Following are the attributes and their meanings.

CAUTION

RFC destinations are not transported. You must maintain them on each system manually.

◆ **RFC Destination**. This entry is a unique name for your RFC destination. You should use the logical name defined for the remote system.

◆ **Connection Type**. Use type 3 to indicate R/3 connections. The ALE process uses type R/3 connections to communicate with a remote SAP system, and the EDI process uses type TCP/IP connections to communicate with the EDI subsystem.

TIP

Press Enter after you enter the type and description of your RFC destination. This step enables the fields necessary for connection type TCP/IP.

◆ **Load Distribution**. This item is useful if you are going to log on to a message server instead of an application server. The message server then decides which application server is least loaded and dispatches the request to the application server. To start, you can select No.

◆ **Target Host**. This item is the TCP/IP host name of the remote system. The target machine can be any application server on your remote system. If you have an account on the remote system, you can find the list of application servers by executing transaction SM51 and looking in the second column, under Host.

- **System Number.** This entry is the system number assigned to the remote SAP system. Your Basis staff can help you with this value. If you have an account on the remote system, log on to the remote system and execute transaction SM51. Under the Server Name column, look at the last two characters of the entry pertaining to your application server. These two digits are your system number for the remote system. You can also determine this value from the SAP logon pad.

- **Logon.** Enter the language, client number, user ID, and password to log on to the remote system. The user ID must have been defined on the remote system.

 CAUTION

This user ID must have all authorizations and should be configured as a background user.

Save your entries, and then test the connection to make sure that the system is accessible. If you get an error, check one of the parameters and make sure that the systems are linked via TCP/IP.

Advanced Settings in the RFC Destination

In addition to the basic settings previously described, you can optionally specify the tRFC options for this RFC destination. The tRFC options control the retry logic when communication errors occur. Refer to Chapter 20, "The Outbound ALE Process," for details on the retry mechanism. Choose Destination, TRFC. This brings up the pop-up window shown in Figure 22.5.

- **Suppress Background Job If Conn. Error.** If this field is blank, the system automatically retries the failed tRFC individually by submitting a background job. Keep in mind that leaving this field blank can severely affect system performance when many messages are exchanged and a connection problem occurs. Therefore, you should select this flag so that the system does not attempt to retry failed connections automatically.

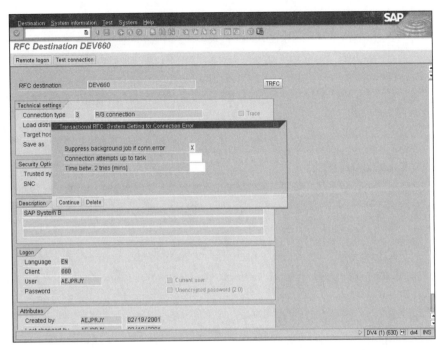

FIGURE 22.5 *tRFC settings for handling connection errors* (© SAP AG)

 NOTE

If you select the Suppress Background Job If Conn. Error field in the tRFC options, you can choose one of the following options to process failed tRFC connections.

- Schedule program RSARFCCP in the background for a destination system. This setting retries all failed tRFC calls for the specific destination.

- Execute transaction SM58 and manually process one entry or multiple entries. This setting is mainly used for debugging.

- Execute program RSARFCEX and selectively execute failed tRFCs.

◆ **Connection Attempts up to Task.** This field specifies the number of attempts the system makes to connect to the remote system before giving up. Using one of the three options just specified then processes the entries.

◆ **Time betw. 2 Tries [Mins].** This field specifies the amount of time to wait between attempts.

The Port Definition

Transaction: WE21

Path: From the ALE customizing in IMG, choose Sending and Receiving Systems, Systems in Network, Asynchronous Processing, Assigning Ports, Define Port

A port defines the medium in which data is exchanged between the two systems. In the ALE process, IDocs are transferred via memory. As of release 4.6, six port types are available.

◆ Transactional RFC (tRFC) ports used for ALE communication

◆ File ports used by EDI

◆ CPI-C ports used to communicate with R/2 systems

◆ Internet ports used to connect with Internet applications

◆ ABAP-PI ports used to process data via the ABAP programming interface

◆ XML ports used to process files in XML format

 CAUTION

For port definitions to be generated automatically, the RFC destination name must be the same as the logical system name.

Port definitions are client-independent objects. The tRFC port used in the ALE process can be generated automatically when you generate partner profiles, or it can be maintained manually.

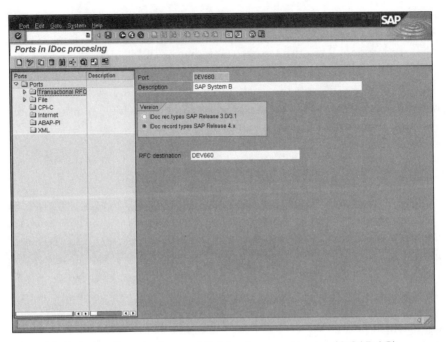

FIGURE 22.6 *Attributes in the port definition for a remote system* (© SAP AG)

A port definition is maintained for each remote system with which your system communicates. Figure 22.6 shows the port definition maintained on SAP System A (DV4630) for SAP System B.

◆ **Port**. Any meaningful name to identify the port uniquely. During automatic generation, SAP assigns it using sequential numbers prefixed with the letter A.

◆ **Description**. Any meaningful description of the port. This attribute is for documentation only.

◆ **Version**. This attribute defines whether IDocs are in the version 3.x format or version 4.x format.

◆ **RFC Destination**. This attribute is the RFC destination maintained in the "Setting Up an RFC Destination" section.

Advanced Settings

This section describes advanced settings that provide an end-to-end view of the state of the system. If you are an ALE novice, you can skip this section; doing so won't have any effect on the ALE process flows. These settings are mainly for obtaining information about the state of the process that is not available with standard settings.

Setting Up Transactional RFC Reporting

Transactional RFC is an asynchronous communication process, meaning that when an IDoc is dispatched, the sender does not wait for the IDoc to be received on the destination system. Control returns as soon as the IDoc is successfully transferred to the communication layer. The IDoc gets a status code of 03 (Data Passed to Port OK). The communication layer must make sure that the IDoc is successfully transferred to the destination system. By looking at an IDoc that has a status code of 03, you cannot say for sure that the IDoc was actually received on the destination system.

A standard program, RBDMOIND, is scheduled or executed online to determine whether the communication was successful. If the IDoc has been dispatched to the destination system, RBDMOIND updates the status of the IDoc to 12 (Dispatch OK); otherwise, the IDoc stays in status 03. The selection screen has the following parameters.

- ◆ **IDoc Creation Date (From)**. This parameter contains the date from which you want to update the status. It selects all IDocs dispatched from this date to the current date.

- ◆ **IDocs per Commit Work**. This parameter specifies the number of IDocs to be checked before a commit is performed. Stick with the default values.

Setting Up Audit Reporting

In the default behavior, after an IDoc is dispatched to a destination system, the sender does not know the state of the process on the destination system. You can configure the system, however, for cross-system reporting. You must model the ALEAUD message between the systems. In the next chapter, you'll learn how to set up various messages exchanged between the systems in the customer distribution model.

Two programs enable cross-system reporting.

- ◆ **RBDSTATE.** This program is scheduled to run periodically on the destination system. It reports the status of incoming IDocs to the sending system, using the ALEAUD message and ALEAUD01 IDoc. This status information is recorded separately from IDoc status information in the audit logs.
- ◆ **RBDAUD01.** This program is executed on the sending system. It analyzes the audit log and displays the output as a report.

The RBDSTATE program returns the following statuses, from the receiving to the sending system.

Table 22.1 Statuses Returned to the Sending System When RBDSTATE Is Run on the Receiving System

Status of IDoc in Receiving System	Status Reported to Sending System via ALEAUD
53 (Application document posted.)	41 (Application document created in receiving system.)
51 (Error: Application document not posted.)	39 (IDoc is in the receiving system.) This status is repeated each time RBDSTATE is run, as long as the IDoc remains in status 51.
68 (Error: No further processing.)	40 (Application document not created in receiving system.)

Summary

The basic IDoc settings for the ALE process establish administrative information for the IDoc interface. The communication settings for the ALE process establish links between two SAP systems so that they can execute any function on each other. These configuration settings are one-time settings you must do at the beginning of the project. The Basis group is likely to carry out some of these settings because doing so involves setting up communication components they typically manage.

Chapter 23

**Distributing
Master Data**

A major use of ALE in an implementation is for the distribution of master data. Companies start with this approach to build very loosely connected, or loosely coupled, distributed SAP systems. *Loosely connected* means that the systems function in a mainly autonomous manner. They can operate independently, without the other being available, for a certain amount of time. This prevents the benefits of distributing the systems from being negated by unacceptable downtime due to the increased complexity of the architecture. This chapter covers distributing master data from one system to another, using the material master object as an example (because of its rich functionality and common use). You will learn to configure the different techniques of distributing master data, and at the end of the chapter you will find some answers to frequently asked questions about master data distribution.

An Overview of Distributing Master Data

This section shows you why distributing data is necessary, what is supported in the standard system, and which techniques are used to distribute master data.

Why Distribute Master Data?

Business units require master data objects such as the material master, vendor master, customer master, cost center, G/L master data, and pricing objects. In a distributed SAP environment, you need to exchange master data with other SAP systems. Companies usually deploy a central SAP system to maintain all the master data in one place, and then they use ALE to distribute the data to other SAP systems. You also need to exchange master data with legacy applications. For example, if you continue to run the production-planning operations on a legacy system, you will exchange several master data objects, such as the material master and material bill, between your SAP system and the legacy system. Thus, distributing master data is necessary in any distributed environment.

ALE is a useful means to distribute data in the following cases.

- **Transferring data from conversion clients to production systems**. Some companies maintain a separate conversion client where data from legacy systems is converted into SAP format. When data is ready, it is used for initial data load into the production systems. ALE can be a useful utility because it requires very minimal setup for distributing master data objects.

- **Transferring master data from production systems to test systems**. After companies go live with SAP, they have the most recent data on the production system. It is often necessary to transfer data using ALE to test development systems or legacy systems.

- **Transferring configuration data**. Configuration data is usually transported using the CTS process. As a special case for cost center grouping, SAP recommends using ALE instead of CTS because it has superior error handling and checks.

Which Master Data Can Be Distributed?

To be distributed, a master data object has to be ALE-enabled. This means that it has an outbound process to generate IDocs and an inbound process to read those IDocs and create master data on the receiving system. Table 23.1 contains a list of commonly distributed master data, with descriptions of each message type.

If your master data is not supported, you should check with SAP to see whether it is planned for future release. If not, you can develop your own distribution scenario by using sample code provided in Section Three, "IDocs."

How Is Master Data Distributed?

There are three ways to exchange master data between systems.

- **Push original copy**. Master data is sent explicitly from one system to another using stand-alone programs. The selection screen allows you to specify object values, the destination system, and the message type. For example, BD10 is used for sending material master data to another system.

- **Push changes**. This is an automated process in which changes made to certain fields of a master data object trigger the process of distributing the object to remote systems. You can customize the fields for which

Table 23.1 Commonly Used Master Data in ALE

Message Type	Description
COACTV	Activity price of cost center and cost element combination
COAMAS	Activity type
COGRP5	Activity type group
BOMMAT	Bill of material (materials)
BOMDAT	Bill of material (documents)
CLSMAS	Classes
CHRMAS	Characteristics
CLFMAS	Classification
COSMAS	Cost center
COGRP1	Cost center group
COGRP2	Cost element group
COELEM	Cost element
DEBMAS	Customer master
GLMAST	G/L account
HRMD_A	HR master and PD-ORG data
MATMAS	Material master
PRCMAS	Profit center
COGRP6	Profit center group
INFREC	Purchasing information record
SRVMAS	Services master
SRCLIST	Source list
CREMAS	Vendor master

changes are to be recorded, which enables you to distribute only the necessary changes. This method provides an automatic and efficient means of keeping the master data synchronized between the systems.

- ◆ **Pull master data**. A system sends a request for a specific master object to be transferred to the requesting system. Because the request is asynchronous, the system does not wait for the object to be transferred. The request is delivered to the sending system, which initiates the process of sending the master data to the requesting system.

Strategies for Distributing Master Data

Master data is critical information shared across several applications. It is important to have a good strategy to allow centralized control yet distributed use. The system offers infinite combinations of ways you can maintain and distribute master data for your organization. The following sections explain two popular strategies.

◆ Central maintenance and distributed use

◆ Distributed maintenance and distributed use

Assume that a company has four plants, PL01–PL04. Material master is to be created for the entire company to provide purchasing information and accounting information. The following sections describe how to implement this scenario using these two strategies.

Central Maintenance and Distributed Use

Master data can be maintained centrally on one system and then distributed to other systems, where it is used for local processes. This simple approach accommodates the needs of most companies. Figure 23.1 shows the data flow.

Users who are responsible for maintaining master data are assigned an account on the central system, for which they maintain the values. Purchasing views for four plants (PL01–PL04), as well as accounting views, are maintained for material MAT01 in the central system. When maintenance is complete, material MAT01 is distributed to all four plants, but each plant gets a view only for its specific plant.

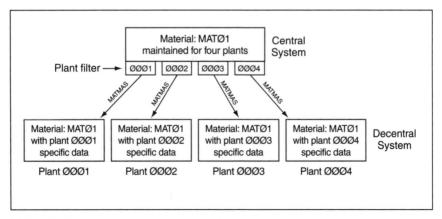

FIGURE 23.1 *Centralized maintenance of master data*

This plant-specific distribution is achieved by setting filters (plant filters) at the IDoc level in the distribution model. The advantages of this simple approach are that there is no unnecessary network load (only the required master data is distributed) and that there are fewer operational and maintenance issues (errors can be monitored and resolved from one system). The disadvantages are that the ownership of data is not clearly defined, the maintenance activities between groups must be coordinated, and users need to log on to a central system.

Distributed Maintenance and Distributed Use

Master data can be initially created on the central system with the minimum amount of information and then maintained on one or more systems, where specific information is added. It is then consolidated in a central reference system, from which it is distributed to the receiving systems (see Figure 23.2).

The data flow steps are as follows.

1. A material, MAT01, is created in the reference system with basic views and is distributed to the financial (FI) and purchasing systems.

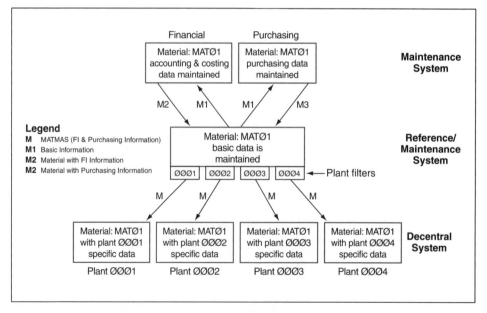

FIGURE 23.2 *Decentralized maintenance of master data* (© SAP AG)

2. Users maintain master data on their local systems for the specific functions. The FI system maintains accounting views for material MAT01, and the purchasing system maintains purchasing views for all plants (PL01–PL04).

3. After maintenance is complete, material MAT01 is sent back to the central system, where additional data can be maintained. Data is then distributed to all four plants but, using plant filters, each plant gets a view only for that specific plant.

The advantages of this approach are that users are grouped by functions and do not have to sign on to a central system, systems are autonomous, and the ownership of data is clearly defined. The disadvantages are that the network can overload (if too much data is transmitted across the systems), there can be more points of failure, and many operational issues must be considered (errors need to be monitored in several places).

The Basic Configuration for Distributing Data

Before you can distribute any data between the systems via ALE, you must put in place the basic infrastructure described in Chapter 22, "Configuring the ALE Infrastructure," and execute the following steps.

1. Maintain a distribution model.

2. Generate a partner profile.

3. Distribute the distribution model.

4. Maintain the workflow settings.

Two systems are used in the following example. System A (logical name DV4630) sends customer master data to System B (logical name DEV660), and System B sends material master data to System A. A distribution model named MASTERDATA will be created on System A and distributed to System B.

Maintaining the Distribution Model

Transaction: BD64

Path: From the ALE customizing in IMG, choose Modeling and Implementing Business Processes, Maintain Distribution Model and Distribute Views

A distribution model is used to model a distributed environment in which you specify messages exchanged between sending and receiving systems. You must create the model on the system that will be the model's owner. This owner is responsible for maintaining the model and distributing it to various systems. Other systems are prohibited from making changes to the model. In the sample scenario, the model MASTERDATA is created on System A, which automatically assigns its own logical system name, DV4630, as the model's owner. You begin by clicking the Create Model View button on the main screen of transaction BD64.

 NOTE

The owning system can be a system other than the sending or receiving system. The only requirement is that the sender and receiver each must have a copy of the model.

Figure 23.3 shows the first screen for creating the model, which contains the following fields.

- ◆ **Short Text**. In this field, you enter a description of the model. It can be any descriptive phrase that helps distinguish the model from others and represents the distribution scenario you are implementing.

- ◆ **Technical Name**. This field contains the name of your distribution model. It can be any meaningful name that represents the distribution scenario you are implementing.

Enter the values and press Enter. On the next screen, you see your new model listed under the Model Views node of the tree display on the left side of the screen. To add a message transfer between two systems, click the model entry to highlight it, and then click the Add Message Type button. A dialog box opens and allows you to enter the sender and receiver systems and the message type, as shown in Figure 23.4. The system allows you to pick any message, including custom-developed messages. This step establishes the sending system, the receiving

FIGURE 23.3 *The initial fields for creating the distribution model* (© SAP AG)

system, and the message exchanged between them. Figure 23.4 shows that the material master (MATMAS) is sent from System B (DEV660) to System A (DV4630).

You can continue to add messages between the sender and receiver. Repeat this step with System A as the sending system, and model the message DEBMAS (the customer master) going to System B using the same model (MASTERDATA).

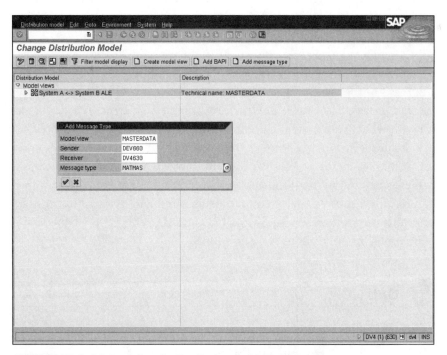

FIGURE 23.4 *Maintaining the distribution model* (© SAP AG)

Here are some important points to keep in mind about the distribution model.

◆ A distribution model is maintained on only one system. It is distributed to other systems for use.

◆ Two models cannot distribute the same message between the same set of senders and receivers.

◆ By default, the client on which you create a model becomes the model's owner. This approach prevents the model from being changed on another client or system.

Generating Partner Profiles

Transaction: BD82

Path: From the ALE customizing in IMG, choose Modeling and Implementing Business Processes, Partner Profiles and Time of Processing, Generate Partner Profiles

Partner profiles can be generated automatically for your partner systems, using transaction BD82. Figure 23.5 shows the selection screen for generating partner profiles. The distribution model and settings in the ALE tables TBD52 and EDIFCT are read to generate partner profiles and port definitions. The partner profiles generated using this utility get you started quickly. However, you will need to fine-tune partner profile parameters later for production purposes because the utility assigns the same values for parameters, such as person to be notified, packet size, and distribution mode. This process generates a partner profile for each system with which your system communicates. Outbound records are created in the partner profile for each outgoing message, and inbound records are created for each incoming message. You can execute transaction WE20 to view the partner profiles generated by this transaction. Refer to Chapter 7, "Configuring Partner Profiles," for details on each field in the outbound and inbound records of a partner profile. A good understanding of the partner profile is very beneficial in analyzing problems later in the execution time.

 CAUTION

This utility does not generate partner profiles for messages based on extended IDocs. Complete details on maintaining partner profiles manually are presented in Chapter 7, "Configuring Partner Profiles."

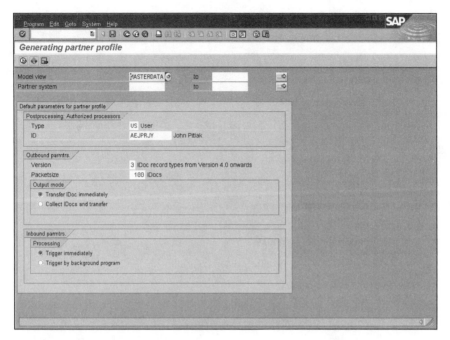

FIGURE 23.5 *The selection screen for generating partner profiles automatically*
(© SAP AG)

This step is to be carried out on all the systems involved in the process. In the example, this step is performed on both System A and System B. However, before you execute this program on System B, that system needs to have a copy of the model.

Distributing the Model

Transaction: BD64

Path: From the ALE customizing in IMG, choose Modeling and Implementing Business Processes, Maintain Distribution Model and Distribute Views

When the maintenance of a distribution model is complete, you can distribute the model to the systems involved in the distributed process. Proceed from the transaction BD64 tree display by clicking the model to highlight it. Then select Edit, Model View, Distribute from the pop-up menus, as shown in Figure 23.6. The system displays a list of logical systems, and System B is already selected. Click the Enter icon to execute the distribution process.

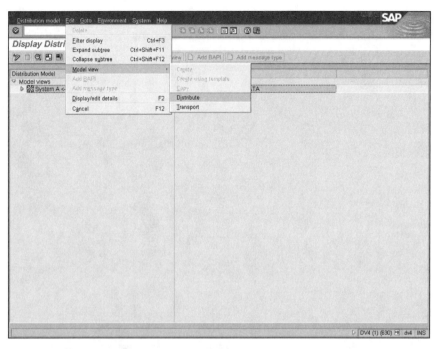

FIGURE 23.6 *Distributing the model* (© SAP AG)

Maintaining Workflow Settings

Workflow is used for sending a work item to the person responsible for errors in the distribution process. The person to be notified is determined from the partner profile. Complete details on how to set up workflow for error notification are discussed in Chapter 9, "Configuring Workflow." This step is to be carried out on all the systems involved in the process. In the example, this step is performed on Systems A and B.

Techniques for Distributing Master Data

Three techniques are used for exchanging master data between systems: push master data, distribute changes, and pull master data.

The Push Approach

For the push approach, data is transferred explicitly from one system to another. This approach does not require any additional configuration settings, so you are ready to test and execute the process.

Testing the Configuration

After you do all the necessary configuration settings, you should carry out sanity tests and process flow tests for the inbound and outbound processes, as described in Chapter 26, "Testing the ALE Interface." The tests help you pinpoint any problems in the configuration.

Executing the Process

Transaction: BD10

Path: From the ALE main menu, choose Master Data Distribution, Cross-Application, Material, Send

The system displays the selection screen (see Figure 23.7) where you can specify different parameters for distributing material master data. The fields have the following purposes.

- **Material**. The material master you want to send. You can select a single value or multiple values by using the range button (the arrow) on the far right of the field.

- **Class**. An advanced option that allows you to send materials based on classification (discussed later in this chapter). You can leave the Class field blank for the moment.

- **Message Type (R/3 Standard)**. The message type associated with the material master object. The standard message type is MATMAS.

- **Logical System**. The system to which you want to send the material master data. If you leave this field blank, the system searches all distribution models and determines the receivers for the message.

- **Send Material in Full**. An indicator also used to create IDocs for the links a material has to other objects (for example, to classification). The objects of these links must exist in the receiver system. You can leave this unchecked for this example.

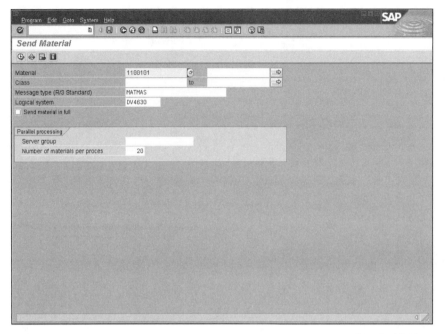

FIGURE 23.7 *The selection screen for distributing material master data* (© SAP AG)

◆ **Server Group**. Also an advanced option, used to control the throughput of the process by executing the process in parallel. Chapter 28, "Managing ALE Process Performance and Throughput," discusses this option, but for the current example you can leave this field blank.

◆ **Number of Materials per Process**. Also an advanced option, used to control throughput by specifying the number of materials processed during parallel processing. This option is also discussed in Chapter 28, but for the current example you can leave this field blank.

Enter the desired values and click the Execute button. The system starts executing the IDoc generation process. At the end, it displays the number of communication IDocs generated. If errors occur in the process, refer to Chapter 27, "ALE Process Troubleshooting and Recovery," for a troubleshooting guide to find the cause of the problem quickly and fix it.

> **CAUTION**
>
> If you leave the Material field blank, the system assumes that you want to send all the materials. You should enter specific values for the materials unless you really want to transfer every single material.

Viewing the IDocs

You can display IDocs by using the IDoc monitoring tools (transaction WE02 or WE05). Refer to Chapter 11, "Monitoring the Interface," for details on how to interpret the information displayed in the IDocs. The IDoc contains the material master data to be transferred to the receiving system. You should check the IDoc status to determine the state of the IDoc. If everything works successfully, the IDoc will be in status 03 (Data Passed to Port OK). If your IDoc is not in status 03, you should refer to Chapter 27 for a troubleshooting guide to find the cause of the problem quickly and fix it. You should also log on to the receiving system and verify that an IDoc was created on the receiving system as well. Execute transaction MM03 to view material master data on the receiving system.

Distributing Changes

In this section, you will learn about the change pointer technique for distributing master data. First, you will learn how the process works, and then you will learn the steps to configure the system.

The Change Pointer Technique

Figure 23.8 shows the process for distributing master data using change pointers. This process involves the following steps.

◆ **The application writes change documents**. SAP maintains change documents for several objects in the system, such as materials, customers, invoices, and bank data, to provide an audit trail for changes made to an object. A change document object represents a set of tables for which changes are recorded. For example, the change document for the material master is named MATERIAL and it contains the various tables of

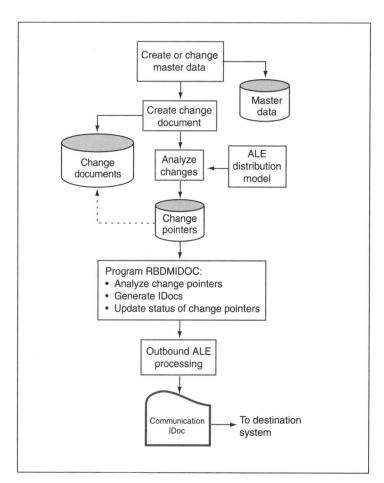

FIGURE 23.8 *Master data distribution via change pointers*

the material master object, such as MARA and MARC. When an application transaction makes changes to an object, the application writes change documents, which are stored in the CDHDR and CDPOS tables for each change made to an object.

TIP

Execute transaction SCDO to see a list of change document objects and their tables.

◆ **The SMD (***Shared Master Data***) tool writes change pointers.** When changes are made to an object, the SMD tool checks the ALE settings and consults the ALE distribution model to determine whether a receiver is interested in the object that was changed. If the system finds an appropriate receiver, the system creates change pointers in the BDCP table that point to change documents in the CDHDR table.

◆ **The ALE programs analyze change pointers and generate IDocs.** SAP provides standard function modules that read the change pointer table and generate IDocs for the objects that were changed. These programs are designed to ignore multiple changes and create only one IDoc. For example, if a material is changed four times before the function module is invoked, only one IDoc with the latest data from the material master data is created. The function modules are invoked by a standard report, RBDMIDOC. The selection parameters of this report allow you to specify the message type for which change pointers are to be analyzed.

Configuration

Besides creating the basic infrastructure described in Chapter 22, "Configuring the ALE Infrastructure," and performing the steps described earlier in "The Basic Configuration for Distributing Data," you must carry out the following configuration steps to enable master data distribution based on changes to the object.

Enable Change Pointers Globally

Transaction: BD61

Path: From the ALE customizing in IMG, choose Modeling and Implementing Business Processes, Master Data Distribution, Replication of Modified Data, Activate Change Pointers (Generally)

This option enables the change pointer process globally. Make sure that the flag is checked.

Enable Change Pointers for a Message Type

Transaction: BD50

Path: From the ALE customizing in IMG, choose Modeling and Implementing Business Processes, Master Data Distribution, Replication of Modified Data, Activate Change Pointers for Message Types

This setting is required for activating change pointers for a specific message type. On this setting screen (see Figure 23.9), make sure that the Active flag is checked for your message type.

Specify the Fields for Which Change Pointers Are to be Written

Transaction: BD52
Path: From the ALE main menu, choose ALE Development, IDocs, Change, Define Change-Relevant Fields

For standard master data objects such as the material, customer, and vendor objects, SAP already provides a list of fields for which change pointers are written. If you are satisfied with the standard set of fields, you can skip this step. If you want to add new fields, you must add entries for the required fields. If you are not interested in IDocs being generated for changes to a particular field, you can remove it from the list. For example, if you do not want to distribute the material master for changes made to the Catalog Profile (RBNRM) field, you can delete this entry from the table.

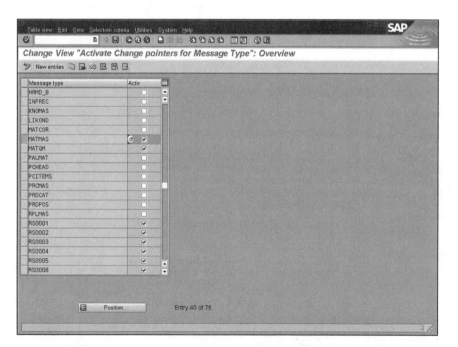

FIGURE 23.9 *Enabling change pointers for the material master* (© SAP AG)

Testing and Executing the Configuration

After you do all the necessary configuration settings, you should carry out sanity tests and process flow tests for the inbound and outbound process, as described in Chapter 26, "Testing the ALE Interface." The tests help you pinpoint any problems in the configuration or with missing elements. You are now ready to execute the process, which involves changing a material master and verifying that an IDoc is generated.

Changing a Field in the Master Data

Change a field in the master data object for which the change pointer is enabled. For example, if you change the net weight of a material in the material master data, a change pointer is written.

TIP

You can verify a change document and change pointer by viewing entries in tables CDHDR and BDCP, respectively.

Executing Program RBDMIDOC to Process Change Pointers

Execute program RBDMIDOC to initiate the process of generating an IDoc. On the selection screen, specify the message type. In this example, you specify MATMAS. After you execute the process, it displays the number of entries processed. If you experience problems, use the troubleshooting guide in Chapter 27, "ALE Process Troubleshooting and Recovery," for details on how to locate the problem and fix it.

NOTE

Normally, you schedule this program to run frequently and start IDoc generation for different message types.

> **TIP**
>
> To view the IDocs, follow the instructions listed earlier in the "Viewing the IDocs" section. To view changes on the receiving system, see the changes made to the material master on the sending system.

Fetching Master Data

The fetch technique is not available for all master data objects. To determine whether a master data object supports a fetch process, go to the ALE main menu. From the menu option Master Data Distribution, drill down to any object and see whether a get option exists. If it does, the fetch option exists. For example, it is provided for the material master, customer master, G/L master, and vendor master objects.

The Fetch Process

Figure 23.10 shows the fetch process. A fetch request originates from the requesting system in the form of a message (MATFET) and contains a list of materials to be transferred. The reference system that contains the materials processes the request and generates material master IDocs. These IDocs are then transferred to the requesting system using the standard MATMAS message.

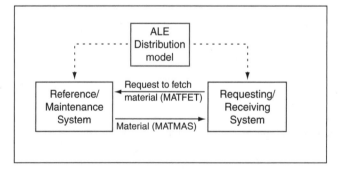

FIGURE 23.10 *The fetch process, requesting a reference system to send material master data*

Configuration and Testing

Besides creating the basic infrastructure discussed in Chapter 22, "Configuring the ALE Infrastructure," and performing the steps described in "The Basic Configuration for Distributing Data" earlier in this chapter, you have to make sure that the message type to fetch master data is modeled in the distribution model. In this case, the requesting system is the sender of the fetch request. For example, if System A can request material master data from System B, the MATFET message type should be included in the model with System A as the sender and System B as the receiver, as shown in Figure 23.11. After you change the model, it must be distributed. You must also generate partner profiles on every system involved in the process.

After you do all the necessary configuration settings, you should carry out sanity tests for the inbound and outbound processes, as described in Chapter 26, "Testing the ALE Interface." The tests help you pinpoint any problems in the configuration or with missing elements.

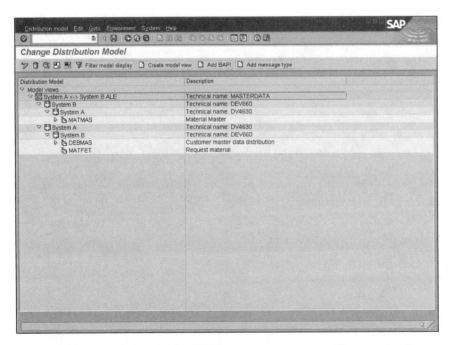

FIGURE 23.11 *Modeling the MATFET message to request material master data from System B* (© SAP AG)

Executing the Process

Transaction: BD11

Path: From the ALE main menu, choose Master Data Distribution, Cross-Application, Material, Get

On the transaction BD11 selection screen, the system displays fields to specify different values for requesting material master data, as shown in Figure 23.12. The fields have the following meanings.

- ◆ **Material**. The material master you want to fetch. You can select a single value or multiple values, using the range button (the arrow) on the far right of the field.

- ◆ **Class**. An advanced option, which you can leave blank for the moment. The Class field allows you to fetch materials based on classification. This field is discussed in "The Advanced Distribution Option via Classification" later in this chapter.

- ◆ **Message Type**. The message type associated with the material master object. The standard message type is MATMAS.

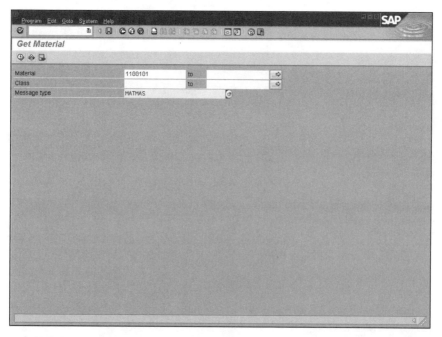

FIGURE 23.12 *The selection screen to specify material master data to be fetched* (© SAP AG)

NOTE

You will notice that there is no option to specify the system that has the material master data. The system that processes the fetch request is determined from the distribution model.

Enter the desired values and click the Execute button. The system sends the MATFET request to the appropriate system. The entire process is asynchronous, so the time the material master objects are received depends on the settings in the partner profile.

Viewing the IDocs and Material Documents

You display IDocs by using the IDoc monitoring tools (transaction WE02 or WE05). There will be IDocs based on the MATFET message. You should also log on to the system that sends the material master to determine the state of the request.

If everything works successfully, the material master should be created on the requesting system. You use transaction MM03 to view the material documents.

The Advanced Distribution Option via Classification

This section explains the details of distributing master data by using the classification system. First, a business scenario is described in which you can use the classification approach. Then, the various steps to configure the process are discussed.

A Business Scenario

Assume that material master data is maintained on a central system for the entire company and there are roughly 20,000 materials. Of these 20,000 materials, approximately 5,000 are to be distributed to System A (the sales system) and the rest to System B (the production-planning system).

You have two choices in the standard system.

◆ Execute transaction BD10, and specify each material to be transferred in the material field, saving the variant for future use. This process can be tedious and impractical because every time a material is added or deleted in the system, you have to update the variant.

◆ Use the classification system to categorize materials based on criteria that allow you to distinguish materials for a specific system. For example, you can classify a material as a sales material, a production material, or both.

How the Classification System Works

In the classification system, you set up a class type that is enabled for distribution. Then you create classes based on this class type, such as a sales materials class and a production materials class. Each material master object will be classified to belong to one or both classes. Then you can distribute materials based on the class.

 NOTE

This option is available for material master, customer master, and vendor master objects only.

Creating a Class Type

Transaction: 01CL

Path: From the ALE customizing in IMG, choose Modeling and Implementing Business Processes, Master Data Distribution, Distribution Using Object Classes, Maintain Class Types

In this step, you create a class type for the object that is to be used in the ALE process (see Figure 23.13). In the example, you create a class type for the material object MARA. Enter a name (beginning with a Z) for the class type, and select the Multiple Classification and Distr. Class Type check boxes.

 NOTE

Only one class type per object can be configured as the distributed class type.

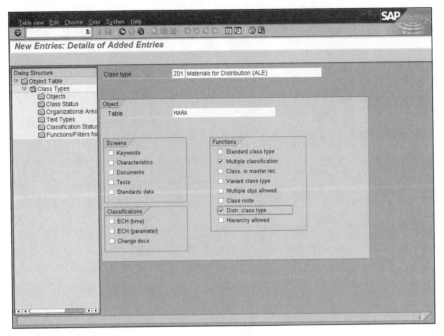

FIGURE 23.13 *Creating a class type for material master data* (© SAP AG)

Maintaining Status for the Class Type

Transaction: 01CL

Path: From the ALE customizing in IMG, choose Modeling and Implementing Business Processes, Master Data Distribution, Distribution Using Object Classes, Maintain Class Types

Maintaining status for the class type is an administrative step for the class type you created earlier. You can assign various status values to your class type and control what can and cannot be done in each state. For ALE purposes, create a Status 1 named Ready for Distribution, and select all four options for the class type, as shown in Figure 23.14.

Maintaining Classification Status

Transaction: 01CL

Path: From the ALE customizing in IMG, choose Modeling and Implementing Business Processes, Master Data Distribution, Distribution Using Object Classes, Maintain Class Types

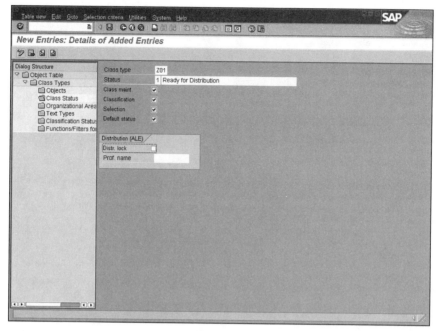

FIGURE 23.14 *Maintaining status for the class type* (© SAP AG)

Maintaining classification statuses is also an administrative step for the status you created earlier. For ALE purposes, select the Incomplete - System flag, as shown in Figure 23.15.

Maintaining Classes

Transaction: CL01

Path: From the ALE customizing in IMG, choose Modeling and Implementing Business Processes, Master Data Distribution, Distribution Using Object Classes, Maintain Classes

Figure 23.16 shows where you specify the classes to be used for your object. The example contains two classes: sales materials and production materials.

FIGURE 23.15 *Additional status maintenance for the class type* (© SAP AG)

FIGURE 23.16 *Creating a class for sales material* (© SAP AG)

To maintain classes, follow these steps.

1. Execute transaction CL01, and assign a name to your class by entering **SALES** in the Class field and **Z01** for the Class Type. Click the Create icon.

2. On the next screen, assign a short description to your class and save it.

3. Repeat steps 1 and 2 for all the classes.

Allocating Classes to the Logical System

Transaction: BD68

Path: From the ALE customizing in IMG, choose Modeling and Implementing Business Processes, Master Data Distribution, Distribution Using Object Classes, Assign Classes to Receiving Logical System

In this step, you assign the class you created earlier to the logical system that will receive data based on the class. Figure 23.17 shows that the SALES class is assigned to System A (DV4630).

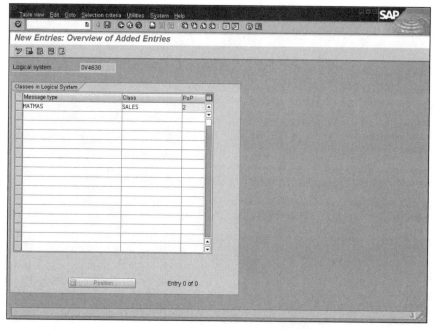

FIGURE 23.17 *Allocating the class to a logical system* (© SAP AG)

Assigning the Object to One of the Classes

In this step, you classify your object into one of the classes created in the preceding section. In the example, the material is classified as sales material or production material (see Figure 23.18). The steps are as follows.

1. Execute transaction MM02. Enter the material to be classified and press Enter. In the dialog box, select the classification check box and press Enter.

2. On this screen, the system allows you to specify the classes you created earlier. Display the options for classes and select the appropriate class. You can select more than one class for your material. Thus, if a part is both a sales part and a production part, you can classify it twice.

Executing the Process

After you classify your objects, you select the class on which you want to carry out the distribution process. This example uses BD10 to distribute the material master. In the Class field, press F4 and select the class on which you want to distribute your materials.

Advanced Formatting Scenarios

The preceding section introduced techniques for distributing master data. For every message, SAP distributes a full-blown maximum IDoc that contains all possible views and data for that object. In the real world, companies often have peculiar situations for which the standard scenarios do not suffice; alternatively, transmitting a complete set of data might not be efficient. Each receiving system can demand a slightly different flavor of the same data. For example, System A can require an older version of data, and System B can require data specific to its area of operation only. You can use various customizing options to meet your company's specific needs. The system generates one master IDoc, which is massaged to suit the needs of each receiver, to generate one communication IDoc per receiver. The options to customize the distribution of master data are described next. First, you examine a business situation in which the customizing option is used. Then, you learn the concept and the steps to configure the system.

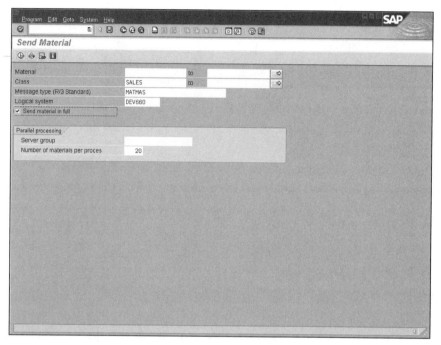

FIGURE 23.18 *Distributing the material master data by class* (© SAP AG)

 NOTE

Refer to Chapter 20, "The Outbound ALE Process," for a discussion of master IDocs and communication IDocs.

Filtering at the IDoc Level

Filtering at the IDoc level creates a communication IDoc in which an object's views are filtered out, based on the filters specified in the distribution model. The following sections describe a business scenario in which you use IDoc filtering and set up filters for the material master object.

A Business Scenario

Consider a company that has 10 plants manufacturing the material MAT01. Each plant operates independently on its own SAP system. The material master data is maintained in a central SAP system for all 10 plants and then distributed to the facilities. The material MAT01 has an MRP view for each plant. If you distribute this material to the plants using the standard scenario, each plant gets the material with MRP views, including the ones for other plants. When the number of materials exchanged between the systems is large and very frequent, this approach can be an unnecessary waste of network resources and can be undesirable from a business point of view.

The technique of filtering at the IDoc level enables you to send a subset of data that is relevant for a receiving system. The system provides several filter objects for each message type to filter data. You will choose the appropriate filter for your business needs and add it to your distribution model. In the business scenario described previously, a plant is a suitable filter. Several other filters, such as company code and sales areas, are also provided.

How Filtering at the IDoc Level Works

When a master IDoc is created, the IDoc consults the distribution model and determines whether any filter objects are specified for a receiver. If so, the value in the filter object is compared to values in the master IDoc's data records. If the values do not match, the data record is dropped. It is also possible to filter out a whole IDoc using a single value filter. This might happen if the field being filtered out belongs to a mandatory segment and the hierarchy in which this mandatory segment resides exists at the top of the IDoc structure.

NOTE

This setting can also be carried out on the receiving system. That is, you can receive a full-blown IDoc and filter it to eliminate unwanted data at the receiving end.

Configuration

You perform the following steps to configure filtering at the IDoc level.

1. Identify the filter object.

Transaction: BD59
Path: From the ALE main menu, choose ALE Development, IDocs, Data
Filtering, Assign Filter Object Type to IDoc Field

A filter object represents a field of an IDoc segment whose values are compared at run time to determine whether a data record is relevant for a receiving system. You must identify the filter object from the list displayed, using transaction BD59. For example, to filter MRP views for a plant, the filter object is WERKS under the E1MARCM segment. You can also create a new custom filter object (if none of the existing filters meets your requirements) by adding an entry to this list. You can use multiple filters within a group, and multiple filter groups, to achieve fairly complex filtering schemes. Refer to the SAP Library for more detail on how this works.

2. **Modify the distribution model.** In the distribution model, you can add filter objects and assign values to be checked. Assume that System B is the central system for material master data and that System A is one of the systems that requires data for plants 0001 and 0002 (see Figure 23.19).

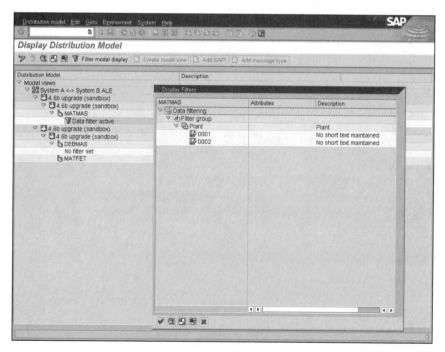

FIGURE 23.19 *IDoc filters configured in the distribution model* (© SAP AG)

Segment Filtering

Segment filtering creates a communication IDoc in which segments of a particular type are completely removed from the IDoc. The following sections describe a business scenario in which you use segment filtering and then set up segment filters for the material master object.

A Business Scenario

Consider a company that has distributed operations based on business functions in the company. System A is the sales system in which all the sales activities are carried out, and System B is the production-planning system in which production-related activities are carried out. A central System C maintains master data information, which is then distributed to systems A and B. The sales system is not interested in the MRP views, and similarly, the production-planning system is not interested in the sales views. Therefore, when the material is distributed, each system requires a subset with a limited number of segments.

The segment-filtering technique is used in this type of situation to send a subset of data that is relevant for a receiving system.

Notice the difference between segment filtering and IDoc filtering. In IDoc filtering, segments that do not contain relevant data for a receiving system are filtered out. In segment filtering, a segment of a particular type is completely removed from the IDoc. For example, consider that a master IDoc for material MAT01 contains 10 data records (segment type E1MARCM, MRP view) pertaining to 10 plants. In IDoc filtering, each plant gets only one data record that is relevant for that plant. In segment filtering, all 10 records are dropped.

How Segment Filtering Works

For each specific sender/receiver combination, you can specify a set of segments to remove from a message. In the standard delivered system, all segments of an IDoc are distributed. You will learn how to customize a message to filter out segments in the configuration steps. When a master IDoc is created, it consults the segment filters and removes any unwanted segments to create the communication IDoc for a receiver. The advantage of this technique is that it determines the segments to be filtered out at run time, so the standard message can be used.

NOTE

This setting can also be carried out on the receiving system—you can receive a full-blown IDoc and filter the unwanted segments at the receiving end. However, filtering at the receiving end doesn't make much sense because you have already used the network resources for transferring a full-blown IDoc.

Configuration

Configuring the segment-filtering technique is a one-step process. All you have to do is specify the segments to be filtered.

Transaction: BD56
Path: From the ALE customizing in IMG, choose Modeling and Implementing Business Processes, Master Data Distribution, Scope of the Data for Distribution, Filter IDoc Segments

Identify the IDoc segment that corresponds to the data you do not want to distribute. The segment names and documentation of the IDoc should help you identify the correct segment. For example, if System A (DV4630) is not interested in MRP-related data in a material master IDoc, you can filter out the E1MARCM segment, as shown in Figure 23.20. Similarly, if a system is not interested in sales-related data, the E1MVKEM segment can be filtered out.

 NOTE

There are some limitations to keep in mind when using segment filtering. You cannot filter mandatory segments. Also, you must maintain correct parent-child relationships. If you want to filter a parent segment, you must ensure that all of its child segments are also filtered.

The Reduced IDoc Type

The reduced IDoc type technique allows you to get down to the field level and specify the fields a receiving system does not need. The system still sends the fields, but this has no effect on the receiving system because each field has a null

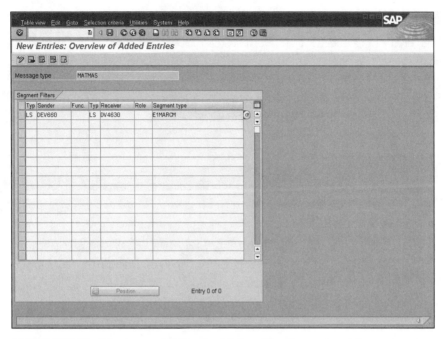

FIGURE 23.20 *Filtering out MRP-related information from a material master* (© SAP AG)

value, represented by a forward slash (/) in the field. The following sections describe a business scenario in which you reduce a standard IDoc type, using the MATMAS02 IDoc type as an example. Only master data IDocs can currently use the reduced IDoc technique.

A Business Scenario

In the preceding scenario, you saw how to filter out unwanted segments at run time. Consider the following situation. The two systems (System A and System B) decide to maintain the standard price for material master data locally on their systems. They do not want it to be wiped out every time the material master is loaded from the central system, where most of the material master information is maintained. This time, you want certain fields of the segment to be filtered out (or not affect) the receiving system. You can use the reduced IDoc technique to filter out fields that are not to be wiped out.

How the Reduced IDoc Type Works

You create a reduced IDoc from a standard IDoc type at definition time by enabling or disabling segments or even specific fields within a segment. Of course, you cannot disable mandatory segments. The reduced IDoc gets a new message type, which is then used in the partner profile to indicate that the reduced IDoc, instead of the complete IDoc, is wanted.

Configuration

1. **Analyze the data.** You first identify the master data fields you want to protect from being overwritten. Then you identify their corresponding fields in the IDoc segments. If you determine that you do not want any of the fields in a segment, you can remove the entire segment.

   You will find the IDoc structure and the documentation of IDocs useful in your analysis. Execute transaction WE60 to view an IDoc type's documentation.

 NOTE

Keep in mind that you cannot remove mandatory segments.

2. **Reduce the IDoc type.**

   Transaction: BD53

   Path: From the ALE customizing in IMG, choose Modeling and Implementing Business Processes, Master Data Distribution, Scope of the Data for Distribution, Message Reduction, Create Reduced Message Type

   Follow these steps to reduce the IDoc type.

   A. On the first screen (see Figure 23.21), enter the message type to be assigned to the reduced IDoc type. This name must start with a Z. It is generally recommended that you give the new message type a name similar to the original message type. For example, the reduced message type for MATMAS could be ZMATMS.

   B. Click the Create button and enter the name of the standard message type. Move down and enter a short description of the new message type.

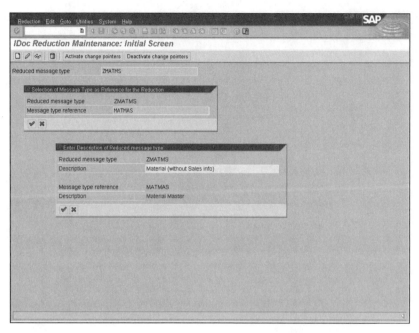

FIGURE 23.21 *The initial screen to reduce a message type* (© SAP AG)

C. The system copies the latest version of the IDoc associated with the message type (see Figure 23.22). By default, only the mandatory (green) segments are activated. You must activate additional segments you want to include in your reduced IDoc. Click the segment you want to activate, and then click the Select button. The color of the segment will turn from red to white. Repeat this step for all the segments you want to activate.

D. Activate the fields in the active segments. Double-click any active segment, including the mandatory segments. The system displays a list of fields in the segment, as shown in Figure 23.23. Mandatory fields are in green and are automatically activated. To activate additional fields, click the check box next to the field and then click the Select button. Core fields change from purple to blue when activated, and normal fields change from red to white. Repeat this step for all segments you have activated.

E. Save your changes, and then from the initial screen, activate the reduced IDoc type.

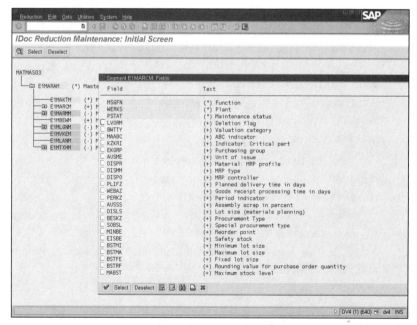

FIGURE 23.22 *Activation at the segment level for the material master* (© SAP AG)

FIGURE 23.23 *Activation at the field level for the material master* (© SAP AG)

3. Change the partner profile to Use New Message Type. You have to add a new entry in the partner profile with the message type created for the reduced IDoc.

4. Change the distribution model. The distribution model also needs to be modified to use the message type assigned to the reduced IDoc type. During execution, the system allows you to select the reduced message type as one of the possible message types for distribution. For the sample scenario, when you execute BD10, the system will have the ZMATMS message type as one of the possible choices for the Message Type field.

Version Change for Segments and IDocs

The version change technique allows you to exchange IDocs with systems using older versions of IDocs. The following sections describe a business scenario to enable version change for an IDoc.

Assume that System A and System B are on version 4.0A of SAP, and to get enhanced functionality, the 4.6A version is now being installed on System B. However, System A will continue to operate on version 4.0A because it's running mission-critical applications. You must determine how to support the version 4.0A IDocs when you transfer the material master IDoc from System B to System A. For example, the material master data that was being exchanged in version 4.0A used the MATMAS03 IDoc and the MATMAS message. In version 4.6A, this IDoc type has experienced several changes, with segments in the IDoc having additional fields that the receiving system cannot interpret.

The ALE service layer reads the partner profile to determine the IDoc version and segment version to be generated. Configuring version change requires just one step—modifying the partner profile. On the sending system, System B, enter the desired segment version in the Seg. Release in IDoc Type field, and enter the IDoc version in the IDoc Type field of the outbound record of the partner profile for the receiving system (System A, logical system DV4630), as shown in Figure 23.24.

Extending IDocs

So far, you have learned how to reduce or otherwise modify the information sent to the receiving system. In addition, you will be required to extend the data exchanged between two systems. Extending an IDoc requires several steps. Refer to Section Three, "IDocs," for details on how to extend IDocs, program the extensions, and configure the system to recognize the extensions.

FIGURE 23.24 *Partner profile settings to generate back-level IDocs and segments* (© SAP AG)

Frequently Asked Questions about Master Data

What if a field in the master data is required on the receiving system but not on the sending system?

In this case, you must change the configuration on the sending system to make the field mandatory or use the user exits to add default values.

What if a field is maintained locally, and I do not want it to be wiped out when master data is copied?

You can customize the standard IDocs to prevent certain fields from being overwritten, by using the reduced IDoc type technique. Refer to "The Reduced IDoc Type" in this chapter for details.

What if the receiving system is upgraded to a newer version?

The sending system will continue to provide the message as usual. The receiving system will be able to process an IDoc from a previous version without any modifications. SAP guarantees backward compatibility. You will not be able to take advantage of the latest upgraded functionality, but the system will work.

What if the sending system is upgraded to a newer version?

The sending system will have to be configured to generate a back-level IDoc for the receiving system via the partner profile. See the "Version Change for Segments and IDocs" section in this chapter for more details.

What if I have 10,000 materials, and I want to distribute a set of materials to System A and the rest to System B?

You have four choices. The first two choices are standard in the system but can limit you in certain cases. The last two choices are custom techniques provided to make your task easy. Readers with less experience might prefer to skip the last two choices.

◆ On the selection screen for distributing materials (transaction BD10), you can specify the material numbers. Save the specification as a variant for later use. This approach is useful when you can easily distinguish the necessary set based on the material numbers. However, it might not be practical for large quantities or systems where new materials are added frequently.

◆ Use the classification system. In this approach, you can classify materials using particular characteristics. See "The Advanced Distribution Option via Classification" for details. This choice is available only for customer master, material master, and vendor master objects because they can be classified.

◆ Create a custom program that allows you to specify or select materials based on your criteria, and then call the RSBDEMAT (transaction BD10) program with the selected materials. For example, to select all materials that belong to a specific plant, you can write a simple program. In the program, you have a select statement that determines all materials that have an entry in the MARC table with your desired plant and then calls the RSBDEMAT program with selected materials.

◆ Create a new customer segment with a field whose value can be used to distinguish the destination system. Attach it to the top-level segment, E1MARAM, and then populate the values in this field in the customer exit for the IDoc. Create a filter based on this custom field, and add the filter to your distribution model. For example, if you want to distribute materials that belong to a plant, create a segment Z1MARAM with a plant field and use this segment to extend the E1MARAM segment. In the customer exit, you can fill the value of the plant in this field. Create a filter using this new field, and add it to the distribution model.

What if I have created purchasing views in the material master for all the plants in our company, but I do not want each plant to get views for other plants?

You can use filters in the distribution model to filter objects for specific plants.

What if I have separate systems for sales activities and FI activities, and the FI system does not care at all about the sales views?

You have two options.

◆ Create a reduced message type for your FI system without the sales segments. The system will assign it a new message type. Use this new message type for distribution.

◆ Filter out segments at run time using segment filtering.

Summary

Master data is critical information shared across multiple applications in an organization. Most companies develop a strategy to maintain the integrity of master data while supporting a distributed environment. SAP provides the ALE process for implementing and controlling master data distribution.

Several customizing options are available to tailor the system to suit your needs, such as filtering, version management, and classification. The overall functionality of master data is very rich, and the system offers a nearly infinite combination of ways to design your distribution strategy.

Chapter 24

**Implementing
Distributed
Business
Processes**

ALE was invented to support distributed processing across multiple SAP systems. This chapter covers the implementation of a distributed system and examines the issues and strategies involved in keeping distributed systems synchronized. The distributed contracts scenario, a standard SAP-delivered scenario, illustrates the steps for implementing a distributed system.

An Introduction to Distributed Processing

As the term *distributed processing* suggests, part of the business process is carried out on one system and part on another. This segregation of business processes is based on the principle of executing a business process on the system best suited for the process. Consider the purchasing process in a company that has several subsidiaries. Each subsidiary procures certain common materials for local use, for which it negotiates rates with its own selected vendors. If the purchasing requirements could be reported to a central corporate system that negotiates rates with vendors based on the collective requirement, the company might receive better rates, quality, and delivery times. To provide autonomy of operations, the purchasing process could continue to operate on individual systems. This example shows how distributed business processes can provide a competitive advantage.

 NOTE

Chapter 18, "Introduction to Distributed Systems," provides full details of the technical and business reasons for distributing processes.

To transform an integrated business process into a distributed business process, you need to re-engineer the business process and enhance the technology component to support distributed processing, as follows.

◆ **Re-engineered business processes**. Business processes typically carried out on stand-alone systems are re-engineered to support distributed yet integrated processing. Process chains are split at appropriate process boundaries. Processing to achieve a distributed yet integrated system is an art. A process chain split at the wrong boundaries can mean unnecessary data exchanges and difficulties keeping the systems in sync. On the other hand, an optimal distributed process provides an independent operating unit with minimal dependence on the other system, resulting in minimal network load.

◆ **Technology to support distributed processes**. Programs that were once used in integrated processes are enhanced so that they are *ALE-enabled*, which means that they understand the syntax and semantics of IDocs that are used to exchange data between distributed processes. The two systems exchange data with each other at appropriate points to stay synchronized. To make optimal use of network resources and maintain autonomy, only necessary data is shared between the systems.

Data Types Exchanged

In a distributed scenario, three types of data are exchanged.

◆ **Transactional data**. Transactional data represents day-to-day business transactions carried out in the system, such as purchase orders, sales orders, and invoices. The ability to exchange transactional data between distributed systems achieves the highest business benefits.

◆ **Master data**. Master data is required to support the creation and interpretation of transactional data across systems. Examples of master data include vendor master, customer master, and material master data. Master data does not change frequently. This data is exchanged via the ALE process when a scenario is first deployed, and on a timely basis if the master data is changed or new relevant master data is created.

◆ **Customizing data**. A set of customizing data must also be the same on the distributed systems. ALE calls this type of data *control data*. Examples include purchase organization, sales organization, and business areas. Because customizing data does not change frequently, this data is exchanged via the existing CTS (*Correction and Transport System*) process. ALE controls who owns the data and what can be exchanged but does not carry out the actual transfer.

Implementing a Distributed Scenario

SAP provides a set of standard preconfigured scenarios in various application areas based on the commonly distributed applications and processes. It has optimally distributed the processes to provide a distributed yet integrated environment.

 NOTE

A complete list of preconfigured scenarios is available in the online help for ALE under Application Scenarios. In addition, a number of white papers and configuration guides are posted on the SAP Labs Web site, at http://www.saplabs.com.

It is impossible to provide general directions for implementing a distributed scenario; each scenario is unique and presents different options, although at the technical level you will find several similarities. This chapter uses the distributed contracts scenario to illustrate the steps for implementing a distributed business process. You can use this example as a guideline for other scenarios.

The methodology used to implement a distributed scenario is similar to that used in the EDI process to configure a transaction. In the analysis phase, you analyze the business requirements and compare them to what SAP provides. In the preparation phase, you identify the parameters used in the interface. The setup phase involves configuring the application components and ALE components. You test the setup in the testing phase, and then execute the process. The results are ultimately verified in the verification phase. Finally, in the support phase, you monitor the system and troubleshoot if it experiences any problems.

The Analysis Phase

In the analysis phase, you study the integrated process, identify process boundaries, identify data flows, study system limitations, and make decisions about customer enhancements.

Studying the Integrated Process

It is important to study the integrated process before you begin analyzing the distributed process. You can use the online help, implementation guide, and reference model to understand the business process. The online help provides a detailed description of a business process, the implementation guide points out the customizing options available in the process, and the reference model helps with process flows and component descriptions.

The distributed contracts scenario in the example is part of the Materials Management module. A purchasing contract or outline agreement is a long-term agreement with your vendor. It describes the total quantity or purchase value you agree to procure from the vendor. It does not contain specific quantities or delivery dates. Those items are specified in individual purchase orders that are released against the contract.

Identifying Process Boundaries in the Distributed System

Process boundaries define the business functions that take place on each system. In the example, a contract is created in a central system, and purchase orders against the contract are created in one or more satellite systems where local operations are carried out.

TIP

A number of distributed scenarios are documented in the Implementation Guide in the SAP Library, and the various settings are discussed in the IMG. The documentation should provide a clear picture of the process boundaries.

Identifying Data Flows

Integration between the systems is achieved by timely and controlled exchange of transactional and master data. Each system maintains a redundant copy of the data necessary to execute business processes on the local system. The systems are responsible for the integrity and maintenance of their local data only. One of the systems is assigned as the owner of the data that multiple systems share and is thus responsible for creating, maintaining, and distributing the data to the other system(s). Data flows help you understand the information exchanged between the systems. From the data flows, you should be able to identify the various transactional and master data exchanged between the systems (see Figure 24.1).

1. A purchasing contract is created centrally without any plant information and is distributed to one or more satellite systems. The contract contains the vendor number, material, and quantity or value of goods to be

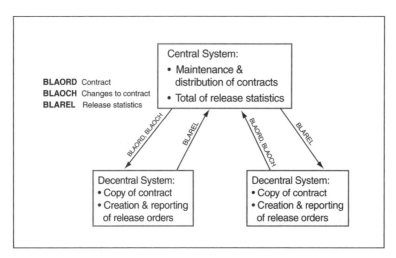

FIGURE 24.1 *Data flow in the distributed contracts scenario*

procured over a period of time. Any changes made to the contract are also distributed. Changes can be made only in the central system.

2. Purchase orders are entered in the satellite systems against the purchasing contract, and release statistics indicating quantity and values used in the purchase order are communicated to the central system and updated locally.

3. The central system maintains the total value and quantity used up so far. The satellite systems do not have access to the statistics on the central system. If the value or quantity exceeds the total value or quantity of the contract, it can be blocked, which results in a change to the contract. The blocked contract is distributed to various satellite systems, which prevents them from entering additional purchase orders against the contract.

Studying System Limitations

A distributed scenario certainly provides business benefits, but in most cases, the application functionality is reduced because the systems are distributed. In a single integrated system, data and processes are readily available and, therefore, execution time is mainly based on the processing time. In a distributed environment, the execution time is based on the processing time and the network distribution time. Waiting that long is not always practical. For example, if a sales order is being entered in a single integrated system, the system calculates the delivery dates and carries out credit checks instantaneously. If, however, the systems are distributed, a real-time availability check performed in another system might not be supported.

The distributed contracts scenario is inferior to an integrated process because the satellite systems can continue to release purchase orders against a purchasing contract that's near its maximum value until they receive a blocked contract from the central system. Such a situation can result in purchase orders exceeding the maximum value set in a contract.

Deciding on Customer Enhancements

As part of the analysis process, you might have discovered gaps between your business needs and the standard SAP functionality. If gaps cannot be filled with one of the customizing options, you often can use a user exit instead. In any IDoc process, one of the common enhancements is to extend IDocs and use the user exits to populate data in the extensions. User exits have been provided at strategic points in the process to add customized code formally to an existing SAP process; they are supported during an upgrade. Refer to Chapter 32, "Programming in the IDoc Interface," for details on locating user exits for the IDoc processes.

The following user exits are available for the messages exchanged in the distributed contracts scenario.

- For message type BLAOCH/BLAORD:
  - **MM06E001 (EXIT_SAPLEINM_001).** This user exit modifies the control record information of the outbound IDocs.
  - **MM06E001 (EXIT_SAPLEINM_002).** This user exit populates IDoc extensions for outbound IDocs.
  - **MM06E002 (EXIT_SAPLEINN_001, EXIT_SAPLEINN_002, EXIT_SAPLEINN_003).** These user exits process incoming data in extended IDocs.
- For message type BLAREL:
  - **MM06E001 (EXIT_SAPLEINM_001).** This user exit modifies the control record information of the outbound IDocs.
  - **MM06E001 (EXIT_SAPLEINM_003).** This user exit populates IDoc extensions for outbound IDocs.
  - **MM06E001 (EXIT_SAPLEINM_004).** This user exit processes incoming data in extended IDocs.

The Preparation Phase

In the preparation phase, the basic objective is to identify the elements that will be used in the configuration process.

Identifying the Central and Satellite Systems

You must identify the SAP systems involved in the process. This scenario allows one central system and multiple satellite systems. A logical name is assigned to each system involved in the process. For this scenario, the central system is System A, and the satellite system is System B.

Identifying Lists of IDocs and Messages

At the technical level, master data and transactional data exchanged between the systems are implemented via IDocs. A list of IDocs and messages should be identified for each type of data exchanged between the systems.

For the sample scenario, the data flow described in Figure 24.1 depicts the transactional data exchanged between the systems. Besides the transactional data, material master and vendor master data must also be kept in sync between the two systems. Table 24.1 lists the IDocs and messages for data exchanged between the systems.

Table 24.1 Messages Exchanged in the Distributed Contracts Scenario

Message	IDoc Type	Description
BLAORD	BLAORD03	Purchasing contract
BLAOCH	BLAORD03	Changes to the purchasing contract
BLAREL	BLAREL02	Release statistics
MATMAS	MATMAS03	Material master
CREMAS	CREMAS03	Vendor master

Identifying Workflow Parameters

You must also identify the organizational object (user ID, position, workcenter, and so on) responsible for handling errors associated with this process and the standard tasks associated with each message exchanged. You can choose from several types of organizational objects. Refer to Chapter 9, "Configuring Work-flow," for details on the workflow component.

To begin, you can use your user ID as the person to be notified in case of errors. Table 24.2 shows the standard tasks for error handling.

Table 24.2 Standard Tasks for Error Handling

Workflow Task	Task ID
BLAOCH_Error	TS00007975
BLAORD_Error	TS00007974
BLAREL_Error	TS00007979

Identifying Lists of Control Data Objects

To make semantic sense of data that is exchanged, the systems must have the same values for customizing objects, such as company codes, plants, and sales areas.

Table 24.3 shows the customizing objects that must be known to all the systems in the sample scenario. The IDocs exchanged between the systems refer to these values, and it is important that these values are known to the systems before IDocs are exchanged.

Table 24.3 Customizing Objects for the Distributed Contracts Scenario

Description	Customizing Object
Company code	V_T001
Purchasing organization	V_T024E
Purchasing group	V_024
Contract type	OMEF
Incoterms	V_INC
Terms of payment	V_T052
Shipping instructions	V027A
Tax indicator	FTXP

The Setup Phase

In the setup phase, you carry out the steps to configure the system, using the information identified in the preparation phase. The setup phase consists of application configuration and ALE configuration.

Configuring Application Components

These settings are specific to the scenario being implemented and must be carried out in the context of the business process. The settings are then distributed to the systems involved in the distribution process via the CTS process. Because each system involved in the process is an independently operating SAP system, companies have different strategies for distributing the customizing data. Control data distribution is explained separately near the end of this chapter.

 CAUTION

Some customizing tables are marked *type A,* which means that they are treated as master data. Therefore, either they must be transported manually, or the customizing steps must be repeated in all the systems. If you make a setting in the IMG and the system does not prompt you for a change request, it is very likely that the setting is treated as master data.

Maintenance of General Application Settings

The customizing objects for the sample scenario are identified in the preparation phase. The settings for company code, purchasing organization, purchasing group, incoterms, terms of payment, shipping instructions, and tax indicator are part of the overall setup of the purchasing module and are outside the scope of this book. You will work with team members in the functional area to make sure that the necessary application settings are maintained and distributed to the various systems.

The Number Range for Contracts

`Transaction:` OMH6
`Menu Path:` From the IMG (SPRO), choose Materials Management, Purchasing, Contract, Define Number Range

The document type for distributed contracts has an internal and external number range associated with it. The *internal number range* is used on the central system for assigning unique numbers to the distributed contracts. The *external number range* is used on the satellite systems when contracts are received from the central system. Therefore, the external number assignment in the document type on the satellite system must contain the range used in the central system, as shown in Figure 24.2.

The Contract Type for Distributed Contracts

Transaction: OMEF
Menu Path: From the IMG (SPRO), choose Materials Management, Purchasing, Contract, Define Document Types

A new document type is required to distinguish distributed contracts from regular contracts created in the integrated system (see Figure 24.3). This document type must exist on the central and satellite systems.

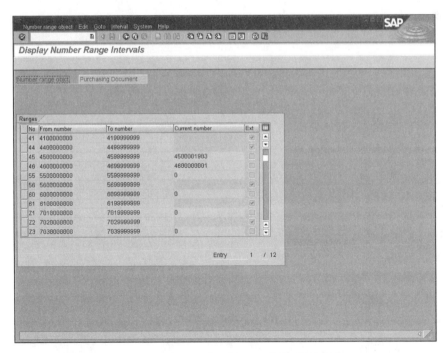

FIGURE 24.2 *Number ranges (external and internal)* (© SAP AG)

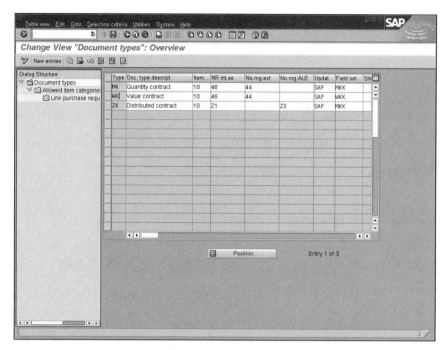

FIGURE 24.3 *The document type for distributed contracts* (© SAP AG)

Message Control Settings to Propose ALE Output

Transaction: MN07

Menu Path: Logistics, Materials Management, Purchasing, Master Data, Messages, Outline Agreement, Create

The outbound IDoc for contracts is triggered via Message control. A condition type, VNEU, exists to distribute contracts via ALE. In the default setting, this condition type is not proposed automatically. Condition records can be created to have the output proposed automatically for the document type used for distributed contracts (see Figure 24.4).

 NOTE

For complete details on the concepts and use of Message control, refer to Chapter 8, "Configuring Message Control."

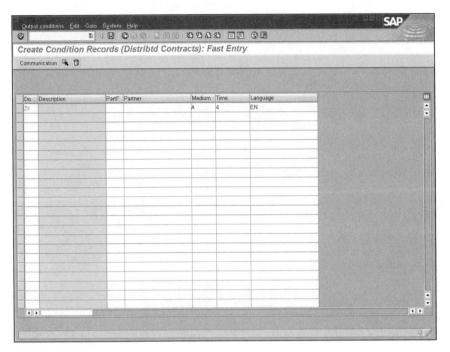

FIGURE 24.4 *Condition records for output type VNEU* (© SAP AG)

Configuring ALE Components

The technical implementation has similarities across several scenarios. The following ALE settings are carried out. Chapter 22, "Configuring the ALE Infrastructure," and Chapter 23, "Distributing Master Data," provide details of these five steps, so only a brief description is provided here.

1. **Maintain the basic ALE infrastructure**. The basic ALE infrastructure, as discussed in Chapter 22, allows the systems involved in distribution to recognize each other.

2. **Maintain the customer distribution model**. A customer model depicts various messages (master data, transactional data) exchanged between the systems and establishes a sender and receiver of data (see Figure 24.5).

3. **Distribute the customer model**. A customer model is always maintained on any system for the entire distributed network of SAP systems, so it must be distributed to various systems in the distributed network.

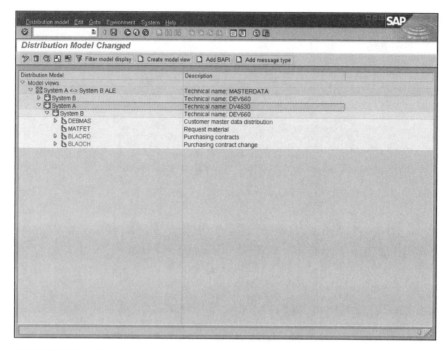

FIGURE 24.5 *The customer distribution model for the distributed contracts scenario* (© SAP AG)

TIP

If a message has been included in another model for the same set of senders and receivers, the system will not allow you to create another entry. Therefore, a good technique is to maintain one model for all master data distribution. That way, several scenarios can use the same master data model and one model specific to the transactional data for the distribution scenario.

4. **Generate the partner profile**. After the model has been successfully distributed, partner profiles can be generated automatically in each individual system. On every system, a partner profile exists for each system with which it communicates, and a record exists for each outbound message and each incoming message.

NOTE

Chapter 7, "Configuring Partner Profiles," gives complete details on partner profile parameters.

5. **Make workflow settings**. Workflow is used for sending a work item to the person responsible for errors in the distribution process. The person to be notified is determined from the partner profile. This step is also carried out on every system involved in the process.

 NOTE

Chapter 9, "Configuring Workflow," discusses how to set up workflow for error notification.

Advanced ALE Settings

The preceding sections described the basic setup without any enhancements or extensions to the process. Depending on your business needs, you can utilize the following options to tailor the process.

◆ **Customer enhancements**. If enhancements such as extended IDocs and user exits are utilized, you will have to transport those objects to the various systems.

 NOTE

See Section Three, "IDocs," for complete details on how to extend IDocs and develop user exits.

◆ **Advanced formatting options**. The advanced formatting options for an IDoc, such as filtering and version control, are discussed Chapter 23, "Distributing Master Data." They can be utilized as necessary.

The Testing Phase

Before you execute the process, you can carry out a basic sanity test of the configuration. The system provides standard tools to test the components. You can test the ALE settings, control data settings, and application settings.

 NOTE

Chapter 26, "Testing the ALE Interface," provides complete details on how to test the components.

The Execution and Verification Phase

After completing the configuration, you are ready to execute the process. The steps to execute a scenario are specific to the scenario. You work in the context of the business process to carry out the various steps. For the distributed contracts scenario, do the following.

1. **Synchronize the master data**. Vendors and materials used in the scenario must be known to the central and satellite systems. Any changes to the master data must also be replicated between the systems. Chapter 23 discusses techniques for distributing master data.

2. **Create a contract in the central system**.

   Transaction: ME31K
   Transaction prior to version 4.6: ME31
   Menu Path: Logistics, Materials Management, Purchasing, Outline
   Agreement, Create

   Enter the material, the quantity or value of the contract, and the validity date, as shown in Figure 24.6. Check the messages proposed on the output control screen via Header, Messages. Output type VNEU should be proposed automatically with medium A (ALE), as shown in Figure 24.7. Save the contract and note the number. When the document is saved, the IDoc processing begins.

   On the central system, you can do the following.

   • Display the results in the output control screen to make sure that the message was processed successfully.

   • Check the IDoc to make sure that it was passed to port successfully.

FIGURE 24.6 *Creating a contract in the central system* (© SAP AG)

FIGURE 24.7 *Output type ALE proposed for the distributed contract* (© SAP AG)

On the satellite system, you can do the following.

- Check the IDoc to make sure that it was posted successfully.
- View the local copy of the contract in the system.

3. **Create a purchase order against the contract**.

Transaction: ME21

Menu Path: Logistics, Materials Management, Purchasing, Purchase Order, Create, Vendor Known

On the satellite system, create a purchase order using the contract as a reference. To select a contract as a reference, choose Purchase Order, Create w. Reference, To Contract from the menu. The system prompts you to enter the contract number. Enter the number and you can copy the material information. Copy the line and enter the desired quantity, delivery date, and plant information, as shown in Figure 24.8. Save the

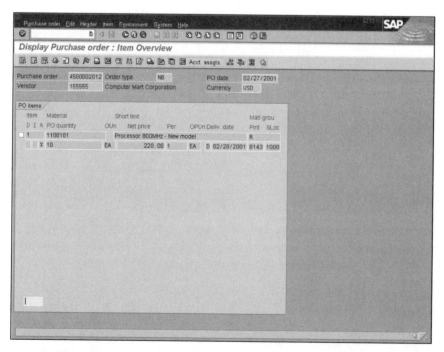

FIGURE 24.8 *Entering a purchase order in the satellite system against the distributed contract* (© SAP AG)

purchase order. The system recognizes that the purchase order is against a distributed contract and automatically generates the BLAREL (release statistics) message to the central system.

4. **Verify the release statistics in the satellite system.** You can check the release statistics on the local system, which will show the quantity consumed. In addition, you can check the release statistics IDoc (BLAREL) sent from the satellite system to the central system, as shown in Figure 24.9.

5. **Verify the release statistics in the central system.** You can check the release statistics on the central system, where it shows the total quantity consumed based on release orders from the satellite systems (see Figure 24.10).

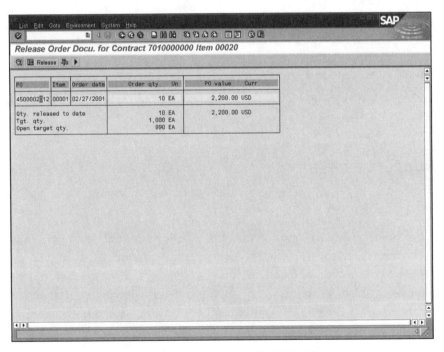

FIGURE 24.9 *Release statistics on the local system* (© SAP AG)

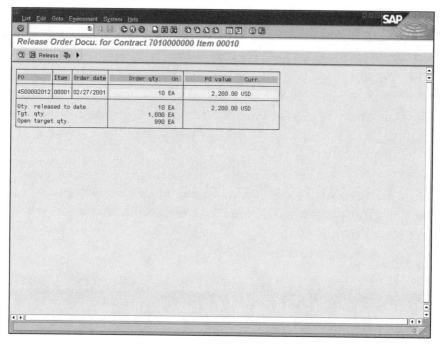

FIGURE 24.10 *Release statistics on the central system* (© SAP AG)

The Support Phase

In the support phase, you monitor the system on an ongoing basis and identify problems if they occur.

It can be necessary to monitor the state of the system at any time. You might be interested in the number of contracts distributed between the systems. IDocs serve as a focal point to monitor the state of the system. You can view the number of IDocs created in the system and drill down to get more detailed information. Chapter 11, "Monitoring the Interface," describes several monitoring tools.

The system can fail at any point. It will be necessary to find the problem, fix it, and restart the system. Complete details are provided in the troubleshooting guide in Chapter 27, "ALE Process Troubleshooting and Recovery."

Distributing Control Data

The biggest challenge in a distributed SAP environment is keeping the customizing data synchronized among the SAP systems. The challenges faced here are similar to those faced with master data, but master data has much richer functionality to maintain backward compatibility, version management, filtering, reduction, and so on. Prior to version 4.6A, these options were not available for control data. Starting with version 4.6A, the tools for keeping customizing data synchronized are improved. The following discussion is based on the tools introduced with version 4.6A. For earlier versions see the "Creating and Maintaining a Control Data Model prior to Version 4.6A" section later in this chapter.

Strategies in Distributing Control Data

The most common approach to managing control data is the centralized approach, shown in Figure 24.11. In this approach, one of the systems is set up as the global configuration system. Any changes to customizing objects are made in this system and then transported to the distributed systems. A control data model is maintained on this system to identify the owner of control data objects and recipients. This locks the recipient systems from making changes to the customizing objects.

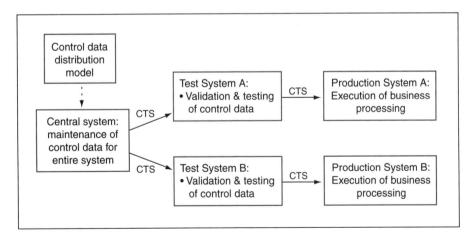

FIGURE 24.11 *Centralized maintenance of control data*

The biggest advantage to this approach is the control over configuration data. Changes are made on one system, and any conflicts are tested immediately. The disadvantage is that systems have customizing data they don't need. This takes away the autonomy of the distributed systems to customize processes for their local needs without having to worry about the effect on other systems. It also requires procedures and rules to make global changes.

Managing Control Data

The following guidelines are offered for controlling configuration across distributed systems.

♦ Start with the distributed scenarios concept from the very beginning without physically splitting the systems. Later, this will help you split the systems easily. It is easier to separate an integrated system than to merge two systems that have drifted apart.

♦ Centralize maintenance of the entire organizational structure if at all possible.

♦ Develop procedures and rules to restrict users from making local changes. You can use the control data model to restrict such changes.

Maintaining the Control Data Model

You can create and maintain the distribution model for control data directly. This is very similar to maintaining the customer model for transactional data and master data objects. Assume that you want to control the maintenance of purchasing organization and company codes in System A and lock other systems from making changes to these customizing objects.

Determining the Object ID for the Customizing Object

The object ID is determined from the IMG. For example, to see the customizing object for the purchasing organization, go to the area in the IMG where the purchasing organization is maintained, click the line, and select Edit, Display IMG Activity. On the next screen, select the tab titled Maint. Objects. (Prior to version 4.6A, select Goto, Document Attributes, Display from the menu. In the drop-down menu that appears, click the Objects button.) For the purchasing organization, the customizing object ID is V_T024E. Similarly, the object ID for a company code is V_T001.

Creating a Distribution Group

Transaction: BDXJ

Menu Path: From the ALE customizing in IMG, choose Modeling and Implementing Business Processes, Synchronization of Customizing Data, Maintain Distribution

You create a distribution group by assigning a group name, a description, and the name of the system that will be the "master" system for the set of customizing data. Click the Assign Customizing Objects button. On the following screen, enter the object types and IDs you want to include in this distribution group. After entering the objects discussed for the distributed contracts scenario, the screen should look like Figure 24.12. Later on, when you define this flow on the distribution model, the distribution group acts as a filter object for the message type for customizing data distribution.

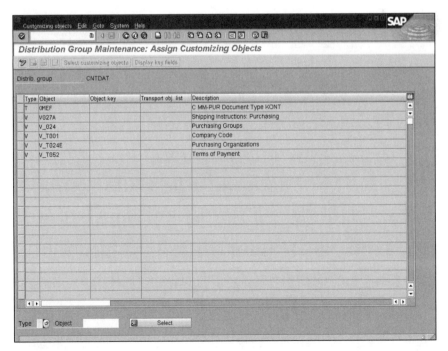

FIGURE 24.12 *The control data model for the distributed contracts scenario* (© SAP AG)

Defining the Customizing Data in the Distribution Model

Transaction: BD64

Menu Path: From the ALE customizing in IMG, choose Modeling and Implementing Business Processes, Maintain Distribution Model and Distribute Views

In this step, you enter values in the control data distribution model. On the Change Distribution Model screen, you see a list of systems in a tree format. The owning system is listed first, and then receiving systems are listed. Select the desired receiving system and click the Add Message Type button. Type **CONDA2** and press Enter. Next, click the line containing CONDA2 and click the Filter Model Display button. On the pop-up window, enter the distribution group name in the Object Name field and fill in the other fields with the appropriate data (the start date, end date, model view, sender, receiver, and message type). Click the Execute icon. When you are done, a Data Filter Active icon is displayed under the CONDA2 message type. Double-clicking the filter icon displays a pop-up window showing the distribution group as part of the filter object, as shown in Figure 24.13.

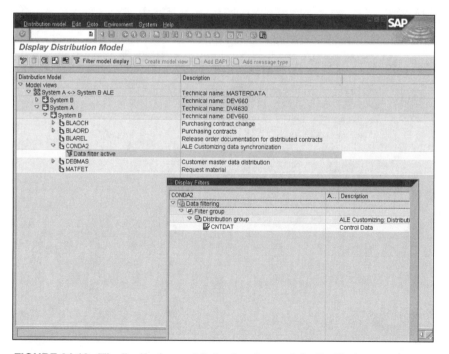

FIGURE 24.13 *The distribution model, showing the use of the distribution group* (© SAP AG)

Distributing the Model

Transaction: BD64

Menu Path: From the ALE customizing in IMG, choose Modeling and Implementing Business Processes, Maintain Distribution Model and Distribute Views

Click the name of the model view on the BD64 screen. Then, from the pop-up menus, select Edit, Model View, Distribute. Select the receiving logical system name from the list that pops up. The model is distributed synchronously. You must have the RFC destinations maintained between the systems.

Creating and Maintaining a Control Data Model prior to Version 4.6A

Prior to version 4.6A, SAP provided a more restricted set of tools for handling the distribution and synchronization of control data. These restrictions are also relevant if you have a distributed system that includes satellite systems running pre-4.6A versions. The main features of the older process are as follows.

- ◆ There is a standard distribution model called CONTROLDATA, maintained via transaction BD64.

- ◆ The message type used is CONDAT, instead of CONDA2.

- ◆ There is no concept of the distribution group. Instead, the customization objects are defined directly in the filter object.

- ◆ A simplified tool for configuring the control data distribution, transaction BD89, is provided.

 NOTE

SAP has provided an add-on tool that gives systems running versions 3.1H through 4.5B similar capabilities for handling distribution and synchronization of customizing data as systems running versions 4.6A and above. See OSS note 120745 for more information.

Summary

In this chapter, you learned how distributed processes are implemented. In a distributed system, three types of data (transactional, master, and customizing) are exchanged between the systems. Each system maintains a local copy of the data needed for the business processes. It is thus responsible for the integrity and maintenance of local data only. Data shared between the systems is assigned an owner, who is then responsible for maintaining and distributing the data to other systems. A well-designed distributed system requires minimum dependency on the other system and operates independently with optimal use of network resources.

True benefits of a distributed system are achieved with a timely and controlled exchange of transactional and master data between the systems. Various messages exchanged between the systems are modeled in a customer distribution model. The ALE process is used for exchanging master and transactional data. Customizing data must be consistent across systems to make semantic sense of master and transactional data. Maintaining and customizing data consistently across systems is a challenge. A control data model is used to model the customizing objects. It defines an owner for the data and keeps other systems from modifying the data.

Chapter 25

SAP to Non-SAP Communication

In this chapter, you will learn why companies have embraced the ALE/IDoc technology for SAP to non-SAP communication. The various technical and business reasons are discussed, and configuration steps to set up the exchange of IDocs between SAP and non-SAP systems are presented. This chapter assumes that you are familiar with the ALE or EDI process.

The technical architecture of ALE technology makes it suitable for communication with external systems. The ALE architecture consists of three layers.

- ◆ **Application services**. The layer responsible for the application logic. This is where all the business rules are encapsulated and IDocs are processed.

- ◆ **Distribution services**. The layer responsible for determining recipients and formatting data according to each recipient's requirements.

- ◆ **Communication services**. The layer responsible for delivering data to the recipients. The settings in this layer determine the medium in which data is to be transferred. This layer allows SAP to communicate with any external system by simply changing the communication settings.

ALE/IDoc Interface Applications

Two of the most commonly used applications of ALE/IDoc technology outside the SAP-to-SAP realm are SAP to third-party products and SAP to legacy systems.

SAP to Third-Party Products

SAP interfaces with several bolt-on products—for example, the production-planning optimizers, shipping optimizers, and warehouse management system—through the ALE/IDoc interface. The use of bolt-ons has been a strategic step in SAP's growth. SAP concentrated on the core business processes and applications, and the bolt-on products provided functionality in specific areas in which SAP was not interested or which SAP needed more time to build. An IDoc interface exists for several application areas. The interface defines the what and the when for the IDocs that must be exchanged between SAP and the bolt-on. SAP certifies products for compatibility with a specific interface.

CAUTION

SAP certification provides an assurance of connectivity only. Evaluating the product's functionality is up to the customer.

The implementation methodology of these scenarios is very similar to the distributed SAP processes discussed in Chapter 24, "Implementing Distributed Business Processes." Technical differences at the communication layer require settings that differ from those for SAP-to-SAP transfer. These settings are discussed later in the chapter.

SAP to Legacy Systems

At some point, all SAP implementations have to interface with legacy systems for a smooth transition to the SAP environment. Any IDoc interfaces developed for EDI, SAP to SAP, and SAP to third-party products can be deployed for integration with legacy systems without any modification to the SAP programs. Several companies have realized the benefits offered by this interface and use it as a standard architecture for all their interfacing needs. Data between SAP and legacy systems is usually exchanged via files.

Why Is ALE/IDoc a Better Approach?

Before the availability of the ALE technology, the BDC (*Batch Data Communication*) technique was the main choice for developing interfaces between external systems and SAP. Although simple to develop, the BDC approach poses several problems, such as differences in screen sequences in batch versus online mode, lack of a standard error-handling process, and complicated management during upgrades. The following list summarizes the reasons why ALE is better suited for the job. These features are discussed in the context of ALE and EDI processes throughout the book, and, therefore, the technical details are omitted here.

♦ **Several standard scenarios**. The standard ALE, EDI, and SAP to non-SAP scenarios can be used without any modification to interface with legacy systems.

♦ **Future support**. The ALE/IDoc technology is the basis for SAP's business framework architecture. The number of IDocs has grown considerably, BAPIs and ALE are well integrated, and this technology is definitely here to stay.

◆ **Use of IDoc structures**. One of the major tasks for integration with external systems is the definition of business rules for data structures. IDocs can be used to represent very complex structures. You can accommodate several business rules within the IDoc structure—such as mandatory versus optional data records, order of data, and arrangement of data—without having to write additional code. These structures are self-documenting as long as the data fields have been documented. You can use standard reports to view, download, and print IDoc documentation.

◆ **Development tools**. Interfaces with legacy systems require quite a bit of development because of proprietary structure and content of the data. SAP provides a complete development environment for new ALE scenarios and IDocs. Custom scenarios blend with standard scenarios to take full advantage of the ALE interface layer tools and utilities.

◆ **Superior error handling**. A major chunk of the program logic for an interface program is devoted to error handling. With ALE, you can focus on the business logic because error handling is built in to the ALE interface layer. It logs information in the IDocs and utilizes workflow, which offers several benefits for notification and resolution of problems. Thus, development time and size of code are reduced considerably.

◆ **Restart and recovery options**. A major operational concern is the restart and recovery procedure. Companies develop procedures that are typically unique for each interface. This environment poses several problems in training and maintenance of procedures. With ALE, the restart and recovery mechanism is similar across the board.

Legacy Interface Development Issues

Although the ALE interface should be an obvious choice, true benefits are achieved if you keep the following points in mind while developing legacy interfaces.

◆ **The learning curve**. The ALE technology has a steeper learning curve than other techniques, and people with ALE, EDI, and IDoc skills are sometimes in short supply. It's advisable to develop templates for inbound and outbound programs to make the development easier and consistent.

♦ **Acceptability of the IDoc format**. In some companies, development on legacy systems is frozen in order to phase them out. An interface with legacy applications might already be defined, and IDoc format might not be an acceptable format. You will require a subsystem (ALE converter) to convert data from IDoc format to the legacy format.

♦ **Reuse of IDocs and processes**. Reuse the standard IDocs and processes as much as possible. Companies often develop new IDocs using new segments without researching the existing repository of IDocs and segments.

♦ **The size of data files**. Data exchanged with legacy applications can grow very large. It's not uncommon to see data files in the range of 200MB. Although technically the IDoc interface does not have any restriction, it is advisable to divide a data file into smaller independent units. For example, you could dump the entire material master data into one single IDoc, but this would consume too many resources, take too long to display, be difficult to manage, and possibly halt a system without enough memory. A good approach is to divide the data being transferred into units that can be used independently.

 TIP

IDocs up to 2MB do not affect performance. A few large IDocs don't matter, but if you consistently exchange IDocs that are about 100MB, you should rethink your design approach.

♦ **Distribution of changes**. A common tendency is to distribute entire sets of data. At one site, a complete load of employee information was being distributed to an external system on a periodic basis to keep the systems in sync. This process caused unnecessary performance hits on the system. SAP provides the change document concept for several objects, enabling you to distribute only those objects that have been modified in some way. This approach can reduce the number and size of IDocs considerably. See Chapter 23, "Distributing Master Data," for details on distributing changes.

Interfacing with Non-SAP Systems

To interface with external systems, you can either employ the direct approach or use converters.

The Direct Approach

In the direct approach, the IDoc file format is sent to an external system without any conversion (see Figure 25.1). The external system is responsible for stripping the control records and administrative information out of the IDoc data records. For data being sent to SAP, the external system is also responsible for appending this information.

 NOTE

In one interesting situation, I saw legacy files brought into the SAP system and converted into an IDoc format using ABAP programs written out to the operating system as IDoc files, and then brought in through the normal IDoc channel. Alternatively, the files could have been reformatted as IDocs by the ABAP program and loaded directly using the function module IDOC_INBOUND_WRITE_TO_DB.

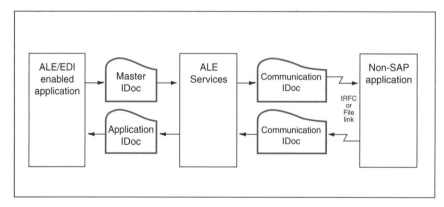

FIGURE 25.1 *Interfacing with an external system directly*

Using Converters

Another way to interface with external systems is to use converters. In this approach, a middleware product called an *ALE converter* handles the transformation between the IDoc format and legacy format, as shown in Figure 25.2. SAP certifies several ALE converters; you can obtain a list from SAP's Web site, or refer to OSS notes 0114714 (for SAP versions 4.0 through 4.6) and 0041365 (for releases prior to 4.0). These converters are based on the same principle as the EDI subsystems that convert IDoc data to EDI standards, and vice versa. The difference lies in how data is exchanged between SAP and the converter. EDI subsystems use a file interface, whereas ALE converters use memory-to-memory transfer. In fact, most products that were certified as EDI subsystems have been enhanced to be certified as ALE converters. If you've already deployed an EDI subsystem for your EDI project, check with your vendor about its ALE certification. You can use a system that is not certified, but certification provides an assurance of connectivity. Several companies that aren't very concerned with memory-to-memory transfer have used their EDI subsystems to perform the conversion process.

The advantage of using the memory-to-memory transfer option is in not having to deal with file permissions and file management. The advantage of using a file interface is apparent when you're dealing with large data packets. For example, if you are going to transfer files of 50–60MB, a file interface is more suitable because the entire file is not loaded into the memory.

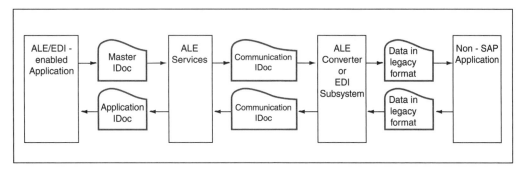

FIGURE 25.2 *Interfacing with an external system via an ALE converter*

Configuration Requirements

To interface with an external system using standard ALE and EDI scenarios, you use components from both the ALE and EDI interfaces. This section does not cover any new settings, but you will need to know which components are used from the ALE and EDI processes. Check the EDI and ALE chapters suggested here for details on how to set up specific components. The configuration settings required are as follows.

1. **Maintain the logical system**. Assign a logical name to the external system (ALE converter, EDI subsystem, or legacy system). The logical name must be unique across the distributed network. This setting is similar to those for SAP-to-SAP communication. See Chapter 22, "Configuring the ALE Infrastructure," for details on how to set up logical names for systems. This step is not required for EDI processes.

2. **Create the RFC destination**. Identify the technical parameters for the SAP system to communicate with the external system. You will want to create an RFC destination of type T. This setting is the same as the setting in the EDI configuration. See Chapter 6, "Configuring Basic EDI Components," for more information.

3. **Maintain the customer distribution model**. A sending system uses the customer distribution model to determine the recipients for a message. You will maintain a customer distribution model for outgoing messages from SAP to the external system. You do not need to model incoming messages from the legacy system to SAP because the distribution model is an SAP concept and does not exist outside SAP. The steps to maintain the customer distribution model for ALE processes are described in Chapter 23, "Distributing Master Data."

4. **Create a port definition**. A port definition controls the medium of communication. If your external system uses files to exchange data, you must create a file port in which the attributes for directory names and file names are specified. If the external system uses memory-to-memory transfer, you must create a transactional RFC (tRFC) port. Section One, "EDI," describes file ports. See Chapter 6, "Configuring Basic EDI Components," for complete details on maintaining file ports. Transactional RFC ports are described in the context of ALE in Chapter 22, "Configuring the ALE Infrastructure."

5. **Create partner profiles**. Create one partner profile for the logical system name identified in Step 1. An outbound record will exist for each outgoing message, and an inbound record will exist for each incoming message. Refer to Chapter 7, "Configuring Partner Profiles," for complete details on establishing and maintaining partner profiles.

TIP

You can maintain incoming messages in a distribution model to depict the distribution scenarios and use it for automatically generating partner profiles, but the model has no business functionality.

6. **Set up the inbound trigger**. The inbound trigger depends on the communication medium used to exchange data with the external system. If IDoc data is exchanged via files, the inbound trigger explained in the EDI section is used. If IDoc data is exchanged via memory buffers, settings for inbound triggers are done on the external system. Because the inbound trigger is specific to the product being used, you have to rely on documentation from the vendor for details.

NOTE

See Chapter 6, "Configuring Basic EDI Components," for complete details on inbound triggering via files.

Testing

The testing tools described in the EDI process are more useful than the testing tools described in Section Two, "ALE," for two reasons.

- ◆ The EDI process is used for SAP to non-SAP communication.
- ◆ During initial development, a great deal of testing is carried out using IDoc files, so the testing described in the EDI process is more appropriate.

Monitoring, Troubleshooting, and Performance

Monitoring, troubleshooting, and performance depend on the communication method being used to exchange data. If you are using the file mechanism, refer to Chapter 13, "Managing EDI Process Performance and Throughput," for details. Otherwise, for details on memory-to-memory transfer, refer to Chapter 28, "Managing ALE Process Performance and Throughput."

Enhancements and Custom Development

Much custom programming and IDoc development is carried out for interfaces with legacy systems. These programs are independent of the communication method and focus on business logic. Section Three, "IDocs," includes complete coverage of extending IDocs, creating new IDocs, programming, and customizing the IDoc interface for customer enhancements.

Summary

The components necessary for configuring SAP to interface with non-SAP systems via the IDoc interface have been borrowed from the ALE/EDI process. Because of the segregation of the communication layer in the ALE/EDI process, you can easily adapt ALE and EDI processes to communicate with an external system. Data can be exchanged via files or memory buffers, depending on the external system's capabilities.

PART IX

Operating and Administering the ALE Interface

Chapter 26

Testing the
ALE Interface

After you configure the ALE interface, you test each component to make sure that the configuration settings work as desired. Perhaps, to meet your business needs, you have developed some components of the ALE interface from scratch, such as Message control, IDoc structure, and IDoc programs. In this case, it becomes all the more important to test each individual piece thoroughly before deploying it in production.

This chapter introduces utilities and techniques for testing inbound and outbound ALE processes. New tools appear in every release, and existing tools are enhanced to support the testing utilities better. Some of the inbound tools mentioned here might not be available in your current release.

For each test, the following topics are mentioned.

◆ Steps to carry out the task

◆ Where to look for errors

◆ Possible causes of errors (to help debug)

◆ How to verify the successful execution of the test

The focus of this chapter is on testing methods and techniques. On several occasions, you will need to refer to Chapter 11, "Monitoring the Interface," and Chapter 27, "ALE Process Troubleshooting and Recovery."

Testing Outbound Processes

The outbound process is relatively simple to test and requires the least simulation because the process originates in SAP and all the major components reside in SAP. The best approach for testing an outbound process is to test each component and then the whole process. The following sections describe the utilities available for testing and explain how to test each component.

SAP provides two types of test utilities.

◆ Utilities for a sanity test

◆ Utilities to test the process

The first type of utility performs a basic sanity test on the configuration of ALE objects such as the customer model, partner profile, and RFC destination parameters. A sanity test enables you to test a component without executing the actual process. These utilities are accessed from within the objects' maintenance screens. The second type of utility tests the process. The outbound process is tested with the actual components involved in the process.

Prerequisites for Testing Outbound Processes

The outbound process is composed of programs that are linked to run one after the other. To test each component separately, you have to disconnect them. In the outbound record of the partner profile for your message, set the Collect IDocs flag. The flag prevents the RSEOUT00 program from running immediately after an IDoc is created in the system.

 NOTE

For reference, use the process flow described in Chapter 20, "The Outbound ALE Process."

Performing Sanity Tests

This section describes the basic sanity tests available for each individual object, such as the partner profile, customer model, and RFC destination. These tests check the validity of various attributes in the objects without executing the process. Although you might have carried out some of these tests while configuring particular components, the tests are mentioned here in complete detail.

Testing Partner Profiles

Partner profiles can be checked to make sure that the parameters specified are still correct. The following checks are carried out.

◆ The process code
◆ The user to be notified
◆ Message control consistency with outbound parameters

You execute the program RSECHK07 to check the consistency of partner pro-files, via transaction SE38 or from the menus of the initial partner profile screen. The output is a color-coded report that contains details about any problems that occur.

Although a check is carried out when the partners are created, some parameters can become invalid over time. For example, if a user ID that no longer exists was spec-ified in the partner profile, this report would flag the invalid user ID as an error.

Testing the RFC Destination

This test confirms the connectivity between the SAP systems. Execute transac-tion SM59. Click the RFC destination being used in the process—typically, the logical system name assigned to the remote SAP system. You can confirm your RFC destination by viewing the details of the port definition that will be used for outbound processes. Click the Test button. If the results are positive, the connec-tivity is okay. In addition, you should test the log on process to make sure that log on parameters are correct. Click the Remote Logon button.

If the test connection returns negative results, the message should indicate the problem. If the message is not self-explanatory, you can turn on RFC Trace to log every step in the RFC test process. This log is slightly cryptic, and knowledge of CPI-C (*Common Programming Interface Communication*) is necessary to interpret the trace information.

If the remote log on test is successful and the user ID is a background user, the system does not display a response. If a problem occurs, the system creates a ses-sion for the remote system and prompts you to enter a user ID and password.

If the connectivity between the two SAP systems is at fault, the possible causes of errors are as follows.

◆ The TCP/IP host name for the SAP system specified in the Target Machine field could be misspelled.

TIP

If the problem persists, you can try to use the IP address of the host on which the EDI subsystem is or will be installed. If this method works, the problem lies in the TCP/IP configuration. Check with your Basis staff.

◆ The value entered in the System Number field could be incorrect. Log on to the remote system and use transaction SM51 to display the application servers. The last two digits in the application server name provide the value for the system number.

◆ The user ID, password, or client number could be incorrect, or the password could have expired.

◆ The physical links and network links might not be working—although this is rare. You execute the ping command at the OS level to make sure that the link is up.

Testing Distribution Model Consistency

This test performs a number of checks for the messages modeled in a customer model (see Figure 26.1).

◆ The existence of a message type

◆ The consistency of segment filtering and conversion settings

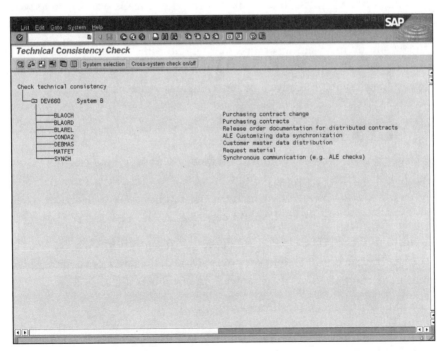

FIGURE 26.1 *The consistency test of the distribution model* (© SAP AG)

◆ Partner profile correctness

◆ The correct definition and existence of process code

◆ The settings for any function module to be called, including event and parameter definitions

◆ The validity of permissions for executing function modules or other application components

◆ The consistency of logical system definitions

TIP

By default, this test does a cross-system check, but you can limit it to your local system by clicking the Cross-System On/Off button.

Execute transaction BDM5. Drill down until you get to the right message and destination system. Click the message and choose Edit, Check from the menu. The system carries out the checks and changes the color of the message type, depending on the results. Red means error, yellow means warning, and white signifies a successful test.

If the tests result in a warning or an error, you select the line and choose Edit, Details from the menu. The system displays the cause of the problem. Double-clicking the problem transfers you directly to the area where you can fix the problem.

Testing Outbound Processes

Message control, change pointers, or stand-alone programs can trigger an outbound ALE process. The outbound process is essentially a sequence of several subprocesses that link together to form the total process. This section describes the testing procedure for each subprocess.

The testing of the Message control process is discussed in Chapter 10, "Testing the EDI Interface." The four subprocesses tested in the outbound process for stand-alone programs and the change pointer process are as follows.

◆ Successful triggering from change pointers

◆ Successful triggering from the stand-alone program

◆ The generation of IDocs

◆ Successful dispatch of IDocs to a remote SAP system

Verifying Successful Triggering from Change Pointers

In this test, you want to make sure that change pointers are written when an application document is changed. To test this process, change the application document for which you want to test the change pointers. For example, to test change pointers for the material master, execute transaction MM02 and make appropriate changes.

This process does not have a formal log for failure, but you can check the BDCP and BDCPS tables. An entry is created in these tables for every change made to a document enabled for change pointers. If an entry is missing, you have a problem.

The change pointer process does not work in the following situations.

- ◆ Changes are probably not recorded for the object with which you are working. Execute transaction SCDO and verify that a change document object exists for your object. The names of the change document objects are sometimes cryptic, so you might have to view complete details (such as the tables included in the change document) to locate the right change document object.

- ◆ Changes to only certain data elements are recorded. Determine the data element for the field you are trying to change. Use transaction SE11 and verify that the Change Document field is selected for the data element. If this field is not turned on, the change document will not be written.

- ◆ The IDoc message type for the object has not been maintained in the customer model. Thus, if you are trying to generate IDocs for the material master, MATMAS should exist in a customer model.

- ◆ Change pointers are not globally active. Execute transaction BD61 to verify this condition.

- ◆ Change pointers have not been activated for the message type. Execute transaction BD50 to verify this condition.

- ◆ The fields for which ALE change pointers are written do not include the field you are modifying. Execute transaction BD52 to verify this condition.

If this step is successful, an entry should appear in the BDCP table for the change. Use transaction SE16 or SE17 to view entries in this table. If everything looks good, you should execute program RBDMIDOC to start the IDoc generation process from change pointers.

Verifying Successful Execution of Stand-Alone Programs

This test is applicable if you are using a stand-alone program to generate IDocs. In this test, you want to make sure that your program is executed successfully.

A program exists for each master data object enabled for ALE. From the ALE part of the SAP standard menu, select Master Data Distribution, and select the appropriate master data to be distributed. For example, Cross-Application, Material, Send executes transaction BD10 to send material master data.

Because this program is executed online, the results are displayed on the screen. If the number of master IDocs or communication IDocs is zero, you probably have a problem. Following is a list of places to check, depending on the type of error.

- If the number of master IDocs processed is zero, check the parameters entered on the selection screen of the stand-alone program.

- Make sure that the message type has been modeled in the customer distribution model and that the customer distribution model is available on the sending system.

- If you have developed a custom program or an IDoc type, check the configuration settings for the message type and IDoc type. Refer to Chapter 33, "Customizing the Interface for New or Extended IDocs," for details on how to configure the ALE process for custom IDocs.

If this step is successful, you should get a message indicating the number of communication IDocs generated.

Verifying the Generation of IDocs

This step verifies the program logic that generates the IDocs. If you have extended the IDoc selection program via user exits, modified the program, or created a new one, you will be particularly interested in this step. This step is simply an extension of the preceding step and doesn't require any new programs or transactions.

There are several possibilities for errors in this step, and if they occur, the status record of the IDoc indicates the problem. You can use transaction WE02 or WE05 to display the IDoc and its status records.

If you are testing a standard SAP-supplied program, errors at this stage are rarely due to program logic. The main cause of errors is a missing or an incorrect partner profile. (The sanity tests you carried out earlier should have caught this error.) If you have done custom development, either of the following factors can cause errors.

- The partner profile is missing or incorrect.
- The IDoc structure or program logic is incorrect.

TIP

If you cannot figure out the problem, start the debugger and begin debugging the program.

If this step works correctly, the IDoc must be in status 30 (IDoc Ready for Dispatch).

Verifying Successful Dispatch of IDocs to Remote SAP Systems

In this step, you test the process to dispatch IDocs from one SAP system to another. One of the major culprits in this process is the RFC destination setting for the remote SAP system. You will experience the most problems with this setting because parameters in the RFC destination pertain to another SAP system. If you successfully carried out the sanity test for RFC destination as described earlier, the chance of error here is minimal.

Transaction: WE14
Menu Path: From the Area menu of EDI (WEDI), choose Test, Outbound Processing from IDoc

The IDoc must be in status 30 (IDoc Ready for Dispatch) to be passed to the communication layer. A standard program, RSEOUT00, handles this operation. Execute program RSEOUT00 via transaction SE38, or execute WE14. The selection screen allows you to select IDocs based on various criteria (see Figure 26.2). You can enter the IDoc number generated in the preceding test, "Verifying the Generation of IDocs." If the process executes successfully, you should execute program RBDMOIND for completeness. The RBDMOIND program updates the IDoc status to 12 (Dispatch OK) when the IDoc is received on the remote system. Refer to Chapter 22, "Configuring the ALE Infrastructure," for details on the significance of the RBDMOIND program.

FIGURE 26.2 *The selection screen for the RSEOUT00 program* (© SAP AG)

Check the last status record of the IDoc and the tRFC log (SM58) for errors. See the errors explained in the "Testing the RFC Destination" section earlier in this chapter. This step is verified by checking the IDoc's last status code. The status should be 12 (Dispatch OK).

> ### CAUTION
>
> The IDoc status 03 (Data Passed to Port OK) does not guarantee that the IDoc has been received on the other system.

Testing Inbound Processes

The inbound process is different than the outbound process in that the former originates outside the local SAP system. The sending system is not always available, or you simply might not want to start the outbound process from scratch every time you test the inbound process. When you test the inbound process, you can use several utilities to simulate the start of the process. The actual processing is carried out by the real components. The best strategy for testing an inbound process is to test each component separately.

As it does for the outbound process, SAP provides two types of test utilities for the inbound process.

◆ Utilities for the sanity test
◆ Utilities to test the process

Prerequisites for Testing an Inbound Process

The inbound process is composed of programs that are linked to run one after the other. To test each component separately, enable the Trigger by Background flag in the partner profile. This setting disconnects the components from one another and prevents them from starting the next process immediately. As a reference, you can use the process flow described in Chapter 21, "The Inbound ALE Process."

Performing Sanity Tests

You can use standard system tools to test the configuration components defined for the inbound process. These tools help do a basic sanity test of the configuration settings without executing the process.

Testing Partner Profiles

You can check partner profiles to make sure that the parameters specified are still correct. The test is the same as the corresponding test defined in the outbound process.

Testing Inbound Settings

The ALE system provides a tool to test the consistency of inbound parameters for error handling. You can use this tool to test all the process codes or one process code at a time. The output is a color-coded report that displays the possible cause of any problem.

You can run this report for all process codes by using program RBDMOINF via transaction SE38. However, if you are interested in testing only one process code, you can run program RBDMOINC to test an individual code. Test results are displayed on the output screen in a color-coded report. Double-click any problem to get additional details. Errors in this test can be due to the following reasons.

- The link between the process code and the function module is not defined.
- The object type for the IDoc of this message is missing. If an object is present, it checks for the presence of a triggering event (INPUTERROROCCURED) and a terminating event (INPUTFINISHED). This error is more likely to occur for the custom-developed processes.
- The object type for IDoc packets for this message is missing. If an object is present, it checks for a terminating event named MASSINPUTFINISHED.
- The task for error handling has not been defined.
- The linkage between the task and triggering events is inactive or undefined.
- The linkage for the terminating events is undefined or inactive.
- The roles for the task are undefined.

Most of these settings relate to workflow settings for a new process. SAP already provides these objects for standard messages. This test is useful for custom-developed processes. Refer to Chapter 33, "Customizing the Interface for New or Extended IDocs," for details on configuring new inbound processes.

Testing Inbound Processes

An inbound ALE process is essentially a sequence of several subprocesses that link together to form the total process. This section describes the testing procedure for the three subprocesses.

- The inbound triggering process
- The successful creation of IDocs in the database
- The posting of the application document

One of the major components for the inbound process is the IDoc itself. If the sending system is not available or you want to quickly start the inbound process repeatedly, you need a way to create an IDoc and start the inbound process. The following section describes a tool you can use to generate an IDoc and start the inbound process, and then explains how to test the subprocesses.

Using the Test Tool

Transaction: WE19

Menu Path: From the Area menu of EDI (WEDI), choose Test, Test Tool

The test tool is a two-step process. In the first step, you create an IDoc by using one of the following options.

- ◆ Copy an existing IDoc.
- ◆ Create an IDoc based on an IDoc type.
- ◆ Create an IDoc based on a message type.
- ◆ Create an IDoc using a file as a template.
- ◆ Create an IDoc with no template.

The option you choose depends on your tastes and program requirements. The first option is most commonly used because it enables you to modify an existing IDoc (inbound or outbound) to suit your needs (see Figures 26.3 and 26.4).

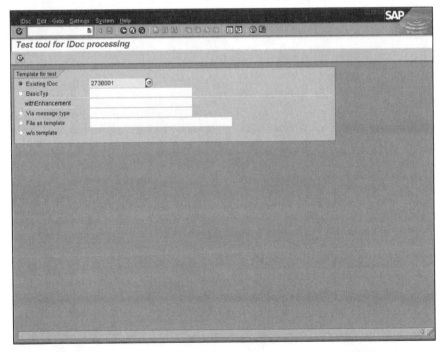

FIGURE 26.3 *Options to create an IDoc* (© SAP AG)

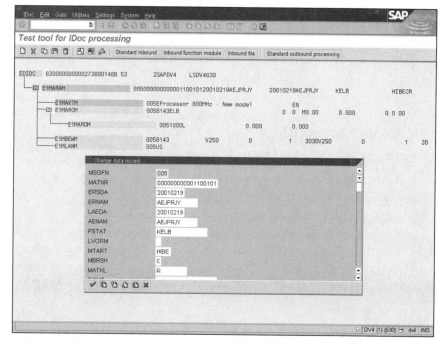

FIGURE 26.4 *The screen to modify the contents of a copied IDoc* (© SAP AG)

In the second step, the IDoc created is passed to the inbound process. You have several options to select the method of starting the inbound process.

◆ **Start the inbound processing via the standard path.** This method uses all inbound components.

◆ **Call the inbound function module directly.** The system bypasses the checks for partner profile and hands the IDoc data to your inbound function module directly. This method is useful for testing an inbound process without having to maintain any inbound configuration. You can also start the function module in debug mode and select the processing option for your posting module.

◆ **Save the IDoc in a file and start the inbound process.** This method is similar to the first method except that you also create an IDoc file at the operating system level. This method is used mainly for EDI processes.

Verifying the Creation of Successful IDocs

This step uses the information in the IDoc's control record to verify that a partner profile is found and that the IDoc is created without any structural errors. This step is useful for checking the structural accuracy of incoming custom-developed IDocs.

Start the inbound process using any of the utilities described earlier. The results are logged in the IDoc's status records. To display the status records, use the IDoc display utilities. If an error occurs, the IDoc gets a status code of 56 (IDoc with Errors Added), and an error workflow is started. The person notified in this case depends on whether a partner profile could be read. If a partner profile is found, workflow is sent to the responsible person specified in the partner profile. If a partner profile entry cannot be read, the message is sent to the EDI administrator.

Common problems in this step are related to data in the control record and syntax errors in the IDoc.

◆ You must make sure that the control record parameters match the key of the partner profile record for that inbound message.

◆ Various factors cause syntax errors. (For more information, see Chapter 30, "IDocs on the Inside.") The status records should pinpoint the problems.

If this step is successful, you should see an IDoc that has a status code of 64 (IDoc Ready to Be Passed to Application).

Verifying the Logic of the Inbound Function Module

Transaction: BD87

Verifying the logic of the inbound function module is the most important step for custom-developed function modules. You must verify that the posting function module is working correctly. You must also verify the logic and the interface of the function module. If problems exist, you debug the process one step at a time.

The IDoc created in the preceding test, "Verifying the Creation of Successful IDocs," is used to test this process. SAP provides a standard program, RBDAPP01, to start the processing of IDocs in status 64. Figure 26.5 shows the selection screen for this program, where you can specify various parameters. Enter your IDoc number and start the process.

FIGURE 26.5 *The selection screen to pass an IDoc to the posting program* (© SAP AG)

Errors in this step are mainly related to data errors and are logged in the IDoc's status records. You can use the IDoc display utilities to display the relevant status records. The IDoc gets a status code of 51 (IDoc with Errors Added). Detailed information about a specific error is also logged in the status record. An error workflow is started to notify the person responsible for handling the error. If your posting program uses the call transaction to post the document, you can step through every screen to determine the exact location of the error. The most common problems in this step relate to data or occur in the application configuration. Make sure that the data values are correct in the data record fields. Also, check your program logic for any errors. If this step is successful, you will see an application document successfully created, and the IDoc will get a status code of 53 (Application Document Posted).

Testing the Workflow Exception Process

After you test the inbound and outbound processes, you can specifically test the workflow component to test the exception-handling process. One obvious test method is to create an error in the process and check for a work item in the Inbox of the responsible user. However, doing so requires you to build error data, which can be difficult. You can test just the workflow component by using the following simple procedure. This procedure applies to all error workflows for outbound and inbound processes.

Transaction: SWUS

Menu Path: From the Area menu of workflow, choose Development, Runtime Tools, Start Workflow (Test Environment)

In this step, your aim is to test the exception-handling process to make sure that the right person is notified when an error occurs. You can use this tool to start the error process manually without introducing a real error. In an actual process, the system starts the error process based on the type of error. The steps are as follows.

1. Identify the workflow task started for a particular exception. Refer to Chapter 9, "Configuring Workflow," for a list of error tasks. For example, the error task for application errors in posting a material master IDoc is MATMAS_Error (TS00007947).

2. Enter the task number in the Task field and click the Input Data button. Press F4 on the next screen and enter an IDoc number.

3. Click the back arrow and click the Start button (see Figure 26.6). This step should start a workflow process.

Errors in this step are communicated in the status bar. For additional details, you click the message. The common problems in this step are related to workflow configuration. If the system reports that you are not one of the possible agents, the task profile has not been maintained or a problem exists with your PD-ORG setup. Refer to Chapter 9 to see how to set up the task profile for workflow tasks. If this step is successful, the responsible person for the task should get a work item in his or her Inbox.

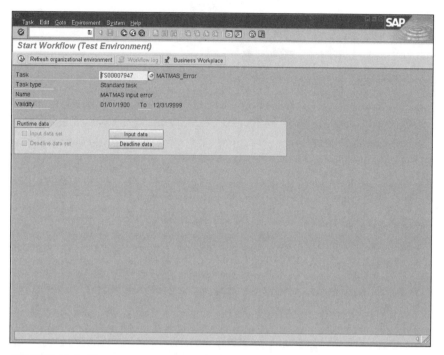

FIGURE 26.6 *Testing a workflow error task* (© SAP AG)

Summary

The tools and techniques for testing outbound and inbound processes are similar. The tests involve doing a sanity test, in which the components are tested without executing the actual process. The sanity tests expose problems in configuration settings. Another set of tests involves testing the process one step at a time. For testing inbound processes, a test tool enables you to create test IDocs on-the-fly. After you create an IDoc, you conduct a three-step test on each component of the inbound process. Each step's results are verified before proceeding to the next step.

Chapter 27

ALE Process Troubleshooting and Recovery

Even if you carry out all the configuration steps exactly as detailed in the configuration section and test all the components thoroughly, any system will experience problems at some point. In this chapter, you'll learn what is considered successful process execution, how to troubleshoot the system when it fails, and how to restart the system from the point of failure.

Where you view the problem depends on where it occurred. This section helps you logically navigate to the point where an error has occurred or a problem exists. In Chapter 11, "Monitoring the Interface," several tools to monitor the system are mentioned—this chapter explains which one to use under particular conditions.

 NOTE

The troubleshooting process for ALE is similar to its counterpart for the EDI process. The main difference lies in troubleshooting errors in the communication process. The restart points are also slightly different because of differences in architecture at the communication level.

How to Troubleshoot

The best approach to troubleshooting any process is to understand the process, identify the possible points of failure, and determine how the system reports problems. This discussion assumes that you grasp the technical concepts of outbound and inbound processes discussed in Chapter 20, "The Outbound ALE Process," and Chapter 21, "The Inbound ALE Process."

Follow this simple approach to troubleshooting.

1. Determine whether a failure has occurred.
2. For a given symptom, use the troubleshooting chart (presented later in this chapter) as your guide to get to the root of the problem quickly.

3. Use the appropriate monitoring tools described in Chapter 11, "Monitoring the Interface," to read and interpret the appropriate log. Use the information in the log to help you analyze the problem.

4. Fix the cause of the problem.

5. Determine the point of restart. Depending on the problem, you restart the process from the point of failure or from the very beginning.

6. Use the technique most suitable for restarting the process. You can restart the process from within workflow (if applicable) or use one of the ALE/EDI tools to restart the process.

Troubleshooting the Outbound Process

An outbound ALE process is triggered in three ways: by Message control, change pointers, or stand-alone programs. Troubleshooting an outbound process started via Message control is discussed in Chapter 12, "EDI Process Troubleshooting and Recovery." Here you will learn how to troubleshoot outbound ALE processes started from either the change pointer process or stand-alone programs.

Points of Failure in the Outbound Process

The outbound process is essentially a sequence of asynchronous processes. Failure can occur within any process. The points of failure in an outbound process are as follows.

♦ An error in the change pointer process

♦ An error in the stand-alone program

♦ An error in the ALE/EDI interface layer

♦ An error in the IDoc structure (a syntax error, conversion problem, and so on)

♦ An error in sending the IDoc to a remote SAP system

How the System Reports Problems

When problems occur in the outbound process, the system uses the technique most suitable at that point to report the problem. The main technique used is the workflow component, but workflow is not started while you are interacting with the system in a dialog mode. After control passes to the SAP system for processing, the system logs any problems and reports them via workflow. An explanation of the outbound process in the context of the error process follows.

1. When the outbound process is triggered, any problems at that point are reported to the user immediately, so workflow is unnecessary. This occurs when you execute transaction BD10 to transfer a material master. If communication IDocs cannot be generated, a workflow is not necessary because the system has already informed you of the results.

2. If Step 1 finds no problems, an IDoc is created in the system. The system performs some basic integrity checks on the IDoc, and a syntax check is done. If an error is found, the IDoc gets a status code of 26 (Error during Syntax Check of IDoc Outbound). A workflow message is sent to the person responsible, as identified in the partner profile.

3. The system then looks for an outbound record in the partner profile. If the outbound record is missing, the IDoc gets a status code of 29 (Error in ALE Service), and a workflow message is sent to the person identified in the partner profile's general view. If the partner profile is completely missing, the EDI administrator is notified via workflow.

4. If Step 3 is successful, the IDoc is passed to the communication layer for dispatch. If errors occur during dispatch, workflow is not started. The system maintains information about failed transmissions in the tRFC logs. Refer to "Restarting Failed tRFCs" later in this chapter for details.

 CAUTION

If the tRFC options have been left at their default values in the RFC destination and there are communication problems, outbound ALE processes have a tendency to take up all the free background processes. In this situation, non-ALE processes will start erroring out and entries will be logged in the system log, but you will not be notified directly.

How to Determine the Success of an Outbound Process

An outbound ALE process is considered successful if the IDoc gets a status code of 03 (Data Passed to Port OK), and no entries in the tRFC log (SM58) are in error.

TIP

The tRFC log is a common log for all tRFC errors. Sometimes it can be loaded with errors from other applications. In such situations, it is best to execute program RBDMOIND (BD75). This program updates the status of IDocs that have been successfully transmitted to 12 (Dispatch OK); otherwise, it leaves them at status 03.

The Troubleshooting Guide for Outbound Errors

For an outbound process, the best approach is to check the IDoc status and then the SAP Inbox. The flowchart in Figures 27.1 through 27.6 depicts the troubleshooting process as a logical sequence of steps. The troubleshooting chart also tells you which log to monitor and identifies the point of restart. Figure 27.1 helps you analyze problems that occur during the initial process to start the generation of IDocs. Figure 27.2 navigates you to the next step in the analysis process. If an IDoc is not present, it indicates a severe error, but if an IDoc was created, most of the error analysis is done based on the IDoc status. If your IDoc is in status 03, it is usually considered a success unless you have the problems depicted in Figure 27.3. Figure 27.4 helps you analyze IDocs that have syntax errors. Figure 27.5 is useful in analyzing problems with IDocs that have an error in the ALE service layer. The main reason is an incorrect partner profile, but additional reasons are

NOTE

The set of Figures 27.1 through 27.6 should be viewed as one logical figure. Like any other flowchart, though, you will find suitable connectors that enable you to navigate from one figure to another.

also possible, as shown in Figure 27.5. Figure 27.6 helps you analyze reasons for IDocs stuck in status 30. IDocs in status 30 are usually due to the settings in the partner profile, but are sometimes due to locking problems.

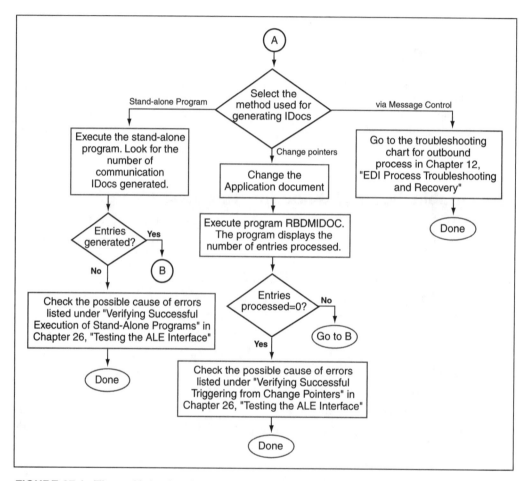

FIGURE 27.1 *The troubleshooting chart for outbound ALE errors—analyzing the initial triggering process*

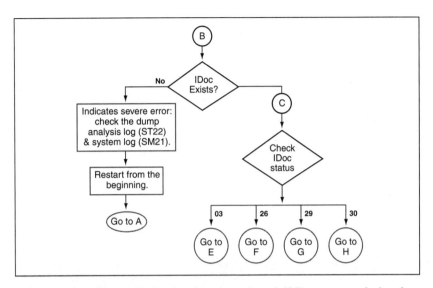

FIGURE 27.2 *The troubleshooting chart for outbound ALE errors—analyzing the next step based on IDoc status*

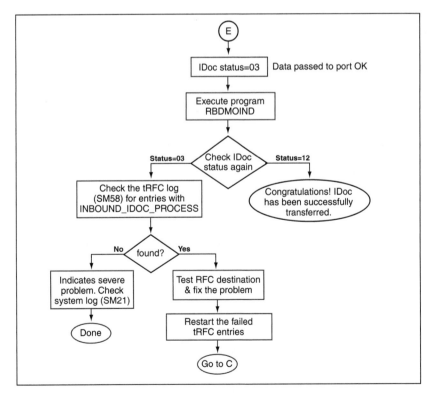

FIGURE 27.3 *The troubleshooting chart for outbound ALE errors—IDoc status 03*

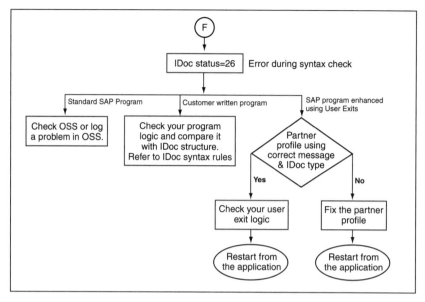

FIGURE 27.4 *The troubleshooting chart for outbound ALE errors—IDoc status 26*

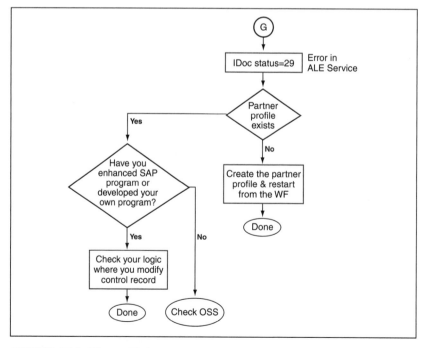

FIGURE 27.5 *The troubleshooting chart for outbound ALE errors—IDoc status 29*

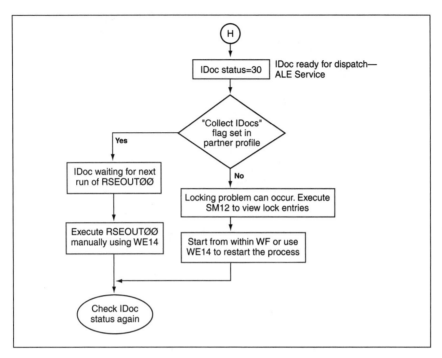

FIGURE 27.6 *The troubleshooting chart for outbound ALE errors—IDoc status 30*

Restart Points for Outbound Errors

A failed process can be restarted from the very beginning or from the point of failure. This section explains the restart points proposed in the troubleshooting chart in Figures 27.1 through 27.6.

Restarting from the SAP Inbox

Transaction: S001
Menu Path: Workplace, Inbox

If a workflow message was generated for the error, you have the option of restarting the process from within workflow. Restarting from the SAP Inbox saves you the trouble of remembering the application transaction and data values. Remember, workflow brings the right task with the right information to the right person at the right time in the right sequence. You can simply execute the work item to start the process. See Chapter 11, "Monitoring the Interface," for details on how to display and execute work items.

If the error was such that several IDocs failed for the same reason, it is convenient to start the process using one of the ALE/EDI tools described in the next section. In my experience, most ALE errors occur in mass numbers, so the SAP Inbox is rarely used for restarting failed ALE processes. In EDI, it is quite common to use the SAP Inbox to restart failed processes.

Restarting with ALE Tools

Transaction: BD87
Menu Path: From the Area menu of ALE (BALE), select ALE Administration, Monitoring, Process IDocs Manually

This method is an alternative to restarting the process from the SAP Inbox. Although it is commonly deployed for mass errors, you can also use it for single errors. There are merits to using this tool instead of the workflow tool in certain cases. For example, assume that you started the ALE process to transfer 10,000 materials, but you forgot to generate partner profiles. The system will generate 10,000 work items. It is very cumbersome to execute each work item individually when the cause of error is the same for all errors. After you fix the problem, you can use the outbound ALE tool to restart all failed IDocs in one step. This tool enables you to process the IDocs from the point of failure without having to restart the process from the beginning. The steps are as follows.

1. Execute transaction BD87.

2. From the screen displayed, make any desired selections to filter the IDocs to be analyzed.

3. On the next screen, you can select the grouping of IDocs to be processed (see Figure 27.7). Highlight the desired grouping and click either the Process button or the Restrict and Process button to start the processing. If you have too many failed IDocs (numbering in the hundreds), processing them all in one run can cause the system to slow down considerably. Refer to Chapter 28, "Managing ALE Process Performance and Throughput," for details on how to utilize packet size and the server group field to restrict the number of dialog processes consumed.

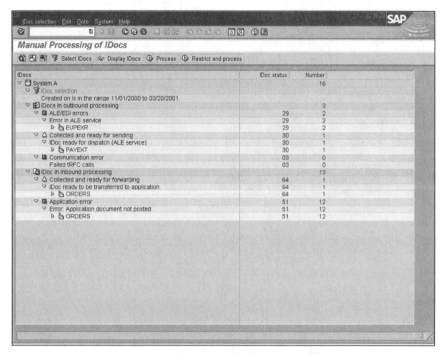

FIGURE 27.7 *The selection screen for restarting IDocs* (© SAP AG)

NOTE

In SAP versions prior to 4.6A, use transaction BD88 to reprocess failed outbound IDocs. The process is similar, except that the first screen of BD88 requires you to select the status condition of the IDocs you want to reprocess. The second screen allows entry of further selection conditions for these IDocs.

Restarting Failed tRFCs

If several tRFCs have failed, you can either restart each one individually or restart them all together. The second option is useful if several entries failed for the same reason.

To restart failed tRFCs individually, execute transaction SM58 and display all the failed tRFCs. Click the desired entry and choose Edit, Execute LUW from the menu. This step restarts the particular entry. If successful, the entry is removed from the log.

TIP

Failures at the tRFC level are frequent. Refer to Chapter 22, "Configuring the ALE Infrastructure," for information on how to automate the reprocessing of failed tRFCs.

To restart several failed entries together, execute transaction BDA1 or choose Periodic Processing, Transactional RFC from the Area menu of ALE (transaction BALE). The selection screen shown in Figure 27.8 allows you to select entries

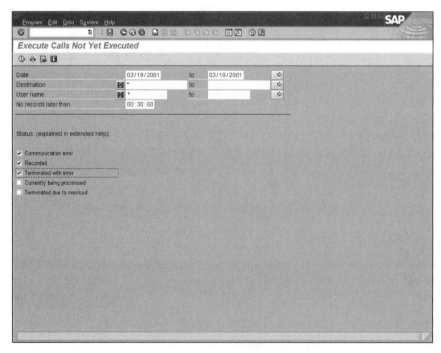

FIGURE 27.8 *The selection screen for restarting failed tRFCs* (© SAP AG)

based on their status, date, time, user, and destination. The status values have the following meanings.

◆ **Communication Error**. These errors are related to network problems.

◆ **Recorded**. Entries in this status were awaiting dispatch when the system was shut down.

◆ **Terminated with Error**. These entries caused a severe error or a dump error on the receiving system. Errors in the user ID and password for remote log on are also classified in this category.

◆ **Currently Being Processed**. These entries are being sent. You should never select this status unless an entry is hung for an extended period. If you select this entry, the IDoc is dispatched again.

◆ **Terminated Due to Overload**. These entries failed because system resources were exceeded.

Purging the Outbound Process

In certain situations, you cannot fix a problem because the data in the IDoc is incorrect, so the process has to be restarted from scratch. If the process in error has created an IDoc, you do not want to leave the IDoc in limbo. You must purge it to prevent it from being processed accidentally.

An IDoc in error can be purged from the work item generated as a result of this error. Execute the work item and look for the Delete button. When you click the Delete button, the IDoc is marked for deletion and gets a status code of 31 (Error—No Further Processing). This status prevents any EDI or ALE tools from accidentally processing the IDoc.

Troubleshooting the Inbound Process

The troubleshooting process for inbound ALE errors is very similar to the troubleshooting process for the inbound process described in Chapter 12, "EDI Process Troubleshooting and Recovery." The only difference lies in how the inbound process is triggered in ALE versus EDI. In ALE, it is triggered from the remote system with a tRFC call, and IDoc data is passed to the inbound process in memory. In EDI, the process is triggered using the startrfc command, and the

IDoc data is passed as a file. After the process is started, it does not matter how it was triggered, so the troubleshooting process is exactly the same from that point on. Errors that can occur in the inbound triggering process are actually part of the troubleshooting process for outbound because an outbound process is the one that triggers the inbound process. An outbound ALE process is not considered successful until an IDoc is created successfully on the receiving system.

The points of failure, points of restart, and methods to purge incoming IDocs are all the same. Refer to Chapter 12 for complete details.

Summary

Errors are possible at various steps in the outbound and inbound processes, and SAP provides extensive log information at various points. Until an IDoc is generated, SAP logs the error in the application initiating the process. After an IDoc is generated, the IDoc becomes the main vehicle for any log information, and errors are routed via workflow to the responsible person.

Because errors are possible at various points, knowing where to start troubleshooting can reduce the time required to fix a problem. The troubleshooting process follows a simple approach. First, determine whether an error has occurred. Then, use the troubleshooting chart to track down the problem. When you find the cause of the problem, fix it and then restart the process from the point of failure, if possible. If not, you must restart the process from the very beginning. Sometimes you will opt to restart the process from the beginning rather than from the point of failure because the data is corrupt. In these situations, you must be sure to purge the items in error.

Chapter 28

**Managing ALE
Process
Performance
and Throughput**

System performance is usually measured by the response time of a user transaction. When a user creates a document or runs a report, the time it takes for the process to complete becomes a starting measure for improving the performance. ALE processes are *asynchronous*, which means that users do not wait online for the IDocs to reach the destination system or post in the destination system. However, ALE processes consume many system cycles in the process of creating IDocs and dispatching them to the destination system. For example, it is not uncommon to see 50,000 materials being transferred via ALE. These huge data transfers via ALE can hamper system performance for other users. One option would be to serialize the process, but this would affect the rate at which data transfer occurs. Moving 50,000 materials could take forever.

On the flip side, if you allow ALE processes to run uncontrolled, they have a tendency to use up all dialog and background processes, which usually requires the system to be shut down. Therefore, managing performance is an important issue for the system's overall health.

In this chapter, you will learn how to manage the performance of ALE processes by controlling their timing, packet size, and parallel-processing options. In addition, this chapter points out general strategies you can adopt to keep your system in good shape, such as data archiving and performance-tuning procedures used for ABAP/4 programs and databases. Those procedures are part of an overall performance-tuning strategy that applies to all modules.

 NOTE

This chapter requires that you understand the technical details of the outbound and inbound processes. For details, refer to Chapter 20, "The Outbound ALE Process," and Chapter 21, "The Inbound ALE Process." Pay special attention to the buffering options available and the processing that occurs in the communication layer.

Methods for Performance Management

You can use three methods to manage the performance and throughput of ALE processes.

- ◆ **Control the process timing**. You control the timing of the ALE process at four stages: the creation of IDocs, dispatch of IDocs to the communication layer, retry of failed transmissions, and posting of IDocs on the receiving system. This approach enables you to select a time that is most appropriate for a process. For example, instead of creating an IDoc every time an object is changed, you can wait until the end of the day to send one IDoc for all changes.

- ◆ **Control the packet size**. You specify the number of IDocs bundled together in a packet used for communication and for posting of documents. The IDocs in a packet are processed one at a time on the receiving end. This way, you make optimal use of network resources, memory buffers, and the number of dialog processes used on the sending and receiving systems. When you are constrained by the amount of resources you can use, you will find this method useful. If you increase the packet size, you get good performance but bad throughput.

- ◆ **Control multiprocessing**. You specify parallel processing for the generation and posting of IDocs. I call this approach "Let the ALE system run wild, but restricted by the number of processes it can consume." This method enables you to make the most of resources allocated to your process. If you increase the number of parallel processes, you increase the throughput but degrade the performance of other processes.

A good strategy is one that strikes a balance among these three methods. The definition of a good strategy is, however, subjective, and attempting to design a common strategy that will work for all companies would be a futile effort. Performance management is an iterative and ongoing exercise in which the goal is to achieve a system that optimally uses its resources. Such a system is subject to change, so you're never truly free of the performance management challenge.

These three options are explained next in the context of the inbound and outbound processes. You will learn where to make the settings and about the benefits and drawbacks of each option.

Managing Outbound Process Performance

This part of the chapter covers outbound processes that use change pointers or stand-alone programs. Performance of outbound processes that use Message control is described in Chapter 13, "Managing EDI Process Performance and Throughput."

Although every company has different needs, you can classify the various outgoing messages into two broad categories.

- ◆ Those requiring near-real-time operation
- ◆ Those that can be operated in batch mode

You do not have any way to control the performance of messages that require near-real-time operation, but such processes exist, and you need to account for system cycles consumed by such processes. For outgoing messages that can be operated in batch mode, you can implement the methods described earlier.

Near-Real-Time Outbound Messages

In near-real-time mode, an IDoc can be generated and passed to the communication layer immediately. From there, the IDoc is dispatched to the destination system in a very short period of time. The actual time lag depends on the load in the system. This technique gives the near-real-time feel, which is useful for critical ALE transactions. For example, if you are interfacing with an external warehouse management system and you create a transfer order in SAP, you want the transfer order sent to the warehouse management system immediately.

 CAUTION

Criticality is a relative term, having a different meaning for each organization. Changes to master data are less likely to be critical than changes to transactional data. This option should not be used for high-volume and non-critical transactions because it causes performance problems.

The configuration options enable you to control real-time behavior at a very granular level. For example, you can enable all messages going to a system for real-time mode or limit that mode to specific messages only. The following settings achieve the near-real-time behavior for a message.

◆ For processes triggered from change pointers, schedule the RBDMIDOC program to execute more frequently (every five minutes) for critical messages.

◆ In the partner profile for the outbound message, set the outbound mode to Transfer IDoc Immediately.

Batch-Mode Outbound Messages

Batch mode is used for non-critical and high-volume transactions. This mode provides the most control from a performance perspective. The choices are

◆ **Control the timing**. The timing for an outbound process has two points of control, depending on the needs of the company.

• **At the change-pointer level**. When master data is changed, the process to analyze change pointers (RBDMIDOC) can be delayed. This type of control achieves the highest performance benefits because there is no load on the system from an ALE perspective. The process can be scheduled to run when the system is not loaded (at night, for example). The only drawback with this approach is that any errors in the outbound process are not discovered until the process is executed.

• **When IDocs are transferred to the communication layer**. This type of control is achieved by setting the output mode in the partner profile to Collect IDocs. The biggest advantage of buffering IDocs at this stage is that they have been generated, so any errors in the IDoc process should have been discovered. The RSEOUT00 program is then used to transfer buffered IDocs in the database to the communication layer. This program must be scheduled on an as-needed basis. Several instances of this program can be scheduled, each with a different variant and different timing to send the buffered IDocs to the OS layer.

◆ **Control error handling**. If errors occur during communication, the system by default creates a background job for each communication failure. This background job retries the process in five-minute intervals. In a large-volume transaction, the system can exhaust all the background jobs in a very short interval and thus prevent other processes from submitting background jobs. Chapter 20, "The Outbound ALE Process," explains the error-handling process in the communication layer. To avoid this avalanche, the tRFC options in the RFC destination should be set to suppress the automatic start of background jobs. Refer to Chapter 22, "Configuring the ALE Infrastructure," for details on how to set up tRFC options and programs required to retry failed transmissions.

◆ **Control the packet size**. The packet size for a message depends on the number of IDocs and the number of data records in each IDoc. You cannot control the number of data records in an IDoc, but you can control the number of IDocs in a packet. The latter, of course, will be small if the number of data records per IDoc is large. The packet size is specified in the partner profile's outbound record in the Pack Size field.

TIP

An average packet size of 2MB to 3MB uses network resources optimally. Each data record occupies roughly 1K, so you can calculate the number of IDocs in a packet depending on the number of typical data records in your IDoc.

◆ **Control parallel processing**. You can specify parallel processing for stand-alone programs that transfer master data, for example, BD10 for material master data. On the selection screen for these programs, you can specify the server group and maximum number of objects for each process.

CAUTION

If you have many objects to be transferred and you have not configured a separate server group for parallel processing, you will exhaust all the available processes. The system will slow down considerably and eventually come to a halt.

To specify the server group, use transaction RZ12. This option limits the number of processes available for parallel processing. Transaction RZ12 is a system-level setting for which you might not have authorization. You will have to work with your Basis staff for this configuration.

Managing Inbound Process Performance

As with the outbound process, you can classify incoming messages into two broad categories.

- Those requiring near-real-time operation
- Those that can be posted in batch mode

In the first option, you cannot control performance, but such processes exist, and you need to account for system cycles consumed by such processes. In the second option, you can implement the methods described earlier.

Near-Real-Time Inbound Messages

In near-real-time mode, when an IDoc is received, it is posted immediately. Although the process is asynchronous, the system feels like a real-time system. This mode is useful for critical ALE processes, as described earlier for the outbound process.

 CAUTION

This option should not be used for high-volume and non-critical transactions because it will cause performance problems.

The configuration options enable you to control the near-real-time behavior at a very granular level. For example, you can enable all messages from a system to be processed in near-real-time mode, or you can limit the near-real-time mode to specific messages from that system. In the partner profile for the inbound message, select the Process Immediately flag to enable this option.

Batch-Mode Inbound Messages

Batch mode is used for non-critical and high-volume transactions and is useful from a performance perspective. The choices to control performance are as follows.

- **Control the timing.** A document is not posted as soon as an IDoc is received. It is batched to run when the system is not busy (at night, for example), to pass it to the posting programs. The Processing Option field in the partner profile's inbound record should be set to Background, No Override with Express Flag.

The RBDAPP01 program passes buffered IDocs in the database to the posting program. This program must be scheduled on an as-needed basis. Several instances of RBDAPP01 can be scheduled to send the buffered IDocs to the posting program, based on the IDoc type. Each instance can be scheduled with a different variant. As an example, suppose that inbound sales orders and material master data are buffered. You want to process sales orders once every hour, but the material master can wait until the end of the day. You need to schedule two instances of RBDAPP01. The first instance runs every hour to process sales orders; the second instance runs, for example, at 10:00 p.m. to process the material master.

◆ **Control the packet size**. When scheduling the RBDAPP01 program, you can specify the packet size, which defines the number of IDocs bundled together for processing in the inbound function module. This approach improves the performance by using one LUW (*Logical Unit of Work*) for several documents. This option is available for a limited set of inbound function modules.

 TIP

Execute transaction BD51. Entries with a 0 in the Input Type field allow mass processing.

◆ **Control parallel processing**. Batched IDocs can be passed to the posting program in a single-threaded or multi-threaded mode. In single-threaded mode, the system passes one IDoc packet and waits for the process to finish before the next IDoc packet is sent. In multi-threaded mode, the IDoc packets are passed to the inbound process simultaneously. If there are several IDoc packets, the system keeps dispatching until it runs out of packets or the number of processes is exhausted.

You enable this option on the selection screen of the RBDAPP01 program by selecting the Parallel Posting field and specifying the server group. Refer to the "Batch-Mode Outbound Messages" section earlier in this chapter for details on setting up server groups.

General Strategies

In addition to the options described earlier to improve the performance of inbound and outbound ALE processes, you should also consider the following items, which can help you further improve performance.

- ◆ **Data Archiving**. Over time, the number of IDocs will grow in the system. A large number of IDocs in the database means longer access times and update times. It is best to archive IDocs on a periodic basis to keep the IDoc database under control. The work item log also tends to grow very quickly and should be cleaned up on a periodic basis. Refer to Chapter 34, "Archiving IDocs and Deleting Work Items," for details on deleting IDocs and work items.

- ◆ **Reorganizing change pointers**. The change pointer table can also become very large. SAP provides a program RBDCPCLR to reorganize change pointer tables. This program should also be run periodically to clean up the change pointer tables.

- ◆ **ABAP Program Performance**. IDoc programs have a large amount of executable code. Some sections of the code might not be optimized for batch input, thereby causing long processing times. Several notes in the OSS system discuss how to improve the performance of individual IDoc programs. These patches can be applied to improve the programs' efficiency. You can also use the SQL Trace and Runtime Analysis tools to optimize ABAP program performance.

- ◆ **Database Performance**. You can significantly improve database operations, such as selecting and posting data for IDocs, by creating indexes for fields commonly used to access information from the database. This procedure is part of the overall performance-tuning task for the entire system.

Summary

ALE processes are asynchronous, but they consume a lot of system cycles, thus potentially causing performance problems for other processes in the system. Three methods are available for managing performance, including controlling the timing of IDoc creation, dispatch of IDocs, and posting of IDocs; controlling the size of communication packets and the number of IDocs processed by a posting module; and controlling the parallel-processing option by creating IDocs in parallel, dispatching IDocs in parallel, and posting IDocs in parallel. In addition, you can configure the error-handling process for failed communications to suppress the automatic start of background jobs for each failed transmission. Apart from these methods, methods such as archiving IDocs, reorganizing change pointers, program tuning, and database tuning can yield additional performance benefits.

SECTION THREE

IDocs

PART X

IDoc Basics

Chapter 29

IDocs from the Outside

This chapter introduces the concept of IDocs without going into any technical details, starting with the basics of an IDoc from an end user's perspective. Various applications and the benefits of the IDoc interface are presented.

What Is an IDoc?

You have probably heard the term *IDoc* many times. This section will help you understand exactly what an IDoc is and what it does.

- **An IDoc is not a process.** The term *IDoc* stands for *Intermediate Document*. It is simply a data container used to exchange information between any two processes that can understand the syntax and semantics of the data. An IDoc is created as a result of executing an outbound ALE or EDI process. In an inbound ALE or EDI process, an IDoc serves as input to create an application document.

- **IDocs are stored in the database.** In the SAP system, IDocs are stored in database tables. Several utilities are available to display the information contained in an IDoc and present it in different ways. For details, refer to Chapter 11, "Monitoring the Interface."

- **Every IDoc has a unique number.** When an IDoc is generated in the system, a unique number is assigned to it. This number is unique within a client.

- **IDocs are independent of the sending and receiving systems.** They can be used for SAP-to-SAP and SAP to non-SAP process communication as long as the participating processes can understand the syntax and semantics of the data.

- **IDocs are based on EDI standards, ANSI ASC X12 and EDIFACT, but are closer to the EDIFACT standards.** The size and format of data elements in an IDoc type are derived from these standards wherever applicable. For example, if a material number is represented by 20 characters in an EDIFACT message, the corresponding data element in the

IDoc is also 20 characters. If there is a conflict in data size between standards, the one with greater length is adopted. This approach ensures compatibility with most standards.

◆ **IDocs are independent of the direction of data exchange**. An inbound and an outbound process can use an IDoc. For example, the ORDERS01 IDoc is used by the Purchasing module to send a purchase order, and it is also used by the Sales and Distribution module to accept a sales order. Using this technique avoids creating redundant IDoc types for the same information.

◆ **IDocs can be viewed in a text editor and do not contain any binary data**. Data is stored in character format. When transferred to the operating system, an IDoc is stored in a file in text format and can be viewed using a regular text editor. However, the contents make sense only if you understand the structure and format of the data in that IDoc. In the Appendix, "FAQs, User Exits, and Miscellaneous Resources," you will find an example of an IDoc file.

IDoc Applications

This section describes various uses of IDocs. Several SAP applications use the robust IDoc interface. The robustness of the interface has been proven since release 2.2, when IDocs were initially used in the EDI process. The following sections describe the applications of the IDoc interface. In all these applications, IDocs serve the basic purpose of transferring data from one application to another.

EDI Integration

EDI is the electronic exchange of business documents between trading partners in a common industry-standard format, such as ANSI X12 or EDIFACT.

Several applications (purchasing, sales, or shipping) in SAP are enabled for EDI. To use EDI, an application first creates an application document, such as a purchase order. Then the EDI interface layer converts the application document (the purchase order) into an IDoc, which is transferred to an EDI subsystem. The EDI subsystem translates the IDoc into an industry-standard format and then transfers it to a business partner over a network.

ALE Integration

ALE enables the exchange of data between two SAP systems. This allows SAP business processes and applications to be distributed across multiple SAP systems. ALE ensures integration in a distributed SAP environment. The IDoc acts as the data container. The introduction and ever-increasing use of ALE technology has made the IDoc a popular component in SAP.

Legacy System Integration

IDocs are independent of the sending and receiving applications. Hence, ALE technology can be used to exchange data between the SAP system and the legacy system. For example, if a legacy application needs to send data to SAP, the application first exports the desired data in an IDoc format or a proprietary format. Using a third-party translator tool, you can convert data exported in a proprietary format into an IDoc format. Using the standard ALE/EDI interface layer, the IDoc data can be passed to the SAP system. This approach allows the use of a functionally rich interface technology to integrate SAP with legacy systems.

Third-Party Product Integration

The products of several CSPs (*Complementary Software Partners*) use the IDoc interface to communicate with the SAP system. A standard IDoc interface has been defined for numerous applications, such as a warehouse management system, production-planning optimizer, and transportation-planning optimizer. This interface describes various IDocs and the sequence in which these IDocs must be communicated to and from the SAP system. CSPs can get their products certified as long as they can support those IDocs in the prescribed sequence. The use of IDocs for integration with third-party products has been the widest implementation of IDocs outside the SAP system.

Workflow Integration

Workflow is used to control and coordinate the sequence of steps in a business process. Workflow uses IDocs in two situations.

◆ To enable the form interface

◆ To enable data exchange between workflows in a distributed SAP environment

The form interface in workflow enables novice or infrequent users of the SAP system to carry out a task in SAP without logging on to the SAP system. This approach shields users who are less familiar with SAP from the complexities of the SAP system.

The form, which can be developed using a product such as Visual Basic, acts as the front end to the SAP system. When a form is executed, the form's data is saved in IDoc format. The IDoc is then passed to the SAP system, where it finds a corresponding workflow task that should be started. The IDoc's data is bound to the workflow process, which then can take necessary action.

The second workflow-related use of IDocs is to support the cross-system exchange of workflows in a distributed SAP environment. If a workflow process is started in one system and one of the steps of this workflow is to be executed in another system, the data required to execute the step in the second system is made available via IDocs.

SAP R/2 Integration

Starting with release 5.0 of SAP R/2, IDocs have been supported for data transfers. Hence, organizations that have part of their business running on R/2 can communicate seamlessly with R/3.

Internet and XML Integration

Web-based applications can be integrated into the SAP business process by capturing the data on the Internet through an interface such as a Web browser. The data collected from the Web in HTTP format is converted to IDoc format, using tools such as SAP's Business Connector. The IDoc data can then be passed to SAP applications via the IDoc interface. You can also import and export IDoc data in XML format instead of using a standard flat-file.

OCR Application Integration

OCR (*Optical Character Recognition*) is a technology that scans and interprets printed matter using pattern recognition. You can integrate an OCR application with SAP via IDocs. Documents in a standard format can be scanned to generate IDocs, which then can be transferred to the SAP system for processing.

ICR Application Integration

A barcode system is an example of ICR (*Intelligent Character Recognition*) technology. Data encoded using barcodes can be captured and stored as an IDoc, which then can be passed to SAP for further processing.

IDoc Interface Benefits

IDoc benefits are especially important if you are considering using the ALE/IDoc interface for integration with legacy systems. The advantage of using the IDoc interface is that you can use existing tools and utilities for custom IDocs as well.

Independence from Applications

The biggest advantage to using the IDoc interface is that it's an open interface. It's independent of the internal structure used by SAP to store data and independent of the sending and receiving applications. Any application that can understand the syntax and semantics of the data can use the IDoc interface.

For example, one of the published IDoc interfaces integrates SAP with third-party transportation-optimization systems. The transportation interface allows third-party products to optimize the mode of transportation and the best route to transport goods. This interface describes the IDocs to be exchanged and the order in which they are exchanged. Any vendor of transportation-optimization application software can use this interface as long as the application can send and receive the specified IDocs in the specified sequence. It does not matter whether the source of the IDoc is an internal application, an Internet application, or a manually created IDoc.

Communication Using Older-Version IDocs

The standard IDocs and the IDoc segments have versions associated with them. Each time a standard IDoc or segment is enhanced, the system assigns it a newer version. Partner applications developed using a previous version of the IDocs are fully supported. SAP can generate and process back-level IDocs. This technology ensures backward compatibility, which offers a major advantage over other interfacing techniques available in SAP.

For example, assume that you have used the standard MATMAS01 IDoc to exchange material master information with your legacy system in version 3.1G.

Now you have upgraded to version 3.1H, in which the MATMAS01 IDoc has been enhanced. You can continue to use the old version and then decide to switch to the enhanced IDoc later.

Exception Handling via Workflow

Handling exceptions is always tricky and tedious. If you have designed sophisticated applications in the past, you can, no doubt, relate to the agony of designing a consistent means of logging errors and exceptions across the board and then developing tools to display that information. In my opinion, about 40 percent of application code is related to error handling in some way.

The standard IDoc interface provides comprehensive log information about the processing of IDocs. Several tools are available to display the logged information. SAP uses the workflow technology to route an error intelligently to the right person. By using the IDoc interface, you automatically take advantage of the exception-handling process for your custom IDocs. This feature helps explain the continued growth in the use of the IDoc interface for legacy integration.

IDoc Enhancement and Creation

Using standard tools (the IDoc editor and Segment editor), you can either enhance standard SAP IDocs or create new IDocs in the system to support custom interfaces. This feature has been the basis for exchanging data with legacy systems using ALE and IDoc technology. The newly developed IDocs integrate seamlessly into the standard EDI interface because they are developed using standard tools provided by the system. IDocs developed in this manner become available in the standard list of SAP IDocs and can take advantage of all the tools designed for standard IDocs, such as IDoc monitoring, error handling, and archiving. Custom IDocs are distinguished from SAP IDocs by their names, which start with Z. You will learn about enhancing IDocs in Chapter 31, "Extending and Developing an IDoc Type."

Standard Monitoring Tools

Several tools are available to monitor the state of the system. They range from simple IDoc display to IDoc statistics. These tools provide a system overview, from which you can repeatedly drill down to view more details. Refer to Chapter 11, "Monitoring the Interface," for details.

Standard Testing Tools

Several tools are available in the system to help with the testing of the IDoc interface. For details, refer to Chapter 10, "Testing the EDI Interface."

IDoc Type Documentation

Each IDoc in the system is thoroughly documented. The usage is detailed down to the field level, with possible values for each field and how it affects the process. Because the entire documentation of the ORDERS05 IDoc cannot fit on one screen, a snapshot of the documentation is shown in Figure 29.1. The IDoc components that the documentation describes are explained more fully in Chapter 30, "IDocs on the Inside," and Chapter 31, "Extending and Developing an IDoc Type." You can obtain complete documentation on any IDoc by using transaction WE60. The report can also be executed to save the output in HTML format or a format suitable for C programming.

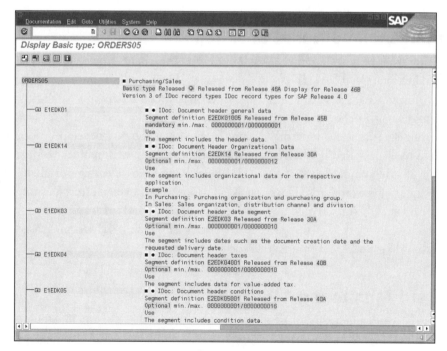

FIGURE 29.1 *A snapshot of the documentation for the ORDERS05 IDoc* (© SAP AG)

Reports for the Subsystem

The system generates output from an IDoc structure for the EDI subsystem. You can use this report to create a hierarchical IDoc structure or type-tree to load the IDoc structure into the EDI subsystem for the mapping process. Figure 29.2 shows a snapshot of the report for the ORDERS05 IDoc.

Starting with version 4.6, you can generate a DTD file for the XML version of the IDoc. The DTD file is for specifying the structure of an XML file—defining the elements, attributes, and entities that can be used, and how they are related to one another. XML-capable software—including the SAP Business Connector and similar products, parsers, and many current EDI translators—use the DTD, along with the XML-formatted IDoc itself, to parse, organize, and format the data correctly.

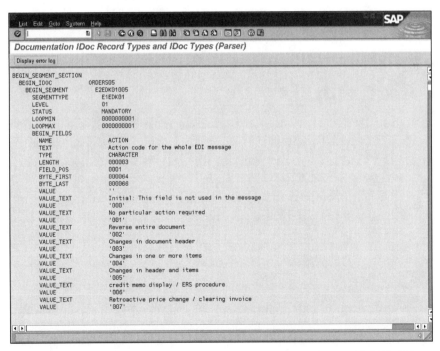

FIGURE 29.2 *A snapshot of an IDoc report generated for the subsystem* (© SAP AG)

Restart and Recovery Tools

Restart and recovery from errors are integral parts of the IDoc interface. Again, several tools are provided to restart the process from the point of failure. For details, refer to Chapter 12, "EDI Process Troubleshooting and Recovery," and Chapter 27, "ALE Process Troubleshooting and Recovery."

Reading IDoc Data

Function modules are available to read and manipulate data in IDocs. You can use the standard function modules contained in the function group EDI1 to develop custom utilities.

Archiving Tools

Tools are available for miscellaneous tasks such as archiving, data cleanup, and restoring information back into SAP. Chapter 34, "Archiving IDocs and Deleting Work Items," describes the archiving process in detail.

Future IDoc Applications

SAP has endorsed IDoc technology in several areas. It is the communication vehicle for the standard approaches to integrating applications from different SAP releases and legacy systems to work together as one logical system. Examples are the interfaces between R/3 and the SAP Business Warehouse and CRM applications. SAP will continue to add functionality, such as better monitoring tools, improved ease of use, and greater robustness, to the standard IDoc interface.

Summary

IDocs act as containers for data exchanged between two applications. The IDoc interface is functionally rich and is used in various applications. It provides a robust environment for interfacing SAP with SAP, as well as with external applications. Using the IDoc interface for integrating external applications with the SAP system offers several benefits, such as a thoroughly documented interface, independence of the application product, numerous testing and troubleshooting tools, and a sophisticated means of error handling via workflow.

Chapter 30

IDocs on
the Inside

By now you should have a good idea of what an IDoc is, what it's used for, and its benefits. It's now time to explore the architecture of an IDoc. The architecture can be best explained by looking at an IDoc's definition and run-time components.

 NOTE

Prepare to encounter some technical jargon in this chapter. By the end, you'll be able to converse with any IDoc geek.

Comparing Flat File Structure to IDoc Structure

The best way to explain the IDoc architecture is to compare your legacy world to how SAP implements the same concept in IDoc lingo. An example of a file structure is used for comparative analysis (see Figure 30.1).

Assume that you have an application that records an employee's weekly hours. At the end of the month, a file containing the monthly report data for each employee is sent to an external system. This application has been replaced by the SAP system, and a standard IDoc has been developed to support the process. Following are some properties of the file.

- ◆ It has three types of records, including employee header information, weekly details, and monthly summaries.
- ◆ Each record type has certain properties, such as whether it's optional or mandatory, number of times it can be repeated, field names, data type for each field, and length of each field.
- ◆ The client site and work description in the weekly details are not always available.

Last Name (10)	First Name (10)	Social Security Number (11)	Date of Birth (8)	**Employee Header** (occurs once, required)
Week Number (1)	Hours Worked (3)	Hourly Rate (3)	Client Site (20)	Work Description (40)	**Weekly Details** (multiple)
Total Hours (3)	Total Amount (10)	**Summary** (occurs once)

FIGURE 30.1 *A flat file structure for a typical monthly report*

The information in Figures 30.2, 30.3, and 30.4 forms the basis of the following explanation of how the flat file information matches up with the IDoc version at definition time and run time.

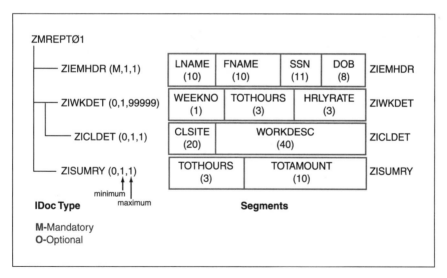

FIGURE 30.2 *The IDoc representation of the flat file structure shown in Figure 30.1*

Smith	John	123-45-6789	102668

1	30	40	Houston Brewery	Beer Testing
2	30	40	Network Computers	High Level Consulting
3	30	50	Network Computers	Programming
4	50	60	DSP Systems	EDI Programming

140	6900

FIGURE 30.3 *An example of the monthly report file for one particular employee*

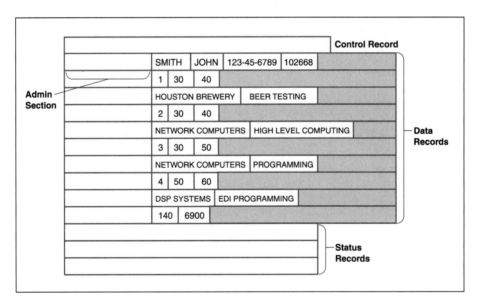

FIGURE 30.4 *The IDoc representation of the employee report shown in Figure 30.3*

IDoc Definition Components

Each of the following sections begins with a formal definition of the component and then compares the file lingo and the IDoc lingo.

Basic IDoc Type

Basic IDoc type defines the structure and format of the business document that is to be exchanged between two systems. Basic IDoc type is commonly referred to as IDoc type, although there is a technical difference between a basic IDoc type and an IDoc type. The difference is important only when you are dealing with extending an IDoc. A basic IDoc type can refer to an SAP-provided basic IDoc type or a customer-developed basic IDoc type. Therefore, concepts discussed in this chapter with a simple customer-defined basic IDoc type should apply to SAP-provided basic IDoc types also. The basic IDoc type for the monthly report example is shown in Figure 30.5.

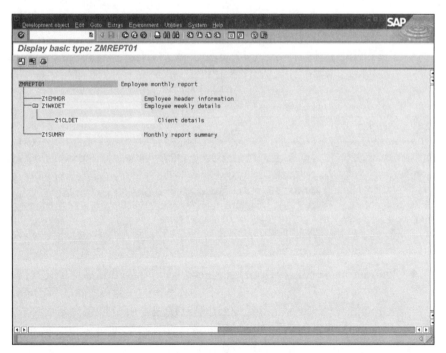

FIGURE 30.5 *The basic IDoc type for ZMREPT01* (© SAP AG)

A basic IDoc type has the following characteristics.

- **Name**. A basic IDoc type can be assigned up to a thirty-character name in release 4.0 and later. To encompass all releases, I am using an eight-character name; for example, ZMREPT01 represents the monthly report IDoc type in this example. Custom IDoc types always start with a Z. The last two characters are the version number. After a basic IDoc type is released and you move to a newer version of the SAP system, any changes to the structure of the basic IDoc type will create a new basic IDoc type. In general, the version number is incremented by one. Thus, ZMREPT02 represents an enhanced version of this IDoc. Segments of a previous version are never deleted. This approach is necessary to maintain backward compatibility. In the standard list of IDocs, you will see ORDERS01, ORDERS02, ORDERS03, and so on.

- **List of permitted segments**. These segments make up the IDoc structure. The current example has four segments: Z1EMHDR, Z1WKDET, Z1CLDET, and Z1SUMRY.

- **Hierarchy of segments**. The hierarchy of segments specifies the physical sequence and any parent-child relationship in the segments. A parent-child relationship signifies that the child segment cannot exist without the parent. In the example, segment Z1CLDET is a child of segment Z1WKDET. Therefore, an instance of Z1CLDET cannot occur unless it follows a related Z1WKDET segment.

 NOTE

In the example, the Client Site and Work Description fields were separated out as another segment. The purpose of this design is to present the concept of a parent-child relationship; this design should not be used as a guide to break up segments. Candidates for parent-child relationships are discussed in Chapter 31, "Extending and Developing an IDoc Type."

- **Mandatory versus optional segment**. When used in an IDoc type, each segment has an attribute that defines whether the segment is optional or mandatory. In the example, Z1EMHDR is a mandatory segment because the monthly report will not make sense without the employee's basic information (see Figure 30.6).

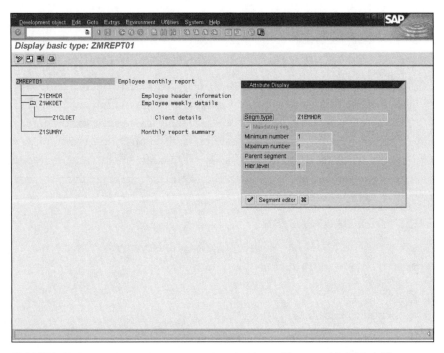

FIGURE 30.6 *Attributes of a segment when used in an IDoc type* (© SAP AG)

- ◆ **Minimum/maximum range for each segment**. When used in an IDoc type, each segment has an attribute that defines the minimum and the maximum number of times a data record corresponding to a segment can exist in an IDoc. In the example, data records corresponding to the Z1WKDET segment can occur multiple times.

An extension type is a customer-defined object that serves as an extension to a basic IDoc type. Extension types are covered in Chapter 31, "Extending and Developing an IDoc Type."

Segments

A segment defines the format and structure of a data record. Segments are reusable components, which means they can be used in more than one IDoc type. A segment consists of various fields that represent data in a data record. Data elements can be of two types: positional or based on qualifiers.

A positional data field occupies a fixed position in an IDoc. In the example, the Z1WKDET segment has fixed fields such as week number and weekly hours. These fields always occur in the same position shown in the diagram.

A field can also be based on a qualifier, in which case the value represented in a field is tied to the qualifier. For example, assume a segment has a date field for three dates: the delivery date, the goods issue date, and the order creation date. Instead of creating three separate fields and assigning a fixed position to each one, the three fields can be represented using two fields—a qualifier field and a date field. The qualifier field identifies the type of date, and the date field contains the date.

Segment Components

A segment in the SAP system is technically implemented as three physically separate pieces, as shown in Figure 30.7.

◆ Segment type
◆ Segment definition
◆ Segment documentation

Segment type is the version-independent name of the segment. SAP-provided segment types begin with E1, whereas custom-defined segment types begin with Z1. In the example, Z1EMPHDR and Z1WKDET are segment types. Segment definition is the version-dependent definition of a segment where you specify the fields that belong to the segment.

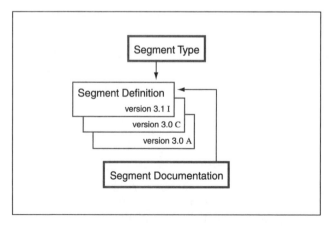

FIGURE 30.7 *Components of a segment and their relationships*

Segment definitions can be no more than 1,000 bytes. SAP segment definitions start with E2, whereas customer segment definitions start with Z2. The name of a segment definition is 30 characters long and is automatically assigned by the system from the name of the segment type. The last three characters represent the version of the segment. For example, the segment definition for the segment type E1EDKA1 is E2EDKA1.

After a segment is released and a new version of SAP is installed, any change to the segment definition creates a new segment definition, as depicted in Figure 30.8. An example of a standard SAP segment E1EDKA1 with two definitions is shown in Figure 30.9. You will notice that the last three characters are incremented by one to reflect the new definition. Thus, a segment can have multiple segment definitions. The first segment definition has spaces in the last three characters.

TIP

A field from a previous segment definition cannot be deleted. This prohibition is necessary to maintain backward compatibility.

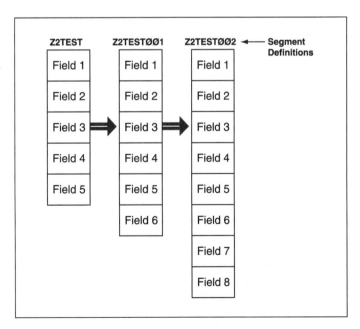

FIGURE 30.8 *Concept of segment definitions*

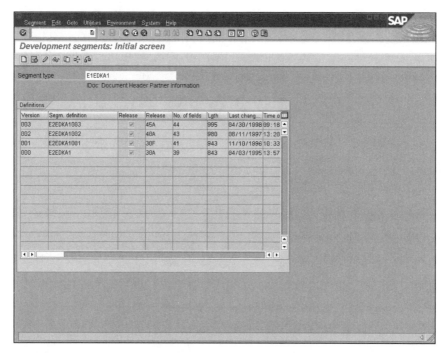

FIGURE 30.9 *Segment definitions of SAP segment E1EDKA1* (© SAP AG)

Segment documentation represents the data dictionary documentation for each field in the segment definition. Segment documentation of SAP-provided segments begins with E3, whereas the segment documentation of customer-defined segment types begins with Z3. There is only one segment documentation per segment.

TIP

When using segments in SAP (for example, in IDoc types and in ABAP/4 programs), you always work with segment types. By default, the type points to the latest segment definition. When you work with segments outside the SAP system, you always use segment definitions. You might have noticed that an IDoc type at the operating system level has data records that begin with E2 instead of the segment type E1.

Data Fields

A data field represents a single data item that is used in a segment. All data field values must be alphanumeric values. The valid data types for a field are CHAR, CLNT, CUKY, DATS, LANG, and NUMC.

IDoc Run-Time Components

An IDoc is an instance of an IDoc type. An IDoc has a record-oriented structure, which is very much like the record structure in a file (refer to Figure 30.4). At run time the following events occur.

- A unique IDoc number is allocated.
- One control record is attached to the IDoc.
- Segments translate into data records.
- Status records are attached.
- Syntax rules are checked. The run time is compared with the definition. Syntax rules checked for IDocs are defined at the end of this chapter.

Although there are several records in an IDoc, they are still classified as one of the three record types. Figure 30.10 shows an IDoc as viewed using the IDoc display tool (transaction WE02 or WE05).

- Control record
- Data record
- Status record

 NOTE

The IDoc number is the element that ties the control records, data records, and status records together.

Control Record

As the name suggests, the control record contains all of the control information about an IDoc; this information basically includes the IDoc number, sender and receiver information, and information such as the message type it represents and

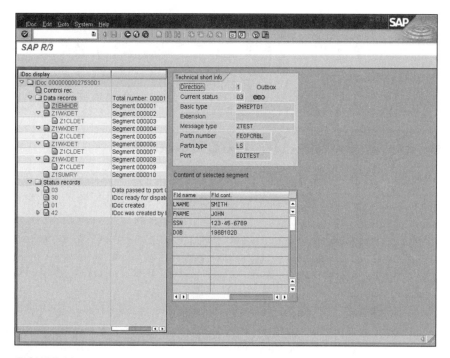

FIGURE 30.10 *An IDoc with control records, data records, and status records* (© SAP AG)

the IDoc type, as shown in Figure 30.11. Think of the control record as the envelope of a letter. By looking at the envelope, you can identify the sender and the recipient.

 TIP

If you look at an IDoc file in a text editor at the operating system level, the control record is always the first record.

A control record has the following characteristics.

◆ There is one and only one control record per IDoc.

◆ The structure of the control record is the same for all the IDocs and is defined by SAP. Of course, the field values are different.

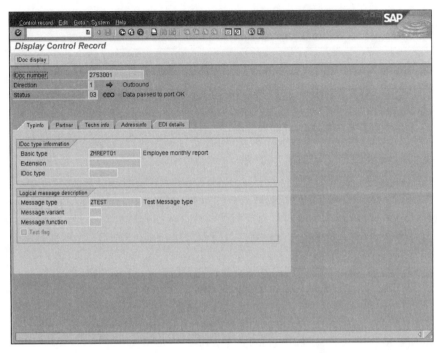

FIGURE 30.11 *Control record of an IDoc as viewed using IDoc display tools* (© SAP AG)

- The structure of the control record is defined by the data dictionary structure EDI_DC40 for IDocs from version 4.0 on; the EDI_DC structure is used for version 3.0–3.1 IDocs.

- The control record data is stored in the EDIDC table. The key to this table is the IDoc number.

- In addition to defining the sender and recipient (fields SNDPRN and RCVPRN), the control record also describes the type of message (field MESTYP). Other fields contain the additional data necessary to define the partner profile (fields SNDPRT, SNDPFC, RCVPRT, RCVPFC, MESCOD, MESFCT, and TEST). Fields IDOCTP and CIMTYP describe the structure and syntax of the data within the IDoc.

The structure of the EDIDC table is shown in Table 30.1. Use transaction SE11 to view this table structure online.

Table 30.1 Fields of the Control Record Table

Field Name	Description	Length
MANDT	Client	3
DOCNUM	IDoc number	16
DOCREL	SAP release of IDoc	4
STATUS	Status of IDoc	2
DOCTYP	IDoc type	8
DIRECT	Direction	1
RCVPOR	Receiver port (SAP system, EDI subsystem)	10
RCVPRT	Partner type of receiver	2
RCVPRN	Partner number of receiver	10
RCVSAD	Receiver address (SADR)	10
RCVSMN	SADR client (receiver)	3
RCVSNA	SADR flag for international receiver address	1
RCVSCA	Communication method (SADR) of the receiver	3
RCVSDF	SADR default flag for the receiver address	1
RCVSLF	Sequential number of the receiver address (SADR)	3
RCVLAD	Logical address of receiver	70
STD	EDI standard	1
STDVRS	Version of EDI standard	6
STDMES	EDI message type	6
MESCOD	Logical message code	3
MESFCT	Logical message function	3
OUTMOD	Output mode	1
TEST	Test flag	1
SNDPOR	Sender port (SAP system, EDI subsystem)	10
SNDPRT	Partner type of sender	2

Table 30.1 Fields of the Control Record Table *(continued)*

Field Name	Description	Length
SNDPRN	Partner number of sender	10
SNDSAD	Sender address (SADR)	10
SNDSMN	SADR client (sender)	3
SNDSNA	SADR flag for international sender address	1
SNDSCA	Communication method (SADR) of sender	3
SNDSDF	SADR default flag for the sender address	1
SNDSLF	Sequential number of the sender address (SADR)	3
SNDLAD	Logical address of sender	70
REFINT	Reference to interchange file	14
REFGRP	Reference to message group	14
REFMES	Reference to message	14
ARCKEY	EDI archive key	70
CREDAT	Date IDoc was created	8
CRETIM	Time IDoc was created	6
MESTYP	Logical message type	30
IDOCTP	Name of basic IDoc type	30
CIMTYP	Name of extension type	30
RCVPFC	Partner function of receiver	2
SNDPFC	Partner function of sender	2
SERIAL	EDI/ALE: Serialization field	20
EXPRSS	Overriding in inbound processing	1
UPDDAT	Date changed: Control record	8
UPDTIM	Time changed: Control record	6
MAXSEGNUM	Number of data segments	6

The complete documentation of the control record as it appears in an IDoc file can be viewed online by using transaction WE61.

Data Records

In an IDoc, data records contain the application data (refer to Figure 30.4). The employee header information, weekly details, client details, and summary information reside in data records. Figure 30.12 shows a data record viewed using one of the IDoc display tools. A data record has two parts, an administrative section and a data section, as shown in Figure 30.13.

◆ The administrative section contains the segment name, client, IDoc number, segment number, and hierarchy level information, as shown in Figure 30.12.

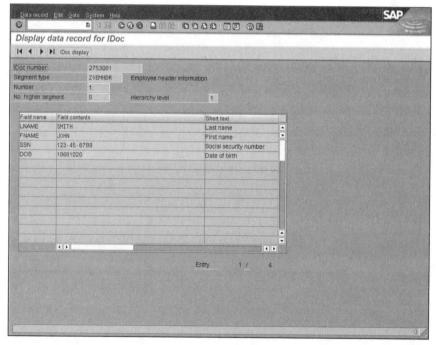

FIGURE 30.12 *Details of a data record viewed using the IDoc display tool* (© SAP AG)

FIGURE 30.13 *Administrative and data sections in a data record*

♦ The data record is defined by the data dictionary structure EDI_DD40 for IDocs from version 4.0 on, and EDI_DD for version 3.0–3.1 IDocs. The structure of the administrative section differs somewhat in the two versions.

♦ The data section of a data record is a stream of 1,000 bytes where the actual data resides. The data section is mapped to a segment type, as defined in the administrative section, to interpret the meaning of various data values in a record. For example, the Z1EMHDR segment translates to a data record at run time. The administrative section of this data record contains the segment type Z1EMHDR. The SDATA field of the data record is mapped to Z1EMHDR to interpret the values in the SDATA field.

Data records for IDocs from version 4.0 on are stored in the EDID4 table, while version 3.0–3.1 IDoc data records are in EDID2. Table 30.2 lists the fields in the EDID4 table. Use transaction SE11 to view this table structure online. The complete documentation of the data record as it appears on IDoc files can be viewed online by using transaction WE61.

Status Records

Status records are attached to an IDoc throughout the process as the IDoc achieves different milestones or encounters an error. At every milestone a status code, date, and time are assigned. The latest status code is also maintained in the control record. Figure 30.14 shows a status record viewed using one of the IDoc display tools.

Table 30.2 Fields in the Data Record Table

Field Name	Description	Length
MANDT	Client	3
DOCNUM	IDoc number	16
COUNTER	Counter in cluster table	3
SEGNUM	Number of SAP segment	6
SEGNAM	Name of SAP segment	30
PSGNUM	Number of the hierarchically higher SAP segment	6
HLEVEL	Hierarchy level	2
DTINT2	Length of VARC field	5
SDATA	Application data	1000

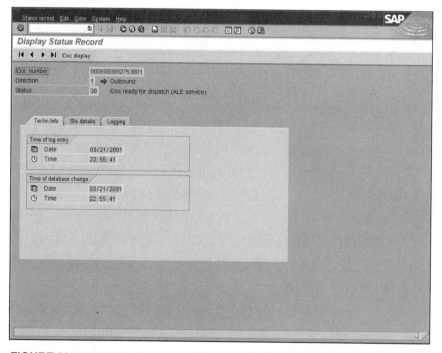

FIGURE 30.14 *Details of a status record as viewed using the IDoc display tool* (© SAP AG)

Status records have the following characteristics.

◆ Multiple status records are usually attached to an IDoc.

◆ For outbound processes, after the IDoc is passed from SAP to the subsystem, the subsystem generates the status records and passes them to
SAP. For inbound processes, SAP generates the status records.

◆ The system defines numerous status codes. Status codes 01 to 49 are
reserved for outbound processes, and 50 and above are reserved for
inbound processes. A status code has several attributes, as shown in
Figure 30.15.

  • A description of the status code

  • Whether it is inbound or outbound

  • A process level that indicates the point in the process at which the
status code is attached

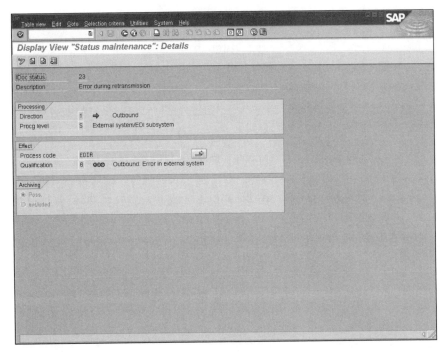

FIGURE 30.15 *Details of a status code* (© SAP AG)

- Whether a workflow is to be started (if the status code represents an error)
- The status group for statistical reporting
- Whether or not an IDoc is suitable for archiving

A list of status codes and their details can be seen by executing transaction WE47.

Fields in a Status Record

The format of the status record is supplied by SAP, and the formats are stored in the EDIDS table. The key for this table is the IDoc number, date and time a message was logged, and a status counter. Table 30.3 shows a complete list of fields in the status record table. Use transaction SE11 to view this table structure online.

The complete documentation of the status records as they appear on an IDoc status file can be viewed online by using transaction WE61.

Syntax Rules for an IDoc

When any IDoc is created, it goes through a syntax check to ensure its integrity. The syntax of an IDoc is governed by the definition of its IDoc type. The syntax rules checked for an IDoc are as follows.

- ◆ Only valid segments as defined in the IDoc type are allowed.
- ◆ Segments specified as mandatory must exist.
- ◆ A data record cannot exceed the maximum number of repetitions defined for the segment type.
- ◆ Segments must occur in the same physical sequence defined in the IDoc structure.
- ◆ A child segment cannot exist without its parent segment. A parent segment, however, can exist without a child segment.

Table 30.3 Fields in the Status Record Table

Field Name	Description	Length
MANDT	Client	3
DOCNUM	IDoc number	16
LOGDAT	Date of status information	8
LOGTIM	Time of status information	6
COUNTR	EDI status counter	16
CREDAT	Date status record was created	8
CRETIM	Time status record was created	6
STATUS	Status of IDoc	2
UNAME	User name	12
REPID	Program name	30
ROUTID	Name of subroutine (routine, function module)	30
STACOD	Status code	8
STATXT	Text for status code	70
SEGNUM	Number of SAP segment	6
SEGFLD	Field name in SAP segment	30
STAPA1	Parameter 1	50
STAPA2	Parameter 2	50
STAPA3	Parameter 3	50
STAPA4	Parameter 4	50
STATYP	EDI: Type of system error message (A, W, E, S, I)	1
STAMQU	Status message qualifier	3
STAMID	Status message ID	20
STAMNO	Status message number	3
TID	Transaction ID	24
APPL_LOG	Application log	20

Summary

An IDoc type represents the definition component of an IDoc. An IDoc type is a version-controlled object that defines a list of permitted segments for an IDoc and the hierarchical arrangement of those segments. A segment consists of a version-independent segment type, several version-dependent segment definitions, and a version-independent segment documentation. The IDoc type effectively defines the syntax of an IDoc.

An IDoc is the run-time instance of an IDoc type. An IDoc consists of a control record, several data records, and a list of growing status records. The control record defines control information such as sender and receiver information. The data records contain the application data that is to be transferred via IDocs. The status records contain status information (success or failure) recorded at each milestone in the process. A status record that represents an error code can contain additional details such as the segment in error.

PART XI

Customer Modifications to the IDoc Interface

Chapter 31

**Extending and
Developing
an IDoc Type**

Understanding the IDoc development process and knowing how to program IDocs are among the most important skills needed to support an SAP ALE/EDI implementation. IDoc development is a three-step process. First, you create a new IDoc or extend an existing IDoc. Then, you create programs for the new and/or extended IDocs. Finally, you customize the ALE/EDI interface layer to recognize the IDocs and their programs. The monthly report IDoc introduced in the preceding chapter is used to explain the various concepts.

This chapter covers IDoc enhancements. The first step is deciding whether to extend an existing IDoc or create one from scratch. This decision is not difficult, but sometimes it is fuzzy. The sample scenarios that follow are designed to help you with this decision. In this chapter, you'll walk through the steps to extend and create an IDoc. You'll learn various design tips to create functionally rich IDocs that make optimum use of segments, thus saving memory and disk space at run time.

IDocs are organized into IDoc types. There are two kinds of IDoc types, the basic type and the extension. The basic type, which I'll refer to from now on as a basic IDoc type, is a standard SAP or customer-developed IDoc structure intended to be used as the container for an entire message or document. An extension, on the other hand, is an IDoc structure that is designed to be inserted into a basic IDoc type to enhance the basic IDoc type's data-holding capability.

 NOTE

Prior to version 4.0, SAP used a slightly different terminology to describe IDoc types and extensions. Basic IDoc types were denoted as standard SAP IDoc types and customer-developed IDoc types. An extended basic IDoc type was called an IDoc type.

Extending versus Developing New IDocs

After careful analysis of the IDoc process and its documentation, you might conclude that the standard basic IDoc type meets most of your requirements. In this case, you can simply extend the basic IDoc type. If the basic IDoc type does not meet your requirements at all, you create a new basic IDoc type from scratch. For example, if you need a field or set of logically related fields from a document placed in an IDoc, and the basic IDoc type you are using does not provide a suitable place for these fields, you could simply extend the basic IDoc type. On the other hand, if you are implementing an EDI document not sufficiently supported by SAP, you might need to develop a basic IDoc type from scratch.

TIP

Always remember that if you create a basic IDoc from scratch, it is considered a modification and is not supported in an upgrade. On the other hand, extending an IDoc is an enhancement and is supported in an upgrade.

Extending IDocs

You extend a basic IDoc type when it meets most of your requirements. Following are some examples.

- ◆ **You have extended the SAP screens to include custom fields, such as in the material master and customer master**. The master data is to be distributed across several SAP systems using ALE. This situation is a perfect candidate and an obvious choice for IDoc extension.

- ◆ **Your business partner sends you additional information or expects additional information on an EDI document**. For example, your customers expect an invoice number and date on an advance shipment notice transaction.

- ◆ **You are interfacing with legacy systems using IDocs**. One of the basic IDoc types fits your needs except for some elements that are specific to your business environment. For example, if you are sending sales orders to your legacy system and it requires engineering information for the materials ordered, you can extend the sales order IDoc to include engineering information.

Creating IDocs

You create a new basic IDoc type when the standard basic IDoc types do not meet your business needs, as is or by extending them. Consider the following situations.

◆ **New basic IDoc types are developed especially for interfaces to legacy systems or third-party products using ALE.** Data to be exchanged with legacy systems is usually in a proprietary format and does not map one to one with a standard SAP business process.

◆ **A basic IDoc type is created when an existing IDoc cannot be mapped to an EDI transaction you want to exchange with your business partner.** For example, to exchange EDI transaction 863 (a report of test results, which is not supported in SAP) with your business partner, you would have to create an IDoc.

◆ **You want to synchronize master data between two SAP systems, and this master data is not supported in the standard system.** For example, to exchange condition record data, which is not supported in the system, you would create an IDoc from scratch.

TIP

The number of basic IDoc types has increased with every new version of SAP. You should check with SAP to see whether an IDoc is under construction for a future release. If so, examine your requirements for an alternative (possibly interim) solution. In addition, new versions of existing types are often created, and they often have increased functionality. For instance, there are currently five versions of the ORDERS IDoc, named ORDERS01 through ORDERS05. (ORDERS05 was just introduced with version 4.6A, adding additional segments to improve support for configurable materials.) It is always advisable to use a standard process whenever and wherever applicable.

CAUTION

Because developing new IDocs is considered a modification—and, therefore, is not supported in an upgrade—you have to review and test your process again after you upgrade.

Creating a New IDoc Type

The process of creating IDocs is presented first because it involves more concepts. Some of the details presented here are also applicable to the IDoc extension process discussed later in the chapter.

To develop a new basic IDoc type from scratch, you need to understand various IDoc design issues. You need to be aware of what is permitted in the system and what is not. You can map your business data into an IDoc in several ways. The first step is to analyze the requirements to determine the best possible way to group data into an IDoc. The next section, "Design Guidelines," presents several design tips to help you get started. Then, the steps to create an IDoc are described. The steps guide you through the complete process, addressing important issues as they arise.

The process of creating a new basic IDoc type is the same for EDI, ALE, or an external process, such as legacy or third-party applications.

Design Guidelines

Here are some design guidelines to help you during the creation of a basic IDoc type.

◆ **Develop an IDoc type for a function, not for a specific application**. For example, the ORDERS02 IDoc is designed for the order process and not specifically for the sales order entry application. This IDoc is used for several documents, such as a purchase order, a sales order, an order response, and an order change. You should follow a similar strategy when creating a new basic IDoc type.

◆ **Use industry standards for your data elements whenever possible**. If you are designing an IDoc for a business document, consult the EDI standards for appropriate length and data types. Use ISO (*International Standards Organization*) codes for fields such as measurement units and currencies.

◆ **Organize the document to contain header information, detail information, and summary information**. This technique is commonly used for SAP documents.

◆ **Do not repeat a segment type in an IDoc definition**. For example, consider the monthly report basic IDoc type (ZMREPT01) from the preceding chapter. If you were asked also to add the client information (Z1CLDET) for the last client to the summary information, your instincts would be to attach the Z1CLDET segment to the summary segment (Z1SUMRY). SAP does not permit placing a segment type more than once in the definition of an IDoc type. Because you cannot use the same segment type more than once in an IDoc definition, the only alternative is to create a new segment type with the same information.

This requirement might seem like a limitation, but it really is not. You can alter your design a little or use the approach suggested here. That SAP has designed its IDocs with the same limitation suggests that it is not a problem.

 CAUTION

Repeating a segment type should not be confused with the Maximum Number field in the attributes for the segment type. The Maximum Number field specifies how many data records for a segment type are permitted at run time.

◆ **Use the parent-child relationship when you are going to permit several entries of the same type in one IDoc**. For example, the current design of the ZMREPT01 IDoc allows only one employee per IDoc, as shown in Figure 31.1. If you wanted to support multiple employees per IDoc to

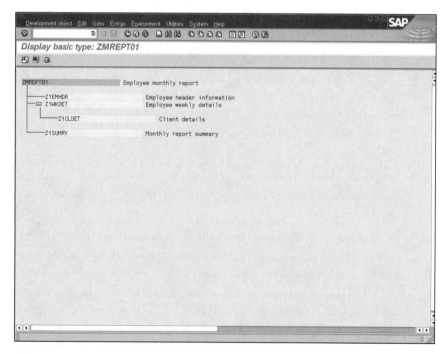

FIGURE 31.1 *The structure of the monthly report basic IDoc type for a single employee* (© SAP AG)

improve performance or because it makes sense for your business, the IDoc design would use the parent-child relationship, as shown in Figure 31.2.

◆ **Avoid having too many mandatory segments**. A segment should be truly mandatory and should not be used just because the person giving you the requirements thinks that it is necessary. Having extra mandatory segments reduces the IDoc's reusability. If a segment is mandatory, every process that uses the IDoc must supply the segment. For example, in the monthly report IDoc, the weekly details segment (Z1WKDET) seems to be mandatory. Consider another process that could make use of this IDoc to send just employee header information and summary information. If the weekly segment were mandatory, the IDoc would not be reusable in that way. By contrast, the employee header information is truly mandatory because this sort of data will not make sense without knowing to whom it belongs.

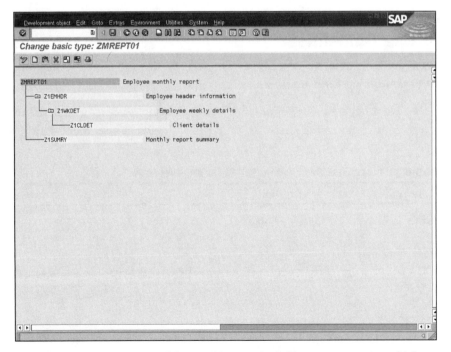

FIGURE 31.2 *The structure of the monthly report basic IDoc type to support multiple employees* (© SAP AG)

- ◆ **Do not make segments larger than 1,000 bytes.** Try to split the segments into functionally separate segments when a segment definition exceeds 1,000 bytes. If not, split the segment into two segments.

- ◆ **Combine IDoc segments that are functionally similar into one segment whenever possible.** Remember, each data record occupies 1,000 bytes at run time. It does not matter whether the record has one field or 50 fields. Don't overdo it, though—leave enough room for expansion.

- ◆ **Create segments that can be reused by other IDocs.**

- ◆ **Avoid qualifiers.** They are difficult to document and manage. They do not necessarily save any space, unless a field has too many variations of the same type. For example, assume that a segment has several G/L account fields for each type of account in a company (for example, a credit account, a debit account, a vendor account, an asset account, and a reconciliation account). You could certainly have a separate field for each type of account, but in this scenario, it would make sense to use a qualifier. A qualifier could represent the type of G/L account, and a field could be assigned for the G/L account number.

Formatting Guidelines

The following guidelines are useful when you are creating segments and when you are programming for your IDocs.

- ◆ Data fields in a segment can contain only alphanumeric values. Table 31.1 contains the allowed data types for fields in a segment definition.

Table 31.1 Allowed Data Types for Segment Fields

Data Type	Description
CHAR	Character strings
CLNT	Client
CUKY	Currency key, referenced by CURR fields
DATS	Date field (YYYYMMDD), stored as char(8)
LANG	Language key
NUMC	Character field with only digits
TIMS	Time field (HHMMSS), stored as char(6)

- Fields should be left aligned. Character fields are automatically left aligned, but number values, when assigned to a character field, are padded with spaces on the left. You must remove these spaces from the fields programmatically, using the condense command.

- Dates are represented as YYYYMMDD.

- Data is not case sensitive.

- Negative numbers are represented with a dash symbol at the end. Thus, −123 is written as 123−.

- Numbers with fractional values use a period to represent the decimal point. Thus, 123.45 represents 123 dollars and 45 cents.

- Floating-point numbers also use a period to represent the decimal point. Thus, 123.45 is written as 1.2345E+02.

- No formatting is used to separate values in the thousands. For example, 29,000.00 is written as 29000.00, without the comma.

Creating a New Basic IDoc Type

Here are the six steps to follow to create a basic IDoc type.

Step 1: Analyze the Data

In this stage, you analyze data that needs to be exchanged between the two processes. Using the guidelines mentioned earlier in the chapter, develop a conceptual picture of the IDoc on a piece of paper.

Follow a top-down approach if you are starting at a business-document level. Break the document into segments, and group the segments that belong together into a segment group. Identify fields in a segment and their data types. Identify any parent-child relationships.

Follow a bottom-up approach if you are starting at the field level. You have been given a document that contains values that must be exchanged between two systems. Group functionally related fields into segments. Group those segments into segment groups, and arrange them in an IDoc type. Identify any parent-child relationship.

You must also consider the planned processing of the new IDoc, which will have to be programmed in a custom function module or ABAP program. After you complete the analysis, you are ready to build your basic IDoc type.

TIP

You can use standard SAP segments in your custom IDocs, so feel free to have a mix of custom segments and SAP segments.

Step 2: Create Data Elements

The second step is to create data elements for the segment definition. The necessity to create new data elements is minimal because if you are extracting data from SAP to put into an IDoc, the data already exists in the database and is represented by a data element. You must create new data elements in the following cases only.

◆ A data element in SAP does not use one of the allowed data types for IDoc segments. For example, the Future Price field (ZKPRS) in the E1MBEWM segment of the MATMAS02 basic IDoc type uses data type CHAR12 instead of ZKPRS. The reason is that the data type for ZKPRS is CURR (Currency), which is not allowed in a segment definition.

◆ A field in SAP is shorter than the industry standard. (This occurrence is rare.)

Follow these steps to create new data elements.

1. Execute transaction SE11. Enter a data element name in the Object Name field and click the Create button.

2. Enter the various attributes (see Figure 31.3). The domain should be based on one of the allowed data types (refer to Table 31.1).

3. Save your entry and generate the data element.

Step 3: Create Segments

You create segments by using the Segment Editor tool. Start the tool by executing transaction WE31 (from the Area menu for EDI, choose Development, IDoc Segments). This tool is very similar to the screen for creating a table or a structure. However, you should not attempt to use the Create Table or Change Table transaction to change or create segment structures.

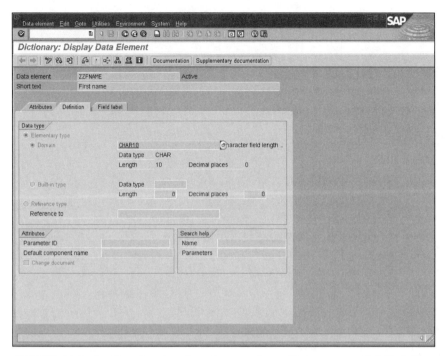

FIGURE 31.3 *Specify values for a data element to be used in a segment.* (© SAP AG)

Follow these steps to create a segment.

1. Execute transaction WE31. Enter the name for your segment type (it must start with Z1), and click the Create icon. The system prompts you with the name of the development class it uses for the segment.

2. Enter the values in the various fields. You are now maintaining the first segment definition. The system automatically assigns a name to the segment definition, based on the segment type. Figure 31.4 shows the segment definition Z2WKDET, which is based on segment type Z1WKDET.

3. Save your values, and if you are working in an environment earlier than 4.6, generate the segment definition. After you save your segment, return to the preceding screen, which will show the status of the segment definition (see Figure 31.5). Use the same procedure to create other segments for your IDoc type.

FIGURE 31.4 *Maintain segment definition in the segment editor.* (© SAP AG)

FIGURE 31.5 *The segment editor, showing the segment definition for the segment type* (© SAP AG)

TIP

After saving your entry, you can click the Check button to test the integrity of your segment. If one of your data elements is not generated or active, the system will report problems.

Step 4: Create the Basic IDoc Type

When you have developed all the necessary segment types, you are ready to create the basic IDoc type. To do this, you use the IDoc editor, which is started with transaction WE30. (From the Area menu for EDI, choose Development, IDoc Types.)

Follow these steps to create a basic IDoc type.

1. Execute transaction WE30. Enter the name for your basic IDoc type (it must start with a Z), select the Basic IDoc Type radio button, and click the Create icon.

2. On the next screen, select the Create New option and enter a description for your basic IDoc type (see Figure 31.6). Press Enter.

3. Click the IDoc name, and click the Create icon. The system prompts you to enter a segment type and its attributes (see Figure 31.7). Choose the appropriate values and press Enter. The system transfers the name of the segment type to the IDoc editor.

4. To add more segments, click the segment created in Step 3 and repeat the procedure described in Step 3. You'll notice that after you create the first segment, the system prompts you for the level (same level or child) at which you want to create the next new segment.

TIP

The IDoc editor has cut and paste features. If you create a segment at the wrong level or in the wrong sequence, you can cut and paste to position it correctly.

5. Save your basic IDoc type.

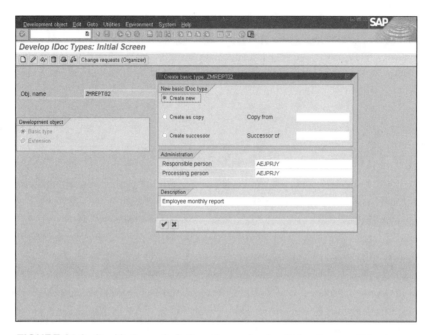

FIGURE 31.6 *Specify the method of creation and a description for your IDoc type.* (© SAP AG)

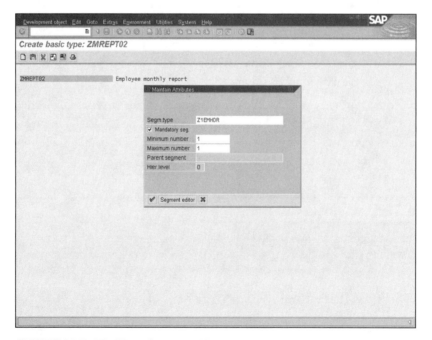

FIGURE 31.7 *The IDoc editor—specify segment attributes for a segment used in the IDoc type.* (© SAP AG)

TIP

From the initial screen, you can click the Check button to test the integrity of your IDoc. The system reports any problems it finds. You can ignore the warnings due to segments not being released, but you should investigate any other problems that are reported.

Step 5: Release the Segment Type and Basic IDoc Type

When you are satisfied with your IDoc structure and segments, you can release them formally to signify their completion and make them available for transport to the test and production systems. First, you release the segments; then, you release the basic IDoc type.

CAUTION

The system checks the release authorizations as you enter the editor. If you do not have authorization, the system grays out the release options. The authorization object checked is S_IDOCDEFT and activity 43.

To release a segment, execute transaction WE31. Enter the segment type and choose Edit, Set Release. The system automatically fills a check box in the segment definitions block.

To release a basic IDoc type, execute transaction WE30. Enter the basic IDoc type in the Obj. Name field and choose Edit, Set Release. The system informs you that it is about to release the object. Confirm the entry, and the basic IDoc type is released. This step prevents further modifications to the basic IDoc type.

TIP

As long as you are on the same release of the SAP system in which the segments, or basic IDoc type, were originally created, you can always cancel the release of a basic IDoc type or a segment type. Canceling a released object enables you to modify it. The steps to cancel a release for a segment type are the same as in the release procedure.

CAUTION

If you are in the process of developing new segments and basic IDoc types, and you upgrade to a new version of SAP, the segments are assumed released, and you will not be able to delete any fields when you are on the new version of SAP. Any changes you make to a segment from that point on will give it a new segment definition. Therefore, you must make sure that segments have the correct fields before you upgrade.

Step 6: Transport the Segments and Basic IDoc Types

Changes to basic IDoc types and segments are recorded in a change request. After you transport the objects, you can also manually re-transport them from the segment editor and IDoc editor screens by choosing Segment, Transport and Development Object, Transport, respectively. Transporting a segment transports all the segment definitions and documentation, but transporting an IDoc does not automatically transport all the segments.

 CAUTION

If you release a basic IDoc type without releasing its segments and then transport the basic IDoc type, the segments will not be transported.

Extending a Basic IDoc Type

To extend a basic IDoc type, you also need to understand what is permitted and what is not. The concept of extending a basic IDoc type means adding one or more custom segments to one or more existing SAP segments of a basic IDoc type. I have seen situations in which users have misinterpreted the IDoc extension process to mean extending the segment tables, using the "append structure" concept. This technique is not permitted (see the "Frequently Asked Questions" section, item 16, in the Appendix, "FAQs, User Exits, and Miscellaneous Resources").

The formal procedure for extending a basic IDoc type is as follows.

1. Start with data analysis. Identify a segment in the basic IDoc type that needs to be extended.

2. Create a custom segment with your fields.

3. Create an IDoc extension that ties the custom segment to the SAP segment that is to be extended.

4. Tie the extension to a basic IDoc type to create an IDoc type. Pay attention to the careful difference in terminology, discussed earlier.

The design and formatting guidelines presented earlier in the IDoc creation process apply to the extension process as well. The steps, however, are different.

 NOTE

The process of extending a basic IDoc type is the same for EDI, ALE, or an external process such as legacy or third-party applications.

Assume that you have extended the customer master screen to incorporate additional sales data information about your customer. This includes two custom fields: delivery priority and customer ranking. To distribute customer master data between two SAP systems, you must also distribute information in the two custom fields. The following steps walk you through the process of extending the basic IDoc type for the customer master (DEBMAS01).

Extending a Basic IDoc Type

Here, in more detail, are the suggested steps to follow for extending a basic IDoc type.

Step 1: Analyze the Data

Analyze the basic IDoc type and identify segments that need to be extended. In this example, the standard SAP segment E1KNVVM contains the sales data information, and Z1KNVVM is a custom segment that contains user-defined fields. Thus, DEBMAS01 is extended by extending the E1KNVVM segment. The segment to be extended is called the *reference segment*. In addition, you need to analyze the processing function module for the message and the basic IDoc type to ensure there is a user exit at a location where programming code for handling the new segment can be inserted.

Step 2: Create Custom Segments

Create the custom segment Z1KNVVM. The Z1KNVVM segment contains two fields: ZZDELPRTY (Delivery Priority) and ZZRANK (Customer Rank). Refer to the "Step 3: Create Segments" section earlier in this chapter for details. Before you create your custom segment, you must also create data elements for the two fields, ZZDELPRTY and ZZRANK. For details, refer to the "Step 2: Create Data Elements" section earlier in this chapter.

Step 3: Create an IDoc Extension

You use the IDoc editor, which is started with transaction WE30, to create an IDoc extension. From the Area menu for EDI, choose Development, IDoc Type.

Follow these steps to create an IDoc extension.

1. Start the IDoc editor. Enter the name for your IDoc extension in the Obj. Name field. This entry can be any meaningful name and does not have to start with a Z. Click the Extension Type radio button, and then click the Create icon.

2. On the next screen, click the Create New button and enter a description for your extension (see Figure 31.8). Press Enter.

3. Click the extension type name, and then click the Create icon. The system prompts you to enter a reference segment type. This item is the segment you want to extend. For this example, enter E1KNVVM as the reference segment, as shown in Figure 31.9. You can repeat this step for additional reference segments you want to include in this extension.

 NOTE

The reference segment is usually an SAP segment. Theoretically, you could extend custom-defined segments, but extending your own segments doesn't make much sense.

4. Now you tie the custom segment to the reference segment identified in "Step 2: Create Custom Segments." Click the reference segment, and then click the Create icon. The system informs you that the segment is added as a child segment. Confirm the entry, and the system prompts you with a dialog box to enter the name of the custom segment and various attributes, such as maximum number and mandatory versus optional,

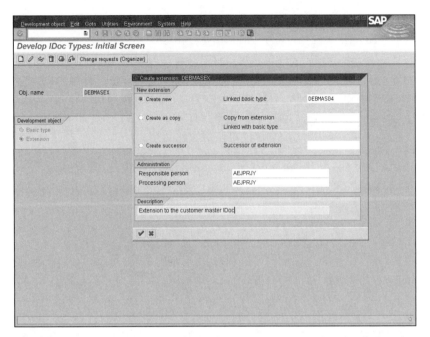

FIGURE 31.8 *Specify the creation method and enter an appropriate description of the extension here.* (© SAP AG)

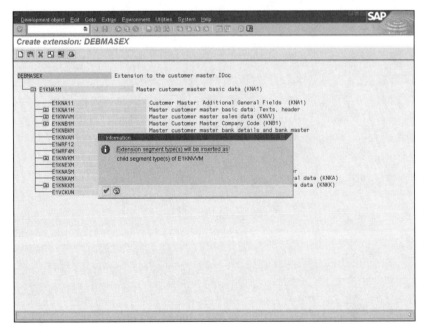

FIGURE 31.9 *Specify the reference segment in the IDoc extension.* (© SAP AG)

as shown in Figure 31.10. Enter the appropriate values and press Enter. Repeat this step for any additional segments you have in your extension.

5. Save your extension. The system might prompt you for a change request if the Changes to Repository Objects option is turned on.

Step 4: Create the IDoc Type

The IDoc type is basically the sum of the basic IDoc type and the extension. To create the IDoc type, follow these simple steps.

1. Start the IDoc editor. Enter the name for your IDoc type in the Obj. Name field. This entry can be any meaningful name that starts with a Z. Click the IDoc Type button, and then click the Create icon.

2. On the next screen, the system prompts you to enter the basic IDoc type and the extension type. Enter the appropriate values. The extension type

FIGURE 31.10 *Specify attributes for the custom segment used to extend a reference segment.* (© SAP AG)

was created in "Step 3: Create an IDoc Extension." The system now checks to make sure that the reference segments in the extension type are present in the basic IDoc type.

3. Press Enter, and the system displays the extended IDoc type (see Figure 31.11). You can expand the reference segment. The system shows the custom segment as a child of the reference segment. It is displayed on a white background to distinguish it from the SAP segments.

Step 5: Release the Custom Segment and IDoc Extension

IDoc extensions and customer segments are to be released, but the IDoc types are not designed to be released. An IDoc type is merely a combination of the basic IDoc type and the extension type. The steps are the same as defined in Step 5 in the "Creating a New Basic IDoc Type" section earlier in this chapter.

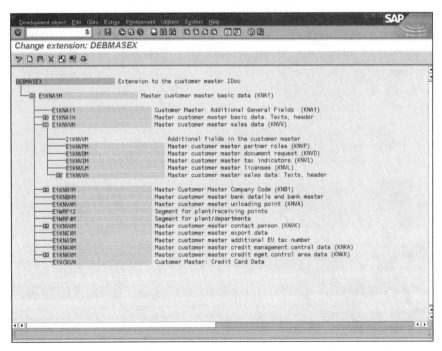

FIGURE 31.11 *The custom segment included in the extended IDoc type* (© SAP AG)

Step 6: Transport the Segments, IDoc Definition, and IDoc Type

It is necessary to transport the IDoc extension and IDoc type to make them available on the production system. The steps are the same as defined in Step 6 in the "Creating a New Basic IDoc Type" section earlier in this chapter.

Summary

The IDoc interface enables you to extend basic IDoc types or create new basic IDoc types to meet your business needs. Extending existing IDocs is preferable to creating new IDoc types because extended IDocs are supported during an upgrade. You extend IDocs mainly to accommodate additional functionality in the business process, such as custom fields in the material master data. You create new IDocs mainly for integration with legacy systems or third-party products.

A functionally rich IDoc requires a good amount of analysis and design. After the analysis, you create segments using the segment editor, and you create and extend IDocs using the IDoc editor. After the segments and IDoc objects are created and tested, they are released to prevent further modifications. Then they are ready for transport to the production environment.

Chapter 32

**Programming in
the IDoc Interface**

This chapter covers the situations in which you have to program in the IDoc interface. Program structure varies, depending on the type of process (inbound or outbound) and the techniques used in the process to generate and process the IDocs, such as user exits, Message control, and change pointers. Although a major programming task is populating and processing the IDoc data, programs can also be written to customize existing process flow and add custom checks. This chapter not only shows you how to write the programs, but also discusses the important issues you need to consider when designing your programs, such as strategic location of user exits and steps to locate user exits. Sample programs are provided for reference.

Writing ABAP Programs

The programming tasks in the IDoc interface can be categorized as follows.

- **Programs for custom IDocs.** These programs are specifically written for new basic IDoc types developed for your process. A separate program is written for the outbound process and the inbound process. The design and program logic of these programs mimics the standard SAP programs for the outbound and inbound processes.

- **Programs for IDoc extensions.** These programs are written specifically for extended IDocs. Standard user exits are available in the outbound IDoc process for populating data in the extended segments. Similarly, user exits are available in the inbound IDoc process for reading data in the extended segments and posting the data.

- **Programs to enhance the process.** These programs are written to enhance the process flow for existing IDocs and add custom checks to the IDoc interface. They also utilize the user exits to implement these checks.

Programs for Custom Basic IDoc Types

Programs for custom IDocs are considered modifications to the SAP system. They are written just like the standard SAP programs for the basic IDoc types. Therefore, the best approach is to copy an existing program of a similar scenario and modify it to suit your needs. The following sections describe various types of outbound and inbound programs written for basic IDoc types.

Outbound Programs for Custom Basic IDoc Types

Outbound programs are also referred to as *IDoc generation programs*. In this section, you will learn how these programs are designed to extract data from an SAP document and create an IDoc. The outbound programs that generate IDocs come in three flavors, based on the triggering mechanism used for the IDoc generation program: outbound IDocs from Message control, outbound IDocs from stand-alone programs, and outbound IDocs from change pointers.

In these programs, the basic principle or core logic for building the IDoc data is the same, but the interfaces of these programs are different. As the IDoc to be generated, these programs use the monthly report IDoc type (ZMREPT01) developed in the preceding chapter. The three variations of the outbound programs are described next.

◆ **Outbound IDocs from Message control**. These programs are implemented as function modules and are specifically designed for applications that make use of the Message control component to generate IDocs. SAP presets the interface for these programs. The Message control component is mainly used by EDI processes for transactional data, although ALE can also make use of Message control for distributing transactional data. For example, the purchase order process uses Message control to generate an IDoc for a purchase order going out via EDI. Purchase orders can also be transferred to an external system via ALE.

◆ **Outbound IDocs from stand-alone programs**. These programs are developed as stand-alone programs with their own interfaces. They can be implemented as reports or separate function modules that can be called from another program. These programs are mainly used for master data distribution in ALE. For example, the process to transfer material master data from one SAP system to another uses this technique to create IDocs.

Some EDI processes also use this technique. For example, the FI transactions use this technique to generate IDocs for the remittance advice and payment order transactions.

♦ **Outbound programs from change pointers**. These programs are specifically designed for generating IDocs from change pointers. The programs are implemented as function modules, and their interface is set by SAP. These programs are mainly used for master data distribution based on changes made to the master data. For example, you can generate an IDoc when a material master is changed or a customer master is changed.

An Outbound Program Triggered from Message Control

This technique is mainly used for creating IDocs for transactional data. EDI-enabled applications use it to generate IDocs for business documents, such as purchase orders and sales orders. This technique is also used in some ALE scenarios to distribute transactional data between different SAP systems. Figure 32.1

FIGURE 32.1 *An IDoc generation program invoked from the Message control component*

depicts how the IDoc generation logic is implemented as a separate piece and invoked from an outbound process that uses Message control to generate an IDoc.

In Message control, the RSNASTED program is used to process outbound ALE and EDI messages. The RSNASTED program calls the appropriate IDoc generation program (implemented as a function module) for a message. The key of the application document to be extracted is passed in the NAST entry, which is one of the function module's parameters. The function module builds the IDoc control record and the data records. The results are passed back to the RSNASTED program, which creates a physical IDoc in the SAP system.

The function modules are generally named IDOC_OUTPUT_<*message_type*> for SAP messages and Z_IDOC_OUTPUT_<*message_type*> for customer messages. This is a guideline and not a rule.

The Interface for the Function Modules

The interface for the function modules follows. You can see the interface at work in the corresponding sample code.

- ◆ **IMPORTING parameters**. The following parameters are passed to the function module by the Message control component.

  - **OBJECT**. The NAST entry that contains the key of the document to be extracted. In the example, an IDoc is to be generated for John Smith. The NAST entry contains the key (his social security number) to identify John's record in the system.

  - **CONTROL_RECORD_IN**. The control record information that is prefilled with information known to the calling program, including the sender system, receiving partner, and IDoc type.

- ◆ **EXPORTING parameters**. The following parameters are returned by the function module to the calling program.

  - **OBJECT_TYPE**. Represents the business object name assigned to the application document. This parameter is used to create a link between the IDoc and the application document.

  - **CONTROL_RECORD_OUT**. The control record with all the information filled out, including the message type, IDoc type, direction, and receiver.

◆ **TABLES parameter**. The following internal table is passed into and out of a function module.

• **INT_EDIDD**. The internal table for data records that are filled by the function module. Data records are filled in the same physical sequence as they are defined in the IDoc type.

◆ **EXCEPTIONS**. Exceptions convey any problems to the calling program. The system starts a workflow for these exceptions.

Program Flow

The program logic contains the following blocks.

1. Copy incoming control record information to the outgoing control record.

2. Populate the remaining fields in the control record.

3. Select application data from the database, using the object key passed in the NAST record.

4. Populate the internal table of data records (INT_EDIDD) with the various segments.

TIP

Before you start developing your program, copy an existing program and make use of its interface.

5. Return control to the calling program. When the control comes back to the Message control component, an IDoc is created in the database.

The following program generates the monthly report IDoc ZMREPT01 from Message control.

```
FUNCTION Z_IDOC_OUTPUT_ZMREPT.
*"----------------------------------------------------------------
*"*"Local interface:
*"       IMPORTING
*"             VALUE(CONTROL_RECORD_IN) LIKE  EDIDC STRUCTURE  EDIDC
*"             VALUE(OBJECT) LIKE  NAST STRUCTURE  NAST
```

```
*"         EXPORTING
*"              VALUE(OBJECT_TYPE) LIKE  WFAS1-ASGTP
*"              VALUE(CONTROL_RECORD_OUT) LIKE  EDIDC STRUCTURE  EDIDC
*"         TABLES
*"              INT_EDIDD STRUCTURE  EDIDD
*"         EXCEPTIONS
*"              ERROR_MESSAGE_RECEIVED
*"------------------------------------------------------------------


*------------------------------------------------------------------
* Constants
*------------------------------------------------------------------


DATA:
*      segment names
       C_HEADER_SEGMENT            LIKE EDIDD-SEGNAM VALUE 'Z1EMHDR',
       C_WEEKLY_DETAILS_SEGMENT    LIKE EDIDD-SEGNAM VALUE 'Z1WKDET',
       C_CLIENT_DETAILS_SEGMENT    LIKE EDIDD-SEGNAM VALUE 'Z1CLDET',
       C_SUMMARY_SEGMENT           LIKE EDIDD-SEGNAM VALUE 'Z1SUMRY',
*      IDoc type
       C_MONTHLY_REPORT_IDOC_TYPE  LIKE EDIDC-IDOCTP VALUE 'ZMREPT01',
*      message type
       C_MONTHLY_REPORT_MESSAGE    LIKE EDIDC-MESTYP VALUE 'ZMREPT'.


*------------------------------------------------------------------
* Data declarations
*------------------------------------------------------------------
* field string for the data records
DATA: FS_INT_EDIDD LIKE EDIDD.
* employee header data
DATA: FS_EMPHDR_DATA LIKE Z1EMHDR.
* employee weekly details data
DATA: FS_WEEKDET_DATA LIKE Z1WKDET.
* client details data
DATA: FS_CLIENTDET_DATA LIKE Z1CLDET.
* employee monthly summary data
DATA: FS_SUMMARY_DATA LIKE Z1SUMRY.
```

```
* total hours and amount for the summary segment
DATA: TOTAL_HRS_MONTH TYPE I,
      TOTAL_AMT_MONTH TYPE I.
* object key (social security number for the employee)
DATA: P_SSN LIKE ZEMPDETAIL-SSN.
*------------------------------------------------------------------
* Database Tables
*------------------------------------------------------------------
* Application data tables
tables: zempdetail, zempwkdet.


*------------------------------------------------------------------
* Internal tables
*------------------------------------------------------------------
DATA:
*     weekly details - application data
      IT_WKDET LIKE ZEMPWKDET OCCURS 0 WITH HEADER LINE.
*------------------------------------------------------------------
* Program logic
*------------------------------------------------------------------


*********************Select Application Data*************************

* determine the object key from the NAST entry
P_SSN = OBJECT-OBJKY.   " employees social security number
SELECT SINGLE * FROM ZEMPDETAIL WHERE SSN = P_SSN.
SELECT * FROM ZEMPWKDET INTO TABLE IT_WKDET WHERE SSN = P_SSN.


*********************Build Control Record***************************

CLEAR CONTROL_RECORD_OUT.
* copy control record from the input parameters to the output parameters
MOVE CONTROL_RECORD_IN TO CONTROL_RECORD_OUT.
* Fill control record information
CONTROL_RECORD_OUT-DIRECT = '1'.
control_record_out-mestyp = c_monthly_report_message.
```

```
control_record_out-idoctp = c_monthly_report_idoc_type.
control_record_out-rcvprt = 'LS'.
CONTROL_RECORD_OUT-RCVPRN = 'LEGHOST01'.


**********************Build Data Records********************************


*-----------------Employee header---------------------------------------

* fill the employee header information
FS_EMPHDR_DATA-LNAME = ZEMPDETAIL-LNAME.
FS_EMPHDR_DATA-FNAME = ZEMPDETAIL-FNAME.
FS_EMPHDR_DATA-SSN   = ZEMPDETAIL-SSN.
FS_EMPHDR_DATA-DOB   = ZEMPDETAIL-DOB.

* fill the administrative section of the data record
FS_INT_EDIDD-SEGNAM = C_HEADER_SEGMENT.
FS_INT_EDIDD-SDATA = FS_EMPHDR_DATA.

* append the employee header data record to the IDoc data
APPEND FS_INT_EDIDD TO INT_EDIDD.

*-----------------Employee weekly details*-----------------------------
LOOP AT IT_WKDET.
* fill the weekly details for each week
   FS_WEEKDET_DATA-WEEKNO = IT_WKDET-WEEKNO.
   FS_WEEKDET_DATA-TOTHOURS = IT_WKDET-TOTHOURS.
   FS_WEEKDET_DATA-HRLYRATE = IT_WKDET-HRLYRATE.

* add administrative information to the data record
   FS_INT_EDIDD-SEGNAM = C_WEEKLY_DETAILS_SEGMENT.
   FS_INT_EDIDD-SDATA = FS_WEEKDET_DATA.

* append the data for the week to the IDoc data
   APPEND FS_INT_EDIDD TO INT_EDIDD.
```

```
* Client details of each week
  FS_CLIENTDET_DATA-CLSITE = IT_WKDET-CLSITE.
  FS_CLIENTDET_DATA-WORKDESC = IT_WKDET-WORKDESC.


* add administrative information to the data record
  FS_INT_EDIDD-SEGNAM = C_CLIENT_DETAILS_SEGMENT.
  FS_INT_EDIDD-SDATA = FS_CLIENTDET_DATA.


* append the client details for the week to the IDoc data
  APPEND FS_INT_EDIDD TO INT_EDIDD.

ENDLOOP.
*------------------Employee monthly summary----------------------------
* compute total hours and amount for the month
LOOP AT IT_WKDET.
  TOTAL_HRS_MONTH = TOTAL_HRS_MONTH +   IT_WKDET-TOTHOURS.
  TOTAL_AMT_MONTH = TOTAL_AMT_MONTH + ( IT_WKDET-TOTHOURS *
                                        IT_WKDET-HRLYRATE ).
ENDLOOP.


* fill the summary information
FS_SUMMARY_DATA-TOTHRS = TOTAL_HRS_MONTH.
FS_SUMMARY_DATA-TOTAMT = TOTAL_AMT_MONTH.


* condense the summary record fields to remove spaces
CONDENSE FS_SUMMARY_DATA-TOTHRS.
CONDENSE FS_SUMMARY_DATA-TOTAMT.


* add administrative information to the data record
FS_INT_EDIDD-SEGNAM = C_SUMMARY_SEGMENT.
FS_INT_EDIDD-SDATA = FS_SUMMARY_DATA.


* append summary data to the IDoc data
APPEND FS_INT_EDIDD TO INT_EDIDD.



ENDFUNCTION.
```

A Stand-Alone Program to Generate IDocs

ALE processes for distributing master data are implemented as stand-alone report programs. For example, the RBDSEMAT report program generates material master IDocs. A stand-alone program can embed the IDoc generation logic in any manner it chooses; in contrast, the Message control component must place the IDoc generation logic in a function module. The program logic is quite similar, except for a call to the ALE layer for creating a physical IDoc in the system. Figure 32.2 depicts how the IDoc generation logic is part of the stand-alone program itself.

The Selection Screen

The selection screen in the stand-alone program enables the user to specify the objects for which IDocs are to be generated. Although the selection screen has not been standardized because of varying needs of the application programs, the ALE programs for master distribution have some similarities. At a minimum, they allow a user to select one or more objects, a receiving system and the message to be generated. Refer to the selection screen for distributing the material master (transaction BD10).

FIGURE 32.2 *IDocs created from a stand-alone program*

Program Flow

The program logic contains the following blocks.

1. Provide a selection screen to enable a user to specify the objects for which IDocs are to be generated.

2. Determine the key of the application document from the object specified in Step 1.

3. Select application data from the database, using the object key identified in Step 2.

4. Populate the control record information.

5. Populate an internal table of type EDIDD with data records for the various segments.

6. Call the ALE service layer (MASTER_IDOC_DISTRIBUTE) to create the IDocs in the database.

7. Execute a Commit work.

The following program generates the monthly report IDoc ZMREPT01, which illustrates a stand-alone outbound process.

```
REPORT ZARNEDI1 MESSAGE-ID ZE.


*------------------------------------------------------------------
* Parameters
*------------------------------------------------------------------
* object key (social security number for the employee)
PARAMETERS: P_SSN LIKE ZEMPDETAIL-SSN.
* message type
PARAMETERS: P_MESTYP LIKE EDMSG-MSGTYP OBLIGATORY.
* destination system
PARAMETERS: P_LOGSYS LIKE TBDLST-LOGSYS.


*------------------------------------------------------------------
* Constants
*------------------------------------------------------------------
```

```
DATA:
*     segment names
      C_HEADER_SEGMENT           LIKE EDIDD-SEGNAM VALUE 'Z1EMHDR',
      C_WEEKLY_DETAILS_SEGMENT   LIKE EDIDD-SEGNAM VALUE 'Z1WKDET',
      C_CLIENT_DETAILS_SEGMENT   LIKE EDIDD-SEGNAM VALUE 'Z1CLDET',
      C_SUMMARY_SEGMENT          LIKE EDIDD-SEGNAM VALUE 'Z1SUMRY',
*     IDoc type
      C_MONTHLY_REPORT_IDOC_TYPE LIKE EDIDC-IDOCTP VALUE 'ZMREPT01'.
*-------------------------------------------------------------------
* Data declarations
*-------------------------------------------------------------------
* IDoc control record
data: control_record_out like edidc.
* employee header data
DATA: FS_EMPHDR_DATA LIKE Z1EMHDR.
* employee weekly details data
DATA: FS_WEEKDET_DATA LIKE Z1WKDET.
* client details data
DATA: FS_CLIENTDET_DATA LIKE Z1CLDET.
* employee monthly summary data
DATA: FS_SUMMARY_DATA LIKE Z1SUMRY.
* total hours and amount for the summary segment
DATA: TOTAL_HRS_MONTH TYPE I,
      TOTAL_AMT_MONTH TYPE I.
*-------------------------------------------------------------------
* Database Tables
*-------------------------------------------------------------------
* Application data tables
TABLES: ZEMPDETAIL, ZEMPWKDET.


*-------------------------------------------------------------------
* Internal tables
*-------------------------------------------------------------------
DATA:

*     weekly details - application data
      IT_WKDET LIKE ZEMPWKDET OCCURS 0 WITH HEADER LINE,
```

```
*       data records
        INT_EDIDD LIKE EDIDD OCCURS 0 WITH HEADER LINE,
*       communication IDocs generated
        IT_COMM_IDOCS LIKE EDIDC OCCURS 0 WITH HEADER LINE.


*----------------------------------------------------------------
* Program logic
*----------------------------------------------------------------


**********************Select Application Data*****************************
SELECT SINGLE * FROM ZEMPDETAIL WHERE SSN = P_SSN.
IF SY-SUBRC NE 0.
   MESSAGE E001 WITH P_SSN.
   EXIT.
ENDIF.


SELECT * FROM ZEMPWKDET INTO TABLE IT_WKDET WHERE SSN = P_SSN.
IF SY-SUBRC NE 0.
   MESSAGE E002 WITH P_SSN.
   EXIT.
ENDIF.


**********************Build Control Record********************************

* Fill control record information
CONTROL_RECORD_OUT-MESTYP = P_MESTYP.
control_record_out-idoctp = c_monthly_report_idoc_type.
control_record_out-rcvprt = 'LS'.
control_record_out-rcvprn = p_logsys.


**********************Build Data Records*********************************

*------------------Employee header----------------------------------------

* fill the employee header information
FS_EMPHDR_DATA-LNAME = ZEMPDETAIL-LNAME.
FS_EMPHDR_DATA-FNAME = ZEMPDETAIL-FNAME.
```

```
FS_EMPHDR_DATA-SSN   = ZEMPDETAIL-SSN.
FS_EMPHDR_DATA-DOB   = ZEMPDETAIL-DOB.

* fill the administrative section of the data record
INT_EDIDD-SEGNAM = C_HEADER_SEGMENT.
INT_EDIDD-SDATA = FS_EMPHDR_DATA.

* append the employee header data record to the IDoc data
APPEND INT_EDIDD.

*-----------------Employee weekly details-----------------------------
LOOP AT IT_WKDET.
* fill the weekly details for each week
  FS_WEEKDET_DATA-WEEKNO = IT_WKDET-WEEKNO.
  FS_WEEKDET_DATA-TOTHOURS = IT_WKDET-TOTHOURS.
  FS_WEEKDET_DATA-HRLYRATE = IT_WKDET-HRLYRATE.

* add administrative information to the data record
  INT_EDIDD-SEGNAM = C_WEEKLY_DETAILS_SEGMENT.
  INT_EDIDD-SDATA = FS_WEEKDET_DATA.

* append the data for the week to the IDoc data
  APPEND INT_EDIDD.

* Client details of each week
  FS_CLIENTDET_DATA-CLSITE = IT_WKDET-CLSITE.
  FS_CLIENTDET_DATA-WORKDESC = IT_WKDET-WORKDESC.

* add administrative information to the data record
  INT_EDIDD-SEGNAM = C_CLIENT_DETAILS_SEGMENT.
  INT_EDIDD-SDATA = FS_CLIENTDET_DATA.

* append the client details for the week to the IDoc data
  APPEND INT_EDIDD.

ENDLOOP.
*-----------------Employee monthly summary----------------------------
```

```
* compute total hours and amount for the month
LOOP AT IT_WKDET.
   TOTAL_HRS_MONTH = TOTAL_HRS_MONTH +   IT_WKDET-TOTHOURS.
   TOTAL_AMT_MONTH = TOTAL_AMT_MONTH + ( IT_WKDET-TOTHOURS *
                                         IT_WKDET-HRLYRATE ).
ENDLOOP.


* fill the summary information
FS_SUMMARY_DATA-TOTHRS = TOTAL_HRS_MONTH.
FS_SUMMARY_DATA-TOTAMT = TOTAL_AMT_MONTH.


* condense the summary record fields to remove spaces
CONDENSE FS_SUMMARY_DATA-TOTHRS.
CONDENSE FS_SUMMARY_DATA-TOTAMT.


* add administrative information to the data record
INT_EDIDD-SEGNAM = C_SUMMARY_SEGMENT.
INT_EDIDD-SDATA = FS_SUMMARY_DATA.


* append summary data to the IDoc data
APPEND INT_EDIDD.


**************Pass control to the ALE layer*****************************
CALL FUNCTION 'MASTER_IDOC_DISTRIBUTE'
     EXPORTING
          master_idoc_control              = control_record_out
     TABLES
          COMMUNICATION_IDOC_CONTROL       = IT_COMM_IDOCS
          MASTER_IDOC_DATA                 = INT_EDIDD
     EXCEPTIONS
          ERROR_IN_IDOC_CONTROL            = 1
          ERROR_WRITING_IDOC_STATUS        = 2
          ERROR_IN_IDOC_DATA               = 3
          SENDING_LOGICAL_SYSTEM_UNKNOWN   = 4
          OTHERS                           = 5.


IF SY-SUBRC NE 0.
   MESSAGE E003 WITH P_SSN.
```

```
ELSE.
   LOOP AT IT_COMM_IDOCS.
     WRITE: / 'IDoc generated', IT_COMM_IDOCS-DOCNUM.
   ENDLOOP.
   COMMIT WORK.
ENDIF.
```

An Outbound Program Triggered from Change Pointers

When important master data, such as customer master or material master, is changed, the system writes change documents for each document to track changes. Change pointers can be written in response to change documents. A standard report RBDMIDOC can be executed to process entries in the change pointer table. To generate the IDocs, this program calls a function module specific to each message. This technique is used in ALE processes to keep master data synchronized across multiple SAP systems. Figure 32.3 depicts how the IDoc generation logic is implemented as a separate piece in case of outbound processes that use the change pointer technique.

The IDoc generation logic is similar to the stand-alone programs except for additional logic to analyze change pointers.

FIGURE 32.3 *IDoc creation triggered from a change pointer*

The function modules are generally named MASTERIDOC_CREATE_SMD_ *<message type>* for SAP messages and Z_MASTERIDOC_SMD_*<message type>* for customer messages.

The interface for these function modules is very simple. It has only one input parameter: MESSAGE_TYPE. This parameter is the message type for which change pointers are to be analyzed for creating IDocs.

The program logic contains the following blocks.

1. Read the change pointers using the CHANGE_POINTERS_READ function module.
2. Analyze the change pointers to determine which documents are valid.
3. Determine the key of the application document from Step 2.
4. Select application data from the database, using the object key identified in Step 3.
5. Populate the control record information.
6. Populate an internal table of type EDIDD with data records for the various segments.
7. Call the ALE service layer (MASTER_IDOC_DISTRIBUTE) to create the IDocs in the database.
8. Update change pointer status.
9. Execute a Commit work.

The following program generates the monthly report IDoc (ZMREPT01) based on change pointers.

```
FUNCTION Z_IDOC_CHGPTR.
*"----------------------------------------------------------------
*"*"Local interface:
*"        IMPORTING
*"                VALUE(MESSAGE_TYPE) LIKE  TBDME-MESTYP
*"----------------------------------------------------------------


*----------------------------------------------------------------
* Data declarations
*----------------------------------------------------------------
```

```
DATA:
  SSN                    LIKE ZEMP-SSN,        "employee's social security
  CREATED_C_IDOCS        LIKE SY-TABIX,        "no. of created IDoc
  CREATED_M_IDOCS        LIKE SY-TABIX,        "no of processed chg.pointer
  CREATED_COMM_IDOCS     LIKE SY-TABIX,        "IDocs of one document
  DONE_SINCE_COMMIT      LIKE SY-TABIX,        "no of IDocs since last com.
  C_MARK(1)              TYPE C VALUE 'X',     "mark for a checkbox
  C_IDOCS_BEFORE_COMMIT LIKE SY-TABIX         "commit after 50 IDocs
                         VALUE 50.


* key structure of change pointer
  DATA:
*    employee key
     BEGIN OF EMP_KEY,
       MANDT LIKE ZEMP-MANDT,
       SSN   LIKE ZEMPDETAIL-SSN,
     END OF EMP_KEY.


* Change pointer (standard structure for any object)
  DATA: BEGIN OF T_CHGPTRS OCCURS 0.
          INCLUDE STRUCTURE BDCP.
  DATA: END OF T_CHGPTRS.


* Change pointer (employee structure)
  DATA:
     BEGIN OF T_CHGPTRS_EMP OCCURS 0,
       SSN     LIKE ZEMP-SSN,
       CPIDENT LIKE BDCP-CPIDENT,
     END OF T_CHGPTRS_EMP.


* written change pointers
  DATA:
     BEGIN OF T_CPIDENT OCCURS 0,
       CPIDENT LIKE BDCP-CPIDENT,
     END OF T_CPIDENT.


*-----------------------------------------------------------------------
```

```
* Program logic
*------------------------------------------------------------------------
* read all unprocessed change pointers
  CALL FUNCTION 'CHANGE_POINTERS_READ'
       EXPORTING
             MESSAGE_TYPE                = MESSAGE_TYPE
             READ_NOT_PROCESSED_POINTERS = C_MARK          " = 'X'
       TABLES
             CHANGE_POINTERS             = T_CHGPTRS.
* create IDocs for all change pointers
  CLEAR:
     CREATED_C_IDOCS,
     CREATED_M_IDOCS,
     DONE_SINCE_COMMIT.
  REFRESH: T_CHGPTRS_EMP,
           T_CPIDENT.
* copy standard change pointers into employee change pointer format
  LOOP AT T_CHGPTRS.
*    extract key information from the standard structure (has client)
     EMP_KEY = T_CHGPTRS-TABKEY.
     MOVE-CORRESPONDING EMP_KEY TO T_CHGPTRS_EMP.
     T_CHGPTRS_EMP-CPIDENT = T_CHGPTRS-CPIDENT.
     APPEND T_CHGPTRS_EMP.
  ENDLOOP.
* sort by employee's ssn
  SORT T_CHGPTRS_EMP BY SSN.

  CLEAR SSN.
  LOOP AT T_CHGPTRS_EMP.
*    if IDoc already created, append CPIDENT (list of same documents)
     IF T_CHGPTRS_EMP-SSN EQ SSN.
        T_CPIDENT-CPIDENT = T_CHGPTRS_EMP-CPIDENT.
        APPEND T_CPIDENT.
        CONTINUE.
     ENDIF.
     SSN = T_CHGPTRS_EMP-SSN.

     CALL FUNCTION 'Z_MASTERIDOC_CREATE_ZMREPT'
```

```
          EXPORTING
               SSN                      = SSN
               MESSAGE_TYPE             = MESSAGE_TYPE
          IMPORTING
               CREATED_COMM_IDOCS = CREATED_M_IDOCS
          EXCEPTIONS
               OTHERS                   = 1.


*    create IDocs for the document
     CREATED_M_IDOCS = CREATED_M_IDOCS + 1.
     CREATED_C_IDOCS = CREATED_C_IDOCS + CREATED_COMM_IDOCS.
     DONE_SINCE_COMMIT = DONE_SINCE_COMMIT + 1.
     T_CPIDENT-CPIDENT = T_CHGPTRS_EMP-CPIDENT.
     APPEND T_CPIDENT.
*    initialize counter variables for created IDocs
     IF DONE_SINCE_COMMIT GE C_IDOCS_BEFORE_COMMIT.
       DONE_SINCE_COMMIT = 0.
*      write status of all processed pointers
       CALL FUNCTION 'CHANGE_POINTERS_STATUS_WRITE'
            EXPORTING
                 MESSAGE_TYPE             = MESSAGE_TYPE
            TABLES
                 CHANGE_POINTERS_IDENTS  = T_CPIDENT.
       REFRESH: T_CPIDENT.
       COMMIT WORK.
       CALL FUNCTION 'DEQUEUE_ALL'.
     ENDIF.
   ENDLOOP.   " AT t_chgptrs_emp
* commit if necessary
   IF DONE_SINCE_COMMIT GT 0.
* write status of all processed pointers
     CALL FUNCTION 'CHANGE_POINTERS_STATUS_WRITE'
          EXPORTING
               MESSAGE_TYPE             = MESSAGE_TYPE
          TABLES
               CHANGE_POINTERS_IDENTS   = T_CPIDENT.
     COMMIT WORK.
     CALL FUNCTION 'DEQUEUE_ALL'.
```

```
        ENDIF.
* Number of master IDocs created
   MESSAGE ID 'ZE' TYPE 'I' NUMBER '004'
           WITH CREATED_M_IDOCS MESSAGE_TYPE.
* Number of communication IDocs
   MESSAGE ID 'ZE' TYPE 'I' NUMBER '005'
           WITH CREATED_C_IDOCS MESSAGE_TYPE.
ENDFUNCTION.


FUNCTION Z_MASTERIDOC_CREATE_ZMREPT.
*"----------------------------------------------------------------------
*"*"Local interface:
*"      IMPORTING
*"             VALUE(SSN) LIKE   ZEMPDETAIL-SSN
*"             VALUE(RCVPFC) LIKE   BDALEDC-RCVPFC OPTIONAL
*"             VALUE(RCVPRN) LIKE   BDALEDC-RCVPRN OPTIONAL
*"             VALUE(RCVPRT) LIKE   BDALEDC-RCVPRT OPTIONAL
*"             VALUE(SNDPFC) LIKE   BDALEDC-SNDPFC OPTIONAL
*"             VALUE(SNDPRN) LIKE   BDALEDC-SNDPRN OPTIONAL
*"             VALUE(SNDPRT) LIKE   BDALEDC-SNDPRT
*"             VALUE(MESSAGE_TYPE) LIKE   TBDME-MESTYP
*"      EXPORTING
*"             VALUE(CREATED_COMM_IDOCS) LIKE   SY-TABIX
*"----------------------------------------------------------------------
*----------------------------------------------------------------------
* Constants
*----------------------------------------------------------------------


DATA:
*     segment names
      C_HEADER_SEGMENT             LIKE EDIDD-SEGNAM VALUE 'Z1EMHDR',
      C_WEEKLY_DETAILS_SEGMENT     LIKE EDIDD-SEGNAM VALUE 'Z1WKDET',
      C_CLIENT_DETAILS_SEGMENT     LIKE EDIDD-SEGNAM VALUE 'Z1CLDET',
      C_SUMMARY_SEGMENT            LIKE EDIDD-SEGNAM VALUE 'Z1SUMRY',
*     IDoc type
      C_MONTHLY_REPORT_IDOC_TYPE LIKE EDIDC-IDOCTP VALUE 'ZMREPT01'.
*----------------------------------------------------------------------
```

```
* Data declarations
*------------------------------------------------------------------------
* IDoc control record
data: control_record_out like edidc.
* employee header data
DATA: FS_EMPHDR_DATA LIKE Z1EMHDR.
* employee weekly details data
DATA: FS_WEEKDET_DATA LIKE Z1WKDET.
* client details data
DATA: FS_CLIENTDET_DATA LIKE Z1CLDET.
* employee monthly summary data
DATA: FS_SUMMARY_DATA LIKE Z1SUMRY.
* total hours and amount for the summary segment
DATA: TOTAL_HRS_MONTH TYPE I,
      TOTAL_AMT_MONTH TYPE I.
*------------------------------------------------------------------------
* Database Tables
*------------------------------------------------------------------------
* Application data tables
*tables: zempdetail, zempwkdet.


*------------------------------------------------------------------------
* Internal tables
*------------------------------------------------------------------------
DATA:

*     weekly details - application data
      IT_WKDET LIKE ZEMPWKDET OCCURS 0 WITH HEADER LINE,
*     data records
      INT_EDIDD LIKE EDIDD OCCURS 0 WITH HEADER LINE,
*     communication IDocs generated
      IT_COMM_IDOCS LIKE EDIDC OCCURS 0 WITH HEADER LINE.


*------------------------------------------------------------------------
* Program logic
*------------------------------------------------------------------------
```

```
********************Select Application Data***************************
SELECT SINGLE * FROM ZEMPDETAIL WHERE SSN = SSN.
IF SY-SUBRC NE 0.
* Employee & not found
   MESSAGE E001(ZE) WITH SSN.
   EXIT.
ENDIF.

SELECT * FROM ZEMPWKDET INTO TABLE IT_WKDET WHERE SSN = SSN.
IF SY-SUBRC NE 0.
* weekly information missing for employee &
   MESSAGE E002(ZE) WITH SSN.
   EXIT.
ENDIF.

********************Build Control Record******************************

* Fill control record information
CONTROL_RECORD_OUT-MESTYP = MESSAGE_TYPE.
control_record_out-idoctp = c_monthly_report_idoc_type.
*control_record_out-rcvprt = 'LS'.
*control_record_out-rcvprn = p_logsys.

********************Build Data Records********************************

*------------------Employee header------------------------------------

* fill the employee header information
FS_EMPHDR_DATA-LNAME = ZEMPDETAIL-LNAME.
FS_EMPHDR_DATA-FNAME = ZEMPDETAIL-FNAME.
FS_EMPHDR_DATA-SSN   = ZEMPDETAIL-SSN.
FS_EMPHDR_DATA-DOB   = ZEMPDETAIL-DOB.

* fill the administrative section of the data record
INT_EDIDD-SEGNAM = C_HEADER_SEGMENT.
INT_EDIDD-SDATA = FS_EMPHDR_DATA.

* append the employee header data record to the IDoc data
```

```
APPEND INT_EDIDD.

*-----------------Employee weekly details----------------------------
LOOP AT IT_WKDET.
* fill the weekly details for each week
  FS_WEEKDET_DATA-WEEKNO = IT_WKDET-WEEKNO.
  FS_WEEKDET_DATA-TOTHOURS = IT_WKDET-TOTHOURS.
  FS_WEEKDET_DATA-HRLYRATE = IT_WKDET-HRLYRATE.

* add administrative information to the data record
  INT_EDIDD-SEGNAM = C_WEEKLY_DETAILS_SEGMENT.
  INT_EDIDD-SDATA = FS_WEEKDET_DATA.

* append the data for the week to the IDoc data
  APPEND INT_EDIDD.

* Client details of each week
  FS_CLIENTDET_DATA-CLSITE = IT_WKDET-CLSITE.
  FS_CLIENTDET_DATA-WORKDESC = IT_WKDET-WORKDESC.

* add administrative information to the data record
  INT_EDIDD-SEGNAM = C_CLIENT_DETAILS_SEGMENT.
  INT_EDIDD-SDATA = FS_CLIENTDET_DATA.

* append the client details for the week to the IDoc data
  APPEND INT_EDIDD.

ENDLOOP.
*-----------------Employee monthly summary---------------------------
* compute total hours and amount for the month
LOOP AT IT_WKDET.
  TOTAL_HRS_MONTH = TOTAL_HRS_MONTH + IT_WKDET-TOTHOURS.
  TOTAL_AMT_MONTH = TOTAL_AMT_MONTH + ( IT_WKDET-TOTHOURS *
                                        IT_WKDET-HRLYRATE ).
ENDLOOP.

* fill the summary information
FS_SUMMARY_DATA-TOTHRS = TOTAL_HRS_MONTH.
```

```
FS_SUMMARY_DATA-TOTAMT = TOTAL_AMT_MONTH.

* condense the summary record fields to remove spaces
CONDENSE FS_SUMMARY_DATA-TOTHRS.
CONDENSE FS_SUMMARY_DATA-TOTAMT.

* add administrative information to the data record
INT_EDIDD-SEGNAM = C_SUMMARY_SEGMENT.
INT_EDIDD-SDATA = FS_SUMMARY_DATA.

* append summary data to the IDoc data
APPEND INT_EDIDD.

**************Pass control to the ALE layer*****************************
CALL FUNCTION 'MASTER_IDOC_DISTRIBUTE'
     EXPORTING
          master_idoc_control            = control_record_out
     TABLES
          COMMUNICATION_IDOC_CONTROL     = IT_COMM_IDOCS
          MASTER_IDOC_DATA               = INT_EDIDD
     EXCEPTIONS
          ERROR_IN_IDOC_CONTROL          = 1
          ERROR_WRITING_IDOC_STATUS      = 2
          ERROR_IN_IDOC_DATA             = 3
          SENDING_LOGICAL_SYSTEM_UNKNOWN = 4
          OTHERS                         = 5.

* get number of created IDocs
   DESCRIBE TABLE IT_COMM_IDOCS LINES CREATED_COMM_IDOCS.
ENDFUNCTION.
```

An Inbound Program for Custom Basic IDoc Types

Inbound programs are also called *posting programs*. This section explains how these programs are designed to read IDoc data and post application documents. You start with the basic design of these programs, in which a single IDoc is passed to the posting programs.

◆ **Basic scenario**. The ALE layer calls the posting program and passes
IDoc data to it. Posting programs are implemented as function modules
and are designed to read IDoc data and create an application document.
The programs can use one of the two methods available for posting an
application document: a direct-input function module or a call transaction. In a direct-input function module, the database tables are updated
directly; in call transaction mode, the system simulates data for each
screen to post a document. The results of posting are passed back to the
ALE layer, which then updates the status records.

◆ **Advanced scenarios**. The function modules can be designed for
advanced scenarios such as mass processing, serialization checks,
advanced workflow programming, and enabling an existing transaction
for ALE. In mass processing, the function module is designed to handle
several IDocs at the same time. This approach is useful for improving
the system's throughput. A serialization check is used when the sequence
in which IDocs are posted is important. For example, if two order-
change IDocs are waiting to be posted, and the first changes the current
order quantity to 100 and the second changes the quantity to 20, the
sequence in which these are posted is important. You want to post them
in the sequence in which they were received. This sequence can be
implemented by using a serialization check. The advanced workflow scenario is used for raising application-specific events after a successful
posting. Finally, enabling a transaction for ALE is useful when you
cannot afford to post the same document twice, even in the worst
possible case of a system failure. In the standard system, only the
IDOC_INPUT_INVOICE_MM function module to process incoming
invoices is designed with this approach.

The scenarios most commonly implemented for the inbound process are the single IDoc and multiple IDoc scenarios. Serialization checks, advanced workflow
programming, and ALE enabling are not commonly deployed. The posting programs are implemented as function modules and are generally named
IDOC_INPUT_*<message_type>* for SAP messages and Z_IDOC_INPUT_
<message_type> for customer messages. This is a guideline and not a rule. Figure
32.4 depicts how the inbound posting program logic is implemented as a separate
piece and invoked from the inbound IDoc process.

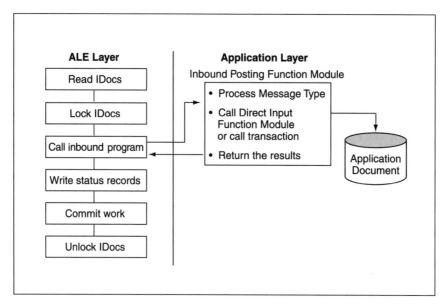

FIGURE 32.4 *Inbound processing of IDocs*

The Interface for the Function Module

The interface for the function module is preset by SAP and is the same for all the inbound scenarios just described. This situation of using the same interface for all possible scenarios makes the interface more involved in comparison with the outbound programs, where the interface is different for each type of program. The various parameters in the interface are described here, using the mass-processing scenario as an example.

◆ **IMPORTING parameters**. The following parameters are passed to the function module by the ALE interface layer.

- **INPUT_METHOD**. Specifies the mode in which the posting program is to be executed, and is valid only for programs that use the call transaction method. The various values are A (Show All Screens), E (Show Error Screen Only), and space (Background Mode).

- **MASS_PROCESSING**. Used for the advanced workflow programming scenario only. The default value is space.

◆ **EXPORTING parameters**. The following parameters are returned from the posting program to the ALE layer to provide information on the results of posting.

• **WORKFLOW_RESULT**. Indicates whether the posting was successful. Workflow is started for the error condition. The value of 0 indicates success and 99999 indicates failure (workflow is started).

• **APPLICATION_VARIABLE**. Used in advanced workflow programming only. Leave it blank.

• **IN_UPDATE_TASK**. Indicates how the piece of code that updates the database tables was invoked in the posting program. The value of ' ' indicates that the update task was not used, and 'X' indicates that the update task was used. This value delays the posting until a commit is done.

• **CALL_TRANSACTION_DONE**. Leave this blank unless you are using an ALE-enabled transaction. An ALE-enabled transaction has been modified to update the IDoc status in its code rather than in the ALE layer. The ALE layer does not update the status information for ALE-enabled transactions.

CAUTION

Don't let the parameter name CALL_TRANSACTION_DONE mislead you. It does not represent whether your posting program uses call transaction.

◆ **TABLES parameters**. These parameters are internal tables used to pass multiple data values to and receive multiple values from the function module. The following entries are used in the posting program.

• **IDOC_CONTRL**. Contains control records of the IDocs to be processed and is passed as an input parameter.

• **IDOC_DATA**. Contains data records of the IDocs to be processed and is also passed as an input parameter.

• **IDOC_STATUS**. Contains status records for each IDoc processed in the posting program and is an output parameter. Therefore,

IDOC_STATUS is populated by the posting program. In the structure BDIDOCSTAT, you can see the various fields that can be filled in the program, using transaction SE11. The structure mainly consists of the IDoc number, status code, message ID, and variables.

For example, assume that three IDocs (100, 101, and 102) were passed to the posting program. The first and third IDoc successfully posted and created application documents. IDoc number 101 failed to post the document. The error was in segment number 3 in the HRLYRATE field, and the error message is represented by error code 15 in the message class ZE. Table 32.1 shows how the IDOC_STATUS table can be populated.

Table 32.1 Values in the IDOC_STATUS Table

DOCNUM	STATUS	MSGTY	MSGID	MSGNO	SEGNUM	SEGFLD
100	53					
101	51	E	ZE	015	03	HRLYRATE
102	53					

- **RETURN_VARIABLES**. Also an output parameter that contains additional processing results for each IDoc. The ALE layer uses RETURN_VARIABLES for workflow processing. This internal table is based on structure BDWFRETVAR, which has two fields: WF_PARM and DOC_NUMBER. The WF_PARM qualifies the document number specified in the DOC_NUM field. The DOC_NUMBER can contain the IDoc number or the document number of the application document created. The various values for the WF_PARM field are Processed_IDOCs, Error_IDOCs, and Appl_Objects.

These values are case sensitive and must be spelled out exactly as shown. For example, assume that three IDocs (100, 101, and 102) were passed to the posting program. The first and third IDoc successfully posted and created application documents 9000 and 9001. IDoc number 101 failed to post the document successfully. The RETURN_VARIABLES table will be populated, as shown in Table 32.2.

Table 32.2 Values in the RETURN_VARIABLES Table

WFPARM	DOCNUMBER
Processed_IDOCs	100
Appl_Objects	9001
Error_IDOCs	101
Processed_IDOCs	102
Appl_Objects	9002

- **SERIALIZATION_INFO**. Also an export parameter, and is relevant only if you are using the serialization object.

◆ **Exceptions**. Exceptions convey problems with control record information, such as incorrect message type.

Program Flow

The program logic contains the following blocks.

1. Read the control record information. Verify the control information (message type). If the message type is incorrect, raise the exception.

2. Read the IDoc data for an IDoc. Remember that several IDocs can be passed together.

3. Parse through each data record. If using the call transaction, build the BDC data table; if not, build internal tables as required by the direct-posting function module.

4. Call the posting program and capture the results.

5. Populate the return parameters.

6. If more IDocs are present, return to Step 2; if not, go to Step 7.

7. Return from the function module. The results of execution are passed to the ALE layer.

 CAUTION

Do not perform commit work in your posting program. The ALE layer is responsible for the COMMIT command to ensure data integrity between the results of IDoc posting and the status table update.

The monthly report IDoc (ZMREPT01) developed in the preceding chapter is used here to illustrate the logic of inbound programs for mass processing. The same program automatically works for a single IDoc. The following listing presents the program code.

 TIP

The MBDCONWF program contains constants used in an inbound program. You should include this program in your inbound program for consistent use of the constant values.

```
FUNCTION Z_IDOC_INPUT_ZMREPT.
*"----------------------------------------------------------------
*"*"Local interface:
*"      IMPORTING
*"              VALUE(INPUT_METHOD) LIKE   BDWFAP_PAR-INPUTMETHD
*"              VALUE(MASS_PROCESSING) LIKE   BDWFAP_PAR-MASS_PROC
*"      EXPORTING
*"              VALUE(WORKFLOW_RESULT) LIKE   BDWFAP_PAR-RESULT
*"              VALUE(APPLICATION_VARIABLE) LIKE   BDWFAP_PAR-APPL_VAR
*"              VALUE(IN_UPDATE_TASK) LIKE   BDWFAP_PAR-UPDATETASK
*"              VALUE(CALL_TRANSACTION_DONE) LIKE   BDWFAP_PAR-CALLTRANS
*"      TABLES
*"              IDOC_CONTRL STRUCTURE   EDIDC
*"              IDOC_DATA STRUCTURE   EDIDD
*"              IDOC_STATUS STRUCTURE   BDIDOCSTAT
*"              RETURN_VARIABLES STRUCTURE   BDWFRETVAR
*"              SERIALIZATION_INFO STRUCTURE   BDI_SER
*"      EXCEPTIONS
*"              WRONG_FUNCTION_CALLED
*"----------------------------------------------------------------

   INCLUDE MBDCONWF.


*----------------------------------------------------------------
* Database Tables
*----------------------------------------------------------------
* Application data tables (Defined in global data)
```

```
*tables: zempdetail, zempwkdet.


*----------------------------------------------------------------------
* Data declarations
*----------------------------------------------------------------------
* employee details - IDoc
  DATA: FS_EMPHDR_DATA LIKE Z1EMHDR.
* employee weekly details data - IDoc
  DATA: FS_WEEKDET_DATA LIKE Z1WKDET.
* client details data - IDoc
  DATA: FS_CLIENTDET_DATA LIKE Z1CLDET.
* employee monthly summary data - IDoc
  DATA: FS_SUMMARY_DATA LIKE Z1SUMRY.


* total hours and amount
  DATA: TOTAL_HRS_MONTH TYPE I,
        TOTAL_AMT_MONTH TYPE I.


* employee details - application data
  DATA:  FS_APP_EMPDET LIKE ZEMPDETAIL.


* weekly details - application data
  DATA:  IT_APP_WKDET LIKE ZEMPWKDET OCCURS 0 WITH HEADER LINE.


*----------------------------------------------------------------------
* Program logic
*----------------------------------------------------------------------
* initialize workflow result
  WORKFLOW_RESULT = C_WF_RESULT_OK.


  LOOP AT IDOC_CONTRL.

*    make sure we have the correct message passed to us
     IF IDOC_CONTRL-MESTYP NE 'ZMREPT'.
       RAISE WRONG_FUNCTION_CALLED.
     ENDIF.

*    clear application buffers before reading new employee
```

```
        CLEAR: IT_APP_WKDET, FS_APP_EMPDET.
        REFRESH IT_APP_WKDET.

*       process all data records in an IDoc and transfer them to
*       application buffers
        LOOP AT IDOC_DATA WHERE DOCNUM EQ IDOC_CONTRL-DOCNUM.

          CASE IDOC_DATA-SEGNAM.

            WHEN 'Z1EMHDR'.                    " employee header
                FS_EMPHDR_DATA = IDOC_DATA-SDATA.
                MOVE-CORRESPONDING FS_EMPHDR_DATA TO FS_APP_EMPDET.

            WHEN 'Z1WKDET'.                    " employee weekly details
                FS_WEEKDET_DATA = IDOC_DATA-SDATA.
                MOVE-CORRESPONDING FS_WEEKDET_DATA TO IT_APP_WKDET.

            WHEN 'Z1CLDET'.                    " client details
                FS_CLIENTDET_DATA = IDOC_DATA-SDATA.
                MOVE-CORRESPONDING FS_CLIENTDET_DATA TO IT_APP_WKDET.
                MOVE FS_APP_EMPDET-SSN TO IT_APP_WKDET-SSN.
                APPEND IT_APP_WKDET.           " append weekly details

            WHEN 'Z1SUMRY'.                    " summary data
                FS_SUMMARY_DATA = IDOC_DATA-SDATA.
          ENDCASE.

        ENDLOOP.

*   verify totals in the data records against the summary record
        CLEAR: TOTAL_HRS_MONTH, TOTAL_AMT_MONTH.
*       compute total hours and amount for the month from weekly details
        LOOP AT IT_APP_WKDET.
          TOTAL_HRS_MONTH = TOTAL_HRS_MONTH + IT_APP_WKDET-TOTHOURS.
          TOTAL_AMT_MONTH = TOTAL_AMT_MONTH + ( IT_APP_WKDET-TOTHOURS *
                                            IT_APP_WKDET-HRLYRATE ).
        ENDLOOP.
```

```
* compare the values with values in the summary record
    IF TOTAL_HRS_MONTH NE FS_SUMMARY_DATA-TOTHRS OR
        TOTAL_AMT_MONTH NE FS_SUMMARY_DATA-TOTAMT.

*       totals in the summary record do not match with weekly details
*       fill IDOC_Status
        IDOC_STATUS-DOCNUM = IDOC_CONTRL-DOCNUM.
        IDOC_STATUS-STATUS = '51'.
        IDOC_STATUS-MSGTY  = 'E'.
        IDOC_STATUS-MSGID  = 'ZE'.
        IDOC_STATUS-MSGNO  = '005'.
        IDOC_STATUS-MSGV1  = FS_APP_EMPDET-SSN.
        APPEND IDOC_STATUS.

        WORKFLOW_RESULT = C_WF_RESULT_ERROR.
        RETURN_VARIABLES-WF_PARAM = 'Error_IDOCs'.
        RETURN_VARIABLES-DOC_NUMBER = IDOC_CONTRL-DOCNUM.
        APPEND RETURN_VARIABLES.
    ELSE.

*       Data looks good. Create weekly report if it does not already exist
*       If weekly report exists, then simply update the records
        SELECT SINGLE * FROM ZEMPDETAIL WHERE SSN EQ FS_APP_EMPDET-SSN.
        IF SY-SUBRC NE 0.
            INSERT INTO ZEMPDETAIL VALUES FS_APP_EMPDET.
            INSERT ZEMPWKDET FROM TABLE IT_APP_WKDET.
        ELSE.
            UPDATE ZEMPDETAIL FROM FS_APP_EMPDET.
            UPDATE ZEMPWKDET FROM TABLE IT_APP_WKDET.
        ENDIF.

        IF SY-SUBRC EQ 0.
*           populate return variables for success
            RETURN_VARIABLES-WF_PARAM = 'Processed_IDOCs'.
            RETURN_VARIABLES-DOC_NUMBER = IDOC_CONTRL-DOCNUM.
            RETURN_VARIABLES-WF_PARAM = 'Appl_Objects'.
            RETURN_VARIABLES-DOC_NUMBER = FS_APP_EMPDET-SSN.
            APPEND RETURN_VARIABLES.
```

```
*          add status record indicating success
           IDOC_STATUS-DOCNUM = IDOC_CONTRL-DOCNUM.
           IDOC_STATUS-STATUS = '53'.
           IDOC_STATUS-MSGTY  = 'I'.
           IDOC_STATUS-MSGID  = 'ZE'.
           IDOC_STATUS-MSGNO  = '006'.
           IDOC_STATUS-MSGV1  = FS_APP_EMPDET-SSN.
           APPEND IDOC_STATUS.
       ELSE.
*          populate return variables indicating error
           WORKFLOW_RESULT = C_WF_RESULT_ERROR.
           RETURN_VARIABLES-WF_PARAM = 'Error_IDOCs'.
           RETURN_VARIABLES-DOC_NUMBER = IDOC_CONTRL-DOCNUM.
           APPEND RETURN_VARIABLES.

*          add status record indicating failure in updating
           IDOC_STATUS-DOCNUM = IDOC_CONTRL-DOCNUM.
           IDOC_STATUS-STATUS = '51'.
           IDOC_STATUS-MSGTY  = 'E'.
           IDOC_STATUS-MSGID  = 'ZE'.
           IDOC_STATUS-MSGNO  = '007'.
           IDOC_STATUS-MSGV1  = FS_APP_EMPDET-SSN.
           APPEND IDOC_STATUS.
       ENDIF.
     ENDIF.
   ENDLOOP.                              "End loop at idoc_contrl.

ENDFUNCTION.
```

Programs for IDoc Extensions

In the preceding section, you learned about programs that are developed for basic IDoc types. In this section, you will learn about programs that are written in the user exits of the SAP programs for extended IDocs. This is probably the most common type of IDoc programming, and therefore the most important to familiarize yourself with. The customer master IDoc that was extended in the preceding chapter is used in this section to illustrate the process of writing user exit programs for extended IDocs. The programs written in the user exits are considered enhancements to the SAP system and are supported on an upgrade. User exits have been provided at strategic locations in the IDoc programs. SAP provides a formal method to develop programs for the user exits. Here you learn about various types of user exits, strategic locations of user exits, how to locate them in the standard SAP programs, and how to use the formal process of developing user exits. Sample programs are provided for reference.

Types of User Exits

It is important to understand the types of user exits available in the system. SAP provides two types of user exits.

- **Old method**. Perform USEREXIT_xxxx
- **New method**. CALL CUSTOMER FUNCTION

In the first type, SAP provides hard-coded user exits in its program logic. There is no formal method of documenting these user exits, and the only way to find them is to search for the string literal USEREXIT in the programs. This process is considered a modification to the SAP code. You have to use the corrections procedure to implement these user exits. Most of the SD applications use this form of user exits. Although SAP is moving toward the new method, as described next, several applications still have the old style of user exits. For example, the user exit in the SD module for incoming orders is implemented in the old style in the program LVEDAF0U. The new method has replaced these exits.

The second type of user exit formally documents and implements user exits without having to go through SAP's correction procedures. These user exits are implemented as function modules that are called from SAP programs. The calling program identifies the user exits with a number. For example, the following code is taken from the inbound program that processes a customer master IDoc. This code calls user exit number 001.

```
call customer-function '001'
     exporting
          idoc_control      = f_idoc_control
          input_method      = input_method
     importing
          workflow_result   = v_workflow_result
     tables
```

```
idoc_data        = t_idoc_data
idoc_status      = t_idoc_status
return_variables = t_return_variables.
```

In the actual implementation, this user exit equates to a function module with the naming convention EXIT_*<program name>_<exit number>*. Thus, exit number 001 implemented in the SAPLVV02 program will be named EXIT_ SAPLVV02_001. The user exit function modules contain an include program that starts with a Z. You write your user exit programs in these include modules. The formal procedure for programming in the user exits is described later in the chapter.

Strategic Location of User Exits

User exits are available at strategic points in the IDoc programs to handle customer extensions. SAP controls these locations, and they are guaranteed to exist with the same functionality on an upgrade. An explanation of the commonly used user exits for outbound, as well as inbound, processing follows. Notice that some of these are not available for every process and that some processes have additional user exits.

Outbound IDoc Processing

The outbound user exits allow you to populate the fields in your extensions, as well as to manipulate or reformat data on standard segments.

- **A user exit is available after each segment is populated.** This exit allows you to add custom logic for any of your extended segments. Technically, the same user exit is invoked after every segment is filled. Therefore, in your user exit program, you must check the name of the current segment being processed.

- **A user exit is also available after the system populates the control record information**. This exit allows you to modify any control information that is necessary. For example, if you have extended an IDoc, you will populate the IDoc type using this user exit. This user exit lends itself to creativity. You can use it to create a variant of your message type to allow special processing or to determine recipients dynamically.

- **A user exit is also available after the system has completely filled out the control record and data records.** This exit allows you to make any final adjustments to the data being sent out.

Inbound IDoc Processing

The inbound user exits allow you to read data on your extension segments and perform custom logic, as well as customize status record processing.

- ◆ A user exit is available when a customer segment is encountered. This exit allows you to add custom logic for any of your extended segments.

- ◆ A user exit is also available after the system populates the status records and is about to return control back to the ALE layer. This exit allows you to modify any status records or add additional status records.

The Common Process

The following user exits occur in procedures that are performed for both outbound and inbound IDoc processing.

- ◆ **A user exit is located in the routine that creates a physical IDoc in the system.** Technically, the exit is called in the EDI_DOCUMENT_OPEN_FOR_CREATE function module, which creates a control record. This user exit is invoked for inbound, as well as outbound, IDocs. It can be used to modify control record information in the IDoc. You typically use this exit to make global changes to your IDocs. For example, you could modify the control record on outbound IDocs for any specific information desired by your EDI subsystem. This user exit (EXIT_SAPLEDI1_001) is implemented in enhancement SIDOC001.

- ◆ **Another user exit is available in the ALE service layer during the version change of incoming and outgoing IDocs.** The exit is not especially valuable on outbound because the system takes care of the version change. On the other hand, on inbound, you will often find this exit useful. For example, if you are on 3.0F and you are receiving IDocs from a back-level system 3.0A, you could modify the segment to include additional fields that are required in the application for 3.0F. This user exit (EXIT_SAPLBD11_001) is implemented in enhancement ALE00001.

Steps to Locate User Exits

The first and foremost task before you start programming is to identify the specific user exit you should use. User exits in the system are grouped under enhancements. Refer to the Appendix, "FAQs, User Exits, and Miscellaneous Resources," for a list of enhancements for the commonly used IDoc programs. If you do not know the enhancement, the steps are listed in the next section. After you identify the correct enhancement, finding the appropriate user exit is very simple, as described in the following steps.

1. Execute transaction SMOD.

2. Enter your enhancement name and click the Components button.

3. Click Display to see the components that are effectively user exits. Click any one, and then click the Documentation button to view the documentation. If no documentation is available, you are at the mercy of documentation in the SAP code to determine the intent behind the user exit.

Steps to Determine SAP Enhancements

The most commonly used approach to locate an enhancement for an IDoc program is explained here, using the customer master IDoc program as an example.

1. Identify the program in which you want to locate a user exit. The IDoc programs follow a naming convention for outbound and inbound function modules. Follow these guidelines to identify program names. Unfortunately, program names are not enforced, so you will notice some inconsistency.

   - Outbound programs via Message control are generally named IDOC_OUTPUT_*<message_type>*.

   - Outbound programs via change pointers are generally named MASTERIDOC_CREATE_SMD_*<message_type>*.

   - For stand-alone outbound programs, the IDoc logic is generally coded in MASTERIDOC_CREATE_*<message_type>* function modules.

   - Inbound programs are generally named IDOC_INPUT_ *<message type>*.

   - The program name for the outbound customer master is SAPLVV01 (MASTERIDOC_CREATE_REQ_DEBMAS).

2. Determine the development class for this program, using the administration attributes of the program via transaction SE37. For the customer master, the development class is VSV.

3. Execute transaction SMOD. You can list enhancements by development class. Press F4 on the Enhancement field. The next screen allows you to enter a development class. Click the Execute button for a list of all

enhancements available in a development class. You can list the components for each enhancement by clicking the Components +/– button. The one that matches your program name is the enhancement for you. In the case of the customer master, the program name is SAPLVV01, so the enhancement for the customer master is VSV00001.

The Process for Developing User Exits

After you identify an appropriate user exit for your process, you can start building the programs by creating a project. A *project* defines one or more enhancements carried out for a module. For example, if you are enhancing the customer master process, one project can encapsulate all developments associated with the process, including the programs for IDoc extension. Follow these steps to create a project and develop programs.

1. Execute transaction CMOD. Enter a project name on the initial screen (see Figure 32.5). The name does not have to start with Z. Click the Create icon.

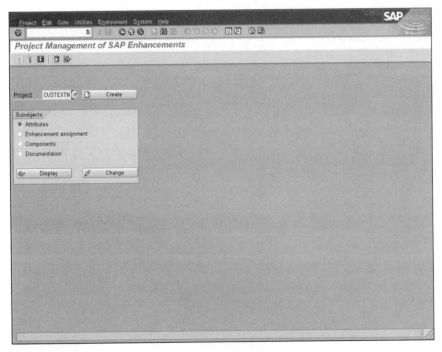

FIGURE 32.5 *The initial customer-modification screen* (© SAP AG)

2. On the next screen, enter a short description of your project, save your project, and then click the SAP Enhancements button.

3. On the next screen, enter the enhancement name as identified earlier (see Figure 32.6). If you've forgotten it, press F4. Save your project again and use the green arrow to return to the main screen of CMOD.

4. Select the Enhancement Components option and click the Change button.

5. On the next screen, click the user exit in which you are interested, and then click the Edit Component button (see Figure 32.7).

6. The next screen shows you the function module (see Figure 32.8); it has an include program that starts with a Z.

7. Double-click this program. The system tells you that it will create the program. Accept the message, and you will be in the ABAP editor, where you can write the necessary code for the user exit.

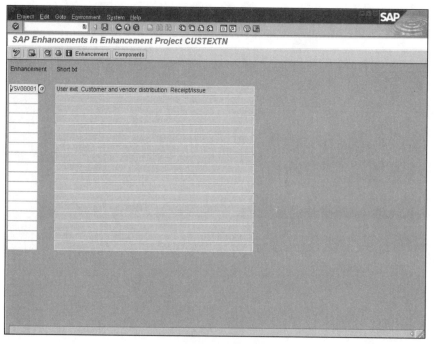

FIGURE 32.6 *An enhancement included in a project* (© SAP AG)

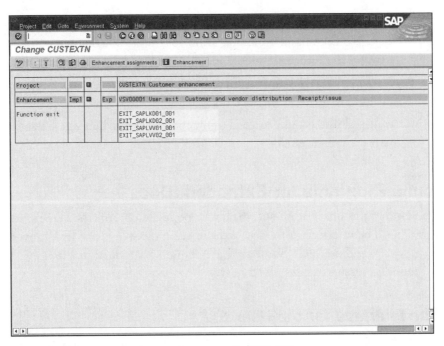

FIGURE 32.7 *User exits in an enhancement* (© SAP AG)

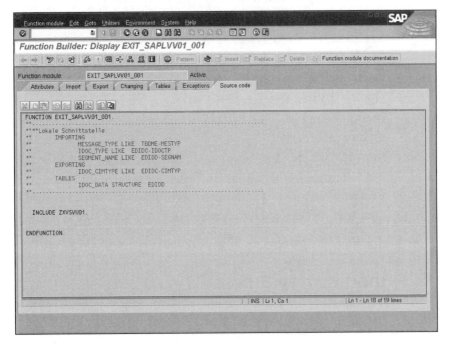

FIGURE 32.8 *A user exit program to enter custom code* (© SAP AG)

8. After completing the program and saving it, go back to the main screen for CMOD transaction and activate your project. This step automatically activates the function module in which you coded your program logic.

9. Test your code by running the process that invokes the user exit. Test until you drop!

10. Transport the project to your production system when you are satisfied with the enhancement.

Outbound Programs for Extended IDocs

These programs are written specifically to populate data in the IDoc's extended segments. The interface of the user exit function module is not fixed; it varies for each process and user exit. Some typical parameters supplied in a user exit for the outbound programs are described next.

The Interface for the User Exits

The interface for the user exits typically contains the parameters shown here.

♦ **IMPORTING parameters**. These parameters are provided as input parameters to your user exit.

- **MESSAGE_TYPE**. Represents the message type being processed. Some user exits are shared across several messages, so checking for the correct message type is important.

- **IDOC_TYPE**. Represents the basic IDoc type in the process. You need to know the IDOC_TYPE because a message can be based on multiple IDoc types.

- **SEGMENT_NAME**. Represents the last segment filled by the system before it calls the user exit. Because the same user exit is called for all the segments, you want to make sure that your code is executed after the segment you have extended.

♦ **EXPORTING parameter**. This parameter is returned by your user exit to the calling program.

- **IDOC_CIMTYPE**. The name of your IDoc extension. IDOC_CIMTYPE allows the system to perform a syntax check according to the enhanced definition of the basic IDoc type.

♦ **Tables**. The following table acts as a two-way parameter for input as well as output.

• **IDOC_DATA**. Represents the IDoc data records that have been populated so far by the system. The IDOC_DATA table is where you will append your data records and pass them back to the caller. This table is always provided as an input parameter.

Program Flow

The program logic typically contains the following blocks.

1. Determine the key of the object for which an IDoc is being generated. If you are writing the user exit for an extended segment in a customer master, you want to know which customer master is being processed. If the key is not available through one of the interface parameters, you can loop through the existing segments that are filled to locate the key.

2. Write whatever code or logic you have to implement. The following sample program extracts user-defined data stored in the customer master table.

3. Create one or more data records for the custom segment.

4. Append it to the internal table of data records supplied in the parameters. You're done!

The following program populates an extended segment (Z1KNVVM) of the customer master IDoc (DEBMAS01). Data for the extended segment is available in the user-extended customer master tables. See Chapter 31, "Extending and Developing an IDoc Type," as a reference when reading the program code.

```
*-------------------------------------------------------------------
*   INCLUDE ZXVSVU01                                              *
*-------------------------------------------------------------------
* In this scenario, the E1KNVVM segment has been extended to accommodate
* user-defined fields in the customer master table KNVV. The name of
* the extended segment is Z1KNVVM. There are two custom
* fields: ZZDELPRTY (Delivery priority) and ZZRANK (Customer Rank)
*-------------------------------------------------------------------
```

```
* Make sure you are processing correct message type
CHECK MESSAGE_TYPE EQ 'DEBMAS'.

*  Make sure data is added after the correct segment
CHECK SEGMENT_NAME EQ 'E1KNVVM'.

* since customer number is not passed in this user exit, you need
* to go through the data records to find the customer number and the
* sales organization, distribution channel, division.
LOOP AT IDOC_DATA.
  CASE IDOC_DATA-SEGNAM.
    WHEN 'E1KNA1M'.                    " has customer number in it
      MOVE IDOC_DATA-SDATA TO KNA1M.
    WHEN 'E1KNVVM'.           " has sales org, dist ch and division
      MOVE IDOC_DATA-SDATA TO KNVVM.
  endcase.
endloop.

* Select data from the user-defined fields in KNVV
SELECT SINGLE * FROM KNVV WHERE KUNNR = kna1m-KUNNR
                    AND    VKORG = KNVVm-VKORG
                    AND    VTWEG = KNVVm-VTWEG
                    AND    SPART = KNVVm-SPART.

* set the IDoc extension name for control record
IDOC_CIMTYPE = 'DEBMASEX'.

* clear and fill extended segment with user-defined fields in KNVV
CLEAR Z1KNVVM.

* copy custom fields from KNVV to the extended segment.
MOVE-CORRESPONDING KNVV TO Z1KNVVM.     "field names must be same

*    condense all fields of extended segment
CONDENSE: Z1KNVVM-ZZDELPRTY,
          Z1KNVVM-ZZRANK.
```

```
* populate segment name in the data record, copy data contents into
* it, and append the data record to existing data records
MOVE 'Z1KNVVM' TO IDOC_DATA-SEGNAM.
MOVE Z1KNVVM   TO IDOC_DATA-SDATA.
APPEND IDOC_DATA.
```

Inbound Programs for Extended IDocs

These programs are written specifically to process data in the IDoc's extended segments. The point in the processing when a user exit is invoked is different for each process. A user exit can be invoked after the end of posting or before posting the document. With the customer master, the user exit is called after data has already been posted. With the material master, the user exit is called before the data is posted. The point at which the user exit is called makes a difference in how you code your logic. The interface of the user exit function module varies for each process and user exit.

The Interface for User Exits

- ◆ **IMPORTING parameter**. This parameter is provided as an input parameter to your user exit.

  - • **IDOC_CONTROL**. The control record for the IDoc.

- ◆ **EXPORTING parameter**. This parameter is returned by your user exit to the calling program.

  - • **WORKFLOW_RESULT**. Conveys any problems discovered in the user exit for which you want to end the inbound processing. The system creates a status record and starts workflow.

- ◆ **Tables**. The following tables act as two-way parameters for input, as well as output.

  - • **IDOC_DATA**. The data record for the IDoc. You can loop through it to locate your extended segment.

  - • **RETURN_VARIABLES**. Represents return variables as required in inbound programs. You can append values to this table in the user exit. This table is optional.

  - • **IDOC_STATUS**. Provides any status records you want to have created.

Program Flow

The program logic typically contains the following blocks.

1. Read the data in your custom segment, typically by looping through the data records unless the system explicitly gives you the custom segment as an input parameter.

2. Determine when this user exit is called. If it is called after the document is posted, you must find the key of the document that was posted. This information is usually available in the data records. You can then update tables per your requirement. With a customer master, for example, the user exit is invoked after the data is posted.

3. If the user exit is invoked before the document is posted, you can move data from the custom segment to one of the tables that can be passed as a parameter. For example, the user exit for the material master IDoc allows you to append data in the customer segment to the extended fields in the material master table before posting.

The wide variety of scenarios makes it impossible to describe every one, but the essence is to know when your user exit is invoked and how to process your data.

A Sample Program

The following program reads an extended segment of a customer master IDoc. This data is then posted to the user-defined fields in the customer master table.

```
*-------------------------------------------------------------------
*    INCLUDE ZXVSVU02                                              *
*-------------------------------------------------------------------
* In this scenario, data in the Z1KNVVM segment is read and processed.
* This user exit is called after the system has already updated the
* customer master. Therefore, data is updated in the SAP tables directly
*-------------------------------------------------------------------


TABLES: KNVV.


DATA: KNVVM LIKE E1KNVVM,
```

```
        KNA1M LIKE E1KNA1M,
        Z1KNVVM LIKE Z1KNVVM.


LOOP AT IDOC_DATA.                       " loop through all data records

  CASE IDOC_DATA-SEGNAM.
    WHEN 'E1KNA1M'.                      " has customer number in it
      KNA1M = IDOC_DATA-SDATA.


    WHEN 'E1KNVVM'.                " has sales org dist ch and division
      KNVVM = IDOC_DATA-SDATA.


    WHEN 'Z1KNVVM'.                      " has custom data
      Z1KNVVM = IDOC_DATA-SDATA.


*     Always a good idea to make sure we have a valid customer number
        SELECT SINGLE * FROM KNVV WHERE KUNNR = KNA1M-KUNNR
                                AND    VKORG = KNVVM-VKORG
                                AND    VTWEG = KNVVM-VTWEG
                                AND    SPART = KNVVM-SPART.
        IF SY-SUBRC EQ 0.                "customer was found
          UPDATE KNVV SET
            ZZDELPRTY   = Z1KNVVM-ZZDELPRTY
            ZZRANK      = Z1KNVVM-ZZRANK
            WHERE KUNNR = KNA1M-KUNNR AND
                  VKORG = KNVVM-VKORG AND
                  VTWEG = KNVVM-VTWEG AND
                  SPART = KNVVM-SPART.
        ELSE.
* The following lines of code will create a status record
* with status 51, and a workflow is started
          IDOC_STATUS-DOCNUM = IDOC_CONTRL-DOCNUM.
          IDOC_STATUS-STATUS = '51'.
          IDOC_STATUS-MSGTY  = 'E'.
          IDOC_STATUS-MSGID  = 'ZE'.
```

```
        IDOC_STATUS-MSGNO  = '005'.
        IDOC_STATUS-MSGV1  = KNA1M-KUNNR.
        APPEND IDOC_STATUS.

        WORKFLOW_RESULT = C_WF_RESULT_ERROR.
        RETURN_VARIABLES-WF_PARAM = 'Error_IDOCs'.
        RETURN_VARIABLES-DOC_NUMBER = IDOC_CONTRL-DOCNUM.
        APPEND RETURN_VARIABLES.

    ENDCASE.
  ENDLOOP.
```

Programs to Enhance the Process

This section describes how user exits can be utilized for tasks other than IDoc extensions. A wide variety of scenarios can be implemented in user exits. Combining your knowledge of the location of exits in the process with a little creativity will enable you to solve many common problems. An example of generating the trading partner for the EDI subsystem is presented here.

Generating the Trading Partner of the EDI Subsystem

You can implement the code shown in the following listing in the user exit EXIT_SAPLEDI1_001 of enhancement SIDOC001 to generate the trading partner of the EDI subsystem for an outbound IDoc.

Program Flow

Here are the necessary blocks.

1. Make sure that the IDoc is an outbound IDoc.
2. Concatenate the SAP trading partner and the value stored in the EDI Message Type field of the partner profile to the Receiver Address field (RCVSAD) in the control record.

3. Copy the incoming control record to the outgoing control record.

```
*----------------------------------------------------------------
*   INCLUDE ZXEDIU01                                           *
*----------------------------------------------------------------
* This exit is used to build a trading partner ID for the EDI
* subsystem. The partner number in SAP and the EDI message type
* fields in the partner profile are being used to build a trading
* partner ID for the EDI subsystem
*----------------------------------------------------------------
   IF CONTROL_IN-DIRECT = '1'.          " needed for outbound only

     CONCATENATE CONTROL_IN-RCVPRN,
                 CONTROL_IN-STDMES
           INTO CONTROL_IN-RCVSAD.

   ENDIF.

   CONTROL_OUT = CONTROL_IN.
```

Summary

Programming in the IDoc interface is carried out to enhance the interface to meet varying business needs. Programs are written for custom-developed basic IDoc types in which outbound programs are written to populate IDocs with data from application documents. Although the core logic for the IDoc generation programs is always the same, there can be different flavors of these programs depending on the triggering mechanism used in the process, such as Message control, stand-alone programs, and change pointers. Each program has a different interface. Similarly, inbound programs are written to read IDoc data and post application documents from it. All inbound programs use a common interface, but the internal implementation of the inbound programs depends on the scenario, such as single IDoc processing, mass processing, serialized IDocs, and ALE-enabled transactions.

Apart from programs for the custom IDoc types, programs are also developed for extended IDocs. These programs are implemented in the user exits that provide a formal method of enhancing the system and are supported on a future upgrade. These programs populate and process data in the extension.

User exits are available at strategic locations in the IDoc interface. Programs are written to carry out additional checks and customize the flow to meet business needs.

Chapter 33

**Customizing the
Interface for New
or Extended IDocs**

After you extend or develop an IDoc type and the necessary programs, you must configure the system to make these components known to the ALE/EDI interface layer. This chapter shows you how to configure the system to recognize new components created for the outbound and inbound processes. These settings can be made in the IMG. Some of the settings are also available from the Area menu of EDI (WEDI). These settings are not required if you are using standard SAP processes and have not made any changes to IDocs or programs.

This chapter contains two major sections: configuring the system for new IDocs and configuring the system for extended IDocs. In each section, you will learn about configuring the outbound and inbound processes. You should read this chapter as a reference. First, you should identify the section that describes your scenario, and then you should branch directly to the steps that pertain to the scenario you are trying to configure.

Configuring the System for New IDocs

This section explains how to make a custom basic IDoc type and its programs known to the ALE/EDI interface layer.

Configuring an Outbound Process for New IDocs

The steps for configuring an outbound process depend on the type of program you have developed for the outbound IDoc. Three types of outbound programs were discussed in the preceding chapter: IDocs via Message control, IDocs from stand-alone programs, and IDocs from change pointers. Each requires a slightly different setup. To describe the procedure, the monthly report IDoc and its programs are used as an example.

Configuring an Outbound Process That Uses Message Control

You carry out the steps listed here if your outbound process uses Message control and you have replaced a standard SAP-provided function module with your custom function module to generate custom IDocs. The following steps describe how you configure the system so that Message control invokes your custom programs and generates custom IDocs.

1. Create a new message type.
2. Link the IDoc type to the message type.
3. Create a new process code.
4. Create or change a partner profile to add a Message control record and an outbound record.

Create a New Message Type

Transaction: WE81

Menu Path: From the Area menu of EDI, choose Development, Message Types

You assign a message type to the data contents transferred in the IDoc and give it a short description. Customer-defined messages begin with Z. This should be the same name used in your IDoc programs. For the monthly report IDoc, message type ZMREPT is chosen.

Link the IDoc Type to the Message Type

Transaction: WE82

Menu Path: From the Area menu of EDI, choose Development, IDoc Type/Message

You assign the message type created in the preceding step to the IDoc type, as shown in Figure 33.1. This step not only serves to document which message is based on which IDoc type, but it also checks this link in the process when IDocs are generated.

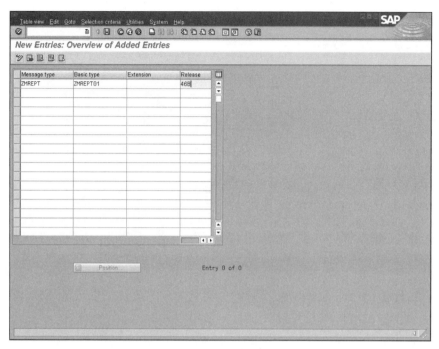

FIGURE 33.1 *Linking the IDoc type and message type* (© SAP AG)

Create a New Process Code

`Transaction: WE41`

`Menu Path: From the Area menu of EDI, choose Control, Outbound Process Code`

This step assigns a process code to the function module created for the outbound process, as shown in Figure 33.2. The process code is an indirect means of identifying the function module.

Create or Change a Partner Profile

`Transaction: WE20`

`Menu Path: From the Area menu of EDI, choose IDoc, Partner Profile`

A partner profile is created for every partner system that sends or receives IDocs. In the partner profile, a Message control record and an outbound record are created for each outbound message that operates under Message control.

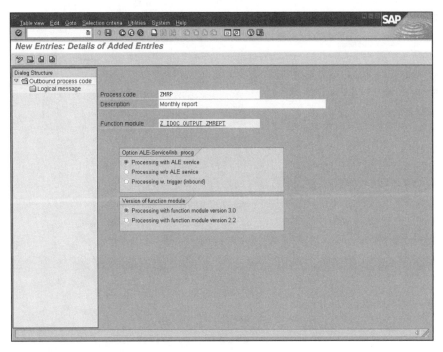

FIGURE 33.2 *The process code assigned to the function module that generates the monthly report IDoc* (© SAP AG)

Create a partner profile if it does not exist. Add the outbound record (see Figure 33.3) and the Message control record (see Figure 33.4) for your message. This step assumes that Message control components such as the Application and Output Type have already been configured. Refer to Chapter 8, "Configuring Message Control," for details on how to create output types and tie them to Message control applications.

Configuring an Outbound Process for Stand-Alone Programs

You carry out the steps listed here if your outbound program is developed as a stand-alone program to generate IDocs. These programs are mainly designed for master data distribution in ALE and interfaces with legacy systems. Here are the configuration steps.

1. Create a new message type.

FIGURE 33.3 *The partner profile—outbound parameters* (© SAP AG)

FIGURE 33.4 *The partner profile—Message control parameters* (© SAP AG)

2. Link the IDoc type to the message type.

3. Add the message to the ALE distribution model (optional).

4. Create or change the partner profile.

Steps 1 and 2 are the same as described earlier in the "Configuring an Outbound Process That Uses Message Control" section. Step 3 is new, and Step 4 is slightly different.

Add the Message to the Customer Distribution Model

Transaction: BD64

Menu Path: From the ALE configuration in the IMG, choose Modeling and Implementing Business Processes, Maintain Distribution Model and Distribute Views

Here you add your message to the distribution model. Figure 33.5 shows how a message type ZMREPT that is sent to legacy system LEGHOST01 is created in the customer distribution model. This step is necessary only if you have not specified the receiving partner in the control record within your program (see Chapter 23, "Distributing Master Data").

FIGURE 33.5 *Adding your message to the customer distribution model* (© SAP AG)

Create or Change the Partner Profile

Transaction: WE20

Menu Path: From the Area menu of EDI, choose IDoc, Partner Profile

In the partner profile, an outbound record is created for each outbound message generated from stand-alone programs. Note that the Message control record is not created in this case because stand-alone programs do not use the Message control component. Refer to Figure 33.3 for attributes specified in the outbound record of a partner profile.

Configuring the Change Pointers
for an Outbound Process

The following steps describe how you configure the system so that RBDMIDOC calls your custom program. You carry out these steps if you have developed an IDoc generation program using change pointers. These programs are designed to generate IDocs based on changes to a document or master data. The RBDMIDOC program reads configuration tables to determine the appropriate IDoc generation program for a particular message type. The settings for those configuration tables are as follows.

1. Create a new message type.
2. Link the IDoc type to the message type.
3. Make sure that the change pointers are globally activated.
4. Activate the change pointers for your message type.
5. Link the message type to the function module.
6. Add the message to the ALE distribution model (optional).
7. Create the partner profile.

Steps 1 and 2 are the same as those described in the "Configuring an Outbound Process That Uses Message Control" section earlier in the chapter. Steps 3, 4, and 5 regarding change pointers are new. Steps 6 and 7 are the same as steps 3 and 4 of the "Configuring an Outbound Process for Stand-Alone Programs" section earlier in this chapter.

Verify Global Activation of the Change Pointers

Transaction: BD61
Menu Path: From the ALE configuration in the IMG (SALE), choose Distribution
Scenarios, Master Data Distribution, Activate Change Pointer, Activate Change
Pointer (generally)

You must make sure that the change pointer process is active. Execute transaction
BD61 and activate the change pointer process if it's not already active.

Activate the Change Pointers for the Custom Message

Transaction: BD50
Menu Path: From the ALE configuration in the IMG, choose Modeling and
Implementing Business Processes, Master Data Distribution, Replication of
Modified Data, Activate Change Pointers for Message Types

Also, for each individual message, change pointers have to be activated. Execute
transaction BD50 and add an entry for your custom message.

Link the Message Type to the Function Module

Transaction: BD60

The message type also needs to be linked to the function module developed for
analyzing the change pointers. Execute transaction BD60 and add an entry for
your custom message, as shown in Figure 33.6.

Configuring an Inbound Process for New IDocs

As mentioned in the preceding chapter, the inbound IDoc process is the same no
matter which outbound process is used to generate an IDoc. The inbound configuration for a new process can be divided into two parts: process configuration
and workflow configuration for exception handling. The steps for process configuration require some of the components defined in the workflow configuration, so
it is necessary to maintain the workflow configuration before maintaining the
process configuration.

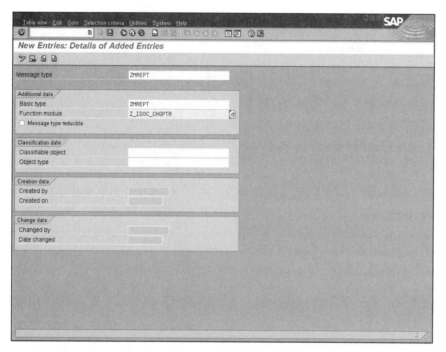

FIGURE 33.6 *Activating the change pointers for a custom message* (© SAP AG)

Workflow Configuration

Workflow configuration is necessary for exception handling in the inbound process. The elements used in the exception-handling process can be understood by looking at the process flow.

♦ When an application error occurs, an event is raised. This event is called a *triggering event*, and it is part of the IDoc application object. For standard messages, the triggering event is named INPUTERROROCCURRED.

♦ The triggering event is linked to a workflow error task. The task is started, and a work item appears in a user's inbox.

♦ The user processes the work item. At the end, the system raises a terminating event to mark the completion of the work item. The terminating event is also part of the IDoc application object. For standard messages, the terminating events are named INPUTFINISHED.

From this process, you will see that the system needs to know the IDoc application object, triggering event, terminating event, task, and the linkage between the triggering event and task.

The steps to make these components known to the system are as follows.

1. Create a new IDoc application object in the business object repository with triggering and terminating events.

2. Create a new task based on the application IDoc object.

3. Create the event linkage.

4. Create a new IDoc packet object in the business object repository (optional).

Create a New Application IDoc Object in the Business Object Repository

Your objective is to create an IDoc application object for your message. The best option is to copy an existing IDoc application object and change the necessary settings. Follow these simple steps.

1. Execute transaction SWO1 or use the path from the SAP standard menu: Tools, Business Workflow, Development, Definition Tools, Business Object Builder.

2. Click the Find icon (it looks like a pair of binoculars), and expand the selection options by clicking the All Selections icon. Enter **IDOCAPPL** in the Supertypes field and click the Execute icon.

3. Click any object and select Business Objects, Copy from the drop-down menu. The system prompts for information required to copy the object, as shown in Figure 33.7.

 NOTE

Make sure that the object being copied has the INPUTERROROCCURED and INPUTFINISHED events. You can confirm this by double-clicking the object and then verifying the event list.

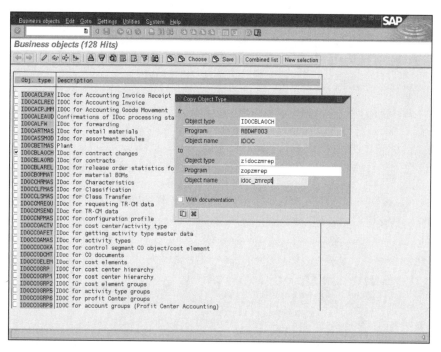

FIGURE 33.7 *IDoc application objects for IDoc messages* (© SAP AG)

4. Assign a name for the object type and the program. The names must start with a Z. Click the Copy button. When prompted, enter the development class. This step should create an entry in the object list at the bottom.

5. Double-click the newly created entry. Click the Basic Data icon (it looks like a hat). Click the Change icon in the application toolbar and change the name and description to match your IDoc. See Figure 33.8 for values entered for the monthly report IDoc. Generate your object type. You can also release the object type.

Create a New Task Based on the Application IDoc Object

A workflow task defines the task attributes that have to be carried out when an application error occurs. You must create a task for your inbound process. A task points to an object method to be executed and to the triggering event that starts the task. The best option is to copy an existing task, such as ORDERS_error (TS00008046). Follow these simple steps.

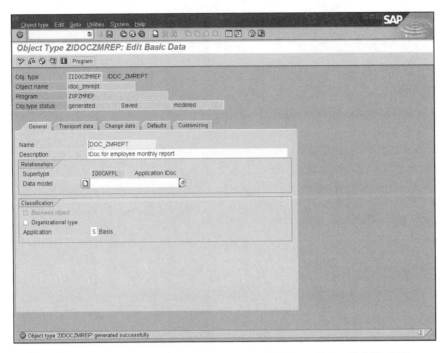

FIGURE 33.8 *The object type for a custom message and its attributes* (© SAP AG)

1. Execute transaction PFTC_COP or use the SAP standard menu path: Tools, Business Workflow, Development, Definition Tools, Tasks/Task Groups, Copy.

2. Click the Tasks button. Select Standard Task for the task type and enter the task number for ORDERS_Error (00008046) as the Task. Click the Copy icon.

3. Enter an abbreviation and name for the task. Press Enter. This should copy the task. Note the number.

4. Execute transaction PFTC_CHG, select Standard Task as the task type, enter the task number noted in Step 3 in the Task field, and click the Change icon

5. Replace the object type field with the IDoc application object you created in the "Create a New Application IDoc Object in the Business Object Repository" section. See Figure 33.9 for task attributes defined for the monthly report IDoc.

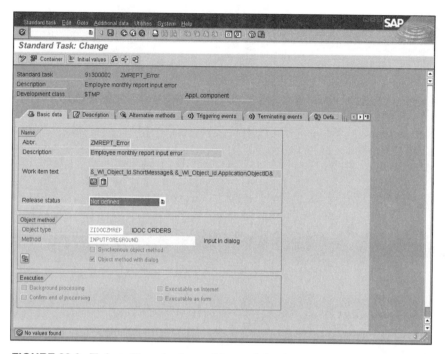

FIGURE 33.9 *Task attributes for the workflow task for the monthly report IDoc* (© SAP AG)

6. Now you change the triggering event. Click the Triggering Events tab to go to the triggering event screen. Delete the existing event, and then create another event based on your object type. Click the Insert Event button. Enter your object type and the INPUTERROROCCURRED event. Figure 33.10 shows the triggering event defined for the customer task for the monthly report IDoc.

7. You are ready to define the binding of data between triggering the event and the task. A binding between two elements is basically saying *a = b* in a programming language. Select the triggering event by clicking the selection button at the left of the line containing your new event. Click the Binding icon. In the Expression column, press F4 and select the default entry (highlighted in green). Perform the same operation for the Exception field. See Figure 33.11 for the binding definition between the triggering event and the task for the monthly report IDoc. You can also click the Check icon for testing the consistency in binding. Click the Green check mark to go back to the triggering event screen.

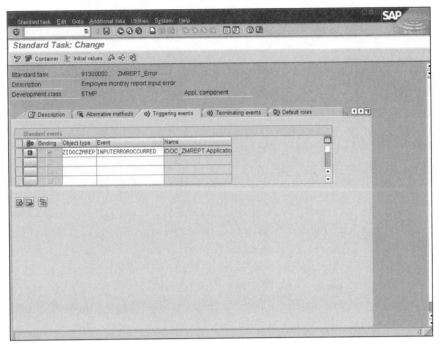

FIGURE 33.10 *The triggering event for the workflow task* (© SAP AG)

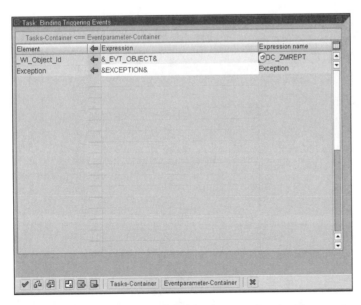

FIGURE 33.11 *The binding definition between the triggering event and task* (© SAP AG)

8. Now you activate the linkage between your task and triggering event. Click the Event Linkage button. This step activates your linkage.

> ### NOTE
>
> Step 8 takes care of the third requirement for maintaining workflow configuration for the inbound process for a new IDoc—creating the event linkage. Now that you've established this link between the event and the workflow task, the workflow system uses the link to start the task whenever the event is raised.

9. You now define the terminating event. Click the Terminating Events tab. Delete the entry that exists from the copy operation. Next, click the Insert Event button and enter the values for Object Type, Event (this should be the terminating event INPUTFINISHED), and Element. For Element, press F4 and select the only entry. See Figure 33.12 for the terminating event defined for the customer task for the monthly report

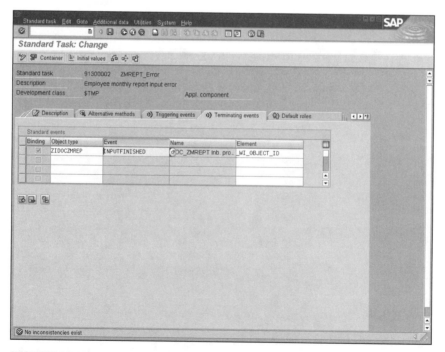

FIGURE 33.12 *The terminating event for the customer task* (© SAP AG)

IDoc. Press Enter and click the green arrow icon in the application toolbar to go back.

10. Make your task a general task so that anyone can execute it. Choose Additional Data, Agent Assignment, Maintain. Click the task to select it, and then click the Properties button. Select the General Task radio button (see Figure 33.13). Press Enter and click the green arrow icon on the application toolbar to go back.

11. Save your task.

Create a New IDoc Packet Object in the Business Object Repository (Optional)

This object is used for processes that are capable of processing many IDocs. Follow the steps outlined in the "Create a New Application IDoc Object in the Business Object Repository" section earlier in the chapter, but this time use IDOCPACKET instead of IDOCAPPL as the starting point.

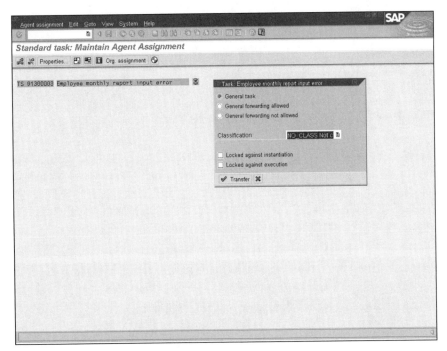

FIGURE 33.13 *Making the customer task a general task* (© SAP AG)

Process Configuration

After you create the necessary workflow configuration, you can carry out the steps for process configuration.

1. Create a new message type.
2. Link the message type to the IDoc type.
3. Allocate the function module to the logical message type.
4. Define the attributes for the inbound function module.
5. Create a new process code.
6. Assign input methods.
7. Create (or change) a partner profile.

Create a New Message Type

Transaction: WE81

Menu Path: From the Area menu of EDI, choose Development, Message Types

Just like the outbound process, the inbound process requires a message type assigned to the data contents transferred in the IDoc. Customer-defined messages begin with Z. The name of the message type should be the same name used in your IDoc programs. For the monthly report IDoc, message type ZMREPT is chosen. If you have already created this entry in your system for the outbound process, you can ignore this step.

Link the IDoc Type to the Message Type

Transaction: WE82

Menu Path: From the Area menu of EDI, choose Development, IDoc Type/Message

You assign the new message type to the IDoc type. This step is also similar to the outbound process. Figure 33.14 shows the linkage between a message and an IDoc type for the monthly report IDoc.

Allocate the Function Module to the Logical Message

Transaction: WE57

Menu Path: From the Area menu of EDI, choose Development, Message/Application Object

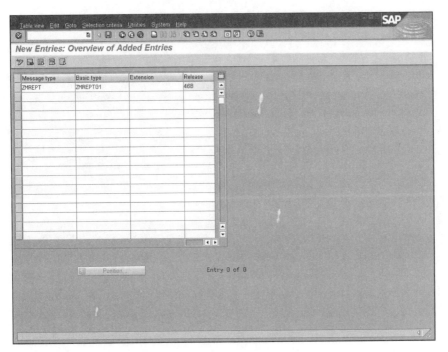

FIGURE 33.14 *Linking the IDoc type and message type* (© SAP AG)

This configuration establishes a link between the function module, message variant (message type, message function, and message code), IDoc type, and business object created by the function module. The Business Object field is optional. Figure 33.15 shows the allocation of the function module to the logical message for the monthly report IDoc.

NOTE

In the case of outbound messages, this link is established in the partner profile. For inbound messages, there is no entry for an IDoc type in the partner profile, so this entry is used to establish a valid IDoc type, message, and business object for a function module.

FIGURE 33.15 *Linking the IDoc type, message type, and business object* (© SAP AG)

Define the Settings for the Inbound Function Module

Transaction: BD51

Menu Path: From the SAP standard menu, choose Tools, ALE, ALE Development, IDocs, Inbound Processing, Function Module, Define Attributes

This configuration step tells the ALE system how your function module has been implemented. The ALE layer uses these settings to invoke the function module with correct parameters. Figure 33.16 shows the settings for the function module written for the monthly report IDoc.

In the Input Type field, the possible values are

- ◆ **Mass processing (0).** This option is for function modules that use a direct input method to create an application document. The ALE layer can pass multiple IDocs to the function module at the same time.

- ◆ **Individual input (1).** This option is for function modules that use the call transaction method to post an application document.

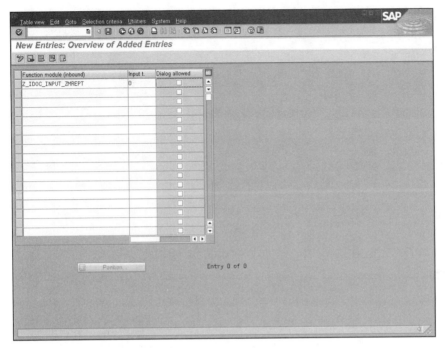

FIGURE 33.16 *Attributes of the input function module* (© SAP AG)

◆ **Individual input with IDoc lock in call transaction (2).** This option is for function modules that use ALE-enabled transactions to post an application document.

The Dialog Allowed field indicates whether the IDoc can be posted in a dialog mode after an error. If this option is turned on, the user can watch each screen during input processing.

Create a New Process Code

Transaction: WE42

Menu Path: From the Area menu of EDI, choose Control, Inbound Process Code

This step defines a process code that points to the function module developed for the inbound process. Process codes provide an indirect means of determining the process (in this case, the function module). Using process codes enables you to change the process without affecting other configurations.

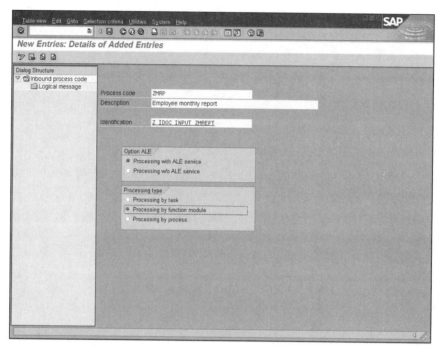

FIGURE 33.17 *Process code pointing to a function module* (© SAP AG)

The process code must start with a Z. Assign a short description, and then save your entry as shown in Figure 33.17. The system prompts you with this message: Please maintain codes added in 'ALE entry methods.' Accept the message by pressing Enter, and you are taken to a screen that shows the existing links between process codes and function modules.

Assign Input Methods

Transaction: BD67 or WE42

Menu Path: From the Area menu of EDI, choose Control, Inbound Process Code

This step creates a link between the process code defined in the preceding step and the function module. Also, this screen contains additional parameters that the workflow component uses for error handling, as well as for advanced workflow programming.

You enter the process code, function module, and workflow components developed earlier in the "Workflow Configuration" section.

You can leave the Application Object fields blank for the monthly report scenario. These fields are used to specify the application event that should be raised after the application document has been posted successfully. To take advantage of this field, the inbound function module has to be coded using the advanced workflow programming technique (see Figure 33.18). For details, refer to the ALE programming guide in SAP's online help.

Create or Change the Partner Profile

Transaction: WE20
Menu Path: From the Area menu of EDI, choose IDoc, Partner Profile

A partner profile is created for every partner system with which you exchange IDocs. In the partner profile, a record is created for every incoming message.

Create a partner profile if it does not exist. Add a record for your incoming message. Figure 33.19 shows the inbound parameters in the partner profile for the monthly report IDoc.

FIGURE 33.18 *Process code details for an inbound function module* (© SAP AG)

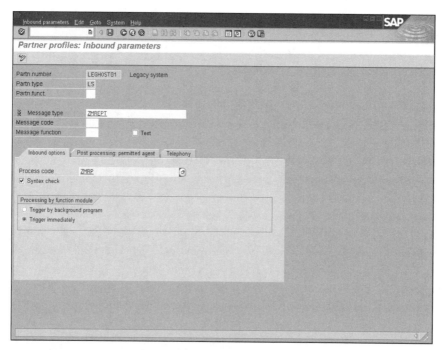

FIGURE 33.19 *The partner profile—inbound parameters for an incoming message* (© SAP AG)

Configuring the System for Extended IDocs

In this section, you will learn how to make IDoc extensions known to the ALE/EDI interface layer. The programs for IDoc extensions are already known to the ALE/EDI interface because these programs are written in the user exits that are part of the standard SAP programs. Therefore, the only requirement is to make the extended IDoc known to the system.

Configuring an Outbound Process for Extended IDocs

The outbound process requires only two configuration settings: establishing a link between the message type, IDoc type, and IDoc extension, and establishing the outbound parameters for the partner profile.

Establishing a Link between the Message Type, IDoc Type, and IDoc Extension

Transaction: WE82
Menu Path: From the Area menu of EDI, choose Development, IDoc Type/Message

This step links the standard SAP message to your new extended IDoc while maintaining the original settings of the SAP basic IDoc type. This arrangement is possible because SAP permits a message type to be based on different versions of the IDocs. Figure 33.20 shows the settings for the IDoc extension created for the customer master data in Chapter 31, "Extending and Developing an IDoc Type."

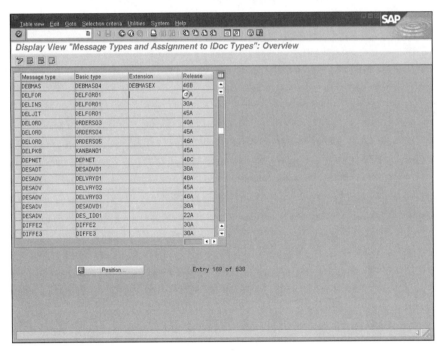

FIGURE 33.20 *The link between the message type, IDoc type, and IDoc extension—outbound process* (© SAP AG)

The Partner Profile: Outbound Parameters

Transaction: WE20

Menu Path: From the Area menu of EDI, choose IDoc, Partner Profile

Here you specify the message type, basic IDoc type, and extension (if any) you want to use for the outbound process, as shown in Figure 33.21.

Configuring an Inbound Process for Extended IDocs

The inbound process needs only one configuration setting to make the IDoc extension known to the system, as described in the following sections. Notice that you do not have to make any change to the inbound record of the partner profile because the inbound view does not have any mention of the IDoc type.

FIGURE 33.21 *Specifying the extended IDoc in the partner profile* (© SAP AG)

Establishing a Link between the Message Type, IDoc Type, and IDoc Extension

Transaction: WE57

Menu Path: From the Area menu of EDI, choose Development, Message/Application Object

This step links the standard SAP message to your new extended IDoc while maintaining the original settings of the SAP basic IDoc type, as shown in Figure 33.22. This arrangement is possible because SAP permits a message type to be based on different versions of the IDocs. Notice that the transaction for the inbound process is different than what you used for the outbound process earlier.

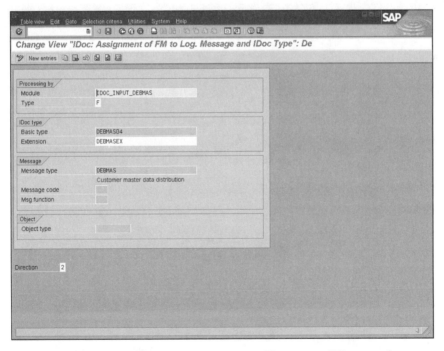

FIGURE 33.22 *The link between the message type, IDoc type, and IDoc extension—inbound process* (© SAP AG)

Summary

Newly created or extended IDocs and programs blend into SAP's existing IDocs and programs repository through various configuration options. This approach enables you to use the EDI interface for custom IDocs and thereby take advantage of the infrastructure's benefits, such as superior error handling, flexibility of process control, and documentation. Configuration for a newly created inbound process is slightly more involved because it requires additional workflow components for exception handling. The rest of the settings, however, are simple.

PART XII

Archiving in the
IDoc Interface

Chapter 34

**Archiving IDocs
and Deleting
Work Items**

When your system is operational and in production, the number of IDocs and workflow run-time logs can grow quickly. A workflow log is maintained for every work item generated for any exception in the IDoc interface. If your transaction volume is high, you need a strategy to clean up IDocs and completed work items from the system. SAP provides archiving programs and deletion programs for several documents in the system. This chapter shows you how to archive IDocs and delete work items, along with work item history.

The major reason to archive is to improve performance, but archiving also helps to reclaim disk space that otherwise would be taken up by obsolete documents (IDocs and work items, in this case). In addition, archiving is often driven by legal document retention requirements.

Archiving is a process in which you offload data in SAP documents to a file at the operating system layer for future retrieval and optionally delete the documents from the SAP system. The important point here is *future* retrieval. SAP provides a workbench for archiving objects and later retrieving objects from the archives.

Deleting is a process in which you permanently remove data from SAP with no provision to restore data. There are two choices for deleting data: use the archiving programs or special deletion programs. In the case of IDocs, there is no special deletion program, so the archiving process is used to delete them. In contrast, for work items you can use a special deletion program, in addition to the deletion program that is part of the archiving program's suite for work items.

You must start the archiving/deleting process soon after you go live with SAP to avoid falling behind. The archiving programs can take a long time to run, depending on the load and amount of data in the system. In some situations, the rate at which documents are created in the system can be close to the rate at which they can be removed. Therefore, it is important to start the archiving process immediately after going live with SAP.

An Overview of the Archiving Module

Before you dig into the archiving process, it is important to know the SAP lingo used in the archiving module. The archiving module is best understood by looking at the functions provided in the system, how the system implements these functions, and how the process is executed.

The Functions of the Archiving Module

The functions of the SAP archiving process are as follows.

◆ **Archiving data**. The capability to archive data is certainly the most important function of the archiving module. Archiving is implemented as a two-step process. First, documents such as IDocs, work items, and purchase orders are offloaded to an archive file at the OS layer. Second, the archive file is read and objects are deleted from the system. This fail-safe mechanism ensures that an object is not deleted until it has been successfully archived to a file. Archiving in SAP is different from database archiving. Database archiving is based on data rules, such as referential integrity rules. Archiving in SAP is implemented at the business level. A document must fulfill certain business rules before it can be archived. For example, an IDoc cannot be deleted if the status is 51 (Application Error).

◆ **Analyzing data stored in archives**. After data has been archived to a file, you can analyze the archived data and obtain details on the objects stored in the archive file.

◆ **Reloading data**. Data from archives can be reloaded into the SAP system. This function is usually not required, but if a situation demands that data be reloaded, it is possible. Reloaded IDocs are set to status 35 for outbound and status 71 for inbound. Once IDocs are reloaded, they cannot be rearchived.

TIP

The function modules used for archiving IDocs are located in function group EDIA.

Implementing the Archiving Module

The following items explain how the system implements these functions using archiving objects, archiving programs, and platform-independent file names. Then you'll learn about the interface of the archiving module with external archiving systems.

The Archiving Object

Each business document that is to be archived is assigned an archiving object name. This name is used in various operations carried out as part of the archiving process. The name assigned to IDocs is IDOC, and the name assigned to work items is WORKITEM.

Archiving Programs

The functions discussed earlier are achieved through programs that are part of the archiving object. An archiving object is composed of four programs: the archiving program, deletion program, analysis program, and reload program.

 NOTE

Not all archiving objects support all four programs.

◆ **Archiving program**. Selects documents that satisfy business conditions established for the object and then writes those documents to a file. The documents are still present in SAP.

◆ **Deletion program**. Takes as input an archive file created by the archiving program and reads the documents in the archive file. Those documents are then deleted from the SAP system.

◆ **Analysis program**. Takes as input an archive file, analyzes data stored in the archives, and displays the results in a report format.

◆ **Reload program**. Takes as input an archive file and allows you to reload one or more objects from the archive back into SAP database tables.

Platform-Independent File Names

Archive files are named using the *platform-independent* naming concept in SAP. As the name suggests, archive files are independent of the hardware platform.

They also provide the capability of dynamic file names, such as naming the file based on the date and time the archive process was started. Complete details on maintaining platform-independent file names are provided later in the chapter.

The Interface with an External Archive Management System

SAP integrates with third-party archive management systems via the archivelink interface, which offloads the management of files to an external system. SAP certifies third-party vendor software for compatibility with the archivelink interface.

Maintaining Platform-Independent File Names

The archiving process starts with establishing names for the archive files. Platform-independent file names can be maintained for the archive files via transaction FILE. First, you define a path name. Then, you define a file name in which you include the path name. Several paths and file names are already set up in the system, based on the standard SAP directory structure. You can elect to use those or copy and modify them to suit your needs. The file names can be dynamic, and they support substitution parameters for file names. Several parameters, such as day, month, system ID, and client, have been defined in the system for substitution.

In the following example, a platform-independent file name is created for IDocs, using the naming convention IDOC_<*date in MMDDYY format*>. This file is located in the /usr/sap/archive/ directory.

Maintaining Logical Path Names

The steps to create a logical path for the archive file are as follows.

1. Execute transaction FILE. The first screen for this procedure, shown in Figure 34.1, displays the paths that exist in the system.

2. Assign a logical name for the path. Click the New Entries button and give a name starting with Z to represent the path, as well as a short but meaningful description. For the IDoc example, call the file Z_IDOC_PATH. Save your entry.

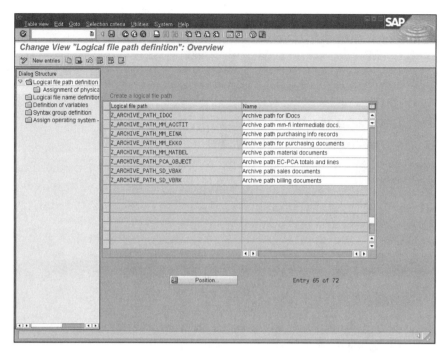

FIGURE 34.1 *The initial screen for platform-independent file names* (© SAP AG)

3. Assign a true physical path to your logical path. Select your logical file path, and click the magnifying glass next to Assignment of Physical Paths to Logical Path. Accept the system's information message and on the next screen, enter the platform on which you are working. For the example, UNIX is chosen but, of course, you should choose whatever is appropriate for you. Enter the physical path and end it with <FILENAME>, as shown in Figure 34.2. This entry is a placeholder for the file name that will be attached to the file. Save your entry, and click the green arrow icon in the application toolbar twice to return to the first screen of file maintenance.

Maintaining File Names

After you maintain the logical path name for the archive file, you maintain a logical name for the archive file.

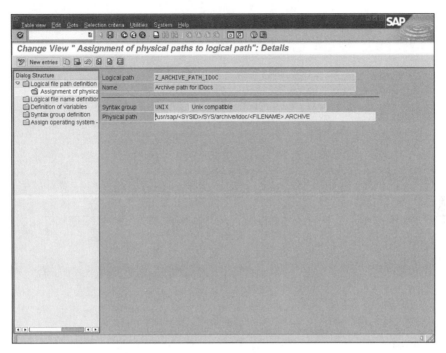

FIGURE 34.2 *Assigning a logical path to a physical path for UNIX* (© SAP AG)

In the Dialog Structure frame on the left of the screen, click the folder titled Logical File Name Definition, Cross-Client to see a list of existing logical file names. Click the New Entries button. Enter values in the fields, as shown in Figure 34.3. The file name contains substitution parameters, which are represented with angle brackets. You can use several standard substitution parameters. Table 34.1 lists the commonly used substitution parameters in the file names.

Archiving IDocs

After you maintain the archive file names, you are ready for the actual archiving process. IDocs can be archived for future retrieval or permanent deletion. There is not much value in archiving IDocs generated in ALE as a result of SAP-to-SAP transfer, because the sending and receiving systems belong to your own company. It is best to delete these IDocs. For EDI-generated IDocs, it is usually best to

Table 34.1 Substitution Parameters for File Names

Parameter Name	Description
<OPSYS>	Operating system in call
<INSTANCE>	R/3 application instance
<SYSID>	R/3 application name in SY-SYSID
<DBSYS>	Database system in SY-DBSYS
<SAPRL>	R/3 release in SY-SAPRL
<HOST>	Host name in SY-HOST
<CLIENT>	Client in SY-MANDT
<LANGUAGE>	Log on language in SY-LANGU
<DATE>	Date in SY-DATUM
<YEAR>	Year in SY-DATUM, four-character
<SYEAR>	Year in SY-DATUM, two-character
<MONTH>	Month in SY-DATUM
<DAY>	Day in SY-DATUM
<WEEKDAY>	Day of the week in SY-FDAYW
<TIME>	Time in SY-UZEIT
<STIME>	Hour and minute in SY-UZEIT
<HOUR>	Hour in SY-UZEIT
<MINUTE>	Minute in SY-UZEIT
<SECOND>	Seconds in SY-UZEIT
<PARAM_1>	External parameter 1
<PARAM_2>	External parameter 2
<PARAM_3>	External parameter 3

leave the archiving function up to the EDI subsystem because it has the document in original form, as sent and received from business partners. EDI documents are legally binding, so it is necessary to preserve the documents in the form that was exchanged with the business partner.

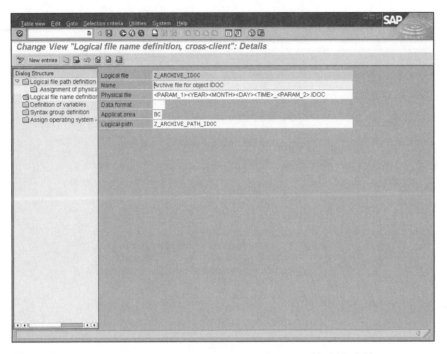

FIGURE 34.3 *Maintaining platform-independent file names* (© SAP AG)

However, some companies require archiving at the source of the data, so it becomes necessary to archive IDocs in SAP. Otherwise, IDocs can usually be deleted. Because the deletion process builds out of the archiving process, the following steps apply to both procedures.

Determining Which IDocs Can Be Archived

You cannot arbitrarily archive IDocs. IDocs must be in a state that makes sense for archiving. An IDoc's status code governs whether the IDoc is suitable for archiving. Table 34.2 lists the status codes in the standard system that allow an IDoc to be archived. This information is stored in table STACUST. For example, it is perfectly okay to archive IDocs that have been successfully posted (status code 53), but it does not make sense to archive IDocs that have not been processed yet (status 64). However, in certain situations you might want to archive IDocs that were created accidentally or, for some reason, you might want to get rid of certain IDocs. You can change the settings of a status code to enable

Table 34.2 IDoc Status Codes That Permit Archiving

Status Code	Description
03	Data passed to port okay
18	Triggering EDI subsystem okay
19	Data transfer for test okay
21	Error passing data for test
31	Error—no further processing
33	Original of an IDoc that was edited
38	IDoc archived
40	Application document not created in target system
41	Application document created in target system
53	Application document posted
57	Test IDoc: Error during application check
68	Error—no further processing
70	Original of an IDoc that was edited
73	IDoc archived

archiving (if it is not already permitted). Execute transaction WE47 and select the status code for which you want to make archiving possible. Click the Detail icon (the magnifying glass), select the Poss. field in the archiving block, and save your changes.

Archiving Programs Used for IDocs

The following programs are utilized for archiving IDocs.

- ◆ RSEXARCA and RSEXARCB are archiving programs. RSEXARCB is similar to RSEXARCA except for the selection screen. The selection options for RSEXARCB are designed for periodic scheduling.
- ◆ RSEXARCD is a deletion program.

- ◆ RSEXARCR reads from the archive.
- ◆ RSEXARCL reloads from the archive.
- ◆ RSRLDREL removes links between IDocs and business documents, such as sales orders and purchase orders.

These programs are documented thoroughly. You can read their documentation from the archiving transaction SARA or use transaction SE38 (Goto, Documentation on the menu bar). For program RSRLDREL, look in the SAP Library under Basis Components, Basis Services/Communications Interfaces (BC-SRV), The IDoc Interface (BC-SRV-EDI), IDoc Interface/Electronic Data Interchange, Archiving IDocs, Archiving: Technical Background, Deleting Links with IDocs.

Customizing

Before you can start archiving, you have to tell the system which file name to use and how big the file can be. Customizing for archiving objects is carried out from transaction SARA. Enter **IDOC** in the Object Name field and click the Customizing button. Select Technical Settings in the Customizing for Archiving: Transaction Selection window. In the technical settings screen (see Figure 34.4), specify the following attributes.

- ◆ **Log.file Name**. This field contains the logical file name you created earlier.
- ◆ **Size in MB**. Contains the maximum size of the archive file in MB. The system checks the current file size before opening the archive file. If the file size exceeds the limit specified here, the system opens another file in which to put the IDocs.
- ◆ **Max. Number of Data Objects**. Specifies the maximum number of IDocs allowed in an archive file. Before adding an IDoc to the archive file, the system checks the number of IDocs in the file against the number specified in the field. If there are too many IDocs, the system creates a new archive file.
- ◆ **Start Automat (under Settings for Delete Program)**. Specifies whether to start the deletion program automatically. Set this option to On. Otherwise, you will have to schedule the deletion program manually.

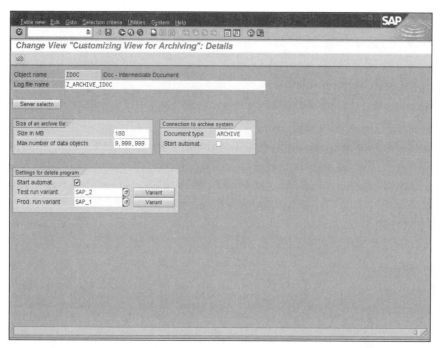

FIGURE 34.4 *Settings to customize the IDoc archiving process* (© SAP AG)

Archiving

Up to this point, you have maintained all the necessary settings. Now you are ready to carry out the actual archiving process.

Start the Main Transaction for Archiving

Execute transaction SARA, enter **IDOC** in the Object Name field, and press Enter. This process enables all the options available for the object, as shown in Figure 34.5.

Maintain Variants for the Archiving Program

This step sets up a variant for the archiving program. Click the Archive button. Choose an existing variant or enter a variant name, and then click the Maintain button. Create your variant as desired. You can select the IDocs to be archived

FIGURE 34.5 *The main screen for archiving IDocs* (© SAP AG)

based on date, message type, message code, message function, direction, or IDoc number range, as shown in Figure 34.6. For example, if you want to delete all the material master IDocs, you can enter **MATMAS** in the message type field. Save your variant and go back to the main screen.

Now you can specify the start time and spool parameters for the archiving program. Click the Start Time button and enter the appropriate values. You can also elect to run the program immediately. After you specify the start time, you can specify the spool parameters that determine where to send the program output.

 CAUTION

In the spool parameters, make sure that the Print Immediately flag is turned off. Otherwise, you could end up killing several trees unnecessarily.

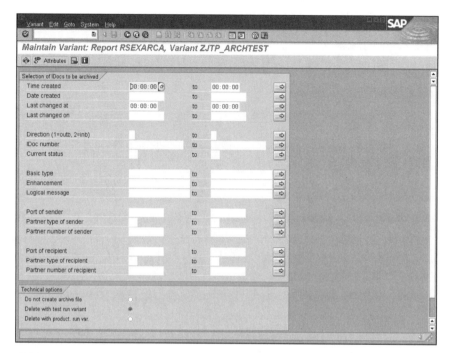

FIGURE 34.6 *Selection parameters for archiving IDocs* (© SAP AG)

Execute the Archive and Deletion Program

Click the Execute button, and the system will begin archiving the objects. The archiving program is submitted as a background job. For security reasons, the system does not permit two background jobs in the system with the same variant. Therefore, you must delete any previous instances of the archiving job before you execute the program. You must have authorization to execute the archiving programs—S_ARCHALL authorization is recommended.

TIP

Archiving jobs are scheduled with a priority class C (the lowest priority). On some application servers, class C jobs are restricted. In that case, you would not be able to run archiving programs. Ask your Basis staff to turn on class C jobs on the application server where you will be executing these jobs.

Check the Results

You can check the results by clicking the Job Overview button. First, check the job log to make sure that the program ran successfully. If it did, display the spool list for the IDocs that were archived.

TIP

If there is a problem in the job log, you can try to execute the RSEXARCA program online by using transaction SE38.

Execute transaction WE05 and make sure that the IDocs have been deleted. If you forgot to check the Start Automat. check box when you customized earlier, the deletion program will not automatically start after the archiving process is completed. In this situation, you must manually run the deletion program from transaction SARA. The steps to execute the deletion program are quite similar to the steps you followed to execute the archiving program. First, you maintain input parameters for the deletion program which, in this case, means specifying the archive file. Next, you maintain the start time and spool parameters. After all the necessary parameters have been maintained, you can execute the deletion program and verify the results.

Deleting Work Items

As mentioned earlier, the workflow management system maintains an extensive log for work items. It maintains a complete history of actions that were carried out on a work item and maintains work items even after they have been completed. Work items can be archived or deleted. If work items are archived, they can be retrieved later. From an ALE/EDI perspective, there is no reason to archive work items.

NOTE

If you are interested in archiving work items, you can follow the steps presented earlier for the IDoc object. The archiving object to be used is WORKITEM. The archiving program for work items is RSWWARCA, and the deletion program is RSWWARCD. These programs are also thoroughly documented. You can view the documentation using SARA or through transaction SE38.

The following programs are used for deleting work items.

◆ RSWWWIDE deletes work items.

◆ RSWWHIDE deletes work item history.

You can use these programs to delete any work item, regardless of its current state. For example, you can delete work items that are still in process. In contrast, archiving deletes completed work items only. Therefore, you must use extreme caution when executing these programs. As a workflow developer at SAP once said, "If you don't, you stand a good chance of losing lots of friends!" If you have a workflow development team, leave the task of deleting work items in their hands. Refer to Table 11.1, "Work Item Statuses," in Chapter 11, "Monitoring the Interface," for a list of status values for a work item. Users often ask whether they can delete work items from their Inboxes. In response, it is important to understand that work items are not treated like e-mail messages, which a specific user owns. A specific user owns a work item only when he or she has executed it at least once. Until then, a work item does not have an established owner. Work items appear in your Inbox because you are designated as a responsible user. They cannot be deleted based on a specific responsible user ID.

The RSWWWIDE and RSWWHIDE programs clean up the work item log and history. You can also use these programs to clean up work items from a user's Inbox that are not required anymore. You must execute RSWWWIDE before you execute RSWWHIDE.

Entering Selection Parameters for RSWWWIDE

Start RSWWWIDE by using transaction SE38. Some fields on the selection parameters screen for the program are self-explanatory (see Figure 34.7), but the following fields need important consideration.

◆ **ID (under Work Item).** This field represents the range of work items that need to be processed. You can choose the default unless you want to delete a specific work item.

◆ **Type (under Work Item).** This field represents the type of work items to be deleted. In the ALE/EDI process, only type W is used.

◆ **Status (under Work Item).** This field defaults to Completed. With this setting, the program deletes only work items that are in a completed

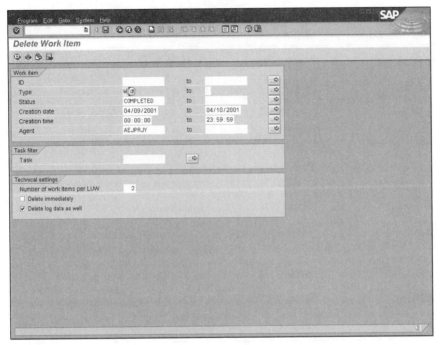

FIGURE 34.7 *Selection parameters for the RSWWWIDE program* (© SAP AG)

state. Work items that are still visible in the Inbox are not completed. Therefore, if you want to clean up work items that have been sitting in the Inbox for a long time, you should leave this field blank.

◆ **Agent (under Work Item).** In this field, enter the user ID of the person whose work items you want to delete. If you leave it blank, the program selects work items for all users. If you enter a user ID, the program deletes only the work items for which a user has been established. Work items that have not been executed at least once will not be selected. Therefore, if you want to clean up the Inbox, leave this field blank.

◆ **Task (under Task Filter).** You can use this field to restrict the work items to a specific task or set of tasks. It is recommended that you restrict them to ALE/EDI tasks only. Table 34.3 contains a list of ALE/EDI tasks.

◆ **Delete Immediately (under Technical Settings).** If this field is not checked, the program runs in a simulation mode, and work items are not

Table 34.3 Workflow Tasks Related to the ALE/EDI Process

Process Code	Task Number	Description
EDIM	TS30000020	No IDoc created yet
EDII	TS00008068	Error in the inbound process
EDIY	TS00008074	Syntax error—inbound
EDIN	TS70008037	Display NAST record with msg.; No IDoc created yet
EDIO	TS00007989	Error in the outbound process
EDIX	TS00008070	Syntax error—outbound
EDIP	TS60001307	Error in the outbound process (IDoc packet processing)
EDIL	TS70008373	Error in inbound status file
EDIR	TS70008125	Error in the subsystem, post-processing allowed
EDIS	TS30000078	Error in the subsystem

deleted. This setting is useful for initial tests, to make sure that the system deletes the desired work items only. When you are satisfied, you must turn off this flag and rerun the program for the work items to be deleted from the system.

In addition to these tasks, you have to include application-specific tasks that exist for each IDoc message. For example, the task name for errors in the DEBMAS message is DEBMAS_Error. The task ID is TS00008039. You can determine the task ID by using transaction PFTC. For the task type, enter **Standard Task (TS)**; for the task, enter the task name. Then press Enter. The system looks up the task number and returns it in the Task field.

 TIP

If you maintain a variant for this program, you won't have to enter the values every time.

CAUTION

The variant shown in Figure 34.8 deletes all work items from the system, regardless of user and work item state. Do not perform this procedure in the production system unless you know what you are doing or you don't care about being fired. In the development and testing systems, it is not uncommon to execute the RSWWWIDE program in the "deadly" mode.

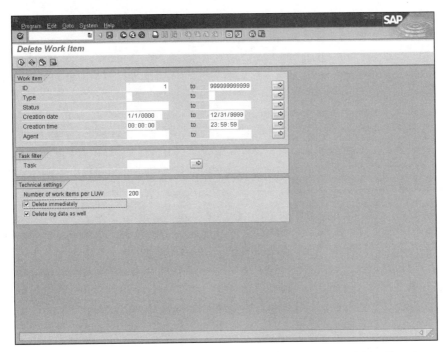

FIGURE 34.8 *Selection parameters for the RSWWWIDE program to delete all work items, regardless of their state* (© SAP AG)

After you enter the necessary parameters, you click the Execute button to start the execution. In the production system, it is recommended that you execute this program in the background mode and schedule it for a time when the system is less busy than normal.

The deleted work items are displayed on the screen. You can also check the Inbox of the user who had ALE/EDI-related work items in his or her Inbox before executing the deletion programs.

Executing the RSWWHIDE Program

After you delete the work items, you can delete the history by executing the RSWWHIDE program. As with RSWWWIDE, the selection parameters for RSWWHIDE allow you to run the program in simulation mode, which you can do until you are satisfied with the results. When you are satisfied, you execute the RSWWHIDE program in real mode to clean up the history log.

Summary

IDocs and work items created in the ALE/EDI process tend to build up in a system and cause performance problems. Thus, on a regular basis, it is necessary to eliminate unwanted IDocs and work items. You can choose to either archive those items or delete them permanently. Archiving and deleting are two separate processes. Archiving is useful if you will need to retrieve archived data in the future. Deleting is useful for removing data you will never need again. In some cases, you can use the deletion programs of the archive module to clean up the documents.

From an ALE/EDI perspective, archiving IDocs or work items is not very useful; rather, it is best to delete them permanently. IDocs are deleted using archiving programs, and work items are deleted using special deletion programs provided by SAP. IDocs must be in a state that allows deletion, but you can customize this option. Work item deletion programs do not carry out any checks, so you must be extra careful with the selection parameters specified for these programs.

Appendix A

Frequently Asked Questions

This appendix provides answers to many of the most frequently asked questions on the EDI list server and in training classes.

1. Where can I get a list of the status codes in the system?

Execute transaction WE47 to get a list of the status codes. For each status code, you can also check details such as status text, direction, and whether archiving is possible. In some cases, this information is easier to see by using transaction SE16 to view table STACUST.

2. How do I remove IDocs from my system?

SAP provides standard programs to archive IDocs (RSEXARCA and RSEXARCB) and then delete them from the system (RSEXARCD). For details, see Chapter 34, "Archiving IDocs and Deleting Work Items."

3. I created an IDoc in the system that is in status 30 (IDoc Ready for Dispatch [ALE Service]). I do not want to send this particular IDoc to our business partner. How can I prevent the system from accidentally processing the IDoc?

Create a status file for the IDoc with a status code of 31 (Error—No Further Processing). Use WE17 to import this file. This IDoc can also be archived. A sample status file is shown in Chapter 10, "Testing the EDI Interface."

4. How can I temporarily suspend EDI transmissions to a business partner?

Set the status of that partner in the General view of the partner profile to Inactive. This setting works for EDI partners (customers and vendors). It does not work for logical systems as used in ALE.

5. How can I temporarily stop sending purchase orders to a trading partner?

It depends on whether you have used a generic business rule (condition table) or a very specific one to propose EDI output. If you have used a very specific rule down to the vendor level, you can delete the condition record for that vendor. This action eliminates the automatic proposal and stops any EDI output for that vendor.

6. I created a purchase order, but the Sender field in the control record is empty. What am I missing?

The Sender field is populated from the Account at Vendor field in the vendor master. Refer to Chapter 14, "Outbound with Message Control: Purchase Orders," for all the required fields from an EDI perspective.

7. A workflow task was started because of an error in the IDoc processing. How can I tell who received the work item?

The person to be notified is determined from the outbound or inbound record of the partner profile, depending on the direction of the process. If these records are not found, you use the General view of the partner profile to determine the person responsible. If a partner profile cannot be read at all, the EDI administrator is notified. To bypass this lengthy process, you can execute transaction SWI1, enter **W** in the type field, and specify the approximate date and time when the process had the error. Locate the work item and go to its detail by double-clicking the work item. Choose Goto, Agent, Selected Agents. This reveals the user who has the work item.

8. Can I delete work items for a specific user?

You can delete work items based on a user ID only if the user has been established as the "owner" of the work item. Until a user executes a work item at least once or specifically reserves a work item, a work item does not have an established owner. You can delete work items based on task, work item ID, date, time, and several other parameters.

9. How do I delete old work items?

SAP provides standard archiving and deletion programs to clean up work items. You can delete work items regardless of their status by using the RSWWWIDE and RSWWHIDE programs. The various parameters for these programs are discussed in Chapter 34, "Archiving IDocs and Deleting Work Items."

10. How can I tell how many IDocs are in error?

You can determine the number of IDocs are in error in several ways. The IDoc statistics tool (WE07) provides a comprehensive picture of the state of the IDocs in the system. Read Chapter 11, "Monitoring the Interface," for details on the monitoring tools.

11. How can I determine the IDoc number generated for a purchase order?

Go to the output control screen of the purchase order (Header, Messages). Click the output type and choose Processing Log from the menu. The log displays the IDoc number.

12. How can I determine the purchase order number from an IDoc?

The purchase order number in an IDoc is stored in the E1EDK01 segment in the BELNR field.

13. I see two IDoc types that look similar, ORDERS01 and ORDERS02. What is the difference?

The last two digits in an IDoc type represent the IDoc version. ORDERS02 is a newer version that supports configurable materials. Each new version contains additional segments to support new functionality. (The current version is ORDERS05.) For instance, ORDERS04 added support for credit cards. Each new version is also a superset of the previous version, to maintain backward compatibility.

14. I see segments with names starting with E1, E2, and E3, such as E1EDK01, E2EDK01, and E3EDK01. What is their significance?

A name starting with E1 is the version-independent name of a segment type. By default, it points to the latest segment definition. A name starting with E2 is the version-dependent segment definition, and a name starting with E3 is version-independent segment documentation.

15. Can I assign multiple message types to an IDoc type?

Of course. In fact, SAP uses this technique for maintaining backward compatibility. For example, message type ORDERS is assigned to ORDERS01 and ORDERS02.

16. Can I use the append structure option to extend an SAP segment?

No, you are not permitted to use the append structure option to extend a segment. You should use the formal method of IDoc extension to create custom segments first and then include the custom segment in the extended IDoc type.

17. A user who has nothing to do with ALE/EDI processes has several EDI-related work items in his or her Inbox. What's wrong?

This scenario is typically the result of assigning ALE/EDI error tasks as General Tasks and incorrect configuration for the EDI Administrator. See Chapter 6, "Configuring Basic EDI Components," for details on maintaining this configuration.

18. Why can't I set certain work items in my Inbox to Done and get rid of them?

Those work items probably require a terminating event to mark their completion. See Chapter 11, "Monitoring the Interface," for details on how to determine whether a work item requires a terminating event. Work items generated for application errors (status 51) in the IDoc require a terminating event.

19. Can someone else execute the work items if the user who handles errors with ALE/EDI processes is on vacation?

This problem has several solutions.

- ◆ Assign more than one user to the position that handles errors. This approach allows more than one user to receive work items, yet only one user can execute a work item at a time.
- ◆ Set up backups in the HR module.
- ◆ Set up Inbox views using evaluation paths.

These options are described in detail in Chapter 9, "Configuring Workflow."

20. Why does data transfer using ALE cause the receiving systems to hang?

When an ALE process transfers an IDoc to the receiving system, the IDoc takes up a dialog session on the receiving system. If numerous objects are being transferred and partner profiles have not been set to collect the IDocs, ALE processes might well have exhausted the dialog sessions currently available in the system. This condition causes a considerable slowdown and eventually halts the system. See Chapter 28, "Managing ALE Process Performance and Throughput," for details on the settings required to control ALE processes.

21. Why do I sometimes get a pop-up message saying that an update task was terminated?

In several outbound processes (especially the ones that use Message control), the task of generating IDocs is detached from the application processing. The IDocs are generated in an update task. SAP uses this method to speed up the update process. If one of the updates has an abnormal termination (usually the result of syntax errors in programs), SAP sends the update-terminated message. Execute transaction SM13 to examine the details.

22. I have written a user exit for the L_IDOC_CREATE_WMTOID01 program called in the asynchronous update task. Is there a way to debug IDoc programs that are called in the asynchronous update task?

Use transaction SM66. You must have authorization to execute this transaction and debug the programs. You don't have long between the time you create a transfer order and the time the system executes the IDoc generation program. The best option is to utilize one of the user exits and add some code to insert the delay in the IDoc processing. This gives you a chance to see an entry in transaction SM66 and then allows you to debug.

23. Why does data transfer using ALE cause background jobs to fail on the sending systems?

When an ALE process transfers an IDoc to the receiving system and encounters an error, the default behavior is to create a background job to retry the transmission later. If many objects are being transferred, the system exhausts all the background jobs. This problem occurs because of the default settings on the tRFC options in the RFC destination. See Chapter 22, "Configuring the ALE Infrastructure," for details on how to set up the tRFC options in an RFC destination.

24. Can I get my work items in my e-mail client?

Yes. SAP provides a MAPI Service Provider component, which is available in versions 3.1G and newer. For more information, look under Basis Components, Basis Services/Communication Interfaces (BC-SRV), Business Workplace and Services (BC-SRV-OFC), SAP MAPI Service Provider (BD-SRV-GBT) on the SAP Library CD. This software allows a MAPI-compatible client, such as Microsoft Outlook or Exchange, to view and execute work items in the SAP Inbox. Before version 3.1G, SAP Labs provided a MAPI connector with free distribution. Check out the SAP Labs Web site at http://www.saplabs.com.

25. Why doesn't the system archive certain IDocs?

Whether an IDoc can be archived depends on its status. You can execute transaction WE47 and change the default settings of the archiving flag for a status value to allow archiving. See Chapter 34, "Archiving IDocs and Deleting Work Items," for details on how to carry out archiving.

26. My organization has hundreds of vendors and customers. How can I build partner profiles without entering them manually?

You can either write BDC programs or use function modules specifically provided for creating partner profiles. For details, see Chapter 7, "Configuring Partner Profiles."

27. When I am processing inbound IDocs that are in error, why is the Process in Foreground button grayed out for some messages?

The inbound function modules for posting an incoming IDoc are programmed using either the call transaction method or a direct input function module. The system enables the Process in Foreground button for function modules that use the call transaction method. The button is grayed out in other cases because there is no provision to step through the screens.

28. How can I tell whether an inbound process uses call transaction or direct input?

Execute transaction BD51. Entries with 1 or 2 in the Input T. field and a check in the Dialog All. field use the call transaction method. Entries with a value of 0 use the direct input method.

29. How do I communicate with back-level versions?

You specify the IDoc version and the segment version in the partner profile.

30. How do I find the IDoc(s) linked to a business document?

While you are viewing the document in version 4.6, select System, Links from the drop-down menu. This also works the other way. While viewing an IDoc, you can see the linked document(s) by using the same drop-down menu path. In previous SAP versions, use the menu path System, Services for Object, View Relationships, or access the link from the Environment menu selection for certain business documents.

31. IDoc user exits are not being accessed. How do I get them to work?

IDoc user exits are managed with transaction CMOD, as described in Chapter 32, "Programming in the IDoc Interface." In transaction CMOD, activate the project that includes the non-functioning user exits.

32. If I have more questions, who can help me?

Drop an e-mail to Arvind Nagpal at arvindnagpal@yahoo.com or to John Pitlak at pitlak@acm.org. We look forward to hearing from you. Another avenue is to pose your question to the many participants in the SAP EDI FAQ list server. To subscribe, send an e-mail to mailto:md@md.faqgcn.com with the following in the subject.

```
SUBSCRIBE SAPFAQ-EDI
```

Transaction Codes

Transaction codes provide shortcuts to functions so you don't have to navigate through the menus. The following transaction codes are frequently used in the areas indicated.

Main Menus

(Note that from version 4.6A on, most of these can be invoked from the command box only when you are at the SAP easy access menu.)

WEDI	Main menu for EDI-related activities
BALE	Main menu for ALE-related activities
SWLD	Main menu for workflow-related activities
SALE	Main area for ALE configuration
NACE	Main menu for Message control configuration

IDoc Definition

SE11	Data dictionary
WE31	Segment editor
WE30	IDoc editor to create and extend IDoc type
BD53	Reduce IDoc types for master data
WE60	IDoc documentation (IDoc structure and segment definition)
WE61	IDoc documentation (control record, data record, and status record)

IDoc Monitoring

WE02	IDoc display
WE05	IDoc list
WE07	IDoc statistics

Configuration (Basic Infrastructure for ALE and EDI)

WE20	Maintain partner profiles manually
BD82	Generate partner profiles automatically
WE21	Port definitions
SM59	RFC destination
BD64	Maintain customer model

Workflow (Definition)

SWU3	Basic workflow settings
PPOC	Create organizational plan
PPOM	Change organizational plan
PPOS	Display organizational plan
PFTC_INS	Create task
PFTC_CHG	Change task definition
SWE2	Event linkage table

Workflow (Run Time)

SO01	SAP Inbox
SWEL	Event log
SWI1	Workflow log
SWI5	Workload analysis

Message Control

NACE	Maintain condition records for various applications
VOK2	Message control components for sales and distribution
VOK3	Message control components for purchasing
VOFM	Maintain requirements for Message control
V/86	Field catalog for condition tables

Testing

WE19	Test tool for IDocs
WE12	Convert an outbound IDoc to an inbound IDoc
WE16	Process an incoming IDoc
WE17	Process an incoming status file

Reprocessing IDocs

BD88	Process outbound IDocs (before 4.6A)
BD87	Manual processing of IDocs

System Monitoring

SM12	Locked entries
SM13	Asynchronous update log
ST22	Dump analysis
SM21	System log
SM66	Debug asynchronous update tasks

Miscellaneous

XD02	Maintain customer master
XK02	Maintain vendor master
MM02	Maintain material master
VA01	Create sales order
ME21	Create purchase order
ME11	Create purchasing information records

Enhancement	
SMOD	Search and locate user exits
CMOD	Maintain projects to code user exits

Configuring New Components	
WE81	Create new message type
WE82	Link IDoc type and message type
WE41	Create outbound process code
WE42	Create inbound process code
BD64	Maintain ALE distribution model
WE57	Allocate inbound function module to message type
BD51	Define settings for inbound function module
BD67	Assign input methods for a process code (inbound)
WE57	Link IDoc to message and function module (inbound)

Programs

The following programs are scheduled to run on a periodic basis for processing at different layers of ALE and EDI processes. One or more instances of each program are scheduled on an as-needed basis.

◆ **RSNAST00.** Processes buffered entries in the NAST table and is used for applications that use Message control to process IDoc output. The use of RSNAST00 in the process flow is described in Chapter 3, "The Outbound EDI Process." Steps to execute the RSNAST00 program are listed in Chapter 10, "Testing the EDI Interface."

◆ **RBDMIDOC.** Generates IDocs by processing change pointers that have been logged for changes made to master data objects. The significance of change pointers and the use of the RBDMIDOC program are described in Chapter 20, "The Outbound ALE Process." Steps to execute the program are listed in Chapter 26, "Testing the ALE Interface."

◆ **RSEOUT00.** Processes outbound IDocs (status 30) that have been buffered to support mass processing. The use of RSEOUT00 in the process flow is described in Chapter 3, "The Outbound EDI Process." Steps to execute the RSEOUT00 program are listed in Chapter 10, "Testing the EDI Interface."

◆ **RBDAPP01.** Processes inbound IDocs (status 64) that have been buffered to support mass processing. The use of RBDAPP01 in the process flow is described in Chapter 4, "The Inbound EDI Process." Steps to execute the RBDAPP01 program are listed in Chapter 10, "Testing the EDI Interface."

◆ **RBDMANIN.** Reprocesses inbound IDocs that failed because of application errors (status 51). This program can be executed directly using transaction SE38, but in most cases, this program is invoked from the ALE tool to process incoming IDocs (transaction BD87). Steps to execute the BD87 transaction are listed in Chapter 12, "EDI Process Troubleshooting and Recovery."

◆ **RBDMOIND.** Updates the status of IDocs that have been successfully dispatched to a receiving SAP system. The use of RBDMOIND in the process flow is described in Chapter 20, "The Outbound ALE Process." Steps to execute the RBDMOIND program are listed in Chapter 26, "Testing the ALE Interface."

◆ **RSEIDOCM.** Can be scheduled to run as a monitoring program. This program starts workflow when the state of the system crosses a predefined threshold. Configuration of this program is described in Chapter 9, "Configuring Workflow."

User Exits in the IDoc Programs

User exits are an important aspect of enhancing the IDoc interface to accommodate extended IDocs. A list of the user exits is provided in Table A.1 for quick reference. Because this list is always growing, you can refer to Chapter 32, "Programming in the IDoc Interface," for step-by-step instructions. The list in Table A.3 shows a cross-reference between SAP messages, ANSI X12 EDI messages, and EDIFACT messages.

To view the latest version of the list in Table A.3, see OSS note 104606.

Table A.1 User Exits in the IDoc Interface: SMOD Enhancements

IDoc Message	Description	Direction	Enhancement
BLAOCH	Contract change	I/O	MM06E002
BLAORD	Contract	I/O	MM06E002
BLAREL	Contract release	I/O	MM06E002
COND_A	Pricing conditions	O	VKOE0001
COND_A	Pricing conditions	I	VKOI0001
CREMAS	Vendor master	I/O	VSV00001
DEBMAS	Customer master	I/O	VSV00001
DELINS	Scheduling agreement	O	MM06E001
DESADV	Advance shipment notice	I	MM06E001
FIDCMT	Distributed general ledger	I/O	F050S001
INFREC	Purchasing information record	O	MMAL0003
INFREC	Purchasing information record	I	MMAL0004
INVOIC	Invoice	O	LVEDF001
INVOIC	FI Invoice	I	FEDI0001
MATMAS	Material master	I/O	MGV00001
ORDCHG	Purchase order change	O	MM06E001
ORDCHG	Sales order change	I	VEDB0001
ORDERS	Purchase order	O	MM06E001
ORDERS	Sales order	I	VEDA0001
ORDRSP	Order confirmation	O	SDEDI001
ORDRSP	Order response for a purchase order	I	MM06E001
PAYEXT	Payment order	I	FEDI0002
PAYEXT	Payment order	O	FEDI0003
REMADV	Remittance advice	I	FEDI0002
REMADV	Remittance advice	O	FEDI0003
REQOTE	Incoming request for quote	I	VEDQ0001
SDPACK	Error handling for input IDoc	I	VMDE0001
SDPACK	Packing	I	VMDE0004
SDPICK	Error handling for input IDoc	I	VMDE0001
SDPICK	Picking	O	VMDE0002
SDPICK	Picking	I	VMDE0003

Table A.1 User Exits in the IDoc Interface: SMOD Enhancements *(continued)*

IDoc Message	Description	Direction	Enhancement
SRCLST	Source list	O	MMAL0001
SRCLST	Source list	I	MMAL0002
SRVMAS	Service master	O	BASO0001
SRVMAS	Service master	I	BASI0001
WMBBIN	Error handling for input IDoc	I	MWMIDI01
WMBBIN	Block storage type	I	MWMIDI04
WMCATO	Error handling for input IDoc	I	MWMIDI01
WMCATO	Cancel request transfer order	I	MWMIDI03
WMCATO	Cancel request transfer order	O	MWMIDO02
WMINVE	Error handling for input IDoc	I	MWMIDO07
WMINVE	Count data inventory	I	MWMIDO09
WMINVE	Count data inventory	O	MWMIDO04
WMMBXY	Error handling for input IDoc	I	MWMIDO07
WMMBXY	Goods movement	I	MWMIDO08
WMRREF	Release reference number	O	MWMIDO03
WMSUMO	Error handling for input IDoc	I	MWMIDI01
WMSUMO	Move storage unit	I	MWMIDI06
WMTOCO	Error handling for input IDoc	I	MWMIDI01
WMTOCO	Confirm transfer order.	I	MWMIDI02
WMTORD	Error handling for input IDoc	I	MWMIDO07
WMTORD	Create transfer order	I	MWMIDO10
WMTORD	Create transfer order	O	MWMIDO01
WMTREQ	Error handling for input IDoc	I	MWMIDI01
WMTREQ	Create transfer request	I	MWMIDI05

Table A.2 User Exits in the IDoc Interface: User Exit Include Programs

IDoc Message	Description	Direction	User Exit Program
ORDERS	Sales order	I	LVEDAF0U
ORDCHG	Sales order change	I	LVEDBF0U
DESADV	Advance shipment notice	O	LVED2FZZ

Table A.3 Cross-Referencing between SAP, ANSI X12, and EDIFACT Messages

IDoc Type	Message	Description	ANSI X12	EDIFACT	Inbound	Outbound
BENEFIT1	BENREP	Benefit enrollment	834			X
PEXR2001, PEXR2002	CREADV	Credit memo display	812	CREADV	X	X
PEXR2001, PEXR2002	DEBADV	Debit display	812	DEBADV	X	X
DELFOR01	DELINS	Delivery schedule	830	DELFOR	X	X
DELFOR01	DELINS	JIT delivery schedule	862	DELJIT	X	X
DELVRY01 (Previously, DESADV01) DELVRY02	DESADV	Shipping notification	856	DESADV	X	X
FINSTA01	FINSTA	Financial statement of an account message		FINSTA	X	
GSVERF01	GSVERF	Cred. memo procedure	861		X	X
INVOIC01	INVOIC	Invoice/billing document	810	INVOIC	X	X
INVOIC01	INVOIC	Invoice/billing document	880	INVOIC	X	X
FINSTA01	LOCKBX	Lockbox	823		X	
ORDERS01, ORDERS02, ORDERS03, ORDERS04, ORDERS05 ORDCHG	ORDCHG	Purchase order/order change	860	ORDCHG	X	X
ORDERS01, ORDERS02, ORDERS03, ORDERS04, ORDERS05		Purchase order/order change	876	ORDCHG	X	X
ORDERS01, ORDERS02, ORDERS03, ORDERS04,	ORDERS	Purchase order/order	850	ORDERS	X	X

Table A.3 Cross-Referencing between SAP, ANSI X12, and EDIFACT Messages *(continued)*

IDoc Type	Message	Description	ANSI X12	EDIFACT	Inbound	Outbound
ORDERS05						
ORDERS01, ORDERS02, ORDERS03, ORDERS04, ORDERS05	ORDERS	Purchase order/order	875	ORDERS	X	X
ORDERS01, ORDERS02, ORDERS03, ORDERS04, ORDERS05	ORDRSP	Purchase order/order confirmation	855	ORDRSP	X	X
ORDERS01, ORDERS02, ORDERS03, ORDERS04, ORDERS05	ORDRSP	Purchase order/order confirmation	865	ORDRSP	X	X
PEXR2001	PAYEXT	Extended payment order	820	PAYEXT		X
PRICAT01	PRICAT	Price catalog	832	PRICAT		X
PRICAT01	PRICAT	Price catalog	879	PRICAT		X
PRICAT01	PRICAT	Price catalog	888	PRICAT		X
PRICAT01	PRICAT	Price catalog	889	PRICAT		X
PROACT01	PROACT	Stock and sale data	852			
ORDERS01, ORDERS02, ORDERS03, ORDERS04, ORDERS05	QUOTES	Quotation	843			X
PEXR2001, PEXR2002	REMADV	Payment advice	820	REMADV	X	X
ORDERS01, ORDERS02,	REQOTE	Inquiry	840	REQOTE	X	X

Table A.3 **Cross-Referencing between SAP, ANSI X12, and EDIFACT Messages** *(continued)*

IDoc Type	Message	Description	ANSI X12	EDIFACT	Inbound	Outbound
ORDERS03,						
ORDERS04,						
ORDERS05						
DELVRY01	SHPCON	Shipping confirmation	945		X	
SHPMNT01,	SHPMNT	Shipping outbound	856	IFTMIN		X
SHPMNT02,						
SHPMNT03						
SHPMNT03	SHPMNT	Shipping outbound	204	IFTMIN		X
SHPMNT03	SHPMNT	Shipping instructions	304	IFTMIN	X	X
DELVRY01	SHPORD	Shipping order	940			X
TRXSTA01	TRXSTA	Shipment status message	214	TRXSTA	X	
TXTRAW01,	TXTRAW	Message for free text in	864		X	
TXTRAW02		SAPoffice format 'RAW'				
DELVRY01	WHSCON	Stock confirmation	945		X	
DELVRY01	WHSORD	Stock order	940			X

IDoc Record Layouts from Version 4.0

Tables A.4, A.5, and A.6 show the structure of the control record, data record(s), and status records respectively, as they appear on IDoc files for version 4.0 IDocs. Each table also gives the name of the corresponding data dictionary structure.

Table A.4 **Layout of the Version 4.0 Control Record (Structure EDIDC_40)**

Component	Component Type	Data Type	Length	Decimals	Short Text
TABNAM	EDI4TABNAM	CHAR	10	0	Name of table structure
MANDT	EDI4MANDT	CLNT	3	0	Client
DOCNUM	EDI4DOCNUC	CHAR	16	0	IDoc number
DOCREL	EDI4DOCREL	CHAR	4	0	SAP release for IDoc
STATUS	EDI4STATUS	CHAR	2	0	Status of IDoc
DIRECT	EDI4DIRECT	CHAR	1	0	Direction
OUTMOD	EDI4OUTMOD	CHAR	1	0	Output mode

Table A.4 Layout of the Version 4.0 Control Record (Structure EDIDC_40) *(continued)*

Component	Component Type	Data Type	Length	Decimals	Short Text
EXPRSS	EDI4EXPRSS	CHAR	1	0	Overriding in inbound processing
TEST	EDI4TEST	CHAR	1	0	Test flag
IDOCTYP	EDI4IDOCTP	CHAR	30	0	Name of basic type
CIMTYP	EDI4CIMTYP	CHAR	30	0	Extension (defined by customer)
MESTYP	EDI4MESTYP	CHAR	30	0	Message type
MESCOD	EDI4MESCOD	CHAR	3	0	Message code
MESFCT	EDI4MESFCT	CHAR	3	0	Message function
STD	EDI4STD	CHAR	1	0	EDI standard, flag
STDVRS	EDI4STDVRS	CHAR	6	0	EDI standard, version and release
STDMES	EDI4STDMES	CHAR	6	0	EDI message type
SNDPOR	EDI4SNDPOR	CHAR	10	0	Sender port (SAP system, external subsystem)
SNDPRT	EDI4SNDPRT	CHAR	2	0	Partner type of sender
SNDPFC	EDI4SNDPFC	CHAR	2	0	Partner function of sender
SNDPRN	EDI4SNDPRN	CHAR	10	0	Partner number of sender
SNDSAD	EDI4SNDSAD	CHAR	21	0	Sender address (SADR)
SNDLAD	EDI4SNDLAD	CHAR	70	0	Logical address of sender
RCVPOR	EDI4RCVPOR	CHAR	10	0	Receiver port
RCVPRT	EDI4RCVPRT	CHAR	2	0	Partner type of recipient
RCVPFC	EDI4RCVPFC	CHAR	2	0	Partner function of recipient
RCVPRN	EDI4RCVPRN	CHAR	10	0	Partner number of recipient
RCVSAD	EDI4RCVSAD	CHAR	21	0	Recipient address (SADR)
RCVLAD	EDI4RCVLAD	CHAR	70	0	Logical address of recipient
CREDAT	EDI4CREDAT	DATS	8	0	Created on
CRETIM	EDI4CRETIM	TIMS	6	0	Time created
REFINT	EDI4REFINT	CHAR	14	0	Transmission file (EDI interchange)
REFGRP	EDI4REFGRP	CHAR	14	0	Message group (EDI message group)
REFMES	EDI4REFMES	CHAR	14	0	Message (EDI message)
ARCKEY	EDI4ARCKEY	CHAR	70	0	Key for external message archive
SERIAL	EDI4SERIAL	CHAR	20	0	Serialization

Table A.5 Layout of the Version 4.0 Data Record (Structure EDIDD_40)

Component	Component Type	Data Type	Length	Decimals	Short Text
SEGNAM	EDI4SEGNAM	CHAR	30	0	Segment (external name)
MANDT	EDI4MANDT	CLNT	3	0	Client
DOCNUM	EDI4DOCNUC	CHAR	16	0	IDoc number
SEGNUM	EDI4SEGNUC	CHAR	6	0	Segment number
PSGNUM	EDI4PSGNUC	NUMC	6	0	Number of superior parent segment
HLEVEL	EDI4HLEVEC	CHAR	2	0	Hierarchy level of SAP segment
SDATA	EDI4SDATA	LCHR	1000	0	Application data

Table A.6 Layout of the Version 4.0 Status Record (Structure EDIDS_40)

Component	Component Type	Data Type	Length	Decimals	Short Text
TABNAM	EDI4TABNAM	CHAR	10	0	Name of table structure
MANDT	EDI4MANDT	CLNT	3	0	Client
DOCNUM	EDI4DOCNUC	CHAR	16	0	IDoc number
LOGDAT	EDI4LOGDAT	DATS	8	0	Date of status information
LOGTIM	EDI4LOGTIM	TIMS	6	0	Time of status information
STATUS	EDI4STATUS	CHAR	2	0	Status of IDoc
STAMQU	EDI4STAMQU	CHAR	3	0	Status for message in status record
STAMID	EDI4STAMID	CHAR	20	0	Message for status notification: Message class
STAMNO	EDI4STAMNO	NUMC	3	0	Message number for status message
STATYP	EDI4STATYP	CHAR	1	0	ABAP message type (A, W, E, S, I) in status message
STAPA1	EDI4STAPA1	CHAR	50	0	First parameter for message in status record
STAPA2	EDI4STAPA2	CHAR	50	0	Second parameter for message in status record
STAPA3	EDI4STAPA3	CHAR	50	0	Third parameter for message in status record
STAPA4	EDI4STAPA4	CHAR	50	0	Fourth parameter for message in status record
STATXT	EDI4STATXT	CHAR	70	0	Status text
UNAME	EDI4UNAME	CHAR	12	0	User name

Table A.6 Layout of the Version 4.0 Status Record (Structure EDIDS_40) *(continued)*

Component	Component Type	Data Type	Length	Decimals	Short Text
REPID	EDI4REPID	CHAR	30	0	Program
ROUTID	EDI4ROUTID	CHAR	30	0	Subroutine (routine, function module)
SEGNUM	EDI4SEGNUC	CHAR	6	0	Segment number
SEGFLD	EDI4SEGFLD	CHAR	30	0	Segment field
REFINT	EDI4REFINT	CHAR	14	0	Transmission file (EDI interchange)
REFGRP	EDI4REFGRP	CHAR	14	0	Message group (EDI message group)
REFMES	EDI4REFMES	CHAR	14	0	Message (EDI message)
ARCKEY	EDI4ARCKEY	CHAR	70	0	Key for external message archive

An IDoc File Example

Listing A.1 contains a dump of an orders IDoc (ORDERS05) to a file. This was generated using transaction WE19. As you can see, everything in an IDoc is character based. The first record is the control record, followed by several data records. Data records start with E2.

Listing A.1

```
EDI_DC40                      46B  3022   ORDERS05
ORDERS                                              EDITEST    LILF0000015555
SAPDEV    LS  SAPDEV
20010125232719
20010125232717
E2EDK01002                                          00000100000001000 USD
E2EDKA1001                                          00000200000002AG 1000000009
VENDOR000001
E2EDKA1001                                          00000300000002WE
1000000009
E2EDK02                                             00000400000002001BP3333377
19990302
E2EDP01002                                          00000500000002010         100
PCE100         PCE      2.002          1000
E2EDP20                                             00000600000603100
19990308
E2EDP19                                             00000700000603001MATERIAL00001
E2EDPT1                                             00000800000603Z019E
E2EDPT2                                             00000900000603LONG TEXT
```

IDoc Status Codes

The status codes in Table A.7 are defined for the IDocs.

Table A.7 IDoc Status Codes

Status Code	Description
0	"Not used, only R/2"
1	IDoc created
2	Error passing data to port
3	Data passed to port OK
4	Error within control information of EDI subsystem
5	Error during translation
6	Translation OK
7	Error during syntax check
8	Syntax check OK
9	Error during interchange handling
10	Interchange handling OK
11	Error during dispatch
12	Dispatch OK
13	Retransmission OK
14	Interchange Acknowledgment positive
15	Interchange Acknowledgment negative
16	Functional Acknowledgment positive
17	Functional Acknowledgment negative
18	Triggering EDI subsystem OK
19	Data transfer for test OK
20	Error triggering EDI subsystem
21	Error passing data for test
22	"Dispatch OK, acknowledgment still due"
23	Error during retransmission
24	Control information of EDI subsystem OK
25	Processing despite syntax error (outbound)
26	Error during syntax check of IDoc (outbound)
27	Error in dispatch level (ALE service)
28	Not used
29	Error in ALE service
30	IDoc ready for dispatch (ALE service)

Table A.7 IDoc Status Codes *(continued)*

Status Code	Description
31	Error—no further processing
32	IDoc was edited
33	Original of an IDoc that was edited
34	Error in control record of IDoc
35	IDoc reloaded from archive
36	Electronic signature not performed (timeout)
37	IDoc added incorrectly
38	IDoc archived
39	Receipt confirmed by target system
40	Application document not created in target system
41	Application document created in target system
50	IDoc added
51	Error: Application document not posted
52	Application document not fully posted
53	Application document posted
54	Error during formal application check
55	Formal application check OK
56	IDoc with errors added
57	Test IDoc: Error during application check
58	Not used
59	Not used
60	Error during syntax check of IDoc (inbound)
61	Processing despite syntax error (inbound)
62	IDoc passed to application
63	Error passing IDoc to application
64	IDoc ready to be passed to application
65	Error in ALE service
66	Not used
67	Not used
68	Error—no further processing
69	IDoc was edited
70	Original of an IDoc which was edited
71	IDoc reloaded from archive
72	"Not used, only R/2"
73	IDoc archived

Release 4.6 versus Prior Versions

You might be wondering what is different between version 4.6 and previous systems. The basic concepts covered in this book apply to version 4.6. However, there are major changes at the user interface level, with many transactions heavily altered and some disappearing. The ability to call area menus such as WEDI just like normal transactions is discontinued. Also, new tools ease such tasks as reprocessing IDocs, maintaining the distribution model, distributing master data, and managing archive files. IDoc extensions are now more intuitive. Throughout this book, wherever applicable, the differences between 4.6 and previous versions are noted.

File Name Changes

The space for object names in the IDoc interface is increased from 4 and 8 characters to 30 characters in version 4.0. For example, IDoc type, segment type, segment definition, process code, and message type names can be as long as 30 characters.

This increase in space affects the structure of IDoc files used in the inbound EDI process. If you have upgraded to release 4.x and want to take advantage of the extended space, you must modify the IDoc files per the new format. You can use the IDoc documentation (transaction WE61) tool to look at the new structure of the control record and data record. Another option is to use the IDoc tool (transaction WE19) to copy an existing IDoc and save the IDoc to a file. Then you can do some cut-and-paste exercises to build your IDocs.

 NOTE

You can continue to use the old format, provided that you do not want to use the extended name space. To support backward compatibility, SAP accepts an IDoc file in 3.x format.

Because of the name space increase, you can run into problems when communicating with systems that are at a lower release level than 4.0. SAP provides a conversion table to map long names to short names for basic IDoc types (transaction WE70), IDoc extensions (transaction WE71), IDoc types (transaction WE72), and message types (transaction WE73). To access the conversion tables, go to the IDoc editor (transaction WE30) and choose Environment, Conversion. Select the appropriate conversion table. Figure A.1 shows the conversion table for an IDoc type monthly report, from its long name to a short name. The monthly report is a sample basic IDoc type used throughout Section Three, "IDocs."

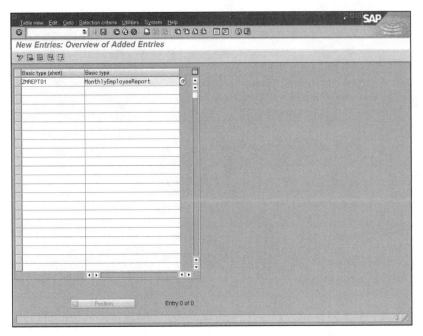

FIGURE A.1 *Conversion between long and short names for basic IDoc types* (© SAP AG)

New Tools to Maintain Partner Profiles

As mentioned in Chapter 7, "Configuring Partner Profiles," the task of maintaining partner profiles can be daunting, especially for large EDI shops where you can have hundreds of trading partners. In release 4.0, you can maintain default parameters for the message types, which can be used later during the maintenance of partner profiles. This saves you a great deal of typing effort. The steps are as follows.

1. **Maintain default parameters for the message type.** In the IMG, choose Basis Components, Basis Services, IDoc Interface/Electronic Data Interchange, Set Default Values for Partner Profiles. From this path, you select the object for which you want to maintain the default parameters. Figure A.2 shows the default values for the outbound message DESADV (shipment notice) to a customer.

2. **Maintain a partner profile.** Execute transaction WE20 and enter your partner number and partner type. Select Utilities, Fast Data Entry from the menu. The system prompts you to select whether you want to maintain inbound or outbound parameters. Then a list of messages for which defaults were maintained in the preceding step is displayed. You select the

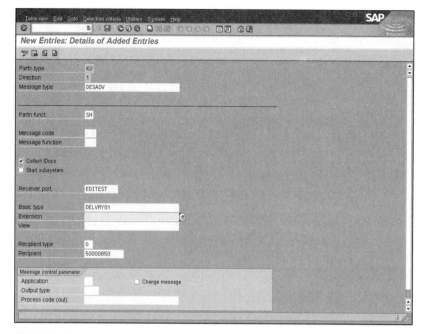

FIGURE A.2 *The default parameters maintained for outbound message DESADV to a customer* (© SAP AG)

appropriate message type, and the system automatically copies the values for you. You then have the option to modify any attributes of your choice.

 NOTE

Similar to a partner profile, you can also maintain default parameters for the port definitions.

Test Tool Changes

The IDoc test tool (transaction WE19) is enhanced to support outbound processing as well. (In 3.x, the IDoc test tools support inbound processing only.) This enables you to send IDocs in bursts to test performance issues.

Cosmetic Changes

As mentioned before, there are many cosmetic changes in 4.x, especially in version 4.6, and most of them are very intuitive. The new interface is, in most cases, more user-friendly and frequently provides more powerful functionality from any given screen. The following points summarize some important cosmetic changes.

◆ **The segment editor has a better display.** On the first screen, you can tell the various segment definitions associated with a segment type. The display has been improved to make it look more like a segment editor than a table maintenance screen (see Figure A.3).

◆ **The general settings for IDocs are easier to maintain and comprehend.** In Chapter 6, "Configuring Basic EDI Components," and Chapter 22, "Configuring the ALE Infrastructure," the basic IDoc settings are discussed. In 4.x, the procedure is simple. Execute transaction WE46, and the system displays the settings that can be maintained. Select the Global Parameters tab and click the Change button. The basic settings for IDocs and additional fields can be maintained here, as shown in Figure A.4.

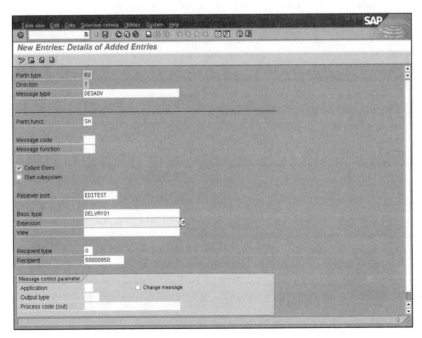

FIGURE A.3 *The segment editor displays segment definitions.* (© SAP AG)

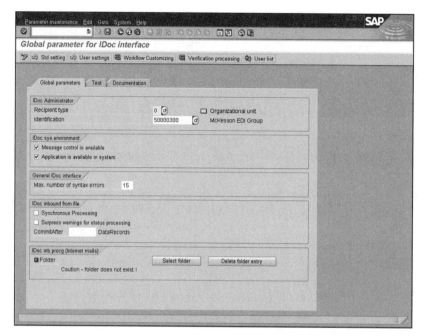

FIGURE A.4 *Global parameters for the IDoc interface* (© SAP AG)

◆ **Configuring the ALE/EDI interface for new processes is easier.** The steps to configure the ALE/EDI interface to recognize custom IDocs and processes are the same, but now the steps can be easily accessed from the ALE section of the SAP standard menu (via Tools, ALE). In 3.x, the steps are partially distributed between the area menu of EDI and the IMG.

◆ **Reprocessing IDocs is simplified through the use of transaction BD87.** The new BD87 transaction combines the functions of the old BD87 and BD88. Using an intuitive tree structure to display IDocs in various statuses, it simplifies most of the IDoc reprocessing tasks you will face. To use this transaction, refer to Chapter 12, "EDI Process Troubleshooting and Recovery."

EDIADMIN Table Settings Prior to Version 4.6

In versions earlier than 4.6, the global EDI parameters are maintained by entries in table EDIADMIN. The valid parameters and their settings are described here. For further information on these settings, see Chapter 6, "Configuring Basic EDI Components."

- ◆ **EDIADMIN.** Specifies the administrator for the IDoc interface at run time. This person is responsible for the integrity of the overall IDoc interface. The format for the value assigned to this field is XXCCCCCCCC. XX is the two-character ID representing the object type (for example, US for User ID, S for Position, or O for Organizational unit). If the object type is a single character, it must be followed by a space. CCCCCCCC is the eight-character object identifier. See Chapter 9, "Configuring Workflow," for details on all the types of objects you can specify here. For example, if the position with position number 12345678 is assigned as the administrator, the value of the parameter in the EDIADMIN field will be S 12345678. If a user with user ID AN000001 is the administrator, the value of the parameter in the EDIADMIN field will be USAN000001. This parameter is used by the workflow system when certain errors occur in IDoc processing, as described in Chapter 6.

- ◆ **MAXSYNERR.** Sets the maximum limit on the number of status records created for syntax errors—a good recommendation is five. If your IDoc gets more than five syntax errors in a production environment, something is terribly wrong. Setting this number higher usually does not help you debug the problem; you need to investigate the process more deeply at the data source.

- ◆ **SEGDVCLASS.** The development class used when developing new segments.

- ◆ **TESTPORT.** (Used for testing purposes only.) Defines the port name that will be used for assigning default parameters during inbound testing. The naming convention used for this port is SAP<*xxx*>, where xxx is a three-character ID assigned to your SAP instance. For example, if the name of your development instance is DV1, the port name will be SAPDV1. This port must be defined in the port definition.

- ◆ **INBOUND.** Starting with release 3.1G, for the inbound process, the creation of IDocs from the input file is disconnected from the processing of the IDocs for posting. However, if you want to maintain the old style, you can use this parameter and set the value to OLD. See Chapter 6 for an explanation of why the two processes were disconnected and the settings required to connect the two processes.

Internet Resources

A great deal of supplementary information on ALE and EDI topics is available on the Internet.

Internet Discussion Groups

The following list servers are useful resources for interacting with your peers. As with any list server, you will find some very useful tips and advice, but the timing is unpredictable.

The *SAP FAQ EDI Discussion List* is a free, e-mail-based forum for the discussion of EDI-related topics of interest to those involved with SAP. To subscribe, send an e-mail message to md@md.faqgcn.com, with the following command in the body of your message.

```
subscribe SAPFAQ-EDI
```

The *SAP EDI Special Interest Group* provides a forum for discussion of EDI-related questions of interest to SAP users. To subscribe to the list, send an e-mail message to listproc@listserver.com, with the following message on a single line.

```
subscribe sap-edi-sig <firstname lastname>
```

The *SAP MIT Listserver (SAP-R3-L)* is for technical and non-technical discussion on any topic related to SAP. For complete details, send an e-mail to listserv@mitvma.mit.edu, with the following message on the first line.

```
INFO SAP-R3-L
```

To subscribe to the list, send an e-mail message to listserv@mitvma.mit.edu, and in the body of the message, enter the following line.

```
subscribe sap-r3-l <lastname firstname>
```

Web Sites

You are encouraged to explore the following Web sites for additional information on various topics discussed in this book.

The *SAP home page* (http://www.sap.com) contains a wealth of information on the products and services offered by SAP. Among other things, you can find a complete list of third-party products certified for ALE and EDI.

The *SAP Intranet site* (http://sapnet.sap-ag.de) contains a wealth of technical literature and white papers on products and services offered by SAP. This site is restricted to SAP customers and partners. You need OSS ID to access this site.

SAP Labs (http://www.saplabs.com) is a completely owned subsidiary of SAP. This site has useful information on products from SAP Labs that make SAP implementation easier.

Also called *ASUG*, the *SAP Americas User Group* (http://www.asug.com) is dedicated to communicating the needs of the user community to SAP. This site is for member companies only. A group within ASUG focuses on EDI-related activities.

The *SAP Fans Club* (http://www.sapfans.com) is a great site for anyone interested in conversing with other SAP professionals in a particular area of interest.

Other Resources

The following sources of information on ALE, EDI, and IDocs are available directly from SAP.

Online Help CD

ALE-related information is available under the version 4.6 R/3 Library, Basis Components, Middleware, Application Link Enabling (BC-MID-ALE).

IDoc-related information is available under R/3 Library, Basis Components, Basis Services/Communication Interfaces (BC-SRV), The IDoc Interface.

Message control information is available under R/3 Library, Logistics, Sales and Distribution (SD), Output Determination (SD-BF-OC) and Logistics, Materials Management (MM), Purchasing (MM-PUR), Entering Text, Printing, and Transmitting Documents, Messages.

Workflow information is available under R/3 Library, Basis Components, Business Management (BC-BMT), SAP Business Workflow (BC-BMT-WFM).

Training Courses

The following training courses pertain to the material in this book and might interest you. These courses are offered at SAP training centers throughout the world. Check SAP's Web site at http://www.sap.com for the course schedule and location.

CA210	EDI Interface
CA910	ALE
BC600	SAP Business Workflow Introduction
BC601	Build and Use SAP Business Workflow
BC619	Application Link Enabling
BC620	SAP IDoc Interface Technology
BC621	SAP IDoc Interface Development
BC615	SAP ArchiveLink
BC660	Data Archiving

Index